SELF-PORTRAITS BY WOMEN PAINTERS

WE DEDICATE THIS BOOK TO OUR MOTHERS AND FATHERS, HUSBANDS AND LOVERS, CHILDREN AND STUDENTS, MENTORS AND TEACHERS, AND MOST OF ALL TO WOMEN PAINTERS WHO HAVE PORTRAYED, ARE PORTRAYING AND WILL PORTRAY THEMSELVES!

Self-Portraits by Women Painters

Liana De Girolami Cheney
Alicia Craig Faxon
Kathleen Lucey Russo

NEW ACADEMIA PUBLISHING   Washington, DC

New Academia Publishing, 2009
First edition, Ashgate Publishing, 2000

Printed in the United States of America

Library of Congress Control Number: 2009934400
ISBN 978-0-9823867-3-6, paperback (alk. paper)

New Academia Publishing, LLC
PO Box 27420 - Washington, DC 20038-7420
info@newacademia.com - www.newacademia.com

Contents

List of illustrations

Note on the authors

Liana De Girolami Cheney is Program Coordinator of Art History at University of Massachusetts Lowell, and author and editor of a number of books, including *Botticelli's Neoplatonic Images*, *The Paintings of the Casa Vasari*, *Readings in Italian Mannerism*, *The Symbolism of Vanitas in the Arts, Literature, and Music* and *Pre-Raphaelitism and Medievalism in the Arts*.

Alicia Craig Faxon, Professor Emerita, Simmons College, and Rhode Island Regional Editor of *Art New England*, is the author of books on Dante Gabriel Rossetti and Jean-Louis Forain, and editor of *Pilgrims and Pioneers: New England Women in the Arts* and *Pre-Raphaelite Art in its European Context*.

Kathleen Lucey Russo is Chair of the Department of Art at Florida Atlantic University. She has published numerous articles and reference book entries on eighteenth-century artists and architects, including Elisabeth Vigée-Lebrun, Rosalba Carriera and Henry Fuseli.

Acknowledgments

The authors would like to express their sincere gratitude to the staff and patrons of museums, libraries, galleries, private collections, photo archives, and universities, as well as photographers, who have generously provided us with photographic assistance, services and permissions: Accademia Nazionale di San Luca, Rome; Accademia, Venice; Anne Adams, Kimbell Art Museum; Alinari Fototeca; Jorg P. Anders, Photographer; Art Institute of Chicago; Art Resource, New York; Ashgate/Scolar Press Staff; Baltimore Museum of Art; Lisa Ben-David; Biblioteca Sarti, Accademia Nazionale di San Luca, Rome; Bibliothèque Nationale and Universitaire, Strasburg; Bibliothèque Nationale de France; Bildarchiv und Porträt Sammlung; Bridgeman Art Library, Wallace Collection, London; British Library, London; British Museum, London; Brown University Library, Rhode Island; City of Bristol Museum and Art Gallery; Martin Bühler, Photographer; Busch-Reisinger Museum, Harvard University Art Museums; Victoria Calhoun; Coimbra University, Coimbra, Portugal; Corpus Domini Convent, Bologna; Deanna Cross, Metropolitan Museum of Art, New York; Delaware Art Museum; Carol Demos, Simmons College; Nancy Desmond, UMASS Lowell; Elizabeth Donnelly, Simmons College; Earl Spencer Collection, Althorp Park; Pamela Edwardes, Ashgate/Scolar Press; Ella Gallup Summer and Mary Catlin Summer Collection Fund; Emma F. Monroe Fund, Museum of Fine Arts, Boston; Rebecca Engelhardt, John and Mable Ringling Museum of Art; Folger Shakespeare Library, Washington, DC; Foto Marburg; Frances Lehman Loeb Art Center; Fratelli Alinari; Gabinetto Disegni e Stampe, Galleria degli Uffizi, Florence; Galerie Chantal Crousel, Paris; Galleria degli Uffizi, Florence; Galleria Doria Pamphili, Rome; Gemäldegalerie, Dresden; Gemäldegalerie, Kunsthistorisches Museum, Vienna; Giraudon, Photographer; Carol Goodwin, Witt Library, Courtauld Institute of Art, London; Catherine Gordon, Witt Library, Courtauld Institute of Art, London; Hermitage Museum, St Petersburg; Hessische Landesbibliothek, Wiesbaden; Daisy Hue, Art Resource, New York; John and Mable Ringling Museum of Art; Kimbell

Art Museum, Fort Worth, Texas; Kunstmuseum, Basel; Kunstmuseum, Bern; John Kuss, New York Historical Society; Jennifer Lapanta, Norton Simon Museum; Schecter Lee, Photographer; Lemme Collection, Rome; Erich Lessing, Photographer; David A. Loggie, Photographer; Marlborough Fine Arts, London; Karin Maul, Staatliche Kunstsammlungen, Dresden; Louis K. Meisel Gallery, New York; Lynn Mervosh, Wadsworth Atheneum; Metropolitan Museum of Art, New York; Musée Condé, Chantilly; Musée du Louvre, Paris; Musée Moderne de la Ville de Paris; Museo Archeologico, Naples; Museo del Prado, Madrid; Museum of Art, Cairo; Museum of Modern Art, New York; Muzeum Zamek, Lancut, Denmark; National Academy Museum, New York; National Gallery of Art, London; National Gallery of Art, Washington, DC; National Gallery of Victoria; National Library of Scotland, Edinburgh; National Museum of American Art; National Museum of Women in the Arts, Washington, DC; National Portrait Gallery, London; National Portrait Gallery, Washington, DC; New York Historical Society, New York; New York Public Library, New York; Nicolo Orsi Battaglini, Photographer; Norton Simon Museum, Pasadena, Ca; Öffentliche Kunstsammlung, Basel; Linnea Olson; Österreichische National Bibliothek, Vienna; Palazzo Barberini, Galleria Nazionale d'Arte Antica, Rome; Phillips Fine Art Auctioneers, London; Pierpont Morgan Library, New York; Pinacoteca delle Belle Arti, Bologna; Pinacoteca di Ascoli Piceno, Marche; Pinacoteca di Brera, Milan; Pinacoteca Nazionale, Ravenna; Pinacoteca Nazionale, Siena; Pitti Palace, Florence; Preussischer Kulturbesitz; Raccolta Scelti, Castel Sforzesco, Milan; Jean Rainwater, Brown University Library; Sandra Rei; Réunion des Musées Nationaux, Paris; Rhode Island School of Design; Rose Art Museum, Brandeis University; Royal Collection of Her Majesty the Queen, Kensington Palace, London; Scala Fototeca; Erich Schleier, Staatliche Museen zu Berlin; Smith College Art Museum; Smithsonian Institution, Washington, DC; Spencer Collection, New York Public Library; Staatliche Museen zu Berlin; Staatsbibliothek, Darmstadt; The State Art Museum of Florida, Sarasota, Florida; Steinberg Krauss Gallery, New York; Tate Gallery, London; Simon Taylor, Art Resource, New York; Joanne Tellier; Barbara Thompson, Witt Library, Courtauld Institute of Art, London; Torno Collection, Milan; Universitätsbibliothek, Erlangen; Universiteits-Bibliothek, Amsterdam; Vassar College; Victoria and Albert Museum, London; Wadsworth Atheneum, Hartford, CT; Walker Art Center, Heard Museum; Wallraf-Richartz Museum, Cologne; Walters Art Gallery, Baltimore; Witt Library, London; Yale Center for British Art; Yoko Terasima, National Museum of Western Art, Tokyo; Federico Zeri Collection, Mentana, Rome.

Preface*

Numerous books exist on artists' self-portraits, but almost all the faces portrayed are those of males. *Self-Portraits by Women Painters* corrects the false impression that there are few self-portraits of females. In this work, various types of female self-portraits are considered: those of the painter, woman of culture, teacher, daughter, mother; of a personification, a mythological or allegorical figure; of a spouse, teacher, family member, physician; or of an admired artist, or group of artists or personifications. Also discussed are artists who produced serial self-portraits, that is, self-portraits in different guises – notably Anguissola, Vigée-Lebrun, Kauffmann, Valadon, Modersohn-Becker, Kollwitz and Kahlo. These images record a continuing life history, and often a journey inward.

Self-Portraits by Women Painters is not a comprehensive encyclopedia of female self-portraiture. Rather, it is an examination of variations in the genre, investigating some of the most challenging and exciting visual works created by women throughout history. The works chosen, culled from several hundred female self-portraits, typify the range of feminine introspection, celebration and even advertisement. Here one meets our foremothers as well as our forefathers, whose lives, loves and achievements give new testimonies of success, imagination and daring.

The analysis engages, to some extent, in an activity that has become fashionable in some intellectual circles, that is, deconstructing the image, particularly in symbolic, disguised and surrogate self-portraits, where the artist assumes another persona in order to communicate with her audience. The female gaze confronts us in many ways and calls into question our suppositions and limitations. There is, of course, always a danger of reading one's own ideas into a painting rather than discovering what the artist sought to communicate. If the artist calls a work a 'self-portrait', there is a good chance she sees it as such. If the painting alludes to some known event in her life, one has the basis for analysis, rather than mere subjective interpretation.

Self-Portraits by Women Painters examines only the most significant self-portraits throughout the centuries, focusing on the Western tradition. Each period has its own identity and is treated accordingly in relation to the relevance of the painter's interaction with her society, moving historically from the image of the self to the symbol and the reflection of the self. In most instances, painters are presented chronologically, based on the art-historical style in which they worked. The painters represented are American (African-American, Latina, Chicana, and North and South American) and European (British, Dutch, Flemish, French, German, Greek, Italian, Russian, Spanish and Swiss).

During the past ten years, a vast literature on women's history and philosophy and the sister disciplines, including the history of art, has flooded the market and challenged the previous 'canon'. The aim here is not to redefine or present an alternative to that canon. Instead, the authors hope to explore a thematic approach to women's art through feminine self-image, pointing out the talents and aesthetic beauty revealed in the works.

Borrowing from Giorgio Vasari's *The Lives of the Most Excellent Painters, Sculptors and Architects*, the best and most interesting female self-portraits have been selected to demonstrate the ways in which women painters have seen themselves. While for thematic reasons and for the sake of historical continuity the focus is on the female self-portrait, the intent is not to isolate women's creativity from the historical current that has been dominated by the art of men. Our thematic approach and interpretations of the self-portraits will, it is anticipated, significantly further scholarship in the field. The authors invite and encourage students, scholars from all disciplines and other interested readers to explore this topic further and close the gaps in this presentation.

The literature on portraiture, in general, is vast. Moreover, the past decade has seen such an escalation in the writings on women that a fully comprehensive bibliography would be both unwieldy and impractical. Therefore, a carefully selected, manageable reference list, with special emphasis on the work of numerous fine scholars whose studies have assisted our own, has been included.

Through self-representation, a painter conveys his or her intimate notions about society and the individual. This book aims to make a wide audience more aesthetically and historically interested in self-portraiture in general and in particular in women painters' self-portraits as they reflect the history of culture and ideas.[1]

Cheney, Faxon, Russo

1999

* This study originated over ten years ago with a series of lecture presentations to national and international conferences discussing the significance of female self-portraits during the Renaissance, Mannerism, the Baroque, and modern times at the Renaissance Society of America (Arizona), Sixteenth-Century Studies Conference (Philadelphia), Fifteenth-Century Studies Conference (Perpignan), South-Central Renaissance Conference (Austin), Medieval Conference (Leeds) and the Visual Resources Association Meeting at the XXIXth International Congress of the History of Art in Amsterdam, 1–7 September 1996.

Introduction:
What is a portrait?

The portrait can be defined in a variety of ways: as 'a human image, individualized by physiognomic specification, subjected to artistic and psychological interpretation, presented as a work of art, and affected by the changing circumstances of perception';[1] or as the image of 'the absent...made present to their friends, the dead...seen by the living many centuries later'.[2] There are a number of factors that must be considered in analyzing a portrait in order to comprehend its full meaning: the identity of the person represented and the motive for painting the work, the role of the background of the work and the period in which it was painted, and the setting, attire, coiffure, ornamentation, gestures and expression, which reflect the taste and style of the era. The context of the portrait is also important. Has the painter created, for example, a likeness, a counterfeit or an idealized image of the sitter, a painting with hidden symbolism or a declaration of the subject's allegiance to a cause or principle? What is the function of the portrait? Who commissioned it and why? These are only a few of the questions which can be raised.

Problems of interpretation, identification and attribution are always a challenge in art history, and they are even more so with portraits. The portrait, like all art, is bound to history and its social conventions. Its stylistic and conventional representation escapes from temporal and spatial limitations – it is, at once, a portrayal of past, present and future. Despite questions of objective and subjective resemblance, it is judged, first and foremost, as a work of art.

When looking at a self-portrait, the viewer is interested in understanding the hidden clues or attributes provided by the artist. Some portraits contain actual writing, an inscription that explains or complements the visual image, such as is found in Catherina van Hemessen's *Self-Portrait* of 1546 (Fig. IV.1). Role-playing in portraiture can also refer to a literary text outside the painting itself, such as in Elisabetta Sirani's *Melpomene, The Muse of Tragedy* of 1640 (Fig. V.5). Signs or symbols (iconography) are employed by painters, especially in a self-portrait; for example, the mirror used by the sitter may become an attribute of the personification of Prudence or of Vanity. The sitter might be engaged in playing the piano, sewing or painting, thereby denoting her occupation, as in Catherina van Hemessen's 1546 *Self-Portrait*, Sofonisba Anguissola's *Self-Portrait at the Easel* of 1556 (Pl. IX) and Elisabeth Vigée-Lebrun's *Self-Portrait* of 1790 (Fig. VI.11).

The variety of functions of a portrait or self-portrait are intriguing. The most common type of portrait was commissioned, and the self-portrait is no exception, as is demonstrated by the collections of self-portraits for the Galleria degli Uffizi in Florence, the Accademia di San Luca in Rome, the French Academy in Paris, the Royal Academy of Arts in London and the Academy of the Arts in Vienna.

The self-portrait is a unique work of art, an intimate record of a sitter's personality. It is an acknowledgement of worth, an exercise in technique, a denominator of era, style and likeness. It is a revelation and a confession. It can be a study in expression or a document in a history of aging. In sum, the self-portrait is far more than a likeness, although that aspect is clearly important. It is a declaration of who the painters are and how they want to be seen: their persona, a personification by the depiction of attributes; and their occupation, demonstrated by the depiction of materials used in the profession – pencils, brushes, color pigments, a mirror.

Dependence on the mirror presents the painter with a challenging dilemma, since the reflected image is reversed. Unless the artist uses a second mirror to right the reversal, the self-portrait is, in a sense, a counterfeit. In Egyptian, Mesopotamian, Greek, Etruscan and Roman times polished metal 'mirrors' provided only indistinct reflections. Once careful observation was introduced in self-representation, artists began to analyze and judge their creations, providing a self-reference and autocriticism that contributed to their intellectual, spiritual and pyschological self-imaging.

Another factor to consider in trying to trace early self-portraiture is the role of the mirror in producing a likeness of the artist, challenging nature 'to show virtue her own feature, scorn her own image, and the very age and body of the time his form and pressure'.[3] The mirror provided the painter with an invaluable image, the reflection of the self, which the artist used to immortalize that self. Until its manufacture in Venice around 1300, the glass mirror as we know it today did not exist.[4] Venetian glass mirrors were usually of circular format similar to that of French ivory mirrors, which in thirteenth-century Paris were produced with two reflecting surfaces: clear glass or polished metals for mirroring, on the recto, while on the verso they were beautifully decorated with an ivory setting.[5]

After the Middle Ages, there are many self-portraits by women painters. However, one dilemma that plagues researchers is whether a painting actually is a self-portrait or not. Obviously one way of identifying a self-portrait is by its title. But titles such as 'Self-Portrait', 'Portrait of the Artist', and the various translations of the concepts, do not guarantee that a given painting is an authentic self-portrait, since owners, art dealers, sellers, and recorders of inventories, wills and other documents have often invented titles to promote their own interests. Compounding the dilemma, discrepancies often occur in nomenclature. To remedy such attribution problems, it is useful to compare, when possible, an artist's other self-portraits to the painting at hand, or portraits of the artist by contemporaries.[6] A further way to help determine the authenticity of a self-portrait is by comparing it to a physical likeness of the artist as revealed by commemorative medals, engravings, photographs, or written descriptions or records.

Another source of identification can be the artistic and critical writings of contemporary artists, theoreticians and travelers, such as the ancient Pliny the Elder's *Natural History* (AD 77), Christine de Pizan's *The Book of the City of Ladies* (1404), the Mannerist Giorgio Vasari's *Lives of the Most Excellent Painters, Sculptors and Architects* (1550), Karel van Mander's *Dutch and Flemish Painters* (1603–4), the Baroque André Félibien's *Entretiens sur les vies et les ouvrages des plus excellens peintres* (1666–8), Denis Diderot's *Salons* and Mariette's *Abécédario*, otherwise known as *L'Histoire et le Secret de la peinture en cire* (1775).

Female self-portraits are as complex as the society in which the artists lived. The intimate revelations exposed to the viewer include a desire on the part of the artist to be discovered, appreciated, and admired for herself as a human being, for her creativity and inventiveness, or her beauty. By observing themselves as objects of beauty and admiration, women painters expanded their role as creator of life into that of artistic creator. If a self-portrait was painted by the artist for herself and not for a patron, it may portray the female interest in assertion and self-advertisement, as seen in Catherina Murphy's daring *Self-Portrait – Pregnancy* of 1970 (Fourcade Droll Collection, New York), and in Alice Neel's *Self-Portrait* of 1980 (Pl. LII), where she has portrayed herself nude at the age of 80.

This examination only treats briefly some different modes of self-portraiture, but it suggests the richness of the genre and the unexpected ways in which artists have dealt with self-representation. What follows concentrates on the many variations of the woman painter's self-image and on what the image discloses about the artist, the era and the style in which it was made, as well as the significance of the mode chosen by the artist in representing herself.[7]

The self-portrait begins as an image of the creative process. In ancient writings the image of the painter was regarded as a reflection of classical culture and the taste of connoisseurs. Only the names of Greek painters are known from this era.[8] Following Plato's theory of art as *mimesis*, mimic or parody, as the imitation of nature, self-portraits of ancient painters can be seen as artists' copies of nature, and their self-images are therefore imitations and not the original of the self.[9] The painted image, the self-portrait, too, is magic; the painter herself becomes a magician.

In the Middle Ages, the self-portrait was rooted in the biblical tradition of the process of divine creation, *Deus artifixe* and representation.[10] The dual characterization of the artist, as at once both admirable and dangerous, was reflected in the medieval theory of art, where the magic quality of the self-image remained mythified, and where a capricious but benevolent ruler became the Creator according to the Judeo-Christian concept of God. God, then, was the first painter and invented the first self-portrait. Examples can be seen in Christ's self-imaging in Veronica's veil, and in the appearances of the Virgin to Saint Luke.

In the Renaissance and Mannerist eras, the notion that the self-portrait reflects God's artistry was changed into the concept of the artistry of Nature. The artist's virtuosity became regarded as that of the *artista divino*, the divine artist, making the artist a superior being, as exemplified by Leonardo and Michelangelo. In the seventeenth and eighteenth centuries, the admiration for *Nature as artist* extended even to the practice of art itself, as honored by the academies of the time. The ways in which the artist either borrowed from Nature, or improved upon it, were of particular concern in the eighteenth century and served as a basis for much theoretical discourse.

In the nineteenth century, the practice of painting became more professionalized, with greater educational opportunities for women. The century witnessed the formation of professional societies for women artists, including the Society of Female Artists in England, the Union des femmes peintres et sculpteurs in France and the Verein der Kunstlerinnen in Germany.

Although the artist's allegiance to a particular style was important during the nineteenth century (Neo-classicism, Romanticism, Realism, Pre-Raphaelite art, Impressionism or Post-Impressionism), it became particularly evident in the twentieth century, when movements have followed one another in rapid succession. There are Fauve self-portraits, Cubist self-portraits, German Expressionist self-portraits, Surrealist self-portraits, and styles in which the figure is abstractly represented. Self-portraits are also more self-analytical and revealing, often an 'inscape' rather than a recognizable representation of a person. The contemporary artist intensifies this search for the inner self, often using symbolic and surrogate forms of representation of both self and others. The Post-Modernist era is also more inclusive of formerly marginal groups, such as African-American, Hispanic, Native American and Asian-American. New areas of formerly neglected art have joined the Western tradition of representation with a recognition of the previous narrow scope of the art-historical canon of acceptable works. Or as Irving Sandler notes, 'Art history is not transparent. It is written by individuals, who bring to it their own personal baggage of appetites, psychological makeups, ethnic identities, social positions, political and religious persuasions, and so on. Claims to objectivity notwithstanding, the historian's idiosyncracies shape art history.'[11] Portraiture is no longer predominantly 'the ape of nature',[12] the dignifying of a ruler or aristocrat, or the representation of a stylish sitter, but rather a confrontation with the limits and possibilities of being human.

Occasionally, artists identify themselves in a painting by the use of a symbolic or surrogate motif. Instead of a signature, a painter may substitute an animal or inanimate object, such as Jehan Pucelle's dragonfly, which symbolizes his name in the *Book of Hours of Jeanne d'Évreux* of 1325 (Cloisters Collection, Metropolitan Museum of Art, New York), or Whistler's butterfly signature. In *Pregnant Rabbit Telling Her Parents* of 1982 (private collection, London), Paula Rego, pregnant by a married man, returns from the Slade School of Art to her home in Portugal to tell her parents. The artist dons the humorous disguise of a rabbit, one of the most fecund of animals.

Particularly popular in the seventeenth and eighteenth centuries was the emblematic self-portrait. Here the artist either assumed a personification or depicted him- or herself with allegorical figures. An example of the first type is Artemisia Gentileschi's *Self-Portrait as the Allegory of Painting* of 1630 (see Pl. XIV). Gentileschi shows herself painting, and identifies herself with *La Pittura*, the personification of painting. In the eighteenth century, the Swiss artist Angelica Kauffmann also took on the allegorical character of painting in her *The Artist in the Character of Design Listening to the Inspiration of Poetry* of 1782 (The Iveagh Bequest, Kenwood). This representation also identifies art with literature, on the principle *'ut pictura poesis'* ('as is painting, so is poetry') from Horace's *Ars poetica*, 1–10, linking painting and poetry as sister arts.[13] Responding to an interest in Greek culture, this allegorical parallelism (*paragone*) had been appropriated and assimilated in the Renaissance and Mannerist periods,[14] was reiterated and elaborated during the Baroque era,[15] and continued into the eighteenth century.

Closely associated with the allegorical self-portrait has been the adoption of a mythological or religious figure bearing the artist's own features: St Cecilia; St Luke (for example Giorgio Vasari, *St Luke Painting the Virgin* of 1567, in the Capella dei Pittori, SS. Annunziata, Florence); Judith (see Pl. XIII, Artemisia Gentileschi's *Judith and Holofernes* of 1615); Goliath (Caravaggio's own features appear on the head of Goliath in *David and Goliath* of 1600, in the Borghese Gallery, Rome); Sappho (Angelica Kauffmann painted herself in her *Sappho* of 1775 (see Fig. VI.17)). This approach usually associates the artist with an identity the artist wishes to assume, for example in Marcia Marcus's *Self-Portrait as Athena* of 1972 (private collection).[16] Here the painter depicts herself wearing Athena's helmet and posing against the Acropolis, claiming Athena's role as goddess of wisdom. An even more audacious identification with deity is found in Cynthia Mailman's *Self-Portrait as God* from Sister Chapel, exhibited at Woman Art in 1977.[17] A towering work, nine feet tall and five feet wide, it depicts the artist nude, with flowing hair and rays of the sun emanating from behind her head.

Sometimes an explanation from the artist is necessary to clarify the subject or content of a painting. For example, in Audrey Flack's *Queen* of 1975–6 (Pl. XLII), Flack appears as the photograph of a child in a double locket in the lower right corner. *Queen* itself is a disguised portrait of Flack's mother. Even more difficult to penetrate is Elizabeth Murray's *More Than You Know* of 1983 (Edward R. Broida Trust), which appears to be an abstract composition, but actually represents the table and chairs where she and her mother sat and talked during the latter's illness, according to the artist.[18]

Often, a self-portrait in a group proclaims an artist's affinities with the group or allegiance to it. This can be observed in Marie Laurencin's *Apollinaire and His Friends* or *Group of Artists* of 1908 (Fig. VIII.3), where the artist portrays Picasso in profile on the far left, and herself standing next to the seated Guillaume Apollinaire. Picasso's lover Fernande Olivier is seen posing coyly on the far right. In this way, Laurencin identified herself with the Cubist movement, begun by Picasso and Braque, and extensively written about and publicized by Apollinaire.

Another function of a self-portrait, particularly in contemporary times, is to express the subject's personality and psychological makeup. This is more difficult to define unless the artist provides some very specific clues. A divided self is shown in Frida Kahlo's *The Two Fridas* of 1939 (Museo de Arte Moderno, Mexico City) in which two self-representations of the artist appear: one on the left in which Kahlo is dressed in lacy Victorian clothing, expressing her German father's European heritage, the other on the right in which she is dressed in a Tehuana skirt and blouse, representing her maternal background and her life in Mexico with her husband, Diego Rivera.

Self-portraits can be seen as having text and voice in several different ways. Beyond the painter's and sitter's voices, contemporary fashions and conventional taste also contribute to the meaning of a work. Vogues come and go for the medallion or full face, single or group portrait, for the isolated, timeless physical image or the portrait in the context of social exchange or surrounded by attributes.

This study is concerned with the function of female self-portraiture in painting as a source of revelation, not merely as signature. It is not meant as an exercise in iconographical reference, but rather an interpretation or statement of the artist's character and self-definition and her relationship to her milieu.

I

Self-portraits in antiquity

Little is known about women artists of ancient times, and even less about their self-portraiture.[1] What information has been gathered comes from legend, and from iconography found on objects in archeological excavations where surviving domestic tools, furniture, ornaments, ceramic vases, coins, fresco and mosaic paintings, and relief and free-standing sculptures help to reconstruct the private and public lives of a few women artists.[2] Although some early records from antiquity[3] do exist for self-portraits by male painters, during the Old and New Kingdoms in Egypt,[4] only the image of the man or woman may be studied, never his or her acconpanying artistic creations. Male self-portraits were subordinate to a more general imagery as part of portraiture, during the Hellenistic period in Greece,[5] and continued to flourish in Rome, as a part of a great quest for naturalism and physical resemblance.[6] But apparently no examples from early antiquity have survived that can be identified with certitude as self-portraiture.[7] Not until the Hellenistic era (400–315 BC) are there records of women artists and their self-portraits.[8] Although men, as artists, have been recorded in Egypt since c.2300 BC,[9] it is unclear when the first surviving male self-portrait was actually executed, although one has been dated to around 1300 BC (Fig. I.1).

The human desire to see oneself or to see one's own image is attested by the ancient world's belief that the individual spirit was contained in his or her reflection, leading to the mythical story of Narcissus. This legend, recounted by Ovid in *Metamorphoses* (3:339–510), is of a handsome youth and the nymph who loved him, Echo, whose love is not reciprocated. As Narcissus' punishment for spurning Echo, the goddess Juno makes him fall in love with his own reflection gazing back at him in a pool. One creative invention of a non-literary kind was the mirror – the principal visual instrument for obtaining an authentic reflection of the self. Surviving mirrors from antiquity reveal two types of perspective: one aesthetic (concern for one's image), the other religious. Many of these mirrors have some sort of inscription. In Archaic Greek funerary art, among the objects of remembrance or gifts to

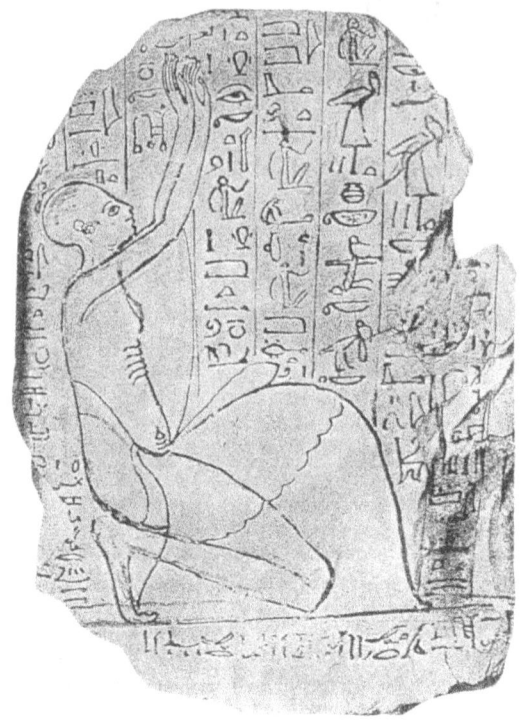

I.1   Egyptian painter, *Self-Portrait*, 1300 BC

goddesses from women were mirrors. They were associated with the women's toilet and femininity, as illustrated in the Archaic mirror of 480 BC dedicated by Hippylla to Artemis (located in the Archeological Museum of Braunau, Germany) and the perfume vase of 460 BC (Bernisches Historisches Museum) which shows two women in a domestic interior by a hanging mirror and a wool-basket.[10]

Classical Greek mirrors were also associated with the celebration of and preparation for nuptial feasts, as illustrated in the tombstone of Pausimache of 390–80 BC (National Archeological Museum, Athens), commissioned by her parents, who were mourning the early death of their unmarried daughter. The image reveals a young woman, standing and looking in a mirror, alluding to her beauty and grace – the aesthetic concerns of Greek society – and to her failure to marry because of her death.[11]

As the use of mirrors expanded in the ancient world, particularly in Etruria, central Italy, so too did their range of design.[12] Their production there began around 530 BC and proliferated until the second century BC. They were cast in bronze in the shape of a disk with a handle in one piece, or in two pieces if the handle was of bone ivory. The disk was convex on the reflective side, producing an image smaller than life size, and concave on the reverse, creating an area for engraved decoration. It was this feature that made Etruscan mirrors striking and original, unlike the plain Greek bronze or Roman silver mirrors. Etruscan mirrors reflected the images of the most liberated women of antiquity as well as the woman's status. Most were both commissioned and owned by women, as the signature on each mirror indicates, since Etruscan women were commonly *mundis muliebris*, or women of the world. Following the funerary ritual honoring the female divinity of Earth Mother (Mater Matuta or Leucothea), all personal accessories were buried with the deceased. If, in her lifetime, the mirror had reflected physical beauty, subsequently the afterworld honored her with eternal fame. Mythological scenes and inscriptions with elaborate literary and religious dedications were added, as in the depiction of Aphrodite and Adonis as lovers in one engraved bronze mirror of the second half of the fourth century BC and in the story of the Judgment of Paris illustrated in an example from the beginning of the third century BC.[13] The mirror became an artistic object with a dual function, to illustrate and to reflect: on the verso or back of the object, usually incised or in relief, a story was illustrated, representing the cultural milieu of the time, and, on the recto or front, most significantly the mirror reflected the image of the self.[14]

The mirror, like other objects in ancient art, communicates much about the role of women, through scenes of child-bearing, nurturing, cultivating, spinning and weaving.[15] Women in antiquity decorated their objects for both aesthetic and spiritual reasons; along with domestic activities went a concern with decorating themselves, creating both their environment and themselves as ornaments of beauty, through occupations learned from female mentors. From the evidence of ancient civilizations, such as Egyptian funerary art and pyramidal texts, it can be assumed that women were skilled in decorating linen fabrics; according to custom they covered the dead with decorative linen cloths, as can be seen in the model of a weaving workshop in the tomb of Meketra from the Middle Kingdom, in the Egyptian Museum, Cairo.[16] From the clay tablet inscriptions of the Ancient Near East it is postulated that women excelled in decorating their houses with draperies and hanging tapestries. Surviving clay tablets further document women's accomplishments in operating weaving workshops and in business transactions over the export of goods.[17] Eastern as well as African and American women designed jewelry, shawls and carpets, and made elaborate quilts.[18] Tools discovered in female gravesites from the seventh millennium BC, during the Neolithic period, suggest that women worked in textiles, ceramics and basket weaving.[19] From various findings it can be assumed that women of the Greek period collaborated in artistic workshops, making materials and weaving textiles, carving in wood and stone, casting metals, and modeling in ceramics – as illustrated in the detail of an Attic red-figure vase of 450 BC by the artist known as the Leningrad Painter, *Caputi Hydria*, where artists are seen at work in a pottery atelier, including a woman completing the design of a krater. Above her hang several vases of different shapes – kylix and lekythos – demonstrating various aspects of her accomplishments as a ceramicist. Other Greek vase paintings depict women engaged in artistic activities such as the construction and production of a loom, recorded on the lekythos vase for oil or perfume attributed to the Amasis Painter, *Women Working Wool on a Loom*, 560 BC (Fig. I.2).[20]

Irrespective of the matriarchal or patriarchal nature of their society, it can be seen that women artists operated in a constrained environment, since their biological function and nurturing qualities overrode their artistic ability. Distinctions between upper and lower classes, however, created varying degrees of free time for royal and priestly or peasant and slave. The woman became mythified as goddess, virgin, and mother, as in the figures of Hera–Juno, Athena–Minerva, Artemis–Diana, Aphrodite–Venus, Demeter–Ceres, and Hestia–Gaia.

Information from this period on women and their creativity relies on a male perspective, of course; one based on interpretation of the literary and visual arts in general and on recorded law accounts, medical treatises and historical texts.[21] In the poems of Homer and Hesiod, there are contrasting views on the roles of Greek women, according to their social status. But both writers reveal a misogynist attitude.[22] As the principal aim of the *polis* was to maintain stability in the existing number of families, the woman's main roles were to procreate and to care for the household. Her legal rights were limited and her assets were deemed to be limited to her biological function.[23] Since

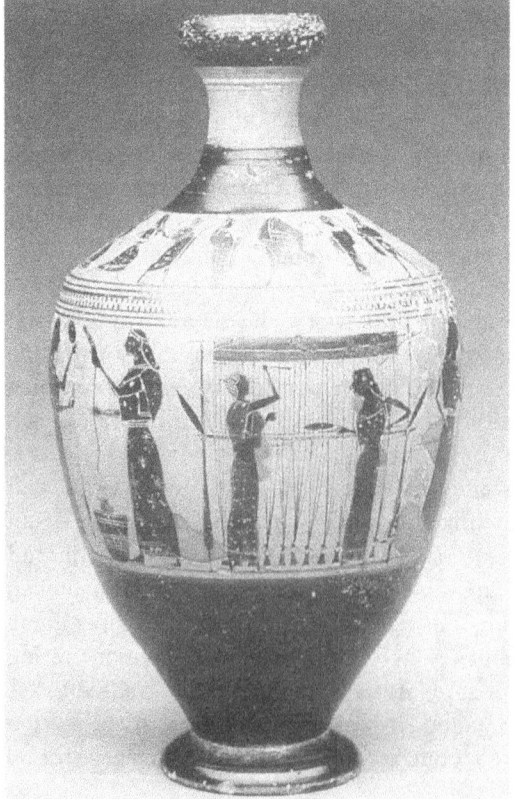

I.2 Amasis Painter, *Women Working Wool on a Loom*, 560 BC

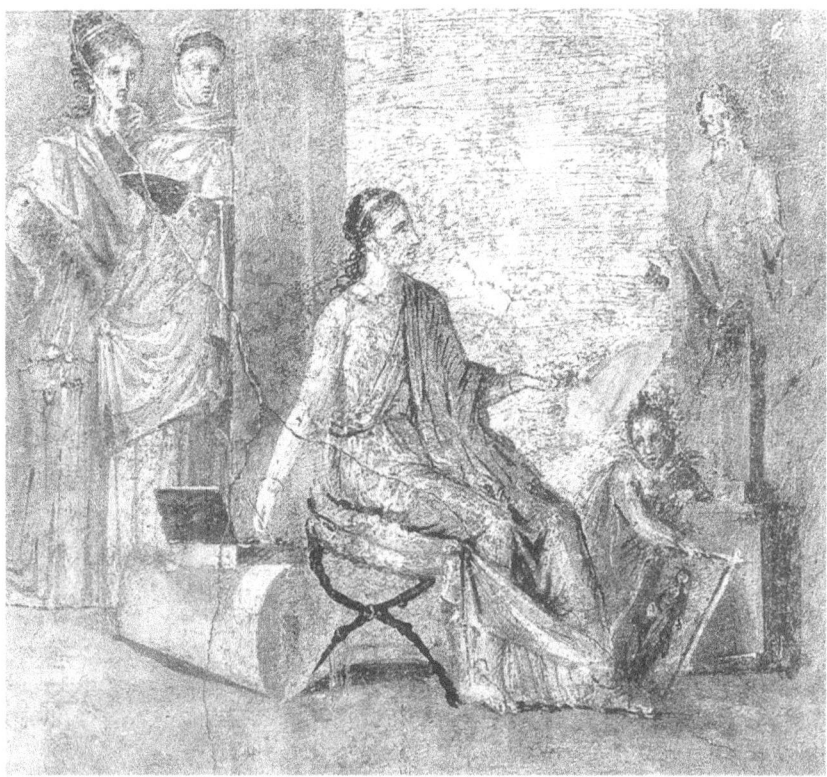

I.3 Marcia, *Marcia in Her Studio*, before AD 79

women were denied a public voice, what limited information is available on the feminine viewpoint comes from fragmented poems composed by women such as Sappho.[24] Those women artists who were recorded were said to have excelled in the arts. That women painters of this period were able to create under their societal constraints was, indeed, remarkable.

In the ancient world in subsequent centuries, women evidently contributed to the arts through singing, acting, dancing and playing musical instruments, as seen in a Roman wall painting from the Villa Boscoreale, in Italy, showing a woman playing the cithara (first century BC, Metropolitan Museum of Art, New York).[25] The Roman environment for women artists continued similar to that of the Hellenistic period. Although Roman laws provided a specific codification of family rights, a dominantly patriarchal society reinforced women's subservient position as individuals. In legal actions a woman had to be represented by a guardian, father, husband or other male relative or by a lawyer.[26] Lacking political rights, women could not hold political appointments and could seldom defend their rights in court without such guardians. While the upper-class married woman, the *matrona*, was highly protected by the law, lower-class concubines or prostitutes had few legal rights.[27] Roman funerary inscriptions reveal that occupations for middle- and lower-class women expanded to include those of laundresses, librarians, governesses, midwives, physicians, dressmakers and hairdressers. Some women engaged in business in conjunction with their husbands. The occupation of a *matrona*, however, was to be a mother, rule the house and entertain guests. She could be involved in patronage of the arts, though this was rare, and honorific inscriptions cite the restoration commissioned by Julia Augusta and Sabina Augusta in the Forum of Trajan in the third century AD, and the commission by Scholasticia of Ephesus of the construction and restoration of two public baths. Women such as Junia Theodora, a Roman resident in Corinth, were also honored for their public generosity and good will.[28]

In wall paintings from palaces and villas at Herculaneum, Pompeii, Naples, and in the Roman dominions, artists have left a legacy of the history of women in Roman times. Gems and coins, in particular, record numerous portraits of unidentified imperial women. Naturalistic portraits were produced by sculptors of busts during Republican times (753 BC to 27 BC), while during the Empire period (27 BC to 337 AD) they were more stylized. The concept of *verism*, being true to self, true to nature, in Roman portraiture, where the unknown artist aimed not only to represent the actual, natural, honest resemblance of the sitter but also to convey the *anima*, the inner being, spirit or soul, made a major contribution to the history of art.[29] Numerous portrait heads and busts also present the state of fashion in dressing, coiffures and crafted jewelry of upper-class women.[30]

The lives of ordinary women can best be reconstructed from archeological and epigraphical documentation, as in funerary art: gravestones and monuments with inscriptions alluding to the domestic virtues of the subject. Ovid's *Ars Amatoria* (*The Art of Love*) was intended as an instruction manual for young women on how to make the best of themselves, in particular in Book Three. There Ovid discusses women's costume and life, offering advice on how to become educated through reading the classics of Greek poetry, as well as mastering the arts of conversation, dancing, singing and playing a musical instrument. The concept of an educated, cultivated woman began in Roman times, but only for women of the aristocracy, or the priestly class, such as the Vestal Virgins.

Although it appears that some women in Roman times were able to lead more satisfying lives, as a result of less restrictive marriage laws and an emphasis on heterosexual relationships, it had been the Greeks who first questioned the traditional role of women. They nonetheless represented females as inferior to men. Plato and Aristotle wrote of women's passive role in procreation and their allegedly limited capacity for mental activity.[31] This view was also expressed in Galen's biological studies and medical treatises, where the female was considered less perfect than the male because she was colder and her testicles were thought to be inside her uterus.[32] Greek philosophers stressed the functional aspect of the woman, her procreational ability, while Roman philosophers directed women's energies to marriage and motherhood.[33]

The earliest written record relating to drawing or painting by a woman in ancient art is recounted by the Roman historian and writer Pliny the Elder in his *Naturalis Historiae* (*Natural History*), Book 35, on the history of art, of the first century AD. Pliny here established a catalogue of famous women in both the visual arts (*pinxere et mulieres*) and in poetry,[34] relying for many of his observations on paintings by women on a contemporary scholar, Marcus Terentius Varro (116–27 BC), and on documentation from Varro's *De vita populi Romani* (*The Lives of the Romans*).

Although few women painters' names are mentioned by Pliny, the particulars he offered help to explain the artistic impact of both genders and allow us to grasp the universality of human expression through the visual arts.[35] The women he cites belonged mostly to one of two schools of Hellenistic art: the Athenian school or the Sicyonia school. The list includes Aristarete, Anaxandra, Kallo, Kalyso, Eirene, Olympias, Helena, Timarete and Lala (Iaia or Marcia), most of whom were said to have painted self-portraits. Many of these women distinguished themselves by their unique inventions and attainments. With the exception of Marcia, they were all said to be married, but documentation on their child-bearing is unclear. All were allegedly trained by their fathers, who were artists. The women assisted their fathers in their workshops, which they sometimes inherited and continued to maintain. Some of them were artistic tutors or mentors and had their own pupils, thus establishing a simple version of an art school or academy.

The women's method of painting was based on the encaustic technique on linen, panel (wood), or ivory, the era's most delicate and expensive painting surface. Pliny reports that this method was introduced by Polygnotus.[36] The procedure of applying the colored pigment involved one of three methods. With the first technique, powdered color was mixed with hot wax and applied with an iron knife to the wood or linen surface. Using the second method, colors were applied to ivory surfaces using a type of spoon-palette with a hollow shape at one end as receptacle for the pigment. This receptacle was heated, to melt and blend the wax with the color, which was then poured over the surface of the ivory (*cestro in ebore*). The artist used the implement's other end, with its long, pointed handle, to level the colors and touch up the details. These techniques were limited by their cost as well as by the slow and tedious nature of the encaustic applications. In the fifth century BC, Aristide the Elder was said to have introduced a third method of painting in which the color was applied with a brush (*penicillo*). While resting the painting on an easel, with this method the artist was able to move with more facility.[37]

With Pliny's account we can reconstruct some of the portraits painted by women, although most of his descriptions of women's art do not focus specifically on self-portraits but concentrate on their education, thematic representation and artistic merit. Even if limited, these data are not without insight for the twentieth-century reader.

Aristarete of Calypso, daughter and pupil of Nearchos, a well-known Athenian painter of genre scenes and portraits during the end of the third century BC,[38] was said to have painted a portrait of Æsculapius (Asklepios), the god of healing, as an *ex-voto* (a painting offering thanks to a deity or saint for saving a person from danger or illness) for his sanctuary in the Athenian acropolis. Because of the S-curve design of her figures, scholars suspect that she may have been active in Rhodes, where her father had a workshop.[39] Her fame was so great that one of her paintings, *A Mother Assisting Her Daughter's Toilet*, was supposedly transferred from the ruins of Pompeii to Naples.[40] This subject derives from the theme of Venus at her toilet, popular as a genre, which related specifically to self-portraiture.

Pliny's text describes a group of accomplished women artists who worked under the royal patronage of Alexander the Great, producing portraits and mythological and genre paintings for the court. The identity of the subjects, though, is sometimes unclear. During the Hellenistic period, the visual arts flourished, thus encouraging artists to experiment. Among the outstanding women painters from this period was Anaxandra (Anassandra; fl. 260 BC), the daughter and pupil of the Greek painter Nealces, who painted portraits in Sicyonia.[41] Another painter, Kallo (Callo), executed a work found in the Temple of Venus at Sicyon which depicts a poetess (perhaps Sappho), 'The fair painter being declared as beautiful as her own work'.[42]

Trained in the Sicyonian school around 200 BC, Kalyso (Calyso) was commissioned to design theatrical stage settings and performances for various festivals.[43] According to Pliny, she presented a portrait of an old man (perhaps a theatrical mask), the famous juggler Theodorus, and the dancer Acistenes, who performed at the festivals at Delphi. Also, the Athenian painter, Eirene (Irene or Cirene), who was the daughter and pupil of the painter, Kratinos (Cratinus),[44] painted a remarkable version of the mythological story of Proserpine for the sanctuary of the goddesses at Eleusis. According to Clemens Alexandrinus (AD 160–215), *Stromata* (IV, 124), Eirene was most likely active during the fourth century or early third century BC and, like her father, she painted commissions for a sanctuary in Attica. Her votive painting at Eleusis was probably placed on the porch of Filone, a Hellenistic sculptor who worked during the reign of Alexander the Great, mostly on bronze statues and bust portraits.

Olympias was another artist from the Hellenistic period. Of her activities as a painter it is only known that Autoboulos was her pupil.[45] From him it is noted that women painters at the time were not only receiving training from their parents but also imparted knowledge of painting to the young, thereby establishing themselves as painters and teachers of the arts.

Although Pliny does not name Helena, other sources recount what were said to be her achievements.[46] She was the daughter of an Egyptian painter who specialized in mosaic. It is believed that she painted a battle scene for the Ptolemies in which Alexander the Great vanquished Darius III, King of Persia, in the fourth century BC. Helena's original painting was rendered in marble mosaic as *The Battle of Issus* in 100 BC for the House of the Faun in Pompeii (now housed in the Museo Nazionale di San Martino). If this mosaic is indeed a version of Helena's painting, then it is the earliest surviving example of a woman painting an historical theme on a grand scale.

Pliny actually viewed many of the works that he discusses. The Athenian painter Timarete (Thamyris),[47] daughter of the artist Micon the Minor, trained in her father's workshop and achieved considerable artistic skill, as Pliny testifies (see Pl. I for a medieval illustration of Timarete at work). Having seen some of her paintings at Ephesus, Pliny considered *Artemis* (or *Diana*), painted on panel and executed in *c.*400 BC as an *ex-voto* for the sanctuary of Artemis at Ephesus, one of the most beautiful paintings of the time. This work apparently represented the traditional style of the Athenian atelier.

Although in private life confined to the role of obedient daughter, faithful wife, and caring mother, Roman women were also involved in *romanitas*, the political, economic and cultural life of the city, as illustrated in historical reliefs such as the Ara Pacis, and fresco paintings from the House of Livia. Priestly women were engaged in spinning and weaving, upper-class women were little burdened with mundane chores, while lower-class women and slaves worked in domestic and industrial settings.[48] However, the economic growth of Rome and the expansion of the Empire, produced more occupations and expanded the power of women artists.

Iaia or Lala of Kyziko (Boccaccio's Marcia), who was active during the first century BC, has been credited with a contribution as a brush painter and ivory carver (again, see Pl. II for a medieval representation of her).[49] Her portraits of women were admired, and she excelled as a miniaturist painter of ivories, executed in tempera and in encaustic on ivory. Pliny relies for the description of Iaia's life on the observations of Varro who in his youth had actually viewed her works. Pliny emphasizes that she remained single all her life, implying that the other women mentioned were married.[50]

Two major periods in Iaia's life are mentioned by Pliny: in Rome, where she specialized in portraits of women, and then in Naples, where she painted a portrait of an old woman in tempera on a large panel, as well as a self-portrait. This new interest in self-portraiture reflects both her own established fame and a cultural development in Rome, where writers such as Lucilius and the circle of Q. Lutatius Catulus developed an interest in autobiography. Pliny specifically states that Iaia composed her self-portrait standing in front of or looking at a mirror ('*ad speculum*').[51] However, his references to the first known female self-portraitist are confusing, as he refers to Iaia at times, but to Timarete in other instances. Pliny also praised Iaia for a new impressionist style, which she achieved using a brush rather than a spoon-palette to apply paint, and for establishing a new school of painting with a group of artists, including Sopolis and Dionysius, whose artistic merits and workshops focused on creating portraits ('*imaginum pictores*') 'whose works filled our galleries'.[52] Iaia's paintings had such merit that they sold for higher prices than those of Sopolis and Dionysius, both well-known contemporary artists. Pliny also commended Iaia for her rapidity in execution ('*velocitas in pictura*').

Painting, in Pliny's account, was the only visual art practiced by women in antiquity, probably because it was less heavy work than casting in bronze, carving in marble or modeling in clay. Accordingly, as early as in the fourth century BC a school, that at Sicyonia, was well known for training women in

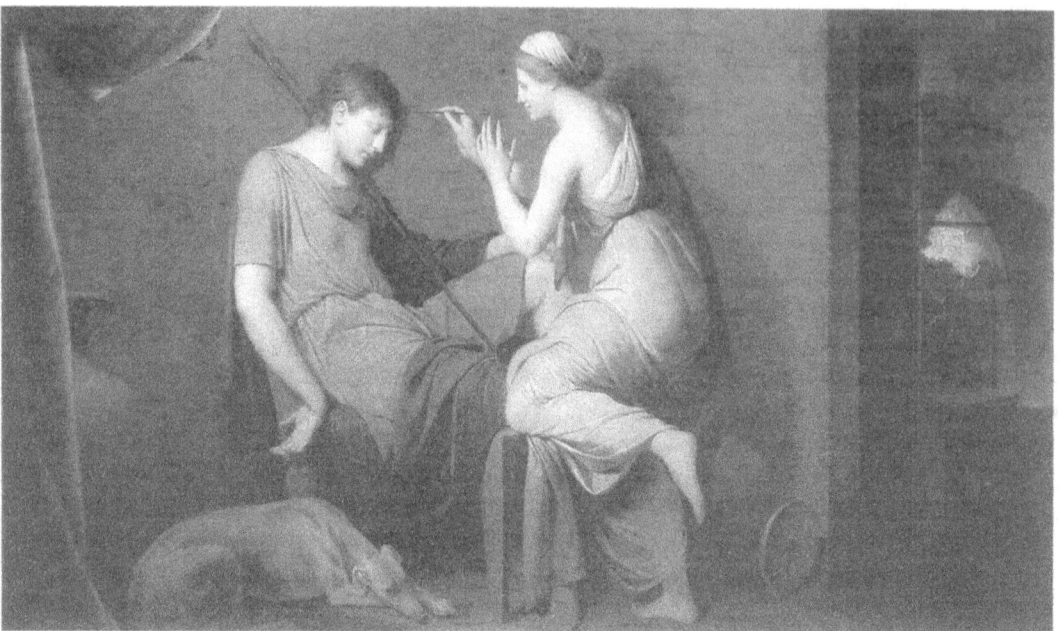

I.4 Joseph Wright of Derby, *The Corinthian Maid*, 1783–4

the liberal arts, including writing poetry, weaving, drawing and painting. Women of the upper class who attended this school learned among other things to apply to painting the use of color employed in textiles.

According to Pliny, a woman played a major part in the development of portraiture. Athenagoras Kora (or Callirhoë) was the daughter of a potter named Dibutades, a native of Corinth, residing in Sicyonia in about the middle of the seventh century BC.[53] Kora assisted her father in modeling clay, maintaining his vase shop, and filling elaborate vases with flowers or perfume. The beautiful maiden fell in love with a young Greek, an apprentice in her father's workshop. In one of the last meetings of the pair, Kora was saddened that evening at news of her lover's departure for war. Desirous of having a remembrance of him, she took a coal from the brazier and sketched his profile with charcoal, tracing the shadow of his face made by a lamp on a wall (see Wright of Derby's reconstruction of this legend in Fig. I.4).[54] Recognizing the likeness of his daughter's portrait, Dibutades was so moved by her affection and her artistic creativity that he filled the outline with clay and completed it in a medallion format, thus creating the first bas-relief. This first portrait (*similitudo*), Pliny recounts, was made in clay and preserved in the Nympheum fountain at Corinth where for two hundred years it honored the Dibutades family until Mummunius sacked the city.[55] Although the first profile portrait was of the image of a man, it was a woman who had created it.

Kora's artistic inspiration originated from a *furor amorus*. In his narrative on the origin of portraiture, Pliny alludes to two types of artistic creativity: intuitive (invention), in the case of Kora, and reasoned or mimetic (imitation)

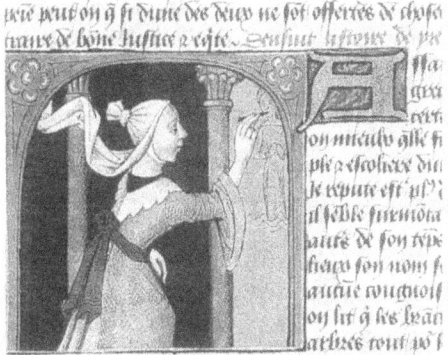

I.5 *Timarete Drawing Herself on a Wall*, in Boccaccio's *Noble and Famous Women*, 1401–2, MS Fr.599, folio 53v

in the response by Dibutades.[56]

Pliny's text was not illustrated. However, a mural painting from a Roman villa at Herculaneum (now in the Museo Archeologico in Naples) dated before the eruption of Vesuvius in AD 79, represents *Marcia in Her Studio*. The scene depicts a female artist painting a male statue in her studio. Attributes of her profession are visible, such as the palette in her left hand, and the painter's box where she is dipping a brush. Below the statue, a crowned putto presents to the viewer a finished panel painting of a woman holding a jug. Behind Marcia stand two female painters. These onlookers, possibly pupils, are also holding professional attributes, while admiring Marcia's work Fig I.3).

The significance of this fresco is threefold. It may be among the first surviving visual images representing Marcia's artistic accomplishments according to Pliny's account, being painted during his lifetime. Furthermore it is the earliest known depiction of a painter's brush and palette being used by a female artist. It may also be one of the first known representations of a woman painter both as a professional artist and as a teacher.

Centuries later, with the revival and appropriation of ancient ideals, medieval writers and artists did assimilate and illustrate Pliny's accounts in their own works, as exemplified by a manuscript of 1401–2 of Boccaccio's *Noble and Famous Women* (*De claris mulieribus*) made for the Duc de Berry (Pl. I; Figs. I.5, I.6).[57] It is in this way that medieval depictions of Greek and Roman women's self-portraiture are found in illuminated manuscripts, as Pascal Bonafoux has demonstrated.[58]

One miniature illustration from Boccaccio's *Noble and Famous Women* illustrates the ancient painter Timarete drawing her image on the wall (Fig. I.4). Another page of the manuscript shows Timarete painting a self-portrait. The illustration of this manuscript may thus allude to the first female self-portrait or to the story told by Pliny of the invention of modeling by Kora.[59]

In a later edition (1470) of the same work another illumination shows *Marcia Painting Her Self-Portrait* (Pl. II). Here, Marcia is seen in her studio

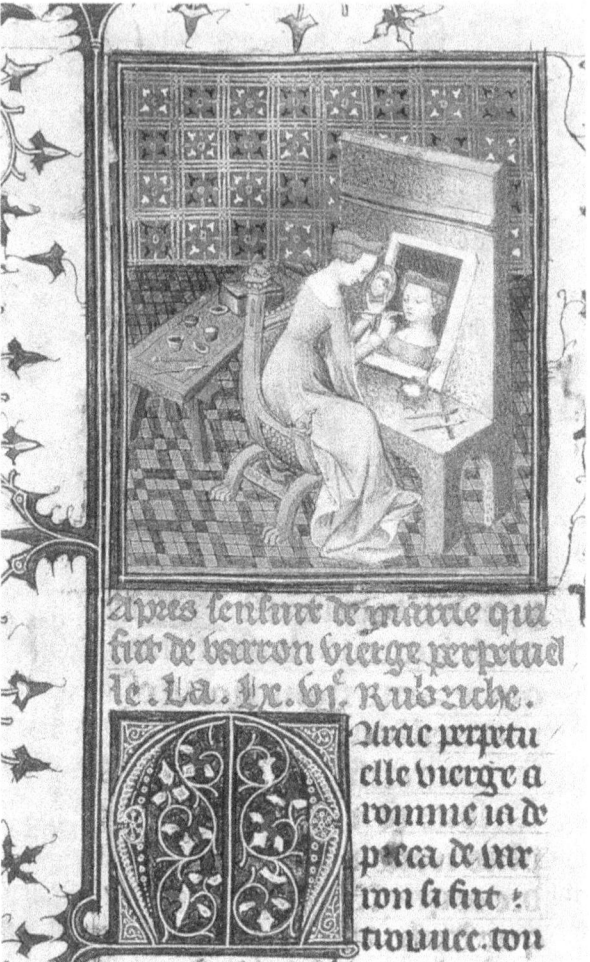

I.6 *Marcia Painting Her Self-Portrait*, 1401–2, in Boccaccio's *Noble and Famous Women*, MS Fr. 12420, folio 101 verso

surrounded by her paintings and sculptures. She stands in front of an easel as she paints, carefully gazing into a mirror, seeing her reflection and comparing it with her painted image.

Timarete can be seen in an earlier illustration (1401–2) of this work, where, in a studio filled with painter's paraphernalia, she is proudly touching up the last details of her self-portrait (Pl. I). Elsewhere in this manuscript, Marcia can be seen painting a self-portrait on a panel, while using a painter's palette with three brushes. Seated at her desk, she holds a mirror (Fig. I.6). Timarete, having completed her self-portrait, no longer needs the mirror and has hung it on the wall, beside her painting. The accouterments of the artist – brushes, jars of paint, and an illuminated book – can be seen resting on Marcia's table.

Around Marcia, finishing the last touches of her portrait, the wall and floor are richly decorated with various patterns that contrast with the simplicity of her dress and coiffure. Her painted self-portrait is larger than her reflected image. Has the painter aggrandized herself or is the large size due to the fact that her mirrored reflection is magnified?[60]

In the illuminated manuscript of Boccaccio's text, the representation of Marcia takes a step further in the examination of a painter in that it shows not only a courtly lady, but also a *persona*, the representation of a character. The depiction of Marcia is a record of the activities of an artist, for example by showing her looking in the mirror and painting what she sees at an easel. Unlike the discrepancies seen in the perspectival rendition of the overall composition – the floor and table are tilted, for example, and the table behind the painter is not proportionate in size – the placement of the seated figure in relation to the mirror, the reflection of the portrait in the mirror and the painted portrait on the easel are all accurately and proportionately rendered. The artist has carefully studied nature and observed its spatial complexity. In the same way Marcia reveals a sense of scrutiny and scientific investigation as she studies the physical reality before her. What she has drawn is carefully conveyed; the portrait is an accurate rendition of reality. Thus, as a painter, Marcia is shown as involved with two realities: the reflection of her image in the mirror that she holds and the painted self-image that she has depicted by viewing herself in the mirror.

Even as a limited subject of visual and historical allusions, it can be seen that the female self-portrait from antiquity paved the way for future representations of the self.

II

The medieval reflection: illumination and miniature self-portraits

After the demise of the Roman empire, there are a few images of women in mosaics in convents, churches and cemeteries but, by and large, records indicate a cessation in painting by women.

For historical simplification, the medieval era can be divided into the Early Middle Ages (from *c.*450, in the Early Christian period, to the reign of Charlemagne, 747–814) and the Late Middle Ages (from the court of Charlemagne to the beginning of the fourteenth century).[1] While this division can enhance our understanding of the contributions of women artists during this fertile period, it unfortunately underscores the limited documentation on their contributions. Few names of women artists occur during the Early Middle Ages; creativity appears to have been limited to artistic and cultural patronage.

As in the Hellenistic period, the Late Middle Ages saw a resurgence of women artists. Documentation from monasteries reveals signatures, self-portraits or both. In the Hellenistic period, female artists were affiliated to their fathers' workshops while in the Middle Ages the accomplishments of women artists were manifest in convent scriptoria. The shift from paternal atelier to convent workshop parallels a social change for women artists from a patriarchal–filial alliance into a matriarchal fellowship, perhaps in response to the art guilds of the time, from which most women were notably absent.

In the Early Middle Ages, the combination of the Judaic tradition with Christian attitudes reduced the role of women in society to the condition of minors who needed to be protected. Marriage laws and associated customs, such as the dowry and nuptial gifts, emphasized placement in the home as mothers.[2] According to some scholars, goddesses in polytheistic systems gave women an important role; however, the role division between male and female – placing women in an inferior position, while gods took over as rulers and patrons of wisdom – prevented women from being free.[3] This dualism was displaced by the Bible, which presented a more equitable view of human nature in which women were not considered inherently inferior. Instead, the woman was viewed as man's spiritual equal, made in God's image (*Genesis* 1:27; Paul, I *Corinthians* 11: 3, 7–9; *Corpus iuris canonici*).[4] The concept of beauty in ancient representations of the female form was associated with paganism and idolatry, and in the Middle Ages was rejected in favor of artistic forms that emphasized spirituality and the denial of naturalistic representation of the human body. This different aesthetic concept in art created a new role for the female where she could express her artistic interests not necessarily as an artist but as a patron of the arts.[5]

The medieval view of woman and her position in society was a function both of her status and of the individual who evaluated her.[6] Usually such opinions came from the celibate clergy and noble aristocracy, who considered women to be inferior, a view also held in ancient times.[7] Disputes about the nature of women continued throughout the Middle Ages, producing a literary controversy lasting three centuries – *la Querelle des femmes* – as exemplified in the writings of Christine de Pizan, who was one of the most learned women of her time. She was perhaps the first woman to enter this dispute; her contribution culminated in her *The Book of the City of Ladies*.[8]

During the Middle Ages, the Church translated the civic laws of subordination into moralistic standards such as relate to the formation of feminine virtue – virginity or chastity. The mythic idealization of woman as goddess in ancient times was transformed into woman as holy being. As a result, the medieval Church expounded the merits of a celibate life, encouraging the woman-virgin to become Christ's spiritual bride by joining a nunnery.[9] Numerous women from the upper class – the unmarried, widows and even wealthy wives – entered convents in order to pursue a spiritual life and freedom from male domination. However, women from the lower classes were seldom able to enter a nunnery, since a dowry was required.

In the convent women could express themselves artistically and intellectually, in circumstances that encouraged their cultivation as artists, providing good working conditions, professional training, materials and moral and psychological support. With the expansion of nunneries, women began to undertake leadership roles such as business management and land ownership.

European monasteries offered their members education, erudition and spirituality, focusing on various aspects of literature, music, the decorative arts and manuscript illumination or painting. Convents and monasteries grew into centers for the preservation of learning and culture as well as for imparting knowledge. Such pedagogical concern manifested itself in copying, decorating, painting and writing illuminated manuscripts, thus providing a training ground for women artists.

From the Early Christian era until the rise of universities in about 1200, book production was centered in monastic scriptoria, with both males and females participating in the work. Scribes and artists worked alone or in teams, copying the text on parchment, and illuminating, correcting and binding the manuscript. Women painters were among the members of two groups: miniaturists and calligraphists. The former added color and ornamentation to the narrative in the text and laid on the gold and silver decoration. The latter, called fair writers (*pulchri scriptores*), copied the books and created the initial letters. Thus, noble women cultivated an art that was eventually to go into decline, that of the miniature painting.

Not all women who were trained in illustration in convent scriptoria were nuns, some being art students. There is documentation on women illuminators such as Anastaise, a Parisian who was a 'skillful and experienced painter of borders and miniatures of manuscripts',[10] as well as of women's self-portraits, as nuns who produced books of illuminations frequently signed their names or painted self-portraits in them.

In Spain, women illuminators fused the Islamic decorative tradition with Christian imagery. The Spanish artist Ende wrote her name on a beautiful Spanish Romanesque manuscript of *Revelations* with Mozarabic ornamentation, the *Beatus Apocalypse* (dated 975), as '*Ende pintrix et Dei aiutrix Frater Emeritus et Presbiter*' (Ende, woman painter and servant of God and Brother Emeritus Presbiter).[11] Interestingly, 'Ende' precedes 'Emeritus', suggesting her principal involvement in the decoration of the manuscript.[12] This work, currently *in situ*, was produced in Spain for the Gerona cathedral. Gisele von Kerssenbroek, another nun employed as illuminator, copied and decorated the *Codex Gisele* of 1300, now in the Bischofiches Generalvikariat of Osnabruck. One of the 52 illustrations depicts the initial P, enclosing the scene of the Nativity, where the artist has represented a congregation and signed her name at the edge of the Virgin's bedspread.[13]

European medieval women artists also excelled in calligraphy. In the ninth century, the court of Charlemagne provided a center for the encouragement of scriptoria, book-making workshops. Charlemagne's sister, Gisela, directed the first Carolingian convent and monastery scriptorium, located at Chelles, northeast of Paris. Although there are no records attributing a specific manuscript to a nun from Chelles, manuscripts signed by non-artists exist in England, Flanders, Germany and Spain. These include the *Beatus Apocalypse* signed by the Spaniard Ende. Reforms within the monastic movement during the eleventh century resulted in the expansion of convents, particularly in Germany, where a large number of nunneries produced signed illuminated manuscripts in which self-portraits and artists' signatures are found.

European monasteries for women were ruled by abbesses, who looked after both the intellectual and spiritual life of the institutions.[14] German convents in particular are notable for their book illuminations; some of their abbesses excelled as both painters and poets, producing literary works accompanied by precious illuminations. Among the renowned abbesses who decorated texts and created self-portraits are Abbess Hitda, Hildegard of Bingen (1098–1179) and Herrade von Landesberg (1125–95).

II.1 Abbess Hitda, *Abbess Hitda Offering the Gospel Book to St Walburga*, 1020

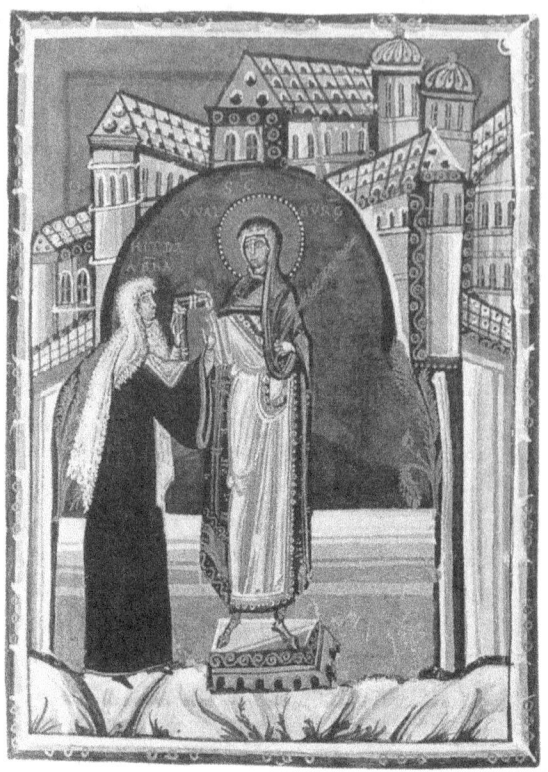

In *Abbess Hitda Offering the Gospel Book to St Walburga*, 1020 (Fig. II.1), Abbess Hitda portrays a schematized landscape of scattered wheat-like stalks, with her own figure silhouetted against the background of her convent. A vision of Saint Walburga appears in front of a round halo-like disk bearing the saint's name. Its background is decorated with ears of wheat. Walburga is the saint of good crops and patroness of the peasants; the first of May is dedicated to her.[15] In the scene she is portrayed as an icon standing on a plinth and holding a stalk of wheat. With great reverence, Hitda offers the manuscript to her holy patron. Hitda's features are sketchily drawn. It is her act of donation and the result of her labor, the illuminated manuscript, that attest to her individualization.

Hildegard of Bingen, one of the most remarkable German women artists, was a writer and Benedictine abbess. She was called the 'Sibyl of the Rhine' because, in addition to being considered a mystic, she was a playwright, philosopher, scientist, physician, theologian, historian, musician, poet and administrator. While nothing about Hildegard's education has been recorded, much can be inferred from her duties at the monastery.[16] Although she was never canonized, she is nonetheless called Saint Hildegard. She built a large convent at Rupertsberg, near Bingen on the Rhine. Her intellectual and religious influence was felt in the church as well as by the state. At the age of 42, Hildegard began to have religious experiences and visions that she translated into visual imagery and literary texts. In 1165 she wrote and illuminated the *Scivias*, a title abbreviated from the Latin inscription *scito vias Domini* ('know the ways of the Lord'), a religious compilation completed in 1152 and written to celebrate the dedication of the cloister church in Rupertsberg to the Bishop of Mainz.

This work was duplicated in the 1930s by Benedictine nuns from the Saint Hildegard Abbey of Rudesheim/Einbingen,[17] with several nuns copying the text and nun Josepha Knipps copying the illuminations. Unfortunately, the original manuscript, Codex One, once housed in the Hessische Landesbibliothek in Wiesbaden, disappeared after its shipment for safekeeping to Dresden during World War II.[18] A facsimile poses questions concerning the 35 illustrations in the text, since it appears either that six different artists illuminated the manuscript besides Hildegard or that the copyist, Josepha Knipps, had inferior artistic skills.[19] Because of the poor quality of the color images of the facsimile and subsequent questions raised by art historians that deal with aesthetic quality, authorship and originality, the nature of the role for Hildegard in the illumination of the original manuscript has been questioned.[20]

In the illustration from the *Scivias*, the *Vision of Hildegard of Bingen* (Fig. II.2), Hildegard is seated in her studio writing her book and talking with a monk. Her commentaries on the imagery help explain the meaning of the flames erupting from her head: 'And it happened in the year 1141 of Christ's incarnation, when I was 42 years and seven months old, that fiery light of great brilliancy streamed down from heaven and entirely flooded my brain, my heart, and my breast, like a flame that flickers not but gives glowing warmth, as the sun warms that on which he sheds his rays.'[21] When comparing the scenes of abbesses Hitda and Hildegard, differences in the depiction of the persona are observable, even though in both representations the physiognomy of the painter is cursory. Hildegard is shown receiving divine inspiration, engaged in the act of writing, exchanging thoughts with a listener (in the painting) or a reader (looking at the manuscript). In contrast, Abbess Hitda is engaged in her private religious world of presenting a gift to a saint, excluding the viewer from her thoughts and sentiments.

Following the path traced by Hildegard, Herrade von Landesberg, abbess of the Alsatian monastery of Hohenburg, completed her encyclopedic 'moralized Bible' *Hortus Deliciarum* (*Garden of Delights*) in 1160–70 (now in the Bibliothèque Nationale and Universitaire, Strasbourg).[22] Her early life and training are obscure. A few documents suggest that she was born into the House of Landesberg between 1125 and 1130. Later she became a member of the congregation of Augustinian canonesses at Mont Ste Odile, Hohenburg, where she received a rigorous humanistic and religious education under the reformist abbess Relindis.[23] The *Hortus Deliciarum* demonstrates Herrade's intellectual training, as inspired by Isidore of Seville's *Etymologiae* on paradise – *hortus* (garden) from the Greek and Latin, and *deliciae* (delights) from the Latin.[24] Unfortunately, the original manuscript, a compendium of medieval learning, was destroyed during the bombing of Strasbourg during the Franco-Prussian War of 1870. Today only

II.2 Hildegard of Bingen,
Vision of Hildegard of Bingen, in
Scivias, 1152

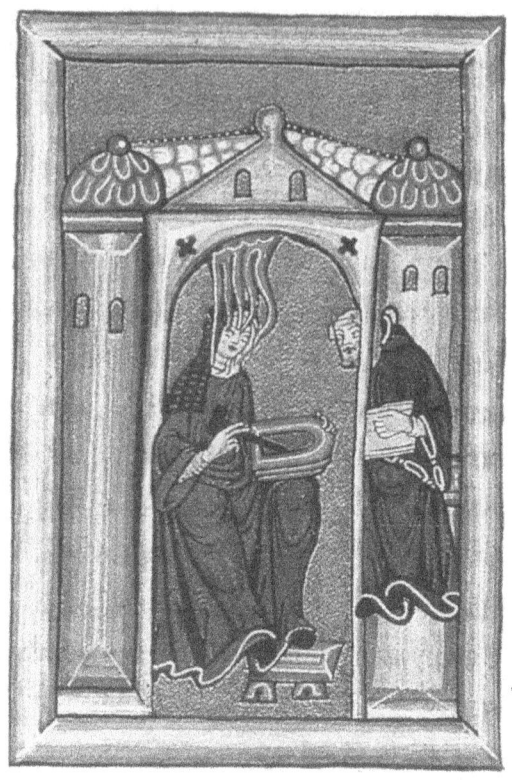

an eighteenth-century tracing exists.[25]

One of the pages from Herrade's text represented a group portrait of the 60 nuns from her convent together with a *Self-Portrait* (Fig. II.3). All the bust portraits are alike and the nuns can only be identified by their names, inscribed above their heads. In the right-hand margin, the abbess Herrade is shown standing and introducing her congregation, herself, and her work: 'Herrade, who through the grace of God is abbess of the church on the Hohenburg, here addresses the sweet maidens of Christ. I was thinking of your happiness when like a bee guided by the inspiring God I drew from many flowers of sacred and philosophic writing this book called the *Garden of Delights*: and I have put it together to the praise of Christ and the Church, and to your enjoyment as though into a sweet honeycomb. Therefore, you must diligently seek your salvation in it and strengthen your weary spirit with its sweet honey drops.'[26]

The bee alludes to the nuns' chaste and pure souls as well as the harmonious and industrious execution of their duties, since their united labor benefits the religious order. Furthermore, the symbolism of the bee's product and the creation in the honeycomb of honey reflects the sweet joy and happiness of monastic living. Herrade demonstrates her knowledge of Christian iconography and medieval bestiaries, as St Ambrose associated the Church with a beehive and its parishioners with bees in the same manner as she connects the honeycomb with the convent and the bees with her nuns.[27]

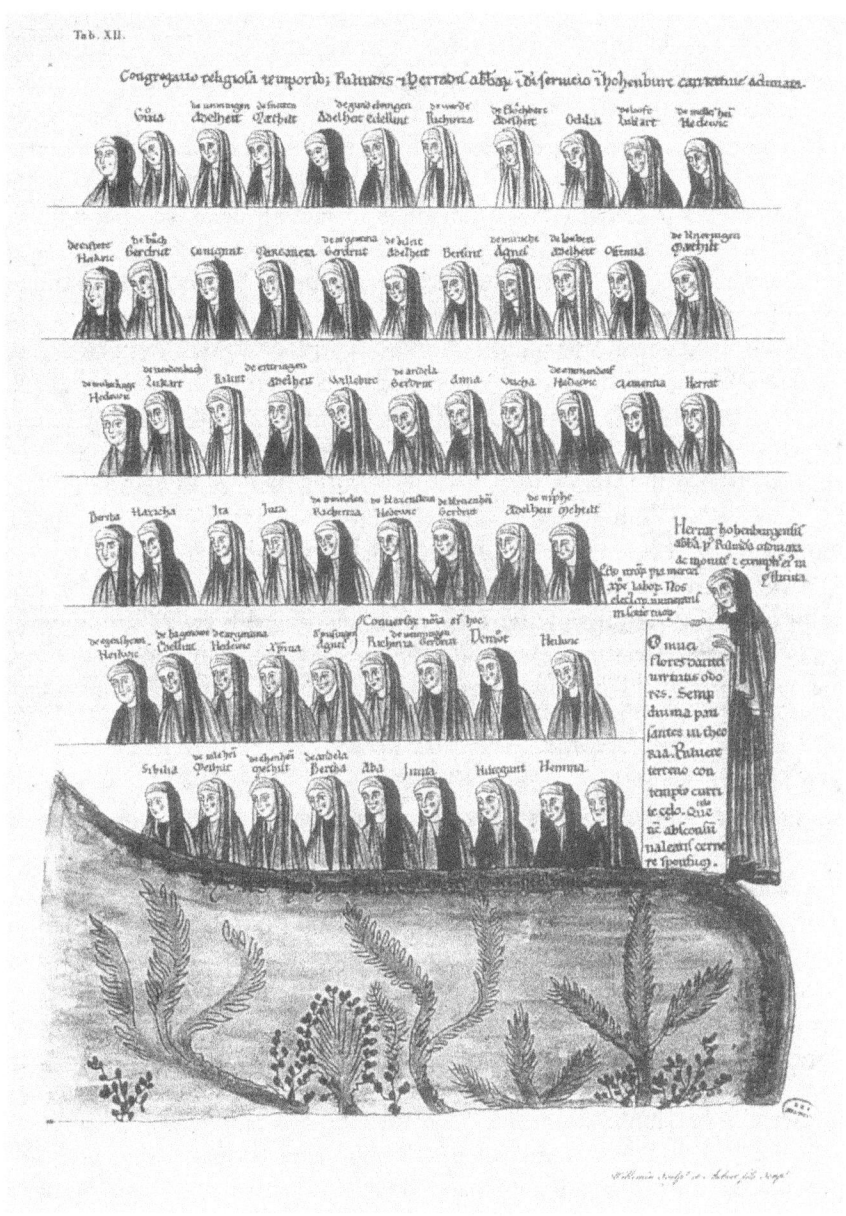

II.3 Herrade von Landesberg, *Self-Portrait*, 1160–70, in *Hortus Deliciarum*

Herrade's group portrait anticipates another seen later in Gisele von Kerssenbroek, who wrote and decorated the *Codex Gisele* of 1300, now in the Bischofiches Generalvikariat of Osnabruck. The imagery of abbess Herrade, as in Hildegard's text, assists in the understanding of the artist's purpose; in these cases, the text defines the image of the self, while the *imago* remains an icon.

Guda, a twelfth-century nun from Westphalia, depicted a *Self-Portrait in*

Letter D, in a homily (a moralizing text about a specific topic) entitled *Homeliary of St Bartholomew* (MS. Barth. 42. folio 110 verso, at the Stadt- und Universitätbibliothek in Frankfurt-am-Main). The work shows a three-quarter view of the artist clad in a habit, standing and addressing the viewer while raising her hand in greeting. She holds, in her left hand, a scroll bearing the inscription 'Guda, a sinner, wrote and painted this book.' The gentle salutation and personal citation, together with the small size of the book, provide an intimate dialogue between viewer and artist, who invites us to experience not only her artistic accomplishment, but also her human experience as a woman.[28]

In the Saint Memin Psalter of 1200 (now in the Walters Art Gallery in Baltimore), Claricia of Augsburg depicted a *Self-Portrait on the Letter Q* (Pl. III). This South German manuscript was a psalter, a collection of Psalms, sacred songs or poems for worship. Claricia depicts herself holding a circular disk in the shape of an 'O' filled with lacertine decoration in red, blue and green. With great ingenuity, she uses a tail to form the letter 'Q' in the shape of the human body, thus placing herself within the design. Claricia has humanized the geometrical and pattern decoration, adding and paralleling the fluidity of the movement of her body with the internal decoration of the letter. She is beautifully dressed in contemporary clothing, indicating that she is not a nun, but a scribe and illuminator in the scriptorium in Augsburg. The red in the ornamentation is repeated in the rendering of her costume.

Both Guda and Claricia focus on the image of the self, even if integrated with the text. Unlike Ende, Hitda, Herrade and Hildegard, their interest is on the visual portrayal of a persona and not the textual interpretation or revelation of the self.

In the Middle Ages the representation of the self-portrait has changed from that of Hellenistic times. In the medieval representation, the painter is not always looking into a mirror for her self-imaging, but also addresses the viewer with some specific gestures, inscriptions, or gaze. It is through the eyes and perception of the viewer that the sitter achieves her reflection. As well as the self-rendition of an intimate, private and subjective experience of the artist in her studio there also developed a public and objective situation of artist and audience, the reader. Although both visual experiences are personal in nature, the painter expanded her artistic world, which is perhaps the reason for the written text as signature and authentication of her work as well as identification of her image. Thus, her image, not her physiognomy, is seen.

Although there was a shift from an oral and aural tradition in antiquity to a more widely written one in the Middle Ages, the self-perception of women painters seems not to have changed. The shift occurs in the perception of the woman painter in relation to her society. Based on Pliny's account, in the Hellenistic period she portrayed herself in assertion of her creative ability, as an acclamation of her beauty and with a challenging desire to perpetuate her image as a woman and artist. In the Middle Ages the restricted society in which she exercised her creativity placed constraints on the representation of the self. Her environment was still private, confined to monasteries, nunneries, and convents, which provided her with a controlled reception to her work. Although she continued to represent herself, she demonstrated her artistic ability without exposing her sexuality, documenting her creation for posterity. In antiquity and in the Middle Ages, the woman painter's interest in self-rendition continues to allude to a whimsical, scintillating and visionary quality in herself and the world, as well as a human ambition to make a mark in history. Thus, in her self-portrait she rises above her present natural existence.

While in the Middle Ages the education of women expanded proportionately with the literature of the time, the development of women painters appears to have been limited to the monasteries. The woman painter identified with the literary aspect of her artistic ability because she could express her creativity in the convent scriptoria or was able to individualize herself in the private environment of her home writing. Education for women in the Middle Ages also included a general training in deportment, good manners, teaching and piety,[29] teachings that are reflected in the self-portraits of the time.

This may be seen particularly in the works of Christine de Pizan (or Pisan) (1365–1430).[30] She excelled in the art of writing books and poetry, and became a painter and a patron of the arts. As a result of her autobiographical writings, a great deal is known about her life.[31] Her father, Thomas de Pizzano, a noted physician and astrologer in Bologna, married the daughter of his colleague, Thomas Mondini. Both Thomas de Pizzano and Thomas Mondini served as counselors to the government of Venice. As Thomas de Pizzano's diplomatic reputation grew, he was rewarded with a post at the University of Paris and a position in the court of Charles V of France. At a young age, Christine de Pizan moved to Paris with her family, where she was educated at the French court. At the age of 15, she married Étienne de Castel, a nobleman from Picardy, who was the king's secretary and notary. De Castel died in 1390. In order to support her six children, Christine began to write poems, ballads, letters and literary works, beautifully illuminated for the great ladies and noblemen of the court, who rewarded her handsomely for her work.

Christine de Pizan was a respected writer on moral questions, education, the art of government, the conduct of war and the life and times of Charles V. In *The Book of the City of Ladies* of 1404, she discusses famous ancient painters, such as Timarete, 'the supreme mistress of the art of painting', Irene from Greece, 'skilled in the science of painting' and Marcia, who 'skillfully painted a self portrait by looking in a mirror in order that her memory survives her'.[32] Her second work, *The Treasure of the City of Ladies* of 1405, is an important study of medieval culture and its perception of medieval woman's place, achievements, perils and pleasures. In essence, it is a survival manual for women as well as a defense of medieval feminism.[33] The authorship of these illustrated books is not in dispute. Some assert however that Christine de

Pizan illuminated her own manuscripts; others suggest that she designed the illustrations and other artists illuminated them, such as the Epître d'Othéa Master, who worked in close collaboration with her.[34] In *The City of Ladies*, her praise of the illumination of another contemporary, Anastaise, suggests that Christine de Pizan might have assisted someone else in illustration. Conversing with Reason about women artists from antiquity, Christine states: 'With regard to painting at the present time I know a woman called Anastaise, who is so skillful and experienced in painting the borders of manuscripts and the landscapes of miniatures that no one can cite a artisan in the city of Paris, the center of the best illuminators on earth, who in these endeavors surpasses in her in any way. And this I know by my own experience, for she has produced some things for me that are held to be outstanding among the ornamental borders of the great masters.'[35]

Some of the illuminations for *The Book of the City of Ladies* have a certain similarity of style, suggesting the participation and supervision, if not the execution, of Christine de Pizan. In the miniature, *Self-Portrait in Her Studio*, 1420, in Christine de Pizan's *Le Livre de la mutation de fortune* (Pl. IV), the writer is seen working at her desk in her study. On the desk is a book bound in bright red leather that contrasts strongly with her pale blue dress. The floor and walls of the studio are depicted as being rich with colored tiles. She is concentrating on her writing, clearly engaged in an intellectual pursuit in the same manner as the ancient painter Marcia.

In *Christine de Pizan Instructing Her Son* (Fig. II.4), from the same work, another elaborate interior is seen with patterned decorations on the wall and floor. That Christine is engaged in teaching is evident by the gesticulation of her hands. Her son stands beside her desk, on which are three books, one of them open. In this example, she is portrayed as an educator as well as a mother, contrasting with the miniature *Reason, Rectitude, and Justice Appear to Christine* in *The Book of the City of Ladies* (1405), which depicts the writer standing in front of her sources of inspiration – personifications of these three qualities. All are crowned with laurels, and hold their emblematic attributes. These personifications assist Christine in the writing of her books, seen scattered on the table. The elegant poses, costume and S-stance are typical of the ornamental style of the Middle Ages. In this miniature, Christine de Pizan portrays herself as a writer and educator, now receiving knowledge instead of imparting it. The ancient application of emblematic associations as attributes of a good moral character, which originated in the Greek concept of *arête* and Roman *virtus*, continued in the Middle Ages, with the addition of a Christian application as illustrated and commented on in Prudentius' *Psychomachia*, an allegorical Latin poem of the fourth century AD in the epic manner about the battle between the forces of virtue and vice. This emblematic association was to intrigue and heighten female self-portraits through several centuries.

The last miniature described here, *Christine Beholds the Paintings in the Salle de Fortune* of 1420 (Pl. V), shows Christine as a cultured woman, a patron of the arts, who admires the frieze collection in the gallery of an imagined Hall

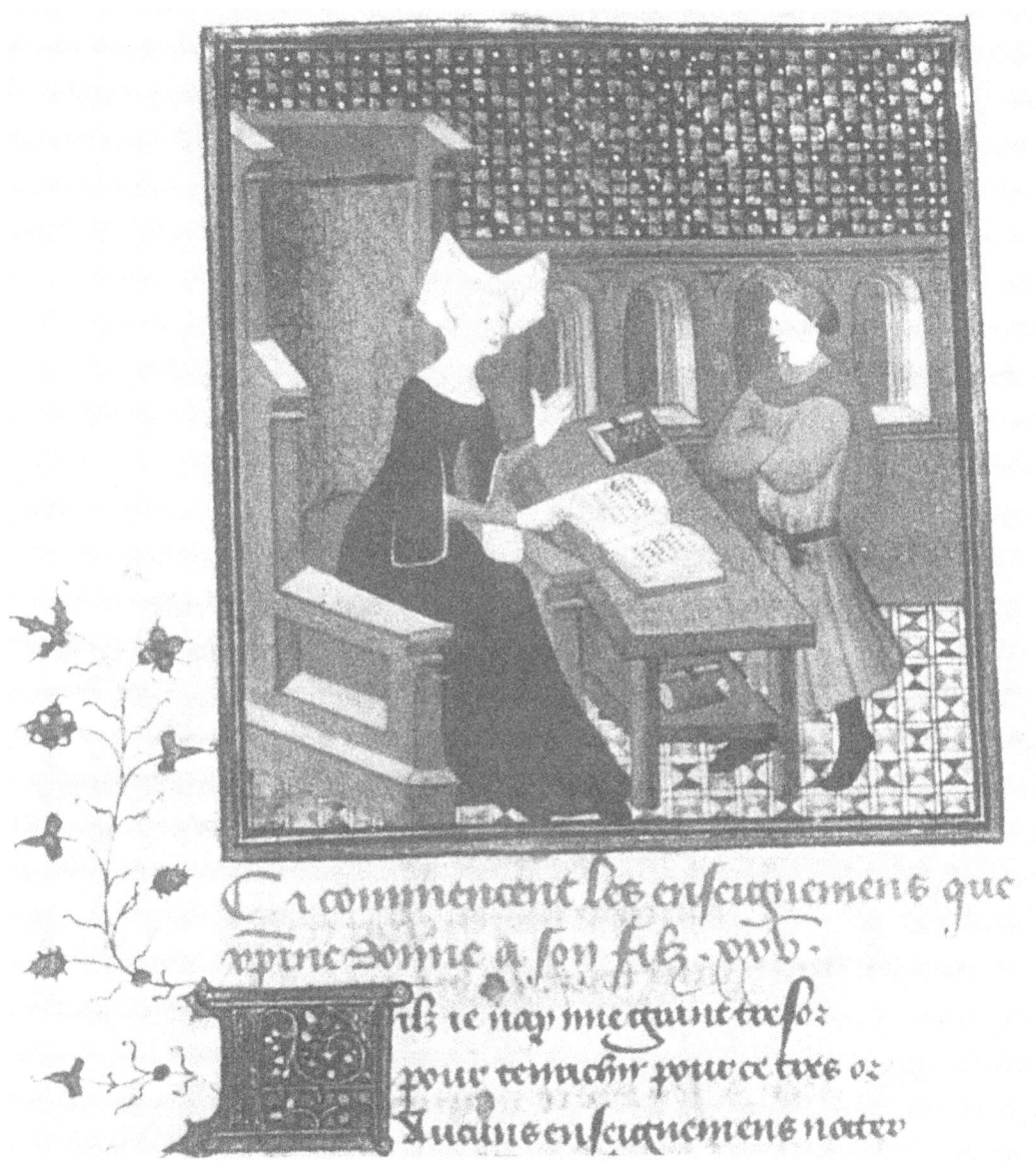

II.4 *Christine de Pizan Instructing Her Son*, 1420, in Christine de Pizan's *The Moral Teachings*, Harley MS 4431, folio 261 verso

of Fortune. In the formation of a visual gallery, she is assisted by the recollection of ancient collections of art (*pinacoteka*) as cited in Pliny's writings. This gallery concept will evolve into *camere picte* (painted rooms) in the Renaissance, *salons* (halls for paintings) in the eighteenth and nineteenth centuries and exhibition halls or galleries in the twentieth century. In all of Pizan's miniatures, the emphasis is on her intellectual and artistic pursuits as mentor and exemplar to other women. The female self-portraits of the Middle

Ages, as exemplified in Pizan's work, provide an understanding of the form's development as a revelation of women's struggles to assert themselves and gain recognition.

III

The Renaissance: interest in self-imaging

The European Renaissance was marked by political, social and economic turmoil. Paradoxically, such calamities as the Hundred Years War, the Black Death and the fall of Constantinople (1453) promoted the spread and rediscovery in western Europe of ancient Greek and Roman culture, its literature and visual arts. Through humanistic teaching and learning, the individual gained importance and secular values were recognized, reshaping the cultural goals of European societies. The Italian city-states, in particular, promoted civic pride and provided artistic competition, thus giving rise to a new type of patronage.

As in the Middle Ages, artistic education and patronage were promoted by the Church, through convents and monasteries. However, artistic growth and commissions were also sponsored by the craft guilds, as well as by wealthy merchants and nobles. Aesthetically and spiritually, art and artistic achievements still served the glory of God, but civic interests and personal pride were added. Artistic and technological changes introduced the use of new painting materials, such as canvas, while fresco was still used on wall surfaces and tempera on panels.[1]

The Renaissance notion of woman depended on the ancient perception and definition of *femina* as 'inferior male'. This long-lived notion of female inferiority continued. Although humanism did much to enhance the dignity of man, it was long in liberating the 'man feminine' from her subordinate status.[2]

The classification of the Renaissance style may be divided into Italian and Northern European, as well as Quattrocento (the 1400s) and Cinquecento (the 1500s).[3] The latter period is subdivided into High Renaissance (1500–1520) and Mannerism (1520–95).[4] The second of these two periods will be discussed in the following chapter.

Portraiture changed during the Renaissance, and in particular during the Mannerist period. In the late Middle Ages, as discussed earlier, and in the early Renaissance, the portrait was subject to religious considerations.

Aesthetic distance between the sitter and God as seen in the Middle Ages was retained in the Renaissance portrait, but with the addition of the element of truth to nature, that is to say the physicality of the sitter.

The Renaissance portrait flourished as a work in which the person portrayed occupied the center of the painting, indicating his or her role in society, as a merchant, member of the nobility or clergy, or public figure.[5] In religious paintings, portraits of donors were relegated to the corners of the panels. Early Renaissance portraits came under the influence of the antique concepts of ancestorship, as illustrated in the relief carving *Roman Patrician with Busts of His Ancestors* (Capitoline Museum, Rome), and of the individual, as found in the writings of the classics honoring famous persons (*uomini famosi*). Portraits were also affected by the general renewal of the visual arts and the practice of public commemoration in medals or displays of civic pride.[6]

In portraits of the Middle Ages and early Renaissance the role of the painted sitter differs a great deal in comparison to those of the sixteenth century, the Cinquecento. In the former, sitters considered their audience or viewed themselves in relation to the image of God, whereas in the latter, sitters viewed themselves in relation to their status in society and contemporary taste. Removed from religious purposes in book illumination, miniatures and panel painting, and seen as a painted medal or commemorative coin in the early Renaissance, the portrait appears with its own identity, unbounded by the page format or group setting. Because of the growing secularization of life and the development of sixteenth-century courtly life, it served several functions.[7]

In the Renaissance, portraiture established a new role in the thematic development of painting. During previous centuries, the portrait was part of an inclusive depiction in religious paintings, as seen in donors' portraits in illuminated books, in altarpieces and in panels, as well as in religious decorative cycles or memorial portraits.[8] In secular paintings, it showed patrons or protagonists expressing their voice or taste by their commissions of decorative cycles or narrative historical legends. Now, however, the portrait was to achieve its own identity. These new types of portraits could represent various things: the individual's position in society, such as pope, prelate, ruler, aristocrat and humanist; his or her occupation, such as artist, dealer, collector and scholar; the voice, text or sentiments of the sitter, such as lover, friend, character, or immortality. As the status of the artist changed from mere artisan to inventor and creator, the self-portrait, too, was transformed into a more closely self-referential image.[9]

The concern for representing the likeness of the sitter, its closeness to life, truth to nature and quality of resemblance, was developed by Northern European painters, in particular the Flemish, including Robert Campin, Jan van Eyck, Petrus Christus, Rogier van der Weyden, Dirk Bouts and Hugo van der Goes. In Italy, Masaccio, Piero della Francesca, Sandro Botticelli, Andrea Mantegna, Antonello da Messina and Gentile Bellini developed a new sense of style in portraiture. The tension created between truth and style provided a new concept of portraiture in Western painting, with lighting, pose, attitude, costume, background and colors all gaining importance. These aspects are both historical and romantic: historical in that the portrait is faithful to the sitter's resemblance, but not without idealization, and romantic in its colorist and atmospheric interpretation of the sitter's psyche.

Humanistic developments, related to the dignity of the individual, the classical revival in literature and the arts, and socioeconomic changes, did not bring about artistic encouragement and recognition of women painters until the sixteenth century. But men's artistic expression soared, especially in Italy and in Northern Europe, in the late Quattrocento and early Cinquecento with the work of geniuses such as Leonardo da Vinci, Michelangelo and Albrecht Dürer.

The male artist's life during the Renaissance moved away from the cloisters and anonymity to participation in guilds and to individualization.[10] However, during most of the Renaissance, there appears to have been one type of life for male painters and a different, although parallel, one for women. Men could express themselves, be trained by masters and enroll for further training and work in the guilds, which commissioned many works at this time and also provided centers for patrons to see works of art. Women continued for some time to rely on the tradition that best offered them opportunities for artistic expression, the monastery. In an extension of this tradition non-monastic female painters were confined to working from home. Since documentation on women's participation in the guilds has not been found, it can be assumed that the guild regulations in Italy excluded them from membership. In Florence, however, in 1530, during the rule of the Medici, women were recorded as involved in other artisan activities, particularly in the textile industry, as male employment shifted to luxury crafts, such as ceramics, books, jewelry and furniture for export to the European aristocracy.[11]

Women's legal rights remained limited. Fathers or husbands of women painters were responsible for administering economic matters and made decisions on their well-being. For most women of all classes, marriage and motherhood were the expected roles. In fact, marriages were arranged by parents as economic contracts or alliances between families or countries. Female chastity was a requisite, regardless of class structure, for any marriage contract. Almost all Renaissance treatises on women view the ideal for them as being chaste and obedient wives. 'All the advances of Renaissance Italy, its proto-capitalist economy, its states, and its humanistic culture, worked to mold the noblewoman into an aesthetic object; decorous, chaste, and doubly dependent on her husband as well as prince', writes Joan Kelly-Gadol.[12]

The female artist, who was usually from the upper class, was encouraged to be gentle, passive, docile and delicate, yet educated. Many clerks during the Middle Ages had written polemics in Latin against women. During the Renaissance, with the spread of humanism, rebuttals continued to appear, defending women; however, women were viewed in an idealized way, and praised for virtues such as obedience, chastity and fidelity, as noted in the writings of Leon Battista Alberti (1404–72). Alberti was a Florentine humanist, theorist, sculptor and architect, who wrote *On the Family*, where he expressed the views of the upper class in the Italian Renaissance on women's role in society.[13]

At the beginning of the fifteenth century, a few humanist scholars influenced the education of a small group of noblewomen, at first in the courts of Italy, then throughout Europe. In Italy, Laura Cereta, Isotta Nogarola, Costanza Varano, Ippolita Sforza, Cassandra Fedele and Cecilia Gonzaga achieved fame for their learning and writings,[14] as did Levina Bening Teerling in Northern Europe.

Although Renaissance men shared a fear of women's intellectual education ('Nothing must be allowed in the training of her mind that would encourage or enable her to compete on even ground with men'[15]), women's education, though restricted, did not consist merely of instruction on being a skilled and domestic wife but included the fostering of moral beauty and counseling in aesthetic beauty. More women learned to write and to read, particularly the classics, paint, play an instrument, and attend to their physical appearance, thus creating internally and externally a *bella figura* (a beautiful image). Therefore, portraits of women represented images to be admired and imitated and to serve as archetypes.[16]

It is important to understand the Italian interest in educating females in the arts of poetry, music, painting and the classics. A decline in the numbers of male students enrolling at the universities played a part as a consequence of warfare, as did the decline of the male population generally because of war and disease, combined with the need for the surviving women to take on responsibilities in society. Women, if they survived child-bearing and disease, or if they maintained a cultivated life in a convent or nunnery, enjoyed greater longevity than men. Another factor was the new intellectual and artistic aspects of humanism, including the revival of classical literature and ideals, as in Boccaccio's *Noble and Famous Women*, 1401–2, where he expressed an Italian humanistic interpretation of the notable women artists from antiquity.[17]

The tradition of patronage that evolved in the Middle Ages from monastic and courtly life continued into the Renaissance. In the northern part of Italy, patronage by women was encouraged at the humanistic courts of Mantua, Ferrara and Urbino. The Renaissance emphasis on the education of the individual provided new possibilities for women and no doubt contributed to their acceptance in universities. At the University of Bologna women were encouraged to become doctors of jurisprudence, medicine and philosophy, producing the noted cases of doctors of jurisprudence Bitisia Gozzadini and Dorotea Bocchi, who lectured at the University in the thirteenth century. Other woman lecturers who became famous at Bologna were Margherita Legnani, who taught from a window in order to be seen by the large crowd of students, and Novella d'Andrea, who lectured completely veiled so that students would not be distracted by her beauty.[18] The city-state of Bologna became an intellectual center where women could pursue artistic quests and patronize the arts. In part their source of inspiration and emulation was Saint Cecilia, who was highly regarded in Bolognese intellectual circles and with whose artistic talents women painters and musicians could identify.[19]

Although most portraits of women were painted by male artists, some examples do exist of women painting portraits of other women. Most are found in manuscripts, continuing a medieval form of women's self-portraiture.[20] The miniaturist tradition continued in the early Renaissance, with heightened interest in nature providing an improvement in the anatomical depiction of the figure. Less rigid poses and stances began to appear, along with variety in the expression of emotions. There also were inventive ideas in architectural design, pattern composition and ornamentation.[21] Among the female artists who created self-portraits in painting and drawing during the Italian Renaissance were Maria Ormani and Caterina de Vigri. In Northern Europe, there are no self-portraits by women painters, although records of their works do exist.

Numerous Italian convents in the early Renaissance nurtured the art and the lucrative enterprises of book-making, book illumination and hand-written transcription of manuscripts. These institutions of learning attracted and honored many accomplished women, creating artistic and competitive centers; for example the convent of Santa Maria in Siena and the Augustinian monastery of Lecceto were honored, and prospered, under the scriptorium directress Giovanna Petroni. The Augustinian monastery in Pavia boasted of having the miniaturist Laura de'Bossi in residence. The convent of Santa Maria delle Grazie in Genoa revered the presence of Tommassina del Fiesco (Fieschi). The convent of San Lino at Volterra, which housed the Poor Clares, benefited from the presence of Dorotea Broccardi, who illuminated and floriated the *Libro dell'Ordine di Santa Chiara* (now in the Biblioteca Guarnacci in Volterra). The monastery of San Giacomo at Ripoli, with nun-artists such as Angelica Miniberti, who signed a *Collectarium*, Angela de'Ruccellai and Lucrezia de Pantiatichi, claimed to have the best scriptorium in all of Italy.[22]

Although panel or canvas painting had been established in the Renaissance and these formats were employed by male painters, no contemporary records are found of a woman's self-portrait on a single panel or canvas. In the Quattrocento, the outlet for a woman's artistic expression was still confined to the courtly monastic life, where artistic recognition resulted from the accomplishments of abbesses or upper-class learned women residing in private convents. This perhaps explains why female self-portraits appeared in illuminated manuscripts, but rarely in panel paintings.

The illustrious Maria Ormani (or Ormand) taught the art of book-making and illumination in an Augustinian convent.[23] Ormani portrayed herself in an attitude of prayer on the illuminated page of a *Breviarium cum Calendrium* (Fig. III.1). The 89th leaf of the manuscript is an elaborate page in the shape of a love-knot scroll containing her inscription: 'A maiden servant of Christ'. In the margin she adds *scripsi*, meaning 'I wrote it.' The knot is a symbol of love and of union – a mystical marriage between Ormani, a nun, and Christ. The depiction of this mystical marriage is a continuation of the tradition of

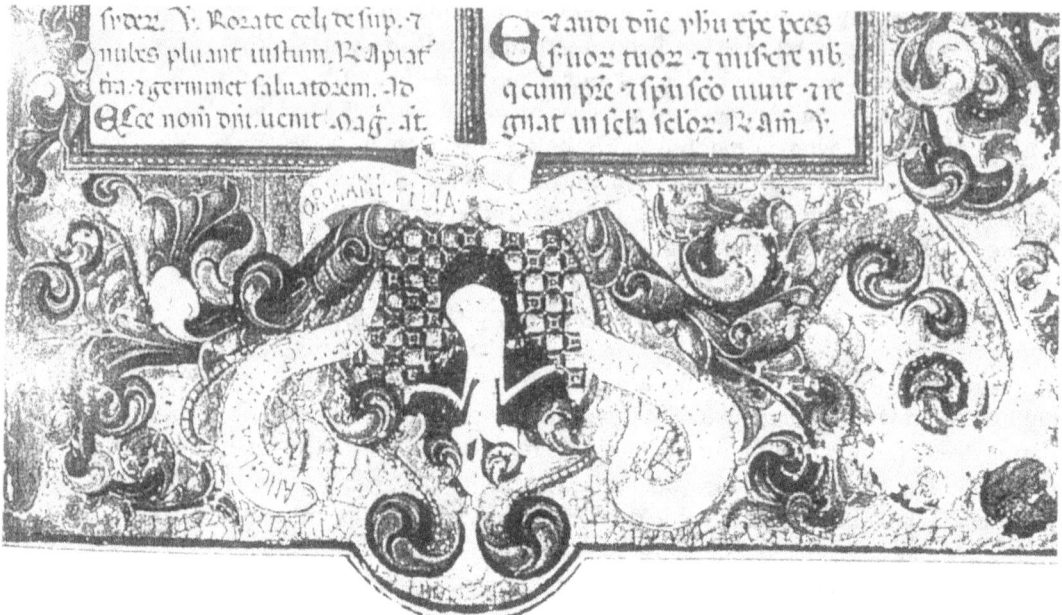

III.1 Maria Ormani, *Self-Portrait*, in *Breviarum cum Calendarium*, 1453, folio 89, vol. 18, codex 1923

portraying holy, virginal women united with Christ for love. This is repeated in later depictions of St Catherine's *Mystical Marriage*. The composition of the checkerboard design in the circle behind Ormani's portrait suggests a stained-glass window pattern as well as a halo motif – Maria is a holy person.

Away from the miniaturist tradition in the Renaissance, the focus turns to religious imagery, where the artist identifies herself with holy figures such as the Virgin Mary, female saints and heroines, particularly the artist's own namesake, by her meritorious and virtuous action (chastity, obedience, prudence and faith).

Another self-portrait from this early Renaissance period is of a Franciscan nun, Caterina de Vigri (1413–63), subsequently called *La Santa* (The Holy Woman) or Saint Catherine of Bologna because she was sanctified in 1703, and she also became known as the patron saint of the fine arts.[24] Later in the eighteenth century, one medal portrayed her as painting an angel.[25] Her room and chapel, with her paintings and her grave at the convent, were sites of pilgrimage through the nineteenth century. Tradition relates that one painting on wood depicting the Infant Jesus had miraculous powers of healing diseases in those who touched the child's lips.[26]

Sufficient documentation exists on Vigri to reconstruct her professional and spiritual life. *Le sette armi spirituale* (*The Seven Spiritual Weapons*), an autobiographical spiritual exercise, composed between 1438 and 1456, describes her religious experiences and the torments and fantasies of celibate life. It served as a manual for training novices.[27] Vigri's illustrated *Breviarium* of 1456–60,[28] and Illuminata Bembo's *Specchio de illuminatione* (*The Mirror of Light*, 1525–30), a biography, provide further information.[29] Caterina was born into a noble family in Ferrara in 1413 and spent her early years in the court of Marchese Niccolò II, where her father served as a lawyer and she as a lady-in-waiting, both for the Marchese's daughter Margarita.[30] In 1427, after her father's death and the betrothal of her patron, Margarita, Caterina entered a Franciscan convent, the Ferrarese Corpus Domini, which was then in the process of becoming a house of the Observant Poor Clares. In 1456 she was sent to Bologna to establish another convent and became the abbess of the Poor Clares of Corpus Domini, a position she held until her death in 1463.[31]

Her youthful experience in the court provided Vigri with the education of a lady, learning to draw, paint and illustrate manuscripts, play a stringed instrument,[32] sing and dance, and to read and write Latin, all in addition to studying classical literature. This humanistic background assisted her in her religious instruction and mystical writings.

Among other books that Vigri illustrated and copied, signed '*Ego Catarina de Vigris soror semper indigna*', are a calendar (*Calendarium*), psalter (*Psalterium*), hymns (*Hymnarium*), commemorations (*Commemorationes*), and saints' lives (*Omnium Sanctorum*). In the last of these, she portrays her patron saint, Catherine, with her own features and wearing a crown of diamonds, in the letter 'D'.[33]

Caterina de Vigri emerges as an erudite Bolognese woman who also mastered the art of painting. 'Her talent, a quiet gentleness and dignified manner gained her general esteem.'[34] She was trained in the Bolognese school as a miniaturist, under Maestro Vitale and Lippo Dalmasii.[35] On folio 10 recto, on the right strip of her *Breviarium*, still located in her chapel in the monastery of Corpus Domini at Bologna, she decorated the initial 'C' with a woman's face, probably a miniature self-portrait (Fig. III.2).[36] A similar visage appears among the pious women on the left side of the altarpiece of *St Ursula and Her Maidens* of 1456 (Pinacoteca of Bologna),[37] another self-portrait. This wooden panel painting represents, on a gold background, a frontal view of the tall, slender figure of a crowned Saint Ursula, embracing with her mantle of mercy very small figures representing holy virgins. Two victory banners parallel Ursula's royal stance. The circular arch behind the figures alludes to their triumphs as virtuous women and martyrs. The impact of Vigri's artistic training in book illumination is especially evident in her ability to handle brilliant and varied colors, and in the richness of patterned details as in the elaborate decoration of Ursula's gold-and-emerald-green mantle and lavender-pink dress ornamented with rich brocade fabric and floral designs.

In Italy Caterina de Vigri continued the medieval monastic tradition of including her self-portrait in religious manuscripts, as had her predecessor Hildegard of Bingen in Germany. Vigri's awareness of the Renaissance style and the importance of the presence of the individual, even in religious painting, caused her to place herself in the altarpiece as a protagonist of the story as well as a participant of the mystical experience, as did other Italian Renaissance artists who stressed the individual in their work. These are said

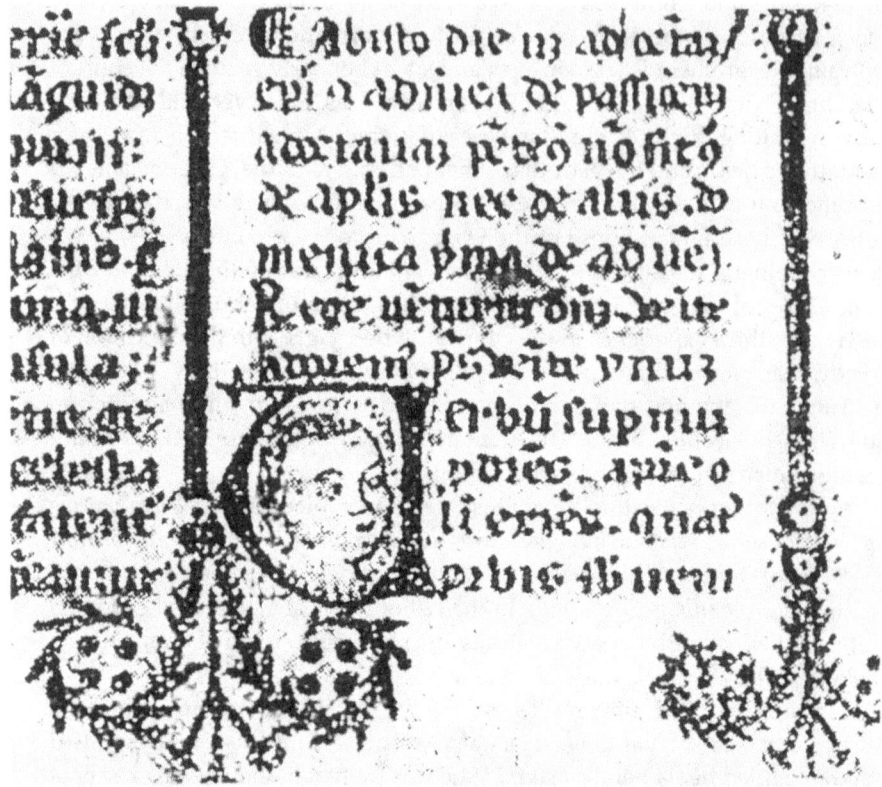

III.2 Caterina de Vigri, *Self-Portrait*, in *Breviarium*, manuscript, folio 10 recto

to have included Masaccio, in the *Tribute Money* of 1425 (Church of the Carmine, Florence), Benozzo Gozzoli in the *Adoration of the Magi* of 1459 (Chapel in the Palazzo Medici-Riccardi, Florence), Fra Angelico in Florence (fresco paintings of 1450–55 for the cells of the monks of San Marco) and Piero della Francesca (San Sepolcro altarpiece of the Misericordia and *Resurrection* of 1460). In Northern Europe Jan van Eyck was said to have included himself in the Ghent Altarpiece of 1426–32 (Church of San Bavo) as was Rogier van der Weyden in *St Luke Painting the Virgin*, 1450 (Museum of Fine Arts in Boston) and Dirk Bouts in the *Last Supper* of 1468–70 (Saint Peter's of Leuven). In Northern Europe the tradition of self-portraiture in a religious context continued to evolve and lingered into the sixteenth century.

The strong monastic tradition in Europe flooded the Portuguese and Spanish markets with magnificent illuminated manuscripts – notably in Portugal by Philippa, daughter of Pedro, Archduke of Coimbra, who illuminated homilies on the Gospels, and in Spain by Doña Angelica, who made choir books for Tarragona Cathedral. In Germany the tradition of illumination continued, with a number of women painters and illustrators. Particularly noteworthy are manuscripts from the Carthusian order by Barbara Gwitchmacherin; from the Dominican order by St Katherine of

Nuremberg (*Novum Testamentum Germanicum* of 1443); and from the Franciscan convent in Cologne by Sibylla de Bondorff (*Das Leben und die Wunderwerke des Heiligen Franciscus*, 1478; now in the British Museum Library). Flemish illuminators were in great demand, with manuscript illumination being practised as a family business. Among the known women painters were Margaret van Eyck, sister of Jan and Hubert, called the 'gifted Minerva', Cornelia Cnoop David, and Clara de Keysere.[38]

Although there are no records of female self-portraits from Northern Europe during the early Renaissance, excellent sixteenth-century examples are found, including work by Levina Bening Teerling or Teerlinc (d.1576),[39] and Hester or Esther Inglis or Anglois (1571–1624), also known as Esther Kello.[40] Teerling's work was to enhance the miniature-painting tradition of Tudor and Jacobean England, known as limning, a style that expressed the artistic taste of Protestant England as a 'unique contribution to the Renaissance unparalleled elsewhere in Europe'.[41] It began with the advent of the Reformation in England in the 1530s and its aesthetic isolation from the Italian Renaissance movement, and lasted until 1620.

Documentation survives of the life, training, and collaboration with her father of Levina Bening Teerling. These records assist us in understanding her art as a woman painter of distinction. Contemporary with the German Hans Holbein (1497–1543) and Nicholas Hilliard (1547–1619), the English miniature painter,[42] Teerling was the only Flemish miniature painter to be invited to work and stay at the court of England in the reigns of Henry VIII, Edward VI, Mary I and Elizabeth I.

Internationally acclaimed, Teerling was paid highly by her patrons – better even than Holbein.[43] She received numerous gifts and commissions from Henry VIII, Edward VI, Mary I and Elizabeth I. While Teerling's career and life are well documented, few of her works are signed and dated. The eldest of five daughters, she was trained and collaborated in the art of miniature painting with her father, Simon Bening, in Bruges.[44] In the 1540s she took an apprenticeship with Giulio Clovio in Italy.[45] By 1545, she was married to George Teerling, and in January 1546 the couple moved to England where Levina became the 'King's paintrix'. With their son, Marcus, the family enjoyed high social status at the court. In 1566, Teerling became an English subject, dying ten years later in the family home in Stepney.[46]

In her *Self-Portrait at Age 50* of 1546 (Fig. III.3), Teerling portrays herself dressed in the English fashion as a noblewoman. Some critics have questioned her age in the picture, claiming that she might be either younger or older than the title says. Its oval shape echoes the shape of a mirror, alluding to the fact that the sitter (Levina) is the painted image of the viewer (Levina). Thus, art imitates or copies nature or reality.[47] Many male self-portraitists of the High Renaissance also adopted a circular or oval format imitating a mirror-image, as seen in Jean Fouquet's *Self-Portrait* of 1450 (Fig. III.4)[48] and English miniatures such as Holbein's *Self-Portrait* of 1543 (Fig. III.5). Holbein painted himself dressed as a painter in the act of painting while gazing at the viewer as if in a mirror. Hilliard's *Self-Portrait* of 1577 (Victoria and Albert Museum,

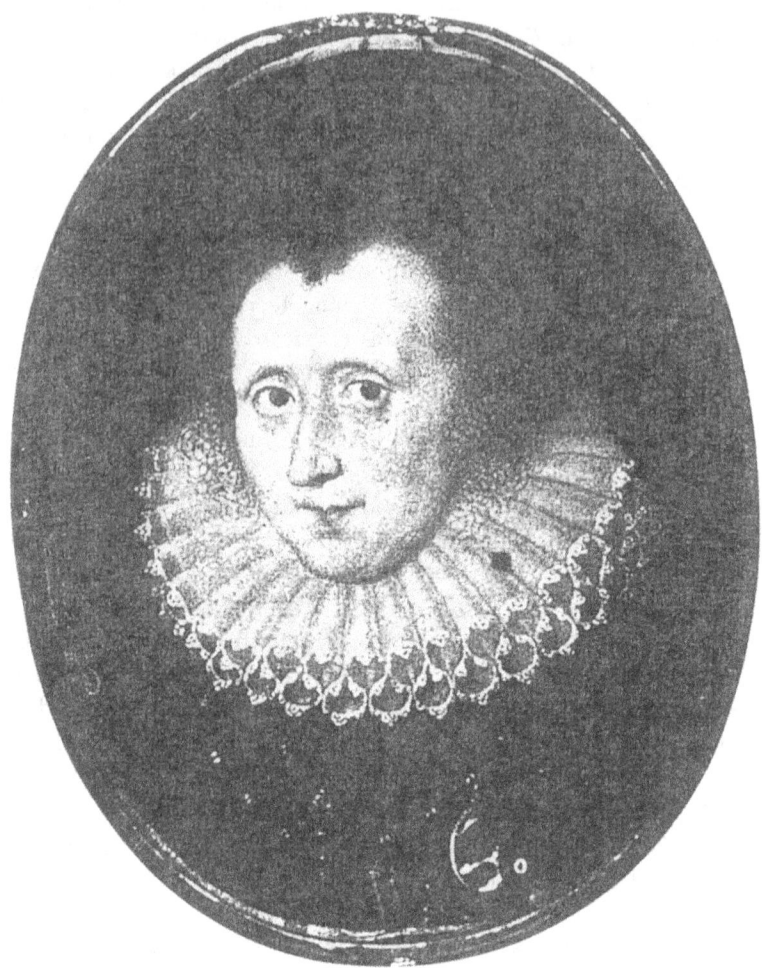

III.3 Levina Teerling, *Self-Portrait at Age 50*, 1546

London) portrays him dressed as a nobleman, with his signature and date inscribed around the tondo, to create a halo design or a triumphal arch motif that honors his courtly position. The medallion shape in these self-portraits recalls the commemorative wreaths or crowns employed by the Romans to pay homage to their heroes, as seen in triumphal arches, sarcophagi and relief sculptures.[49] This honorific motif was assimilated into Renaissance art to laud poets, writers, inventors, rulers and artists, and Teerling, Fouquet and Hilliard employed its format to honor themselves as creators.

Another outstanding miniature painter was Hester (Esther) Inglis or Anglois, also known as Esther Kello, who excelled as an emblematist. Few women artists are known to have cultivated this art form. She was born in Dieppe, France, and died in England. Sometimes the training of women painters was not solely with their fathers, but also with their mothers,[50] and it was Inglis's mother, Marie Priscott Langlois, also a painter, who trained her.

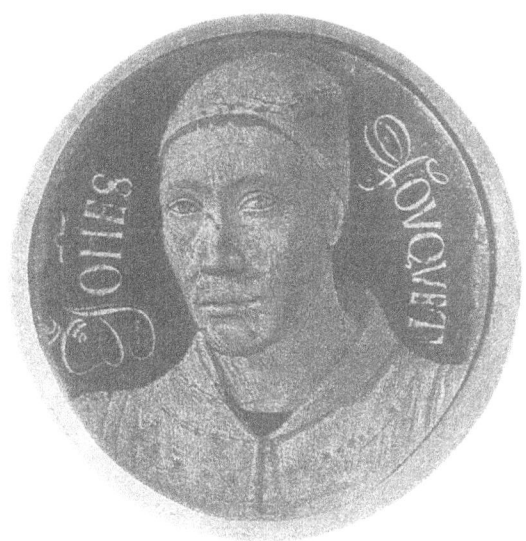

III.4 Jean Fouquet, *Self-Portrait*, 1450

In 1596 Inglis married a minister, Bartholomew Kello. She was patronized by the highest nobility in Great Britain, including Queen Elizabeth, and worked for a long time in Edinburgh, illustrating emblem and religious books, even illustrating and writing by 'her hand a "Book of Emblems"'.[51] In her numerous beautifully designed and written books she frequently depicted herself, as can be seen in the *Self-Portrait* of 1599 in her book of psalms (Fig. III.6), showing her in an oval cartouche decorated with flowering motifs and inscribed with the name 'Esther Anglois Franchoise'. Her stance at a desk, writing in an open book next to a musical score, denotes that she is an educated woman. Inglis copied many books demonstrating the difficult task of miniaturists and calligraphers, as indicated by the large epigraph below her portrait describing the text. In the *Self-Portrait* of 1615 (Pl. VI, National Library of Scotland, MS 8874, folio 4 verso), Inglis depicts herself in English attire, a tall hat and a ruff, honoring her position as a woman of the court and a creative artist.

These two Northern European artists achieved fame in their own time because of their accomplishment in the art of the miniature, Teerling as limning painter and Inglis as emblematist illuminator. With de Vigri, a religious scholar, Ormani, a nun, Teerling, a noblewoman, and Inglis, a humanist, they represent four different female roles. Their portraits reveal their talents for observing nature: by so depicting herself, the woman painter assumes the role or persona of a creator.

Self-portraits by female painters of this period have not been discovered outside of the miniature tradition, notwithstanding numerous recorded self-portraits by male painters. Meanwhile women artists preserved and continued their creativity and self-imaging in illuminated manuscripts, and

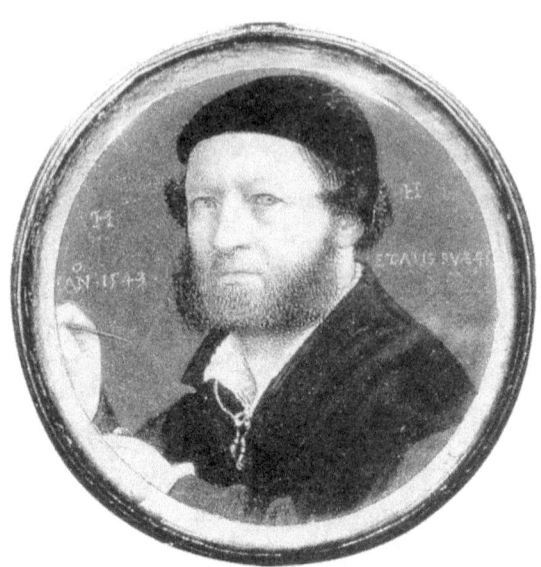

III.5 Hans Holbein the Younger, *Self-Portrait*, 1543, enamel on vellum on a playing card

by maintaining this visual tradition, they also preserved the aesthetic quest of portraying a beautiful image through a delicate, laborious and decorative technique. And as with their Renaissance male counterparts, they stressed the observation of nature and an interest in self-imaging while retaining their concern with ornamentation and beautification. Female painters were to make the leap of aggrandizing themselves on canvas and panel in the following century – the Mannerist period.

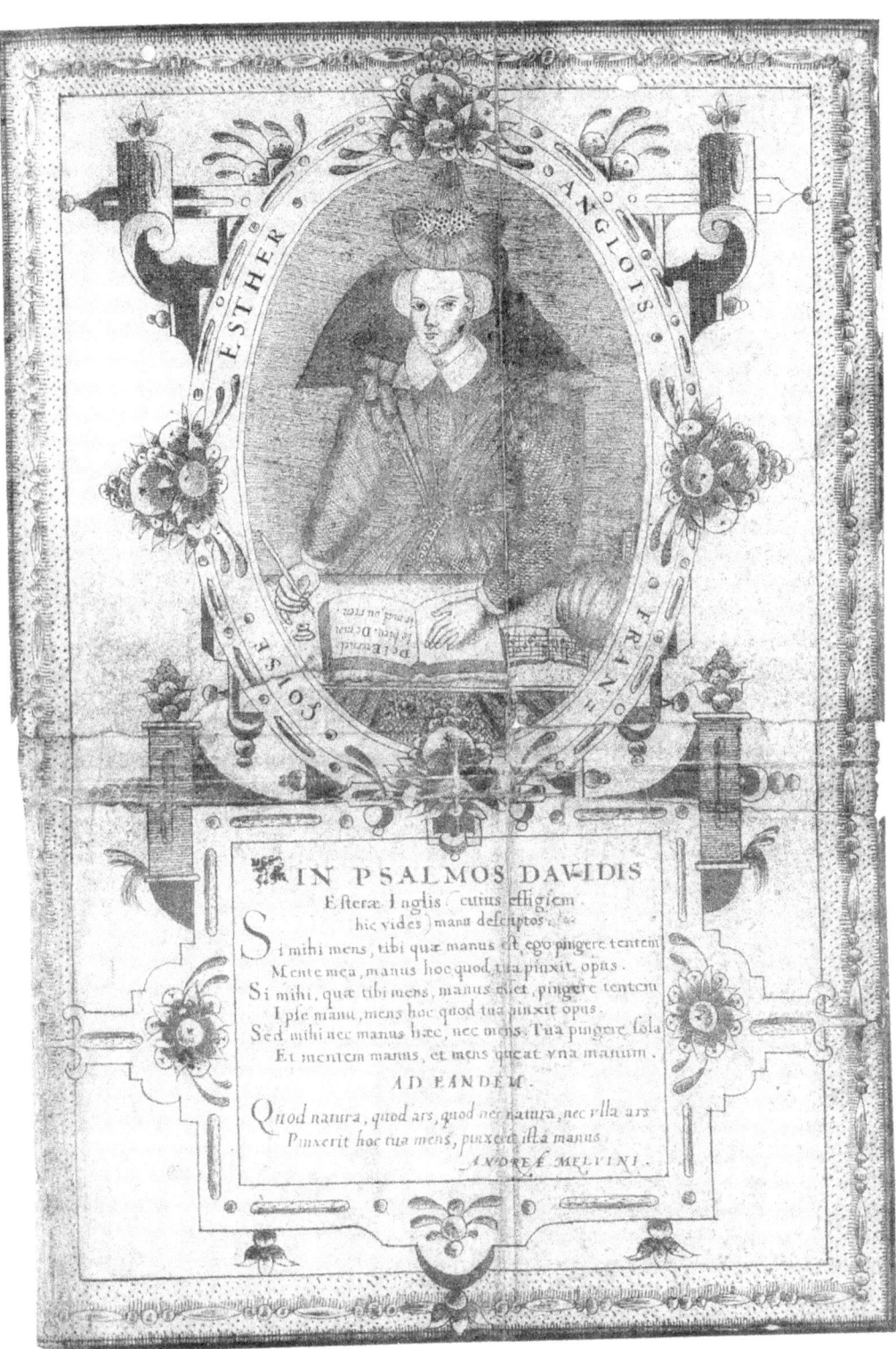

III.6 Esther Inglis, *Self-Portrait*, 1599

Mannerism: the self-portrait of the *nobil donna*

'If the fifteenth century was the time to work, the sixteenth was the season of harvest.'[1] During the sixteenth century the Mannerist period was a controversial and exciting time in European history. Economic chaos and religious turmoil altered the balance of power in political, social, economic and religious life. Notwithstanding these transformations, the arts flourished, including that of portraiture.[2] The impact of social and cultural changes led to a new, complex relationship between the wealthy patron and the artist. Until the Middle Ages patronage had been controlled by rulers and an imperial government, and by the Church. With the Renaissance and the development of Mannerism in art, wealthy private patrons came to control the creation of art, its taste and its style.[3] During the same period the Reformation and Counter-Reformation provided different types of patronage, and a new social status for the successful painter: a recognized place in society.[4]

The status of woman underwent a similar transformation, from inferior creature to *nobil donna* or courtly lady. In 1527, Baldassare Castiglione, a noble diplomat and humanist in the courts of Milan, Mantua and Urbino, wrote an influential book, *Il Cortegiano* (*The Courtier*), that offered another perspective on women.[5] Going beyond the nun of the Middle Ages or the mother and wife of the Renaissance, Castiglione examined women's role outside the boundaries of religious conventions and family structure. *Il Cortegiano* presents the role of the woman as a lady of the court, the *nobil donna*, a learned patron of the arts who could participate in intellectual debates, and read and write in Latin and Greek.[6] For Castiglione, the education of a woman was as vital as that of a man: 'Many virtues of the mind (prudence, magnanimity and continence) are as necessary to a woman as to a man.' It was largely he who paved the way for the sixteenth-century view of women. He considered them as having *virtù*, the ability to perform great deeds, without the need to resort to male assistance and dominance.[7]

While in his celebration of women, *De mulieribus claris* (*Noble and Famous Women*), Boccaccio had expressed revolutionary views for his time, he had still viewed women as subservient to men.[8] Castiglione, on the other hand, placed women on an equal intellectual level. Moved by the humanist concern for the revival of *virtù*, as well as the philosophical position of Renaissance Neoplatonists on love and beauty, he also exalted the beauty of women, a necessary requirement for a *nobil donna*: 'I do think that beauty is more necessary to a Lady and to a Courtier.' *Il Cortegiano* gave rise to a series of polemics in Italian literary circles on what constitutes 'beauty' in a woman.[9]

These Cinquecento treatises were inspired by Marsilio Ficino's philosophical discourses on love, *De amore* (*On Love*, 1474) and *Commentary on Plato's Symposium on Love*.[10] In addition to Neoplatonic philosophy, theories of beauty drew on the Cinquecento literary tradition established by such authors as Mario Equicola, Leone Ebreo, Benedetto Varchi and Agostino Nifo. In his *Libro di natura d'amore* (Venice, 1525), Mario Equicola asks 'What is beauty?' ('*che cosa é bellezza?*'). These writers drew heavily on Plato, Virgil and Ovid. Equicola asserts that the the image of the goddess Venus embodies beauty and her perfect proportions delight the viewer.[11] In his *Dialoghi d'amore* (Rome, 1535), Leone Ebreo defines beauty in terms of delighting the spirit and moving it to love ('*la bellezza che dillettando l'animo...il muove ad amare*').[12] Benedetto Varchi, too, comments on the concept of beauty and grace in relation to love, in his *Lezioni sull'amore* (1540). Another Neoplatonic poet, Leone Orsino, saw 'Beauty as nothing else than a certain gracefulness that delights the spirit of any individual who sees it and knows it, and in delighting moves the spirit to desire to unite, that is it moves it to love' ('*La bellezza non è altro che una certa grazia, la quale diletta l'animo di chiunche la vede e conosce, e dilettando lo muove a desiderare di goderla con union, cioè lo move ad amarla*'). Here, Varchi paraphrases Ebreo's concept of delight, and continues his definition of beauty by stressing the interconnection between beauty (*bellezza*) and grace (*grazia*): 'What is beauty and what is grace; and the best way to know and the most assuring way is through the understanding of their definition' ('*che cosa sia bellezza e che cosa sia grazia; e questo non si puo sapere con miglior modo e più sicuro e certo mezzo, che mediante la deffinizione loro*').[13] Agostino Nifo in *Del bello: il bello è nella natura* (Lugduni, 1549) discusses the quality of beauty, adding the Aristotelian concept of subjectivity. For Nifo, beauty is judged in terms of relativity – compared with beasts, a young woman is beautiful; when compared with goddesses, she is ugly.[14]

In the Quattrocento and Cinquecento such poets as Baldassare Castiglione, Angelo Poliziano and Pietro Bembo adhered to Petrarch's and Dante's models of female beauty, and assimilated those poets' Neoplatonic aesthetics.[15] For them, a beautiful female image reflected a 'celestial beauty that leads the poet or philosopher upward to the experience of divine or heavenly beauty'.[16] Correspondingly, Agnolo Firenzuola in *On the Beauty of Women* (1548) declares: 'A beautiful woman is the most beautiful object one can admire, and beauty is the greatest gift God bestowed on His human creatures. And so, through her virtue we direct our souls to contemplation, and through contemplation to the desire for heavenly things.'[17]

In the Mannerist period, the status of portraiture changed from subordination to Church and state, as in previous centuries, to that of a genre in its own right.[18] Portraits assumed many functions: as historical records, such as the Venetian portraits of the Doges; as instruments of glorification and means of attaining immortality and fame; as remembrances of a loved one; as tokens of friendship; and as gratifications of vanity, in as much as they were *fine* or fashionable portraits; and as marital contracts. (*Fine* portraits were seldom posed for, while in true portraits, real physical likeness was sought, requiring the posing of the sitter.) Leonardo observed: 'The good painter must depict two principal things: that is, man and the concept of his mind.'[19] Bronzino's portraits depict a sitter with the mask of a person; he leaves completion to the viewer's imagination.[20]

As the need to educate women evolved, books of instructions on how to be a good Christian woman or a nun proliferated. These didactic books were written by male clerics, such as Pietro Aretino (*Dialogues*, 1540) and Jan Luis Vives (*Instruction of a Christian Woman*, 1523).[21] Paradoxically, the interest in educating women lay in the spiritual realm, because in the intellectual realm women were usually discouraged from studying the humanities (*studia humanitatis* – logic, grammar, history, literature, philosophy, Greek and Latin). Even so, the period produced intellectually eminent women, such as Vittoria Colonna, Veronica Gambara and Gaspra Stampa.[22]

It is important to examine how female painters of the Mannerist period were viewed during their own time, as well as how they thought about themselves, as illustrated in engravings and commemorative medals. The significance of this topic occurs on three levels. How did women painters reveal themselves to the viewer? What *personae* did these artists assume and why? How did these self-portraits provide new insights into the artists' conception of themselves as creators?

The function of women's self-portraiture in the Mannerist period can be seen not as an exercise in iconographical reference, but rather as an interpretation or statement of the artist's character, her self-definition, and her relationship to her milieu.[23] When self-portraits in the Mannerist style are compared, it can be seen that both male and female painters were concerned with portraying themselves as inventors and creators, that is to say, as artists. The concept of persona emerges as the same for both genders and reflects the impact of the revival of classical values on the individual and on the Neoplatonic philosophy of the Renaissance, which provided a nurturing atmosphere for humanistic awareness of the self.[24] Where the differences between male and female self-portraits appear is in the presentation of the occupation or interests of the individual man or woman.[25] Self-portraits by male artists focus on status or a specific occupation, whereas self-portraits by women artists include educational or cultural accomplishments, for example the woman artist as musician, poet, teacher or art collector.[26]

Also, with Mannerism the female painter expands her role as a natural creator into that of artistic creator, by observing herself as an object of beauty and admiration.[27] Inasmuch as the self-portrait was painted by the artist for herself and not for a patron, it portrays female interest in self-gratification and self-aggrandizement.

The existing female self-portraits of the sixteenth century in northern Europe stand out for their originality, notably the self-portraits by Catherina van Hemessen (1526–87). Her unique self-portraits, establishing the first known self-imaging by a woman on panel, provide insight into her life as both a painter and an educated woman. She was the daughter of the Antwerp artist Jan van Hemessen, who provided her early instruction. Catherina most likely assisted her father in doing the background detail of his genre paintings and collaborated with him on some book illuminations. All of her ten extant paintings were executed before 1552, and there is no record of subsequent activity. Two years later, she married Chrétien de Morien, a musician renowned for his performances at the spinet. The couple were invited to the Spanish court and, in 1556, entered the service of Mary of Hungary, sister of Charles V, with 'a good salary'.[28] Van Hemessen's works are clearly signed and dated in her own hand – perhaps not only to avoid confusion with her father's work but also to affirm herself as a painter.[29]

Self-Portrait at an Easel, at the Kunstmuseum in Basel (Fig. IV.1), is dated and inscribed 'Ego Caterina De Hemessen me pinxit 1546, Aetatis sua 20' ('I Caterina De Hemessen painted myself in 1546, at the age of 20').[30] Seated at the easel, she portrays herself in the act of sketching a female face (perhaps her self-portrait) on a small wooden panel, holding a palette and brushes in her left hand. Van Hemessen depicts herself pausing in her artistic task of painting her self-image to observe the viewer or herself in the mirror. She rests her right hand on the maulstick, holding the brushes and the palette in a staged manner, and carefully regards the viewer (or the sitter), all the while demonstrating her skills and artistic instruments. The double-portrait illusion – one in process on the easel and the completed one as the painting – signifies her ability to draw as well as paint, in keeping with the artistic theory of the sixteenth century that emphasized the importance of good drawing as the basis for a successful painting.[31] Van Hemessen's inventive illusionism is in creating a double portrait, seen in time and space by the viewer but not by her, while she can observe both the viewer looking at her and her mirror's reflection, unseen by the viewer.

The *Self-Portrait at the Spinet* of 1548 (Fig. IV.2), dated and signed 'Caterina De Hemessen Pingebat 1548, Aetatis Sua 22' ('I Caterina De Hemessen painted myself in 1548, at the age of 22') and in the virginal or spinet, 'Habet [E]r[go] Manus' ('Painted by my hands'), retains the same melancholic expression on the part of the artist, but adds another dimension to her achievements – that of van Hemessen's social position as a cultured woman who can play a musical instrument, the spinet or clavichord.[32] This second self-portrait can be viewed as an accompaniment to the earlier portrait of 1546, alluding to the sister quality of the arts of painting and music (*ut pictura musica*).[33]

Two portraits by van Hemessen at the Musée des Beaux Arts in Brussels signed and dated 1549 depict her and her husband. Judging by the compositional design, their size and the inscribed dates, van Hemessen

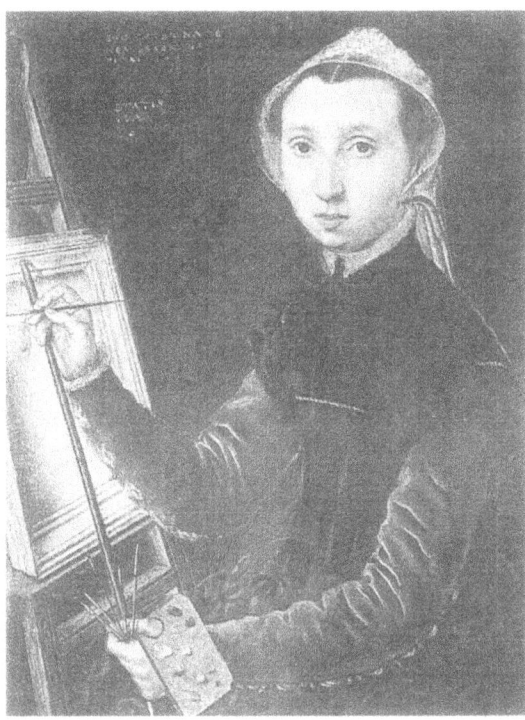

IV.1   Catherina van Hemessen, *Self-Portrait at an Easel*, 1546

intended them to be pendant portraits, most likely commemorating a special event in their lives, perhaps a birthday or their engagement.[34] Italian Mannerism likewise offers numerous examples of female self-portraits that include depictions of a friend or a husband, as we shall see in the paintings of Sofonisba Anguissola and Lavinia Fontana.

In sixteenth-century northern European art, the female artist came to portray herself consciously as a painter and as a cultivated woman. Male self-portraits of the time did not focus on asserting this kind of status. Rather, a male self-portrait might appear in wedding commemorations or, most often, in religious commissions for paintings or altarpieces, such as Albrecht Dürer's *Adoration of the Trinity* of 1511 (Kunsthistorisches Museum, Vienna) and Lucas Cranach's *Self-Portrait* of 1550 (Galleria degli Uffizi, Florence) and *Crucifixion* of 1550 (Stadtkirche, Weimar).[35]

Cinquecento literature applauded the cultivated woman, as we have seen, and noted the implications of social limitation on her artistic success. Castiglione suggests in *Il Cortegiano* that the system of education and patronage during the Renaissance, particularly in Italy, precluded women from developing a full range of themes in art and, therefore, from achieving recognized excellence.[36] That is, women focused on such acceptable 'female topics' as religious paintings and portraits, in particular self-portraits.

Among the women artists who created self-portraits in painting and drawing during the sixteenth century in Italy were Sofonisba Anguissola, Lavinia Fontana, Barbara Longhi and Marietta Robusti.

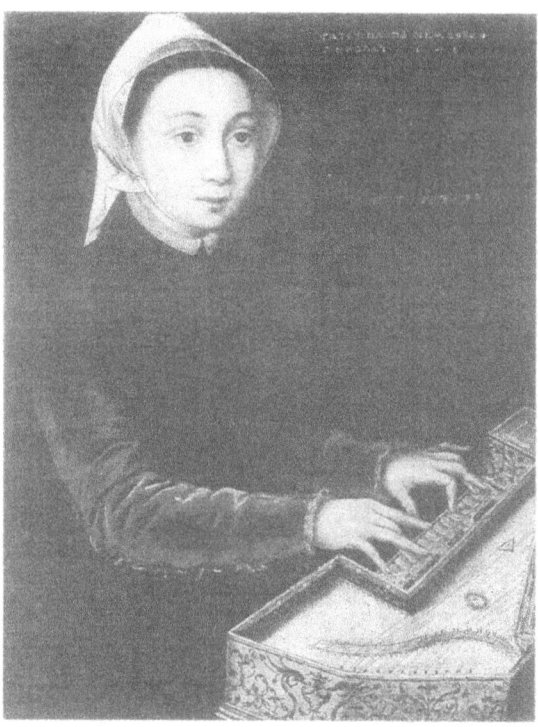

IV.2   Catherina van Hemessen, *Self-Portrait at the Spinet*, 1548

Sofonisba Anguissola (1532–1624) was born in Cremona and died in Palermo. The first modern insight into her work was provided by Giulio Bora's exhibition in Cremona in 1985,[37] and recent exhibitions in Cremona, Vienna, Milan and Washington, DC, and pioneering books on Sofonisba and her sisters by Flavio Caroli (1987), Maria Kusche (1989–92), Ilya Sandra Perlingieri (1992) and Mina Gregori (1994) have documented both Anguissola's art and her life.[38]

Sofonisba's merchant father had six daughters – all painters – and a son. Sofonisba was the first-born, and trained in the Bernardino Campi workshop during 1546. Fifteen years later, after trips to Rome and Madrid (1559), she moved to Bernardino Gatti's studio in Milan. In 1571, during a period at the court of King Philip II and Queen Isabella, she met and married Don Fabrizio de Moncada, a Sicilian nobleman. The king and queen provided her with an artistic environment during her stay at the court, and on her marriage they honored her with precious gifts, including a wedding gown adorned with pearls and a generous dowry. They also presented a substantial annual pension for the couple and their future children on Sofonisba's departure for Sicily in 1571.[39]

Anguissola commemorated the marriage with *Self-Portrait with Her Husband* (1571–5, Fig. IV.3). In this double portrait, marking a wedding as well as an anniversary, the innocent, girlish smile of Anguissola's earlier self-portraits is replaced by the intense and warm expression of a loving matron. The artist indicates the bond of affection by situating her husband close

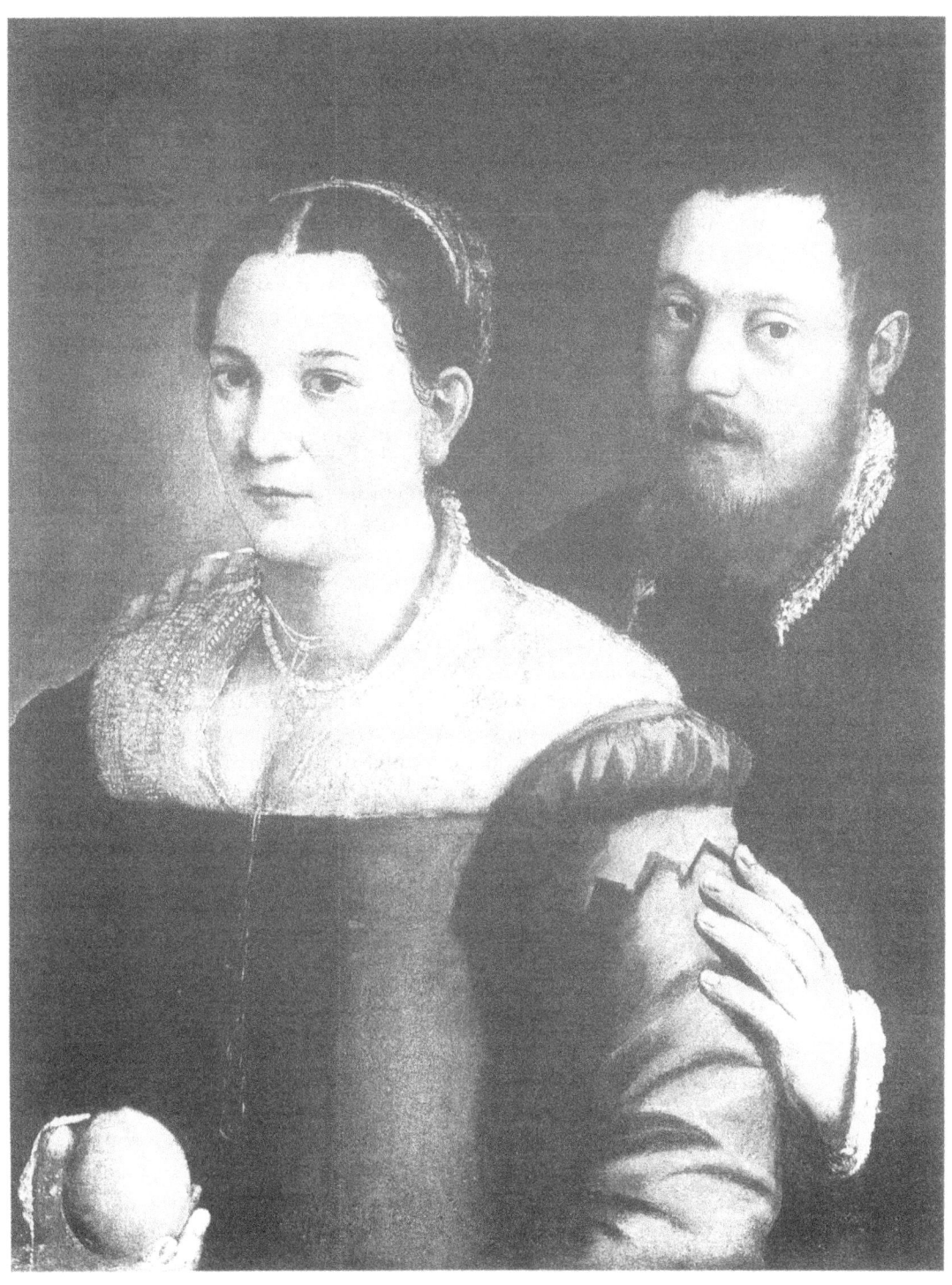

IV.3   Sofonisba Anguissola, *Self-Portrait with Her Husband*, 1571–5

behind her, his hand resting on her shoulder to denote love and support. A pomegranate alludes to marital fecundity. This type of marriage portrait, where the artist includes a self-image, became popular in the sixteenth century with Hans Burkgmair's *Self-Portrait with His Wife* of 1529 (Alte Pinakothek, Munich), where husband and wife pose together while the wife holds a mirror reflecting their images, alluding to their transient marital bliss. Double or marital portraits with the inclusion of the artist's own likeness continued in the seventeenth century with Peter Paul Rubens, Jacob Jordaens, Frans Hals and Rembrandt.[40]

Ten years later, after Moncado had died, Anguissola left Palermo to visit her family in Cremona. During the sea voyage, she met a Genovese widower, Orazio Lomellijno, whom she married in Genoa in 1581. Once again the king of Spain demonstrated his generosity, by providing Anguissola with a new dowry of 400 golden scudi for her and any future children. From 1584 to 1599 she stayed in Genoa, subsequently returning to Palermo, where she remained until her death.[41]

Through Anguissola's numerous depictions of herself, in both paintings and drawings, the rich development of her style, life and career are obvious.[42] In a few of her early self-portraits she represents herself as a painter,[43] but in most she appears as a cultivated woman, reading a book or playing a musical instrument. In subsequent portraits, she chooses the double image, representing her dual status as an artist and as a wife. Anguissola's self-portraits reveal her sense of freedom and natural expression, her boldness, spontaneity, softness and simplicity, as well as her ability to create an image that is alive and engages the viewer. Her self-portraits incorporate a variety of thematic images, moving from the traditional representation of the self to the artist as poet, as musician, as painter, or as mother and wife.

Anguissola's self-portrait of 1552, an oil on copper (Museum of Fine Arts, Boston), is fashioned in an oval shape, harkening back to miniature painting (Pl. VII; and the likeness held up by Giulio Clovio in her portrait of 1556; Fig. IV.4). The artist holds a large medallion, which is a coat-of-arms honoring her. The inscription on the border reads: '*Sofonisba Anguissola Virgo Seipsus Manu Ex Speculo Depicta Cremonæ*', while the center motto, in superimposed lettering, reads: '*A[nguissola] Familia Pittrice C[remonese]*', also with the superimposed letters 'E', 'L', 'M'. The letter 'A' stands for the Anguissola family, and 'C', for Cremona, 'E', for her sisters Elena and Europa, 'L', for Lucia, and 'M', for Minerva. The words *familia* and *pittrice* reveal and affirm that Sofonisba is part of the Anguissola family, the painters of Cremona, validating not only her artistic ancestorship, but also her nobility.[44] This tondo format may have been used not only to advertise her artistic talents but also to affirm a family tradition of dealing in antique coins or medallions.[45]

In the collection of artists' portraits at the Uffizi (Corridorio Vasariano) hangs the first full-size self-portrait by Anguissola of 1552–4, signed and dated: '*Sophonisba Aunguisciola Crem. Pictrix Aeta Sue Ann XX*' (see Pl. VIII). She is clad in somber clothes, without any accessory, focusing on her role as a draughtswoman and painter.[46] Seated at a table, she presents to the viewer the

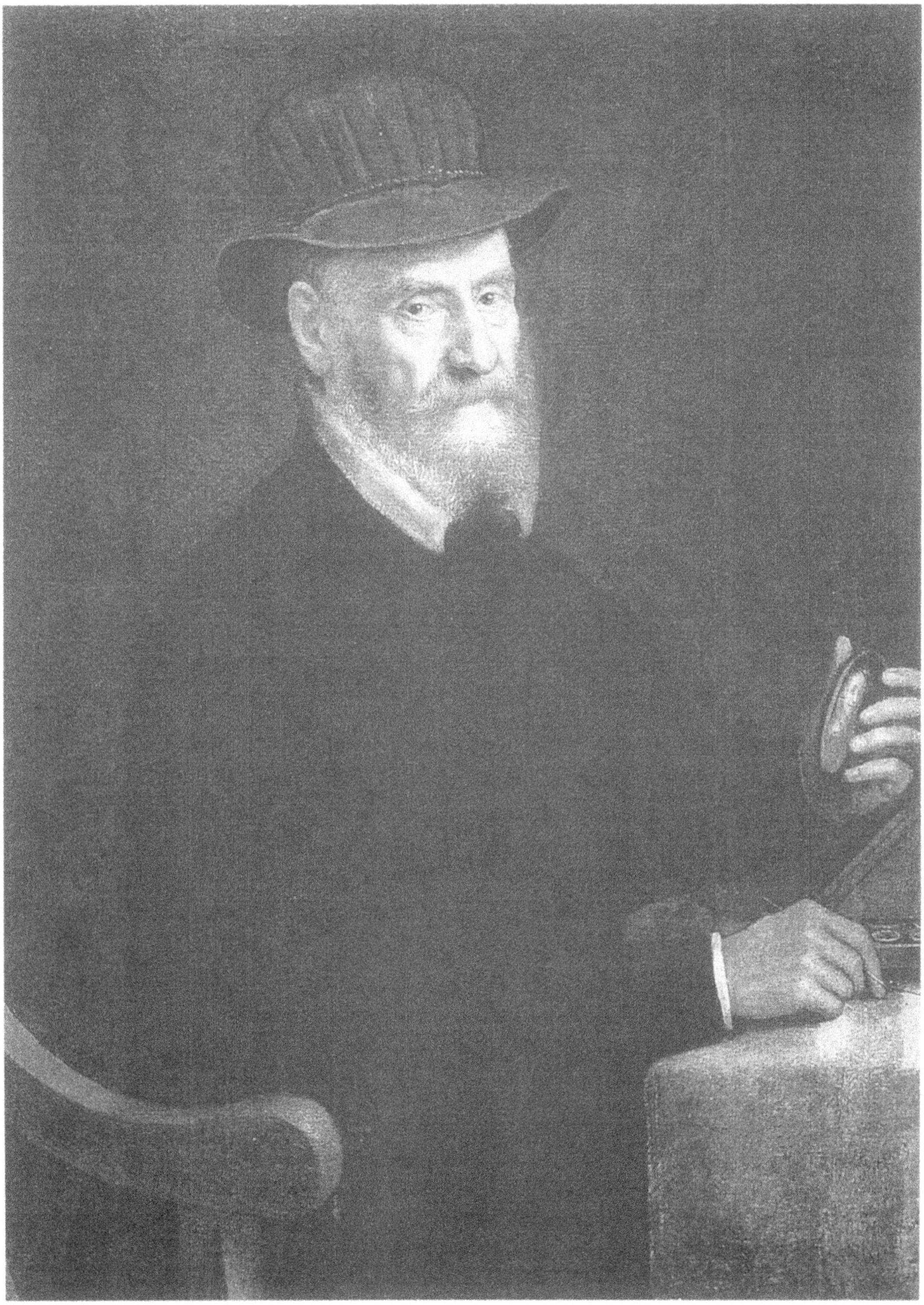

IV.4   Sofonisba Anguissola, *Giulio Clovio*, 1556

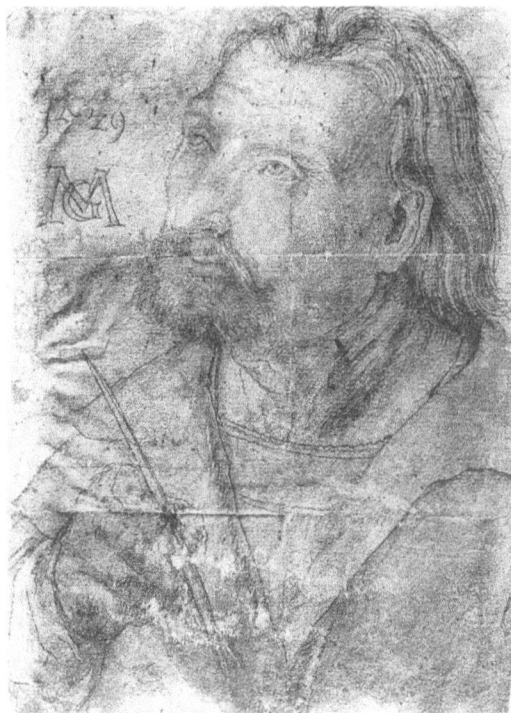

IV.5   Matthias Grünewald, *Self-Portrait*, 1529, drawing, inscribed '1529 MG'

instruments for her work: drawing paper, a palette with color pigments, and brushes.

In depicting herself surrounded by artist's paraphernalia (see also Fig. IV.6), Anguissola shows the influence of northern European conventions of portrait composition, where the subject often sits behind a table or parapet and items are displayed to denote his or her interests, as in Matthias Grünewald's *Self-Portrait* of 1529 (Fig. IV.5). The originality of such work rests on self-portraiture as a testimony of the sitter's occupation – Grünewald being the first male and Anguissola the first female painter known to have used such a device. Another *Self-Portrait* was executed by Anguissola between 1552 and 1554, in pencil on blue paper (Fig. IV.6).[47] The portrait is meticulously drawn, as is revealed by details in the treatment of the hair, hands, facial expression, and garments, as well as technical rendering such as shading. The artist depicts herself as an educated woman, a *nobil donna* – no accoutrements of her profession (as a painter) are visible in this drawing. She is seated, reading. The viewer is the audience, who has interrupted the sitter's concentration.

Besides the Grünewald drawing mentioned above, there are drawings of male self-portraits from the sixteenth century by Raphael, Leonardo, Pontormo and Parmigianino, all reflecting a humanist emphasis and a focus on the individual. If Anguissola's drawing of herself at a young age is compared with Albrecht Dürer's silverpoint *Self-Portrait, at the Age of 13* of 1484 (Graphische Sammlung, Albertina, Vienna) and with Raphael's drawing

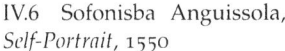

IV.6   Sofonisba   Anguissola,
Self-Portrait, 1550

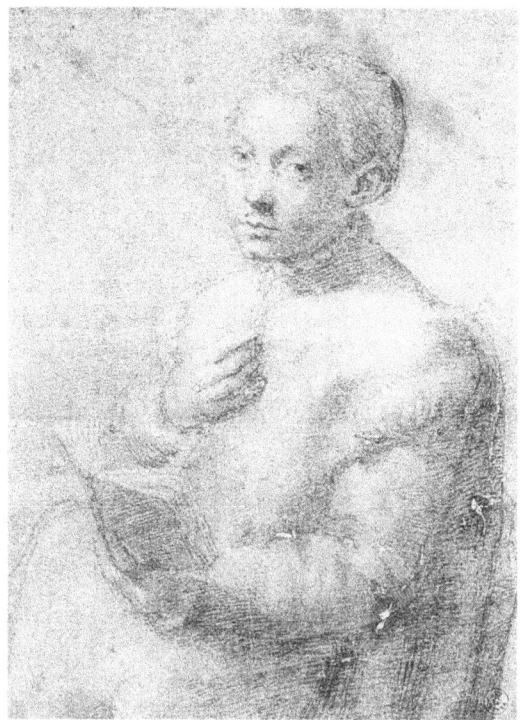

in black chalk, *Self-Portrait the Age of 17* of 1500 (British Museum, London), it can be seen that these artists in their youth explored and observed their persona as well as demonstrating their experience in the drawing techniques of the time.

Anguissola's *Self-Portrait* of 1554 (Fig. IV.7)[18] is signed and dated: '*Sofonisba Anguissola Fecit 1554.*' It derives from the Uffizi drawing, and shows the painter presenting an open book to the viewer. In a similar manner, Bronzino portrayed the poet Laura Battiferi (1560; Palazzo Vecchio, Florence) holding a book and pointing to a special passage in the text.[49] Like Bronzino, Anguissola instructs the viewer on the nature of fame, not only through painting but also through the printed word.

The recently discovered *Self-Portrait at an Easel* (Pl. IX), painted in 1556, is similar to versions found in other collections in Italy, England and Canada.[50] Anguissola is shown seated in front of an easel with a palette filled with colors, holding a brush and a maulstick. The painting on the easel is a depiction of a Madonna and Child in a loggia through which the setting sun can be seen. The composition is based on the traditional subject of Saint Luke painting the Virgin, which was popular in Renaissance and Mannerist paintings as an indication of the artist's divine inspiration and the status of the artist working in his own studio. It also alludes to the theory of the *paragone* (comparison) between drawing and painting, as seen in Rogier van der Weyden's *St Luke Painting the Virgin* of 1435 (Museum of Fine Arts, Boston), Raphael and his assistant's *St Luke Painting the Virgin* of 1517

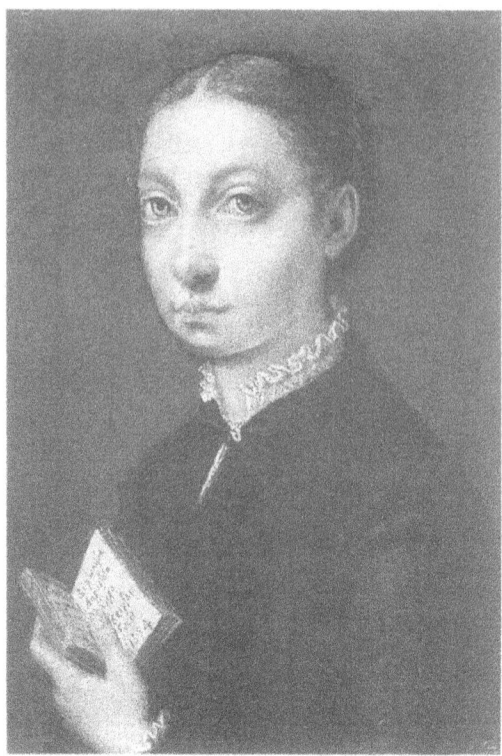

IV.7   Sofonisba Anguissola,
Self-Portrait, 1554

(Accademia di San Luca, Rome), and later in Giorgio Vasari's *St Luke Painting the Virgin* of 1560 (SS. Annunziata, Florence), as well as in books of illuminations. Early Christian legend has it that the Virgin, wanting herself portrayed, appeared in the studio of the painter St Luke, where she instructed and assisted him in doing the portrait. Although there was no muse of painting in the early Renaissance, the prominence of St Luke established the association of a founder figure with a patron saint of painters. Depictions of the saint commonly show him seated at an easel painting a *Madonna and Child*, in an interior setting and surrounded with painter's paraphernalia. The use of a painter's studio as background is also seen in *St Luke Painting the Virgin* by an anonymous Italian painter of the fourteenth century in the church of Santa Maria Maggiore, Rome; also in the illuminated page of *Marcia Painting a Madonna and Child*; in the 1401–2 manuscript of Boccaccio's *Noble and Famous Women* (MS Fr.12420, folio 86, Bibliothèque Nationale, Paris), where Marcia is represented at work painting the image. In contrast Timarete, in painting a *Madonna and Child* in a later manuscript (*c*.1470) of the same work (MS Fr. 598, f. 100 verso, Bibliothèque Nationale, Paris), is seated in the same position as Sofonisba, facing the viewer while depicting the holy image.

The imagery of St Luke painting the Virgin was a source of inspiration for both female and male artists. Anguissola's painting manifests her desire to continue this imagery.

The claim has been made that Anguissola's *Self-Portrait at an Easel* was

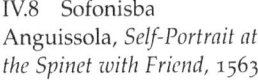

IV.8   Sofonisba
Anguissola, *Self-Portrait at
the Spinet with Friend*, 1563

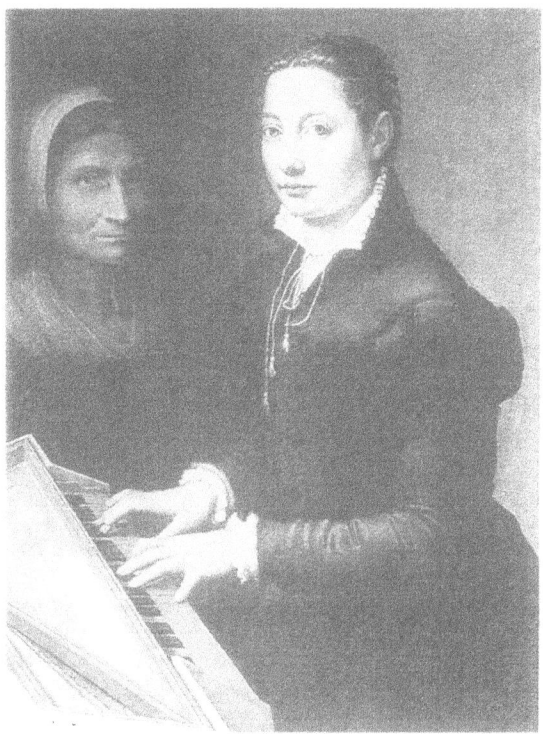

inspired by Catherina van Hemessen's pose in her *Self-Portrait at an Easel*,[51] but there is a noteworthy difference in the subject matter (Fig. IV.1 and Pl. IX). Van Hemessen depicts a likeness of herself or of another woman, not an image of the Madonna and Child. She engages the viewer in the dialogue of the *paragone* – drawing being the mistress of the arts and painting being subordinate to it – and illustrates the notion of artistic process, the drawn image being still visible. Anguissola, on the other hand, involves the viewer in a discussion of the theory of artistic invention; she is guided by divine inspiration, and her execution of the work of art is almost finished. Both artists represent their status as painters in their studio and comment on their merits. Both are likely to have derived their compositional pose from the representations of Saint Luke painting the Virgin.[52]

In several self-portraits, Anguissola plays the spinet or clavichord, as in *Self-Portrait at the Spinet* of 1556 (Galleria di Capodimonte, Naples), where she is depicted alone, and pausing, as if the viewer's gaze has disturbed her concentration; others show her with another figure. Attributions of these works vary; some maintain that the performer is actually her sister, Lucia.[53] Two other self-portraits by Sofonisba at the spinet or clavichord exist in the Earl Spencer Collection, at Althorp, in Northamptonshire. In the version illustrated in Fig. IV.8 an unclear inscription on the lower left reads: '*Sofonisba Anguissola Virgo Seipsum Pinxit Jussu Ami (Caris) Patris 1563*.' A larger version, of 1561–3, now without an inscription, hangs in the Goodwood House

IV.9   Sofonisba
Anguissola, *Bernardino
Campi Painting the Portrait
of Sofonisba*, 1550

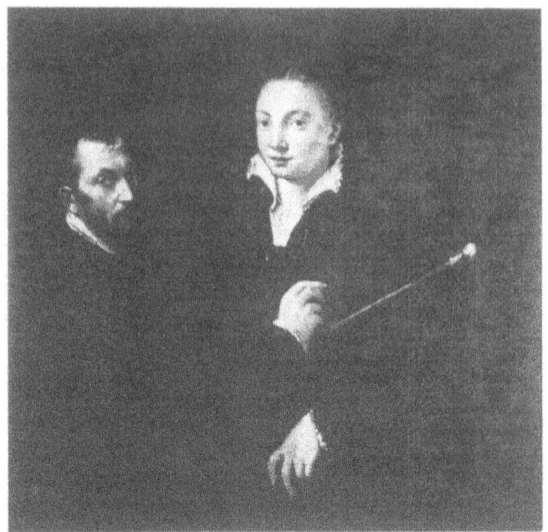

Collection, West Sussex. The original inscription in these paintings paid homage not only to the artist as a painter but also to an old family friend. This dual portrait shows complexity of space and realism in the portrayal of an old and a young woman.

As was traditional in the upbringing of a *nobil donna*, Anguissola was taught to play a musical instrument; thus she is seen at the spinet or clavichord. In addition, she pays homage to Cremona, which since the Renaissance had been a center for making musical instruments. By playing one, Anguissola is making reference to the musical fame of her native city as well as to herself. Comparing her *Self-Portrait at the Spinet* with van Hemessen's painting of the same title, a difference between their interactions with the viewer or audience can be observed – Anguissola performs for and entertains the viewer whereas van Hemessen plays for her own enjoyment.[34]

Anguissola's double portrait of 1559–60, entitled *Bernardino Campi Painting the Portrait of Sofonisba* (Fig. IV.9),[35] reveals the artist's sense of humor. Bernardino Campi, her tutor, is shown painting a portrait of his pupil, Anguissola. The work comments on her achieved fame by showing her being painted by her teacher. At another level, it can be seen as a gift of gratitude to her teacher. Anguissola is the only known artist, female or male, who depicted her teacher in a painting with the following illusions or *trompe l'œil* effects: a painter painting a portrait, a painter painting a self-portrait, and a painter painting another painter painting what is in fact her self-portrait – a Mannerist way of teasing the viewer. The innovative compositional arrangement of this self-portrait prefigures the self-portraits of women painters as teachers in the eighteenth century.[36]

Anguissola was widely recognized during her lifetime by artists, art critics and theoreticians such as Giorgio Vasari, Annibale Caro and Giovan Paolo Lomazzo. Before her death, Anthony van Dyck visited Palermo and drew her portrait. The praises she received from Vasari were numerous; in his biography of the Bolognese sculptress, Properzia de' Rossi,[57] in commenting on Anguissola, he cites Ariosto's sonnet from *Orlando Furioso* (Canto XX, Stanza 2): '*Le donne son venute in eccellenza, Di ciascun'arte, ov' hanno posto cura*' ('Women have come into excellence, in every art where they have taken pains').[58] In the biographies of Benvenuto Garofalo and Girolamo da Carpi, Vasari writes: 'More than any other woman of her time with more study and greater grace, she has labored on every thing connected with drawing. Not only has she drawn, colored and painted from life, and made excellent copies, but she has drawn many beautiful original pictures.'[59] The biographer further notes that, to her creativity (*alla virtù*) and natural talent (*inclinazione*), Sofonisba added artistic training, and diligence in her studies, demonstrating that she, as well as her sisters, was gifted with unusual creative talent, in particular in the art of drawing ('*sono immanorate d'ogni più rara virtù, e in particolare delle cose del disgeno*').[60]

Vasari is also making reference here to the artistic theory of the sixteenth century whereby drawing is the mistress of 'Nature'.[61] In the second edition of the *Lives*, Vasari continued to explain the concept of drawing (*disegno*) and explains what he meant and why drawing ruled creation in the visual arts and has its origin in the intellect. 'Afterwards, when it is expressed by the hands and is called drawing (design), we may conclude that drawing is none other than a visible expression and declaration of our inner conception and of that which others have imagined and given form to in their ideas.'[62] It is this that is exhibited in Anguissola's self-portraits.

In painting, Vasari observes that 'the lines are of service in many ways, but especially in outlining every figure, because when they are well drawn, and made correct and in proportion, the shadows and lights that are then added give the strongest relief to the lines of the figure and the result is all excellence and perfection'.[63] Vasari's conception of artistic creativity is related to this Mannerist theory of painting. He asserts that there are two alternatives in a painter's development or achievement of artistic creativity: imitation (*imitazione*), the copying of works of art as a method of learning; and invention (*invenzione*), independent of imitation, which constitutes the means of conceiving artistic ideas. Imitation serves to guide and teach the artist in composing and creating perfection. For Vasari, imitation draws on three different sources. The first two are copying from nature (*copia dal vero*) and selecting from one's work (*imitare se stessi*). Copying from nature teaches artists to create forms that are alive. It also helps the artist to learn how to draw in such a way that eventually he or she is capable of drawing anything merely from memory.

Vasari praises Anguissola's paintings and drawings, for copying nature as well as creating from memory; for her good judgment (*giudizio*); because she has originality; and because, like Titian, Michelangelo and Raphael, she has in her paintings surpassed nature itself. Vasari includes her drawing, *The Putto Bitten by a Lizard*, in his *Libro dei Disegni* (now in the Gabinetto di Disegni e Stampe [Inv. n. 1039], Museo di Capodimonte, Naples).[64] It is noteworthy,

Vasari concludes, that Sofonisba and her sisters not only create such lively portraits but also paint them so well.[65]

Anthony van Dyck paid homage to Anguissola by drawing her, noting the following on the drawing: 'Portrait of Signora Sofonisba, painter, copied from life in Palermo on the 12th day of July of the year 1624, when she was 96 years of age, still of good memory, clear senses and kind. While I painted her portrait, she gave me advice as to the light, which should not be directed from too high so as not to cause too strong a shadow on her wrinkles and many more good speeches as well as telling me parts of her life-story, in which one could see that she was a wonderful painter after nature.'[66]

Anguissola's sisters also excelled in the art of painting. Several of her paintings represent them in a group, as in *Three Sisters Playing Chess* of 1555 (Muzeum Noradowe, Poznan, Poland). This painting was highly praised by Vasari, who described it as: 'Painted with so much skill and care, that the figures wanted only to be alive.'[67] Among other works the Anguissola sisters all painted each other at different stages in their lives. Anna Maria (active 1568–85), the youngest, married a nobleman, Jacopo de' Sommi. Virtually nothing is known about her, except that she painted portraits and religious objects. At the age of 15 she painted a *Madonna and Child with St John* (also called the *Scala del Correggio*) in which classical temples are portrayed in the background.[68] Elena (active 1560–84) studied with Bernardo Campi along with Sofonisba, and entered the convent of San Vicenzo at Mantua in 1584.[69] Europa (d.1578), who also married a nobleman, Carlo Schinchimelli, painted a few portraits and religious works, among them *The Calling of St Andrew* for the church of Saint Elena, which was destroyed in 1808.[70]

The most gifted of Sofonisba's sisters was Lucia (1540–65), whose portraits are sometimes mistaken for hers. Lucia studied with Sofonisba and painted several portraits, including a *Self-Portrait* of 1557 (Castello Sforzesco, Milan), with an inscription on the lower left: '*MCLVII Lucia Anguissola Virgo Amilcaris Filia se Ipsa Pinxit*' ('1557 Lucia Anguissola, Single, Daughter of Amilcaris, Self-Portrait').[71] Minerva (active 1560–80)[72] also depicted herself, in a miniature *Self-Portrait* of 1559–61 (Uffizi, Florence) and the *Self-Portrait* of 1561 (Pinacoteca di Brera, Milan), which should be attributed to her instead of to Sofonisba.[73] Lucia died young, but during her lifetime she was a painter, a teacher and a scholar of Latin, as Vasari pointed out, a paradigm of a *nobil donna*.[74]

Just as Cremona honored its native woman painter in Sofonisba Anguissola, so too did Bologna with Lavinia Fontana (1552–1614). As discussed in Chapter III, since the Middle Ages Bologna, partly through the presence of its university, had been a center for women's intellectual and artistic development and the fostering of education for both genders.

Lavinia Fontana was trained under her father, Prospero Fontana, and Ludovico Carracci. She worked in Rome under the patronage of several popes, including Gregory XIII and Clement VII.[75] During her lifetime, she received significant appointments, including that of Portraitist in Ordinary at the Vatican by Pope Gregory XIII, and she became the first female to be

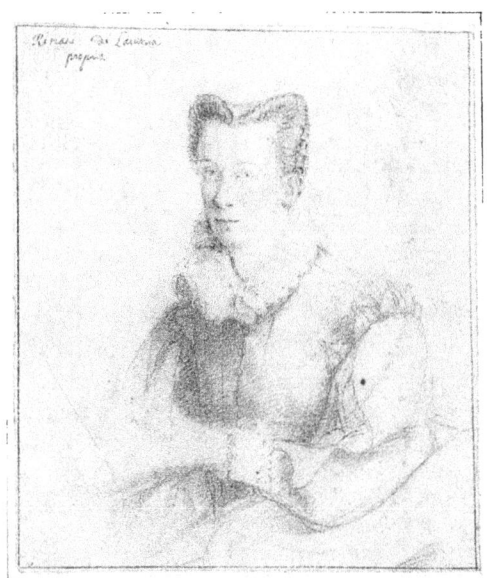

IV.10   Lavinia Fontana, *Self-Portrait*, 1575, drawing, red and black chalk

accepted at the Roman Accademia di San Luca.[76] This honor had not been given to any woman painters of the Renaissance: in the Florentine Accademia del Disegno, they were excluded even from entering their name.

Carlo Galli's *Lavinia Fontana* of 1940 was, for some time, the seminal and most important art-historical source on its subject's life, but the recent elegant and scholarly publication by M. T. Cantaro, *Lavinia Fontana Bolognese* of 1990, and Vera Fortunati's exhibition catalogue on Lavinia Fontana of 1994, present elaborate and accurate accounts of the artist's life and works with illustrations and vast documentation.[77] Very beautiful, Lavinia constantly received marriage proposals. In 1577, she married the Count of Imola, Giovan Paolo Zappi, who had trained in her father's studio.[78] Zappi collaborated with Fontana in painting backgrounds and details, such as drapery. Lavinia was a prolific painter and a fecund woman, bearing eleven children.

Only five self-portraits – three of them paintings – are known: *Self-Portrait at the Spinet* of 1577 (Accademia Nazionale di San Luca, Rome); *Self-Portraits* of 1579 and 1585 (both at the Uffizi, Florence); and two unfinished drawings, both entitled *Self-Portrait at the Age of Nineteen* and executed in 1571 (both at the Pierpont Morgan Library, New York). The two drawings are studies that manifest the painter's interest in the practical, technical and experimental qualities of the art (Fig. IV.10). In them Fontana focuses on her elegant attire rather than on her status as an artist.[79] When comparing the early self-portraits by Fontana and Anguissola, it can be observed how both painters set out to demonstrate their knowledge, meanwhile abiding by the theory of art and the artistic conventions prevalent in the sixteenth century, particularly in the consideration of drawing as the 'mistress of Nature'.[80]

Recently this author discovered another *Self-Portrait*, probably painted around 1577, in a private collection in Seattle.[81] It is a frontal, waist-length

IV.11 Lasinio's engraving after Lavinia Fontana's *Self-Portrait*, 1579

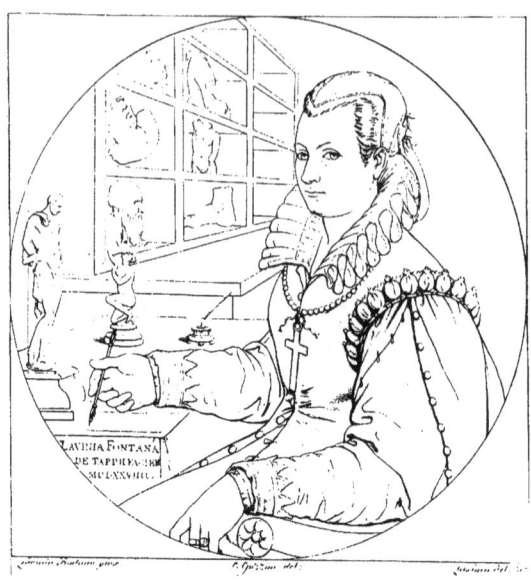

portrait with elaborate and careful rendition of the garments, recalling another self-portrait recorded by the engraver, Lasinio, in the Uffizi collection of artists' self-portraits (Fig. IV.11).[82] The overly fussy depiction of detail, and the aristocratic or aloof stare of the sitter, both reflect the Mannerist style. The rendition of the costume suggests a wedding or ceremonial portrait, as observed in Bronzino's *Lady in Green* of 1540 (Collection of Her Majesty the Queen, London). In Bronzino's portraits of women, the attire reflects the social position of the sitter. Also, unlike her two later self-portraits, emphasizing her role as painter and creator, in the Seattle portrait Fontana focuses on herself, her beauty, her jewelry and her garments.

The *Self-Portrait at the Spinet* of 1577 (Accademia di San Luca, Rome), like its second version done in 1579 (Fig. IV.12),[83] is painted in oil on canvas. It is signed and inscribed: '*Lavinia Virgo Porsperi Fonatane/Filia Ex Speculo Imaginem/Oris Suis Expresit Anno/MDLXXVII*' and portrays Fontana as a Bolognese lady. She is dressed in elaborate satin and lace, and beautified by a braided hairstyle, and corals and pearl jewelry. In the background is a studio. An empty easel stands in front of the window, giving the painter access to natural lighting. The spinet and the easel allude to Fontana's dual artistic role as a painter and a musician. On the spinet rests a coral piece in the shape of a love knot, a symbol of betrothal,[84] and behind her an attendant holds an indecipherable musical score. Perhaps Fontana is playing a love song.

The placement of the coral on the spinet may allude to symbolism associated with the powers of music over love or vice versa. Therefore Fontana, in her self-portrait, is affirming her femininity, her amorous sentiments, and her artistic talents as a *nobil donna*. The knot as a symbol of love and union had also been depicted in the manuscript tradition of the early Renaissance, as seen in the illuminated page of the *Breviarium cum*

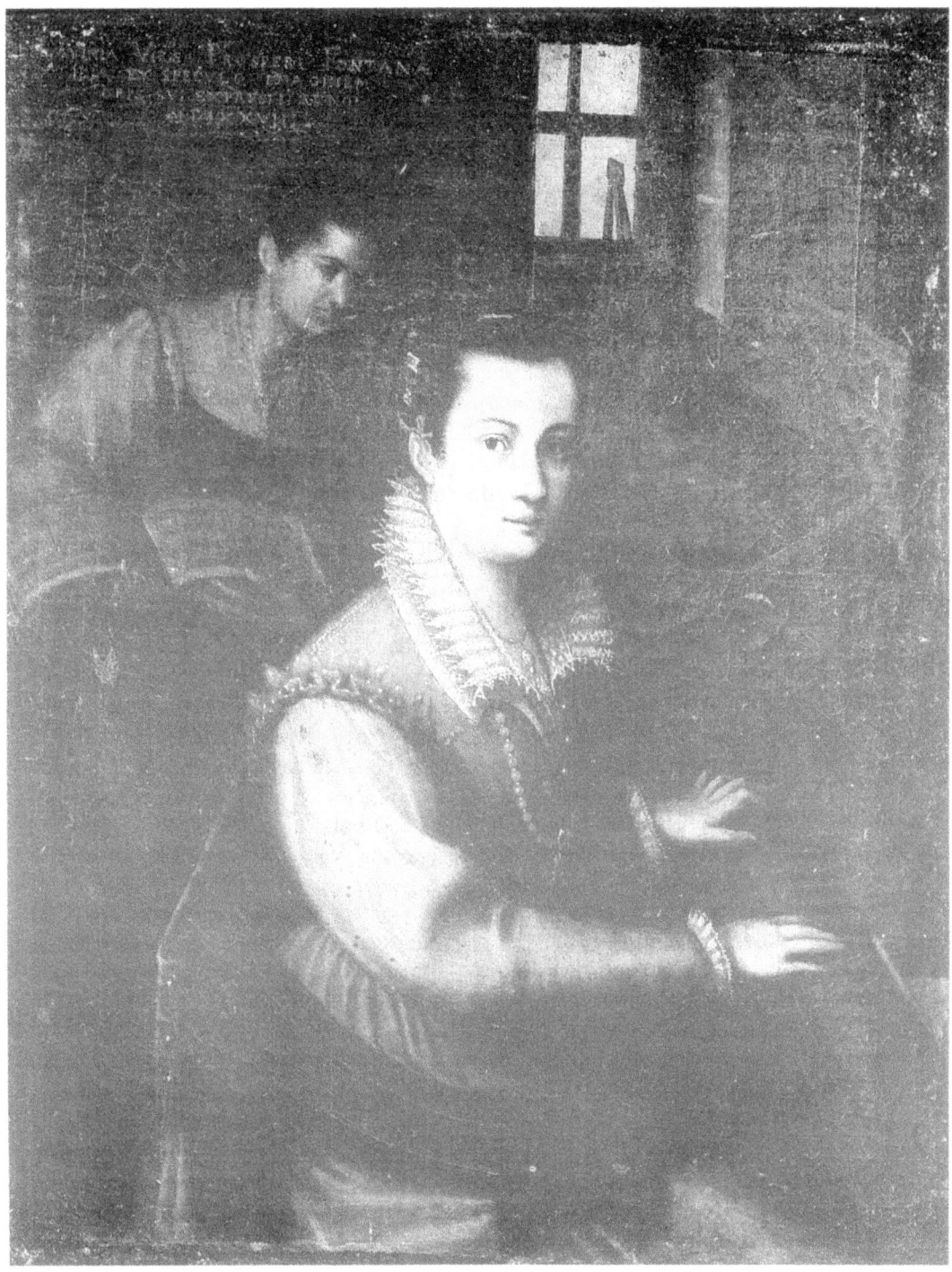

IV.12   Lavinia Fontana, *Self-Portrait at the Spinet*, 1579

Calendarium, 1453 (see Fig. III.1), by the nun Maria Ormani.[85] The elaborate *bas-de-page* of the 89th leaf in this manuscript shows the shape of a love-knot scroll containing Maria's signature as follows: 'A maiden servant of Christ'. And in the margin of the unwritten texts Maria wrote '*scripsi*' meaning 'I wrote it' or 'I recorded it.' In Ormani the love knot symbolizes the mystical marriage between herself – a nun – and Christ, in a continuation of the tradition of portraying holy, virginal women united with Christ for love. Fontana also adopted the emblematic tradition of the love knot but, in contrast to Ormani's religious symbolism, the signification in her portrait is secular, alluding to her betrothal to Giovan Paolo Zappi.

The coral love knot, like another that holds her coral necklace in place, and her signature without 'Zappi', indicate that this portrait was painted before her marriage.[86] The inscription records indeed that she is the daughter of Prospero Fontana, and unmarried. Most significantly, it further states that she has painted a self-image, '*ex speculo imaginem*', an unprecedented inscription in sixteenth-century portraiture in that it uses the word 'mirror' (*speculum*), referring to her portrait as both image and object, reflected and reflection, and invention and imitation.[87]

Sixteenth-century women artists portrayed themselves not only as painters, musicians or *nobil donne*, but also as collectors of art. The contemporary fascination with collecting antiques can be seen in Fontana's *Self-Portrait in Her Study* of 1579, in oil on copper (Pl.X), signed and inscribed '*Lavinia Fontana/Zapii Facieb (M)DLXXVIIII,*' on the edge of the working table. She is beautifully dressed. Her wedding rings on her left hand, although no longer visible in the painting, appear in the engraving by Lasinio (Fig. IV.11).[88] A large cross hanging from a pearl necklace, different from the small coral cross ornamenting her coral necklace in the Accademia portrait, alludes to her Christian and pious qualities as a married woman. But the focus of this portrait is on her talent and her artistic activities, showing a prosperous artist, collector and humanist.

In her studio, seated at her desk, Fontana turns to address or observe the viewer. A collection of plaster casts – a foot, a hand, a torso, and old and young men's heads – is glimpsed in the background (gifts received from her patrons – popes and aristocrats), plus objects she collected for her work.[89] Lasinio's engraving assists in identifying the classical objects in her collection. [90] Fontana's work table holds two antique bronzes on pedestals – a crouching Venus and a standing Apollo – which she may be planning to draw, since she holds a stylus in one hand. In the other hand, resting on the arm of the chair, she holds a handkerchief for correcting errors in the drawing. The same attribute can also be seen in Francesco Salviati's *Self-Portrait* of 1560 (Uffizi, Florence), where the Mannerist painter holds only a handkerchief in his hand as a tribute to his art. Fontana's composition attests to her understanding of current artistic theory, where not only is drawing fundamental to the creative process of a painting (*invenzione*), but importance is given to studying ancient art (*imitazione*). The implication may be that even though it was difficult at this time for a woman to attend art school where drawing classes were held with live models, she could overcome this inadequacy by relying on her

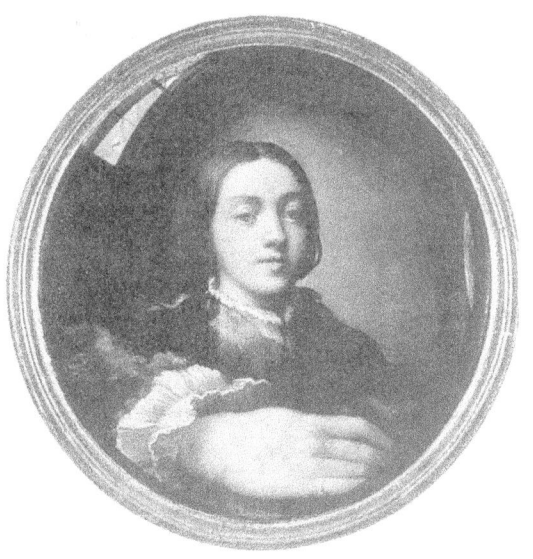

IV.13   Parmigianino, *Self-Portrait*, 1523

artistic talent and her good artistic judgement (*giudizio*), and by the study of antiquity.

The mirror shape of the painting recalls the male *Self-Portrait* of 1523 by Parmigianino (Fig. IV.13). When comparing the self-portraits of Italian sixteenth-century male artists with those of contemporary female painters, it may be seen that both female and male painters are concerned with portraying different levels of reality – the natural reflection of the mirror and the painted image of the reflection.

Another Fontana self-portrait (Fig. IV.14) signed and inscribed: '*Lavinia Fontana De Zappis Faciebat MDLXXIX*', is a three-quarter-length figure, in the manner of Parmigianino's *Antea* of 1515, now at the Capodimonte Museum in Naples. Exquisitely dressed, Fontana reveals in this portrait her artistic ability, her knowledge and her position in society.[91] She portrays herself as a courtly painter – she holds a palette and brushes, while an easel is visible in the background.[92] Dressed with splendor – several strings of pearls, lace, velvet and brocades – and crowned with jewels, she is represented as famous, wealthy and accomplished, anticipating the elegant self-portraits of French women painters in the eighteenth century.[93]

The elaboration and fastidiousness of detail in Fontana's self-portraits are lacking in Anguissola's work. Fontana's portraits are a study of rich minutiae and ornamentation, while Sofonisba scrutinizes herself, her image, her persona. The difference between the conception of the self-image of these two painters is related to their artistic training and teachers (Cremona *vs.* Bologna), to stylistic changes between 1540 and 1590 and to the patronage they cultivated. Both painters traveled extensively outside their native towns, and each was widely recognized during her lifetime by other artists, as well as drawn by them: Anguissola by Anthony van Dyck and Fontana by Paolo Veronese.[94] Both women were praised in their time and honored with

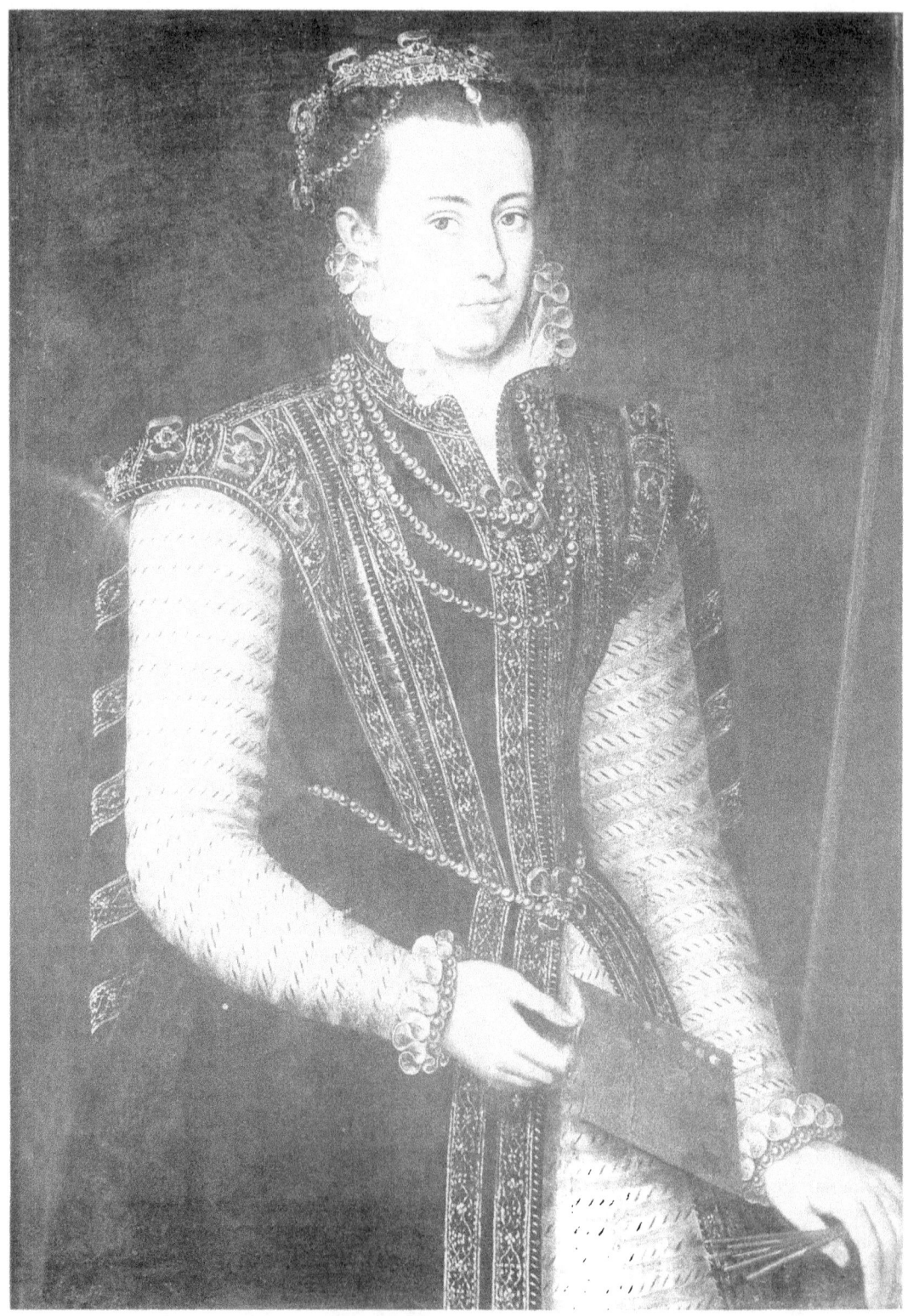

IV.14   Lavinia Fontana, *Self-Portrait*, 1579

commemorative medals. Jacopo da Trezzo, a Cremonese sculptor, designed Anguissola's medal of honor in 1560 (London, British Museum), with the inscription: '*La bella e saggia dipintrice, La nobil Sofonisba da Cremona*' ('The beautiful and wise painter, The honorable Sofonisba of Cremona'), while Felice Antonio Casoni sculpted a commemorative medal of Fontana at present in the Pinacoteca e Musei Comunali of Imola.[95]

Another Northern Italian self-portraitist was Barbara Longhi (1552–1638).[96] Born in Ravenna, she was the daughter of Luca Longhi (1507–80), a regional Mannerist influenced by the Roman school, notably Raphael, and by the central Italian schools of Florence and Bologna. Her brother was the painter and poet Francesco Longhi (1544–1620). While Francesco remained a dilettante, Barbara diligently produced many small altarpieces of the Madonna and Child. Vasari notes in *The Lives of the Artists* (1568, Vol. III) that these paintings are unique for 'their purity of line and soft brilliance of color'.[97] Longhi was trained under her father, copying many of his works and assisting him in his large altarpieces. She also posed as a model for him. She can be seen as a saint (possibly St Barbara) in the *Altarpiece of the Madonna and Saints* of 1570 (Pinacoteca Comunale, Ravenna), and as one of the female guests in the foreground of *The Marriage at Cana* of 1575 (Biblioteca Classense, Ravenna), undoubtedly a fresco painting done collaboratively by her father, her brother and herself.

St Catherine of Alexandria, a self-portrait of 1589 (Pl. XI), was painted by Longhi for the Monastery of Classe near Ravenna. As St Catherine she holds a palm, the symbol of the saint's martyrdom. Her attribute, a broken wheel with spikes, is situated between her arms. It is interesting that Longhi did not select her own patron saint, St Barbara, as a subject, as her father had done. In a recent exhibition of her works, several previously unknown versions of Longhi's self-portraits as St Catherine were displayed in the Pinacoteca Comunale in Ravenna, her native city; they are now in the National Museum of Art in Bucharest and in the Hermitage Museum in St Petersburg (the latter copy is attributed to her father). The claim has been made that Longhi's father painted a replica for one of his patrons. But it might also be that Longhi painted more than one copy of the same theme, a common practice in sixteenth-century Italy.

Her artistry was praised and commented on by sixteenth-century painters, museum directors and prelates, such as Muzio Manfredi, director of the Accademia dei Confusi in Bologna, who wrote: 'Her art is quite marvelous, and even her father is surprised by her art, especially her portraits.'[98] In his *Discorso sulle immagine sacre e profane* (1582), Cardinal Gabriele Paleotti referred to her as 'a person of honor, virtue and beauty reflecting this image in her self-portrait'.[99]

Engravers of the sixteenth and seventeenth centuries recorded the portraits of numerous women painters, including Marietta Robusti (1560–90), also known as Tintoretta, Jacopo Tintoretto's favorite child. She was an apprentice in his studio, and accompanied him everywhere, but dressed as a man.[100] As was customary, Robusti assisted her father by painting the backgrounds of his huge paintings. Greatly admired in the art of portraiture, a fitting subject for a woman at this time, she was invited to several courts, including those of Emperor Maximilian of Germany, Philip II of Spain and the Archduke Ferdinand. Unfortunately, her father declined on her behalf and as a dutiful daughter she remained in his workshop. Tintoretto arranged a marriage for her to Jacopo d'Augusta, head of the Venetian silversmiths' guild, on condition that she remained under the paternal roof.[101]

Marietta Robusti was renowned for her achievements in creating beautiful portraits with rich and unusual jewelry decorations. Many of her male portraits were of her husband's associates. Sensitive to their occupation, Tintoretta embellished them with exceptional garments covered with precious stones and gold, demonstrating that men, too, liked to be portrayed as having wealth and culture. In these portraits, she follows a new type of genre, the representation of men of the merchant class as courtly patrons.

Many of Robusti's portraits have erroneously been attributed to her father or her brother, Domenico Robusti. One such example is the *Portrait of Veronica Franco* of 1575–80 (Worcester Art Museum, Ma), which is attributed to Jacopo Tintoretto or his school, but which should, instead, be attributed to Marietta.

In *Il riposo* (1584) Ridolfo Borghini praised Robusti for her beauty and grace and her ability to play the clavichord or harpsichord, the lute and other instruments, as well as for her painting.[102] In her *Self-Portrait* of 1580 (Uffizi, Florence), attributed to Robusti, she opens the *First Book of Madrigals* (Venice, 1533), by the French composer Philippe Verdelott, at page 24, where the inscription reads: '*Madonna per voi ardo*' ('My Lady for you I burn').[103]

In *The Life of Tintoretto and of His Children Domenico and Marietta*, Carlo Ridolfo records Robusti's musical training under the Neapolitan Giulio Zacchino, who tutored her in singing and playing the clavichord or harpsichord.[104] The depiction of a *nobil donna* playing a musical instrument – the spinet – as we have seen in the work of Catherina van Hemessen, Sofonisba Anguissola, Lavinia Fontana and Marietta Robusti, carries an echo of Christian imagery. For these painters, St Cecilia, the patron saint of musicians, was a talented musician herself as well a chaste woman and spouse – indeed an admirable image for women to see and emulate.[105]

The Uffizi *Self-Portrait* of 1580 (Pl. XII) clearly illustrates Robusti's accomplishment as a musician, while the *Self-Portrait* of 1580 (Fig. IV.15) in the Kunsthistorisches Museum, Vienna, shows her as a Venetian *nobil donna*. This portrait's composition suggests the influence of Titian, for example, his portrait of *La Bella* of 1520 (Pitti Palace, Florence.)

Other self-portraits exist which have been attributed to Robusti, one at the Museo Civico in Padua, one at the Museo del Prado in Madrid and one at the Doria-Pamphili in Rome; they express a skillful use of coloring and light, good sense of design, and originality.[106] One of these, the *Self-Portrait* of 1575–80 (Prado, Madrid), presents a problem of attribution. While it bears a strong physiognomic resemblance to the Uffizi and Vienna portraits, its composition compares more with the artist's portrait of Veronica Franco, where the sitter is painted with an elaborate hairstyle, a pearl necklace and a

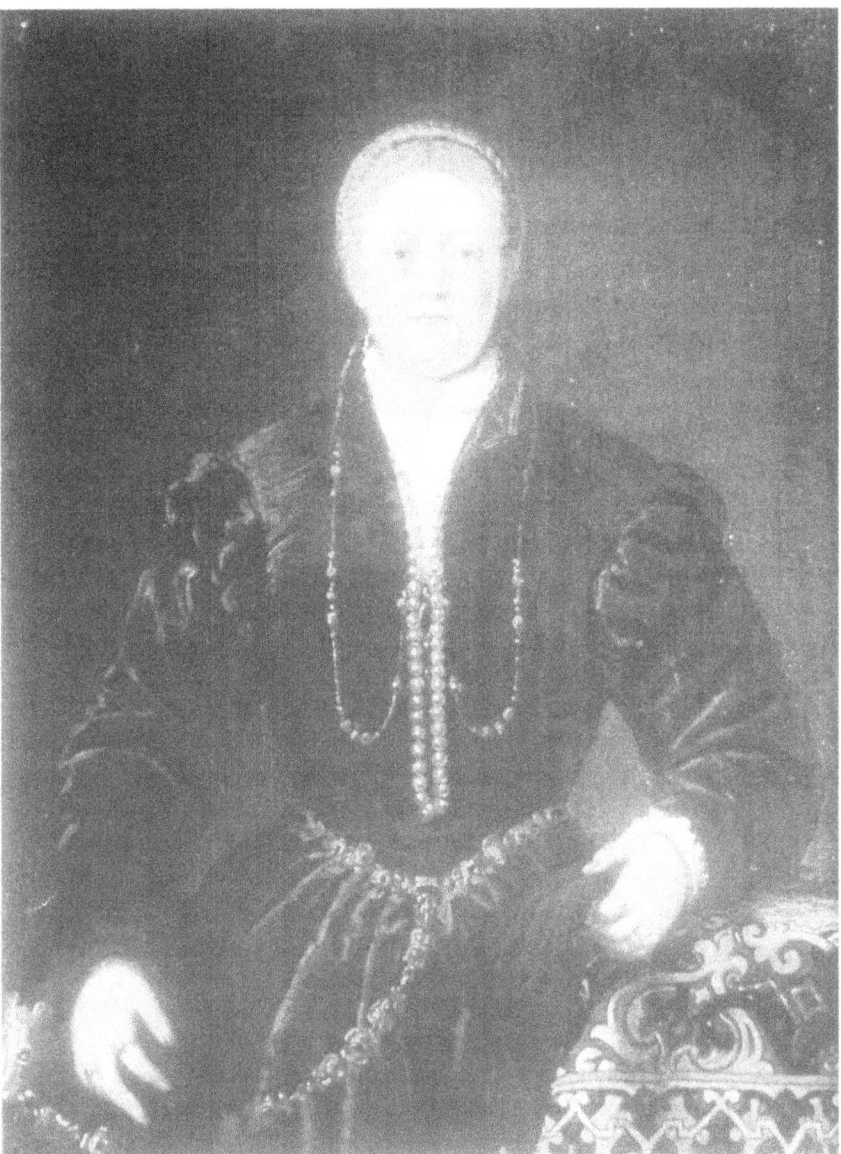

IV.15   Marietta Robusti, *Self-Portrait*, 1580

breast partly revealed through her chemise. Seeing herself at the mirror, she modestly and coquettishly points to herself, surprised and pleased with the beautiful woman she sees reflected back at her. The viewer becomes her mirror, who gazes at her image as she perceives it. This fusion between image and perception or reflection and reflected is a manifestation of Mannerism's interest in lighting effects and optical illusion.

In this portrait Robusti has created a fanciful and idealized portrait of herself. This type of secular portrait recalls the Venetian mythological paintings of Venus beautifying herself, for example Titian's *Venus at her Toilet* of 1540 (Accademia, Venice), and allegorical paintings of poetesses or courtesans, such as Giorgione's *Laura* of 1506 (Kunsthistorisches Museum, Vienna) and Titian's *Flora* of 1540 (Uffizi, Florence).

Robusti died in her thirties in childbirth and is buried in her husband's funerary chapel in the church of Santa Maria dell'Orto, Venice.[107] After her demise she continued to be praised by foreign artists, including Joachím von Sandrart, who engraved her portrait in 1675.[108]

In their self-portraits, Cinquecento women painters are distinguished by various features: emphasizing a self-image as an object of beauty; promoting the art of drawing as a principle of art; emphasizing a single image that portrays the artist's occupation; repetition or serial depictions of the self-image represented in drawing and painting; and representation of the female artist as an educated *nobil donna*, a musician and a humanist. These self-portraits provide the viewer with access to a personal situation in which the female is seen as an artist at close quarters, and through her own eyes. The painter portrays herself out of curiosity, to explore her outer and inner images. She exposes her individual talents, well aware of her artistic merit as a painter and a musician. She does not ignore her *bella figura*, thus emphasizing her exquisitely designed attire, mannered gestures, and carefully selected jewelry. In Anguissola the courtier is seen, in Fontana, the art collector, and in Robusti, the musician.

These women painters provided a new visual vocabulary of portraiture for sixteenth-century artists, prefiguring and shaping the expansion of the self-portrait as an entity in its own right. They shared with male self-portraitists of their generation the practice of including painter's attributes – brush, pencil, palette, easel – in their self-representation, as seen in the self-portraits of Hans Holbein of 1543 (Wallace Collection, London), Ludger Tom Ring of 1547 (Sammlung von Frupp, Essen), Giorgio Vasari of 1567 (Uffizi, Florence), Titian of 1570 (Prado, Madrid); Anthonis Mor of 1558 (Uffizi, Florence) and the Bassani Brothers of 1575 (Uffizi, Florence).

Through their manifestations of the self, the self-portraits of Mannerist women painters provide a heightened level of aesthetic awareness, beauty and artistic excellence. They offer a vivid contrast, as well as a prelude, to the daring innovations of seventeenth-century self-portraiture.[109]

V

The Baroque: power, vision and the self

In the seventeenth century the Baroque period brought further challenges for the female painter. The Counter-Reformation, war and the struggle for a balance of economic power in Europe had precipitated religious and political changes that, in turn, produced an artistic turmoil, which was to be reflected in the drama and diversity of the Baroque style.[1]

With shifts in the class system, political power was in some cases concentrated in the hands of a few noblemen or princes, as in Italy and Spain, or in one person, the absolute monarch, as in France. In some societies the rise of the bourgeoisie had meanwhile created a new class of wealthy burghers, as in the Netherlands. New social conditions formed around the place of women in society. But women were still housebound and confined to housewifely duties, and still considered objects of idealization, demonization or both. The attribution of this dual nature to women by Church and society induced male painters to create complex representations. Some women were identified with holy figures or saints, such as Mary Magdalene and Saint Theresa and heroines from the Old Testament, including Judith and Salome, or were depicted as personifications of virtues or vices.

Patronage was well established in the courts and royal houses. The churches, now divided into Protestant, mainly in Holland, England, Germany and Switzerland, and Catholic, principally in France, Spain, Italy and Portugal, continued to sponsor religious paintings, but with a different intention, piety and fervor. The Catholic Church postulated standardized criteria for religious and devotional imagery, whereas the Protestant churches generally did little to encourage the representation of holy images. The changes in patronage and taste also provided novelty in the visual arts and new opportunities for the artist, starting with an expansion of secular subject matters and themes, such as genre, landscape and still-life paintings. Religious art now conveyed exemplary Christian behavior, as typified by saints, where conversion, piety and the demands of the institutionalized Church and its beliefs became fundamental. The imagery had to appeal to the general public, particularly to the lower classes, who could see in the painted image similar struggles to their own and who could emulate the lives of saints in the hope of gaining Christian salvation.

This new educational message in the subject matter of the visual arts was accompanied by a development in the profession of the artist. Academies of art were founded, where artists were trained to satisfy the religious taste of the time as well as secular or royal fashion. In part, these academies developed in opposition to the monastic scriptoria, the guilds and the drawing academies of the past. The Baroque academies provided artistic protection, professional artistic training, and standards for artists and their subjects, thus establishing a hierarchy of art and elitism. Unfortunately, in this revisionist and selective approach toward the visual arts, women painters had to surpass the achievements of men in order to be honored or even accepted.

The scientific revolution embodied in the discoveries of Copernicus, Galileo, Pascal, Newton, Bacon and Descartes provided new avenues of intellectual and cultural discourse. With the improvement of artistic practices and materials, artists could expand their imagery, thereby creating a monumental, decorative and theatrical art. Painters also began to examine nature with a new interest, as seen in Caravaggio's naturalism of forms, immediacy of space, and invention of tenebrism, a sharp contrast of light and dark emphasizing the use of candlelight in the process of painting.

Where in previous centuries paintings were balanced, refined, static, private and mesmeric, the Baroque provided drama, contradiction and energetic movement, and a desire to obtain an immediate emotional reaction from the viewer. The artist's workshop continued to follow the same educational principles as in the previous century, as the student of art, the apprentice, was meant to learn from the master, but the period of training expanded to six years. Traditionally, the student needed to learn how to grind pigments, prepare canvases, make preliminary sketches, and add background or details to the master's painting. Later on, if the artist was successful in his training, he attended an academy of art, where he would practice drawing from nature by looking at nude models in drawing classes. But this option was rarely given to women, and painters such as Artemisia Gentileschi had their own models who visited their studios.[2] Likewise, women painters were still trained by their fathers or other members of their family.

The Reformation and Counter-Reformation, with their interest in a variety of artistic subjects, provided the female artist with new grounds for artistic independence. During the Renaissance and Mannerist periods, only 35 women are known to have been professional artists; by the Baroque period, the number had increased to 200. Women painters now explored subject matter genres and techniques as diverse as still-life, landscape, seascapes, battle scenes, enameling, engraving, the decorative arts, portraits and self-portraits. Despite often having to be trained by their fathers, women painters could now also be recognized for their own merits and honored accordingly.

In the seventeenth century, the public role of women focused largely on teaching. Witch hunts in Europe had placed women in fear that if they were not viewed as holy virgins, chaste mothers, or good wives, or as nurses and teachers, they would be seen as prostitutes or promiscuous and evil witches.[3] Notions of portaiture were accordingly governed by the social standards of decorum, as well as by the artistic conventions of truth and beauty. The French art critic Roger de Piles identified four aspects to the portrait: the air or features and personality of the sitter, the color, the attitude and pose, and the costume and accessories. Decorum in pose and attire were part of social convention. These types of moralizing portraits connected sitter and viewer, leaving no doubt as to the type of person portrayed.

The different parts of portraits were ranked according to the artists responsible for them and vice versa. In an atelier or studio, assistants were allowed to paint the background, accessories and ornamentation, while the painting of the features and personality of the sitter were the prerogative of the master painter, who was supposed to paint the sitter's soul. A portrait with this quality was said to be speaking (*parlant*) to the spectator, as exemplified by Frans Hals, Anthony van Dyck, Diego Velazquez, Judith Leyster and Artemisia Gentileschi.

In the sixteenth century female painters had tended to execute serial self-portraits, whereas in the seventeenth century they were more apt to focus on the depiction of a single self-portrait in an inventive manner. These self-portraits demonstrate their subjects' self-assuredness, spontaneity and directness, as well as emphasizing another level of meaning – the emblematic quality or personification of the self as a muse of life.

In the seventeenth century women painters worked on a greater number of themes than before and on a variety of sacred and profane subjects, consequently producing a smaller proportion of self-portraits. Innovations in style and technique in self-portraiture occured mostly in paintings by men. The self-portraits of this century further explore the sixteenth century's approach of teasing viewers or engaging them with an element of surprise. The Baroque self-portrait combines naturalism and scientific experimentation with the allegorical or mythological, not only demonstrating realism in the representation, but also the sophistication and erudition of the individual painter, as seen in Nicolas Poussin's *Self-Portrait* of 1650 (Louvre, Paris), Caravaggio's *Medusa* of 1585–90 (Uffizi, Florence), Artemisa Gentileschi's *La Pittura* (Pl.XIV) and Elisabetta Sirani's *Melpomene, The Muse of Tragedy* of 1640 (Washington, DC, National Museum of Women in the Arts). When comparing female with male depictions of the self, one notes the expansion, variety and originality of representation that occurs mostly in paintings by men, while women focus on portraying themselves as personifications.

If the self-portrait in previous centuries had been intimate, personal and limited, with the aim of aggrandizing the painter in a selected environment, the Baroque self-portrait now sought to expand its audience and function as well as to mark a place in the history of portraiture. This artistic quest was paralleled by the development and establishment of wider social, cultural and intellectual boundaries in European courts and republics. It finds expression in the self-portrait of Diego Velazquez in *Las Meninas* of 1656 (Prado, Madrid), where the artist represents himself as a court painter with the Spanish royal family; in Adriaen van Ostade's *Self-Portrait: Artist in his Studio* of 1663 (Gemäldegalerie, Dresden); in Jan Miense Molenaer's *Self-Portrait: Artist in his Studio* of 1631 (Kaiser-Friedrich Museum, Berlin); and in David Teniers's *Self-Portrait: Artist in his Studio* of 1670 (Collection of Sir William J. Farrer, London). In addition to such painters showing themselves in their ateliers with models, collectors and props, Jean-Baptiste de Champaigne and Nicolas de Platte-Montagne's *Double Portrait of the Two Artists* of 1654 (Museum Boymans-van Beuningen, Rotterdam) represents two self-portraits done by two separate painters in one scene.

Two of the most intriguing male self-portraits of the Baroque age are Annibale Carracci's of 1595 (Fig. V.1) and Johannes Gumpp's of 1646 (Fig. V.2), where the illusionism inherent in portraiture is presented at its highest level of audacity and canniness. Carracci's *Self-Portrait* shares the *trompe l'œil* effect of Anguissola's *Bernardino Campi Painting the Portrait of Sofonisba Anguissola* of 1550 (see Fig. IV.9). In Carracci's studio, an easel holds his unframed self-portrait and the instruments of painting it: palette and brushes. Carracci plays with reflection and perception, as the viewer sees the painter's mirrored image captured in the painting on the easel. Conversely, the self-portrait resting on the easel appears to be scrutinizing the viewer. Thus Carracci creates the possibility for the viewer and painter to be one and the same. He represents a traditional self-portrait, which rests on the easel, but by its placement and his absence from the studio scene, Carracci has invented a painted self-portrait within a picture without including himself. As with Anguissola, Carracci claims that his self-portrait is more than a representation of an image, it is a testimony to the art of painting and a manifestation of Baroque illusionism.

Gumpp's *Self-Portrait* likewise embodies a complicated portrayal of self, in which the painter is shown depicting himself in his studio.[4] Two self-portraits of the painter are depicted, one on an easel looking at the viewer, the other reflected in a mirror looking at the painter. The painter himself is seen from the back. In front of him is the easel, where he renders the self-portrait. The painted image is looking inquisitively and humorously at the viewer. Beside the painter, there is another self-portrait. The mirror's image reflects the artist's observation, scrutinizing himself in the mirror in order to copy what he perceives onto the easel painting. The triple illusionistic effect, noted in Anguissola's painting in the sixteenth century, is explored further in Gumpp's portrait, where the viewer sees the double self-portrait and the painter looking at both. The *trompe l'œil* effect is extended to his signature and the date, which are placed on the upper hand of the canvas within the painting; adding to the sense of ambiguity is the question of whether the mirror is really a mirror or another completed self-portrait that the painter is copying in the easel-picture. Most strikingly, as a piece of *trompe l'œil*, the mirror image is treated with loose and painterly brushstrokes, while the canvas painting reveals a more linear treatment. Also fascinating in Gumpp's *Self-Portrait* are the eyes of the painter, which seem to gaze at the viewer from two

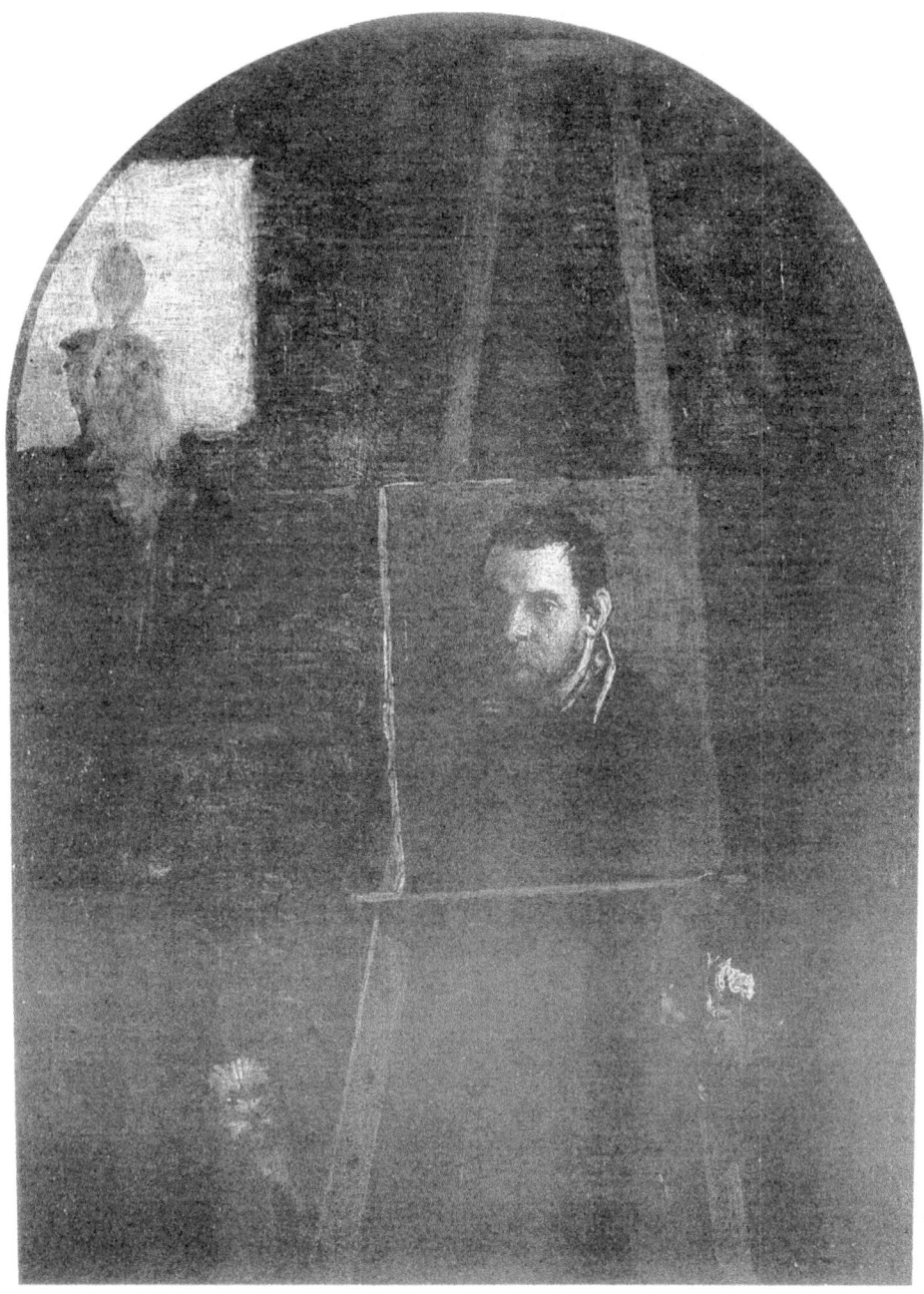

V.1   Annibale Carracci, *Self-Portrait*, 1595

different angles, in a demonstration of the skills of observation required of the painter. The Baroque quest for naturalism is manifested in this self-portrait.

In Italy, Bologna continued to be a center of artistic innovation. Climatic conditions in the north Italian province of Lombardy encouraged a preference

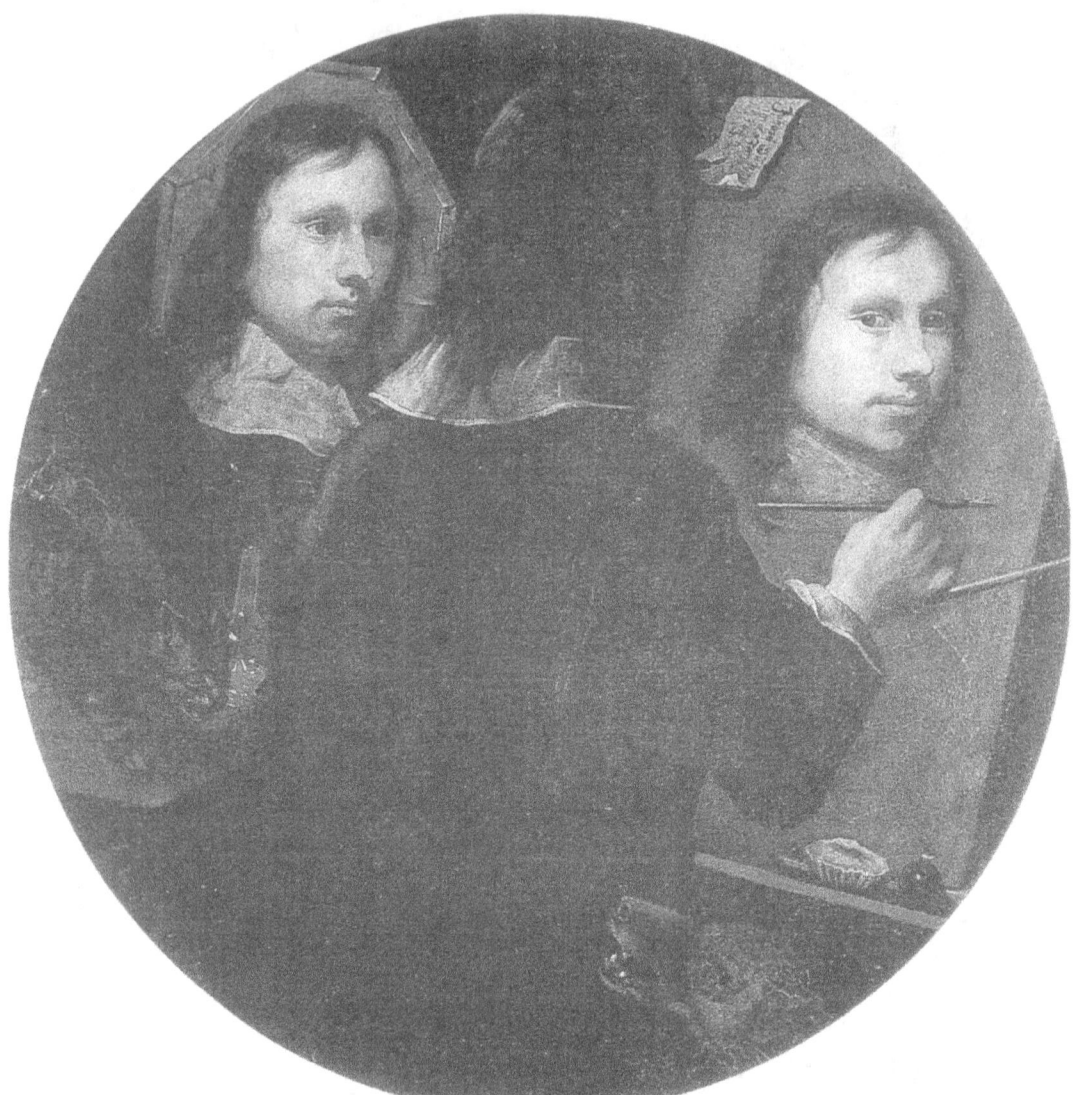

V.2   Johannes Gumpp, *Self-Portrait*, 1646

for oil on canvas over fresco, and oil is a technique that facilitates or prompts naturalism. Oil painting also provided freedom for artists, enabling them to journey from city to city while completing a commission. The new technique was embraced by Caravaggio, some of whose followers, as also of the Carraccis, fathered and taught some of the most important female artists of this period, including Artemisia Gentileschi, Elisabetta Sirani and Fede Galizia.

The educational and militant impact of the Counter-Reformation, the expansion of lay orders, confraternities and, in particular, the Jesuit order, along with the proliferation of didactic books on the life of saints, spiritual exercises and emblematic depictions, influenced the way religious imagery was presented. Some painters depicting martyrs and saints portrayed themselves in the story. They emphasized the significance of their narrative by being a living participant in it while satisfying the new codification of images according to the Counter-Reformation, or, at a practical level, achieving naturalism by the use of themselves as models. With the expansion of patronage and the demand for large commissions, artists began to use a more standardized repertoire of imagery, based on academic criteria and the tastes of the time.

As a result, emblematic books such as Cesare Ripa's *Iconologia* (Rome, 1593 and 1603 with illustrations) had a significant impact in artistic circles, serving as a visual encyclopedia and recipe book on how to depict certain images, whether allegorical, such as the Seasons and the Rivers, or personifications of virtues and vices, such as Charity or Envy. Painters regarded these in a way that fused the self with the represented image, whether secular or religious, which is why so many artists are seen portraying themselves in representations of Old Testament stories, such as those of David and Goliath, Judith and Holofernes and Salome and John the Baptist.

A precedent for this kind of identification had earlier occurred with the representation of St Luke painting the Virgin; now artists sought to portray themselves as personifications of the visual arts, painting, sculpture or architecture, as well as of music and poetry. The emphasis on the intellectual similarity between the sister arts prompted artistic theories on the theme of *ut pictura poesis* ('As is painting so is poetry'), *ut poesis musica* ('As is music so is poetry'; see p. xxv) and variations on these comparisons. In both Italy and France, academies promulgated this type of endeavor.[5]

Seventeenth-century female painters took part in this development, presenting their self-portraits in religious and secular images, and identifying themselves with the protagonists of a story. If the persona was represented in women's self-imagery in the sixteenth century, now in the Baroque the self surfaced as a protagonist in the form of a variety of characters. This phenomenon may be explained in two ways: by the impact of the religious fervor and drive for conversion attained by the Counter-Reformation in Catholic countries and by the theatrical glamor in the visual arts sponsored by both courts and the Church, in order to declare their absolute power, temporal and spiritual respectively. The non-Catholic countries, and absolutist regimes, encouraged a type of visual imagery in which religious and mythological subjects were discouraged or eschewed, and fostered subjects that related closely to their social activities, such as group portraiture of civic and military bodies, still-lifes, landscapes and cityscapes that showed natural and everyday surroundings.

If religious or mythological images were painted in Protestant countries, their representation was minimized and their meaning tended to be diffused or visually translated into local or regional proverbs. This new approach to representation led to development of a new subject matter, the genre scene, where the images exemplified daily and domestic living as well as providing a moral message. If the Counter-Reformation had placed all its efforts in reforming and converting Christians to Catholicism through the power of religious imagery, the heirs of the Reformation, on the other hand, focused on the importance of ethical behavior in daily activities.

In the Baroque period, a certain uniformity in the visual arts was created as a consequence of the academies' criteria, which encouraged the imitation of ancient and Renaissance masters, and promoted two styles: classicism and naturalism. Paradoxically, these two styles were not considered incompatible. The painters who imitated nature associated its beauty with art; some, inspired by this analogy, wrote poetry expressing this similitude.[6] The artists who championed this combination of classicism and naturalism were the Bolognese painters Ludovico (1555–1619), Agostino (1557–1602) and Annibale Caracci (1540–1609), who together founded an academy in their native city, and the Milanese Michelangelo Merisi da Caravaggio (1569–1609), who settled in Rome.

The Academy of the Visual Arts of Bologna provided training and tutelage for many female painters. Ludovico Caracci, for example, trained the talented designer and painter Antonia Pinelli Bertucci (d.1644), the wife of Giovanni Battista Bertucci, a painter of historical subjects and portraits. Domenichino, another member of the Bolognese Academy, taught Teresa del Po Patino, who also trained her daughter and Artemisia Gentileschi in the art of painting. Guido Reni instructed the renowned Elisabetta Sirani in the art of drawing and painting.[7]

Other accomplished painters from this period included Arcangela Palladini, who was said to have excelled in painting as well as in poetry and music; Beatrice Appafave and Augusta Tarabotti, both of whom studied with Chiara Varotari, a poet highly recognized for her writings on women, such as 'An Apology for the Female Sex'; Fede Galizia, daughter of a miniaturist, who lived in Milan and excelled in the art of design and coloring; and Ginevra Cantofoli, who executed portraits, small pastel paintings and large religious works for churches in Bologna.[8]

The writing of Mary D. Garrard has shed new light and understanding on the work of Artemisia Gentileschi.[9] This famous and infamous woman (1593–1652) was born in Rome and trained as a painter in the studio of her father, Orazio Gentileschi. In 1612 Orazio sued the painter Agostino Tasso for defiling his daughter while being married to another woman. In a trial which lasted seven months, Gentileschi courageously defended her rights and virtue, although she was subjected to torture and legal abuse. After the dismissal of the case, she married the Florentine painter Pietro Antonio di Vincenzo Stiattesi in Rome and moved to Florence. While residing there, she was sponsored by the Grand Duke, Cosimo II de' Medici, who assisted her in becoming the first woman member of the Accademia del Disegno in 1616. After bearing four children, Gentileschi separated from her husband in 1626 and focused on her career. Her travels extended to Venice, Naples and England, where she enrolled in the service of Queen Henrietta Maria in 1639

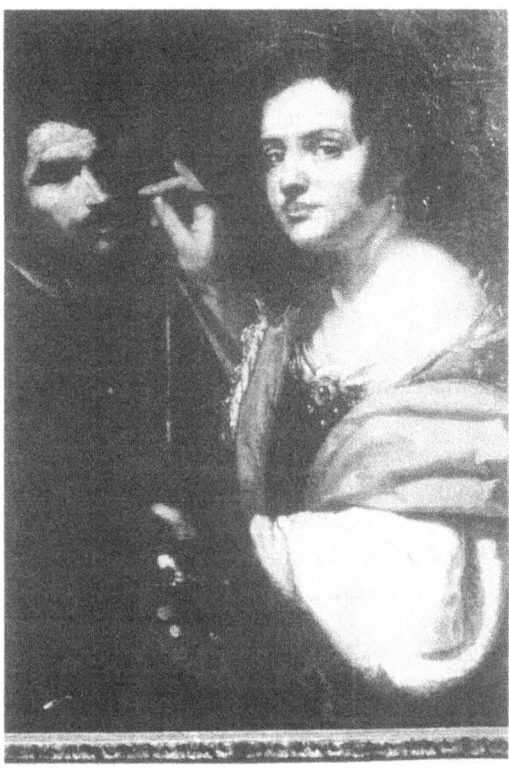

V.3   Artemisia Gentileschi,
*Self-Portrait as the Allegory of
Painting*, 1635–40

to assist her father in completing the decoration of the ceiling of the Queen's
House at Greenwich (now dismantled and at Marlborough House, London).
Years later, she returned to Naples where she died in 1652.

Gentileschi painted numerous versions of the theme of Judith and
Holofernes (for example, Pl. XIII).[10] Interestingly, almost all of her depictions
of this biblical heroine could be seen as self-portraits. In these paintings,
Gentileschi seeks to understand Judith as a paradoxical figure, but also relates
her subject's story to the cultural mores of her own century. The legend of
Judith parallels Artemisia's own artistic successes. Satirical epigraphs such as
'To carve my husband's horns, I put down my brush and took up a knife'
reflect her complex misanthropic imagery.[11]

Gentileschi's artistic activities extended to collecting art, and writing
letters to European dignitaries such as Cassiano del Pozzo, the Duke of
Alcalá, Francesco I d'Este and scholars including Galileo.[12] She also
discovered new levels of meaning in portraying the self and the identity of a
woman. In *The Self-Portrait as the Allegory of Painting* of 1630/1640 (Collection
of Her Majesty the Queen, London), Gentileschi embodies her image as both
a painter and the muse of painting (Pl. XIV; see also Fig. V.3).[13] The impact of
the emblematic tradition, in particular of Cesare Ripa's book, *Iconologia*, is
evident in this self-portrait. Gentileschi paints Ripa's visual representation
(*figurazione*) of Painting (*La Pittura*) as a beautiful woman with thick, black,
unruly locks and wearing a gold chain with a pendant mask. She holds the

attributes of the painter, a brush and a palette. For Ripa, this personification is the amalgamation described by the ancient motto of *ut pictura poesis*.[14]

This fusion of visual energy and poetical inspiration is a self-portrait. Gentileschi portrays herself in the process of her *furor poeticus* (artistic frenzy), or the inventive state of the artist, as she begins to paint on the canvas. As Elizabeth Cropper has pointed out, decoding her name, Arte-mi-sia ('May art be me'), evokes this creative ardor.[15] In the painting, Gentileschi parallels the fertility of her mind and of her body; as in nature, so in the richness and prosperity of her art, symbolized by the beautiful gold chain that decorates her torso. Her working attire reveals the fullness of her breasts. However, Gentileschi appears to imply that art is a device that can also camouflage nature, as is implied by the mask that hangs from the chain. She alludes to Ripa's Imitation (*Imitazione*); this image is of a woman holding brushes and a mask, while a monkey sits at her side. The painter's attributes, including brushes, allude to the artist's imitation of colors, lines and shapes in nature, and the mask demonstrates how the artist imitates human actions.[16] For Ripa, a good painter imitates nature, and Gentileschi interprets this concept not only with the design and composition of the image but also by using green as a dominant and natural color.

Gentileschi's second *Self-Portrait as the Allegory of Painting*, of 1635–40 (Fig. V.3), perhaps a thematic pendant to the London *Self-Portrait*,[17] depicts another aspect of the personification of painting – the actual imitation or copying of nature, the execution of painting. In this instance, Gentileschi is painting, at an easel, the portrait of her father Orazio.[18] As he has done in the past by using her as a model for his painting, she is honoring him by portraying his image, in an oval-shaped composition. Gentileschi ventures to create a dual signification by both thanking him as her father and honoring him as her teacher. Another dual signification is noted in the placement of her brushes. In the lower left of the painting, on the foreground section of the table, Gentileschi has painted her brushes to create the initial 'A', alluding to the activity of the painter who creates art (*arte*) as well as to the painter's name, Artemisia, herself. In contrast to the London self-portrait, Gentileschi's attire is that of a noble lady. A large crown of laurel leaves alludes to her professional achievements. Here the mirrored image is actively engaged in her task, scrutinizing the observed object outside the picture plane – the subject is the object and vice versa. With this portrait, Gentileschi was among the first women to include a member of their family in their self-portrait, while at the same time the painting overtly honors art, painting and the artist by the crown given to the main image.

A century later, the imagery of the personification of painting would be reinterpreted by the academic painter Giandomenico Campiglia in *The Genius of Painting* (1740, Accademia di San Luca, Rome), where, crowned with laurels, Painting holds a brush, a canvas, and a reversed mask. The viewer is presented with the back of the canvas, which hides with tenebrist light effects the reverse mask – a counterfeit of art. The Baroque self-portrait takes on a new meaning, as seen also with Gentileschi, as the correlation between painter and occupation evolves into its embodiment in the protagonist portrayed in the paintings.

One outstanding Bolognese painter was Elisabetta Sirani (1638–65). As with Lavinia Fontana, Sirani was a beautiful woman who painted large religious compositions. Her numerous representations of the Madonna, Mary Magdalene, Salome, and muses and sibyls (female prophets) reflect the Baroque predilection for showing virtuous women depicted as triumphant heroines.[19] Overshadowed by Gentileschi's fame and limited by her short life span, Sirani is not very well known today; however, documents and her diary indicate that her patrons and collectors included many of the most prominent Bolognese families, as well as members of learned and royal society.[20] It was speculated that her mysterious death at the age of 27 was caused by a jealous maid poisoning her, although an autopsy revealed that Sirani actually died from gastric ulcers.[21]

Sirani was trained by her father, Giovanni Andrea Sirani, whose chronic illness facilitated the development of her career, since she was able to take over his important commissions. During her brief lifetime she assisted the eminent Bolognese painter Guido Reni, and was probably taught in the art of painting using her sisters, Barbara and Anna Maria, as models. With them, Sirani developed an artists' workshop and a school for young girls, training also daughters of painters such as Antonia Pinelli and Ginevra Cantofoli. The necessity of assisting, and eventually economically supporting, her family, as well as her artistic talents, provided a platform for Sirani's brief but successful career. At 17, she received her first commission, giving her an excellent beginning. Her fame grew as a professional artist and teacher, making her, with Artemisia Gentileschi, a welcomed member of the Accademia di San Luca in Rome.

Count Malvasia, Sirani's first biographer, praised her as *Pittrice Eroina* (valiant painter) noting that she was a prolific artist and recording 150 of her works, including the *Self-Portrait* (or *La Pittura*) of 1640 in the Uffizi, Florence (Fig. V.4). Sirani depicts herself with confidence and assertiveness, conveying her natural beauty with artistic skill. Beautifully dressed, she stands holding brushes and a palette. She pauses to gaze at the viewer, obviously the model for her painting. Her mysterious look creates a pleasant uneasiness for the onlooker. Is she coquettishly teasing the viewer or is she carefully scrutinizing the subject she is depicting? Unlike Gentileschi, Sirani exalts her own beauty and femininity, enhancing the role of the woman as an object and subject of love and admiration. Both painters, though, were concerned with the aesthetic issues of Baroque art, which included the mixture of illusionism and idealism with naturalism, and the mastering and appropriation of the classical academic style with the vivacity of emotionalism.

Sirani's self-portraits, as was typical of Italian Baroque female painters, represent the traditional image as well as the emblematic appropriation, as seen in another of her self-portraits, *Melpomene, The Muse of Tragedy* of 1640 (Fig. V.5). Here, the artist personifies herself as a muse with the attributes of books and a tragic mask. Several implied meanings can be found in this self-

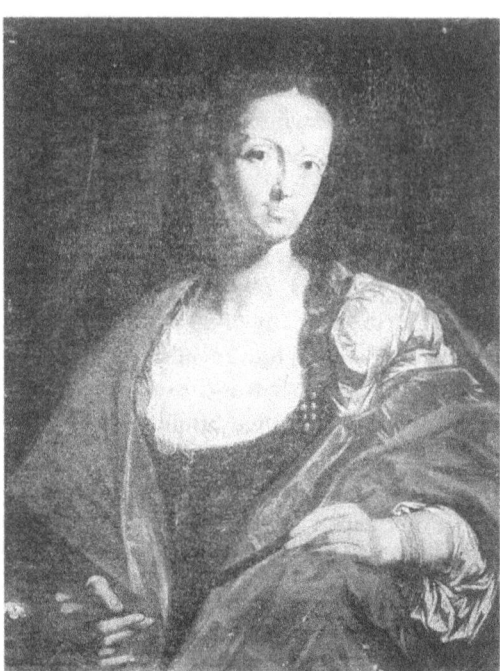

V.4   Elisabetta   Sirani,   *Self-Portrait*, 1640

portrait. A dramatic red curtain emphasizes the theatrical aspect of the muse, who is seen in a frontal pose. Elegantly dressed in Jewish or Mediterranean garments, turban crowning her head, and wearing a yellow and white scarf, Melpomene meditates as one who foresees the doom of humankind. Melpomene, originally the personification of Singing, was one of the nine muses, but in spite of her joyous-sounding name, she became the muse of tragedy as she was the mother of the Sirens, who lured sailors to their death upon the rocks with their singing. The placement of the mask in Sirani's painting is not accidental, as the expressionless mask, with its similar features, compares with the sad face of the muse. According to the beliefs of antiquity, the mask alludes to the supernatural powers of gods and demons as well as warding off evil and enemies, and the muse represents a combination of the intellect and the emotion behind inspiration. This connection of the muse and the mask parallels the quest of Sirani and other Baroque painters to explore the paradox between the freedom of intellectual pursuit in creativity, or invention, and constrictions in the imitation of nature.

Gentileschi's London *Self-Portrait* reveals a similar aesthetic complexity to Sirani's *Self-Portrait*; however, Sirani emphasizes the paradox in selecting Melpomene to personify this artistic challenge. As to another level of meaning found in the painting, Sirani might have implied the inevitability of divine purpose by painting Melpomene's gesture of holding a book while hiding the mask from herself. Her selection of the tragic muse is not fortuitous, since Sirani empathizes with and projects into her own life the image and meaning of the muse of tragedy.

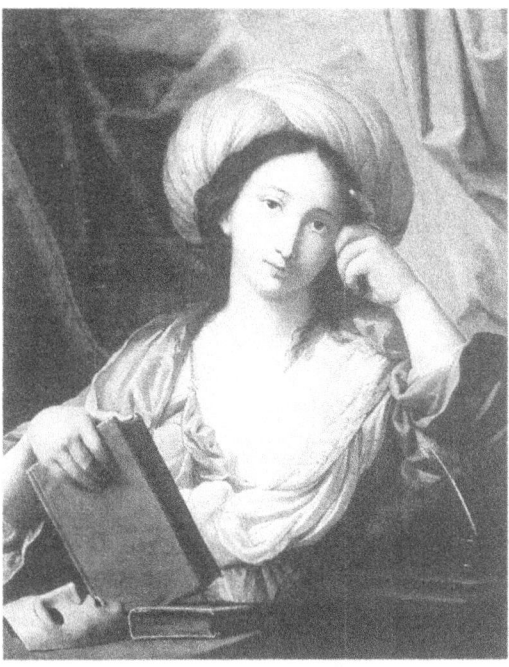

V.5   Elisabetta Sirani,
*Melpomene, The Muse of
Tragedy*, 1640

Information on other female painters who executed self portraits during the Baroque period in Italy is still sketchy and unclear.[22] What information there is mainly concerns painters who depicted self-portraits in traditional style – a painter seated or standing at an easel holding a brush and palette gazing at the viewer or a mirror. These include Ginevra Cantofoli, who painted *Self-Portrait in the Act of Painting* of 1656 (Fig. V.6).[23] Cantofoli was born in 1608 and died in 1672 in Bologna. She married a certain Landi and received her artistic training from Emilio Taruffi, Pasinello, Giovanni Gioseffo del Sole and, in particular, Elisabetta Sirani. Another legend has it that it was not her maid but Cantofoli, a rival in love and art, who was accused of murdering Sirani. Nonetheless, influenced by her teacher, Cantofoli's *Self-Portrait* reveals a purposely designed ambiguity between the real and the painted portrait, with the intent of intriguing and teasing the viewer. Cantofoli – like her predecessor Anguissola painting Campi or her contemporary Gentileschi depicting her father – may have portrayed her mentor and teacher Sirani, honoring not only the art of painting, but also the instructor. In this painting, the portrait on the easel gazes at the viewer, as noted in the self-portraits of Carracci and Gumpp, and paradoxically expresses greater vitality than the image of the artist, who obviously looks at a mirror and not at the viewer.

The Paduan painter and poet Chiara Varotari (1600–1660) depicted herself in a *Self-Portrait*, now at the Uffizi, in 1650. Varotari was not only a trained painter, who depicted religious themes and portraits, but also an art critic who wrote a defense of women's rights, 'Apology for the Female Sex'. This

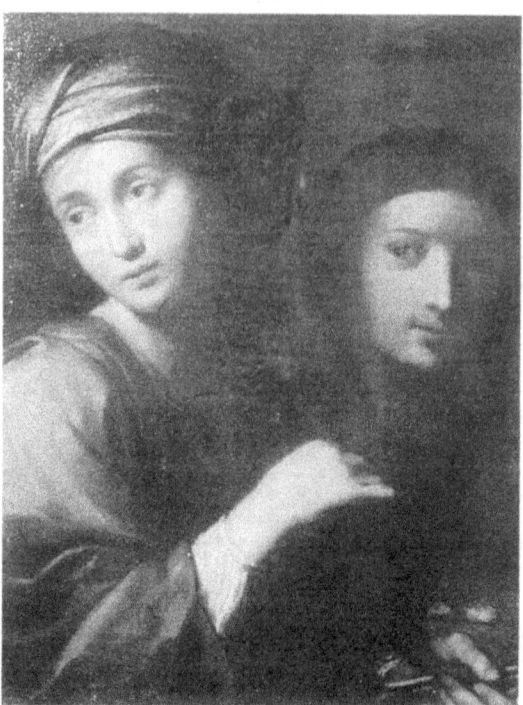

V.6 Ginevra Cantofoli, *Self-Portrait in the Act of Painting,* 1656

feminist essay was partially motivated by her desire not to marry, and to live with her brother, Alessandro. Her critical writings on gender issues recall the pioneer endeavors of Christine de Pizan's *The Book of the City of Ladies,* and other treatises of the late Middle Ages. Varotari was trained by her father, Dario, as well as her brother, Alessandro Varotari (il Padovanino), also assisting him in Padua and Verona.[24]

Having completed her dramatic *Self-Portrait,* Varotari sent it to Florence to be part of the artists' portraits collection of the Uffizi sponsored by Grand Duke Ferdinand II de'Medici. This bust-length work reveals the painter in a state of disarray, looking at a mirror, and partially clothed, with uncombed black hair embellished by a red passion flower. Like Gentileschi, she represents the personification of Painting (*La Pittura*) by holding its attributes, brushes and palette, and expressing the early state of artistic frenzy or process of invention, since no easel or painted image is yet created. Varotari is part of a group of female painters from northern Italy who reflect in their self-portraits the impact of current theories about art as seen in the writings of Giovanni Bellori, Vincenzo Giustianini, Giovanni Battista Agucci and Giulio Mancini.[25] For these writers and painters, Torquato Tasso's lines on art and nature in *Gerusalemme liberata,* XVI, 10, clearly explains the Italian Baroque aesthetic: 'Nature appears like art, that for delight; / Jestingly imitates her imitator.'

Under the spell of the era's scientific revolution, Baroque painters explored new subject matter in addition to portraiture, focusing on the study of nature, in particular flora and fauna, as seen in still-life paintings such as breakfast-pieces or kitchen scenes. Some artists who also portrayed themselves in an unconventional manner through still-lifes include Fede Galizia and Giovanna Garzoni in Italy; Louise Moillon in France; Judith Leyster and Clara Peeters in the Netherlands; and Josefa de Ayala D'Óbidos, in Portugal and Spain.

Fede Galizia (1578–1630) was born in Trento and died in Milan, where she lived most of her life. She was trained by her father, Nunzio Galizia, a miniaturist, and collaborated on several commissions with him. A child prodigy, Galizia was already established as a portrait-painter by the age of 16. Father and daughter were highly valued in Milanese artistic circles, notably by the art theorist Giovan Paolo Lomazzo, who wrote a sonnet praising them both for Galizia's ability as an artist.[26] Highly esteemed by the eminent Jesuit scholar Paolo Morigia,[27] Galizia returned the compliment by painting his portrait in 1596 (Pinacoteca Ambrosiana, Milan).[28] Her fame extended outside the Savoy court to northern Europe: Emperor Rudolph II of Prague purchased several of her paintings. She never married, dying during the plague of 1630 in Milan. The location of her burial site is unknown, perhaps being in the demolished church of Santa Maria Magdalena, where Galizia had strong affiliations with the nuns, or in the church of Santo Stefano, also in Milan. In her testament, signed 21 June 1623, Galizia left her belongings to her cousin Anna Galizia and her nephew Carlo Henrico, and enumerated the collection of paintings she owned by other painters, including a *St Catherine* by Luini, a follower of Leonardo.[29]

Galizia's training under her father in the miniature tradition schooled her in the delicacy and fantasy of this singular subject, and in its many variations of color, texture and detail. Similar to that of Marietta Robusti, a century earlier, Galizia's fascination with the depiction of jewelry and precious stones, and her treatment of their color, reflection and refraction, demonstrate the northern Italian interest in color and light, in part due to the Byzantine mosaic and miniature traditions, as well as to the technology of optics and mirrors developed in Venice.

Galizia's artistic career relates her to a variety of religious as well as to secular themes. Several versions by her of *Judith and Holofernes* are located in private collections, including the Borghese Gallery in Rome and the John and Mable Ringling Museum of Art in Sarasota, Florida (see for example Pl. XV). The differences between them are minuscule, such as variations on the size of Holofernes's head and in Judith's attire and jewelry. The best of these commissions is the *Judith and Holofernes* of 1596 in Florida, signed and inscribed, on the edge of Judith's knife, *'Fede'*, which means 'Faith' in Italian. Although there is no conventional portrait of Galizia in her studio, holding the attributes of her occupation, she identified herself with the Old Testament heroine, her embodiment of the essence of womanhood and religious faith. Galizia's painting recalls the numerous depictions on this subject by Gentileschi. Both identify with the biblical protagonist, but unlike Gentileschi, Galizia avoids misogynistic overtones by idealizing Judith, with her self-image and beautiful physiognomy, and with rich attire and accessories.

Galizia's secular commissions included numerous portraits of prelates.[30] She also figured among the leading Italian seventeenth-century painters of *natura morta* (still life).

Another Italian still-life painter was Giovanna Garzoni (1600–1670). Recent writings and an exhibition of her paintings, with members of her circle, present a complete picture of her contributions to the form.[31] Garzoni came from a Venetian family of painters of no great fame, which moved to Ascoli Piceno, in the Marches, in the middle of the sixteenth century. It is likely that she trained early on with her father, Giacomo Garzoni, and later with her uncle, Pietro Gaiga, who, in turn, had trained in the Venetian school of Palma the Younger, and with the calligraphist Giacomo Rogni.

Garzoni was born in Ascolo in 1600, a date confirmed by the inscription on her *Holy Family* (1616, private collection): '*Iona de Garzonibus Fanno sue etatis XVI, 1616*'.[32] Documentation is unclear as to when Garzoni moved to Venice, perhaps to train with her uncle; however, records reveal that she resided there from 1617 to 1630, when she moved to Naples to work for the Spanish Duke of Alcalà, painting religious subjects.

Records are unclear as to why Garzoni left Naples for Rome in 1631 and dedicated herself to miniature illustrations, as well as to botanical studies and representations. Then living in Turin in 1631–7 after being invited by the Duke of Savoy, Vittorio Amedeo, Garzoni became involved in portraiture as well. Subsequently, under the influence of her mentor and tutor Cassiano dal Pozzo of the Accademia dei Lincei in Rome, she moved to Florence to work under the Grand Duke of Tuscany, Ferdinando II de'Medici. Garzoni likely entered the Accademia di San Luca between 1631 and 1633. While corresponding from Naples with Pozzo in Rome, her name appeared in the list of new members attending in 1633.[33] Around 1654 she settled in Rome and became an active participant and patron of the arts at the Accademia di San Luca, contributing to the annual feasts. In 1670 Garzoni died in Rome, leaving her inheritance to the academy with the stipulation that a monument in her honor be erected in the church of SS. Luca e Martina.[34]

Garzoni became fascinated with the study of botany. Her paintings were done with a stipple technique in tempera and watercolor on vellum, giving a textural illusion to the surface of the page.[35] She also painted religious, mythological and portrait paintings, but excelled in the study of plants and flowers.

Although Galizia and Garzoni were both trained in the miniature tradition, their approaches to still-life arrangement and botanical studies are as different as their stylistic and technical approaches generally. Garzoni painted stippling with tempera and watercolor on vellum, creating a transparent effect, as if looking at nature through an optical lens, then creating a recession into the picture plane. Galizia, on the other hand, used oils on panel or canvas, producing a painterly and overtly tactile quality, and inducing an impression of outward projection from the painting. Garzoni's approach is paradoxically both scientific and decorative, and provides a beautiful and accurate illustrative record of insects, plants and flowers. In

V.7 Giovanna Garzoni, *Self-Portrait with the Letter 'G'*, 1625

contrast, Galizia's subjects are imaginary paintings, created merely for the visual delight of the viewer.

The *Self-Portrait with the Letter 'G'* of 1625 (ink and tempera on vellum) from Garzoni's compiled book of *Caratteri cancellerischi corsivi* (now in the Biblioteca Sarti, Accademia di San Luca, Rome) was designed while she attended the school of calligraphy of Giacomo Rogni in Venice (Fig. V.7).[36] The letter 'G' stands for her first name, Giovanna. She embellishes this calligraphic initial with flowers and birds, a parrot, butterflies and bees. Garzoni also includes a male peacock that makes a wheel placed at the beginning of the curvature of her name 'G', honoring herself with fame, since the peacock is the symbol not only of vanity but also of immortality.

Being familiar with the medieval manuscript tradition whereby miniaturists decorated the initial of the first letter of their name, Garzoni's work is here comparable to Claricia's *Self-Portrait on the Letter 'Q'* from her illustrated manuscript of the St Memin Psalter or Guda's *Self-Portrait in the Letter 'D'* from her painted codex. Garzoni also painted a self-portrait to be placed on her funerary monument, and although it has been lost, two copies were painted by Giuseppe Ghezzi, a member and secretary of the Accademia di San Luca, who was charged with painting the members' portraits in 1674.[37] Of these, Ghezzi's copy of 1698 (now in the Pinacoteca Comunale of Ascoli

V.8   Giovanna Garzoni, *Self-Portrait*, 1660, as copied by Giuseppe Ghezzi, 1698

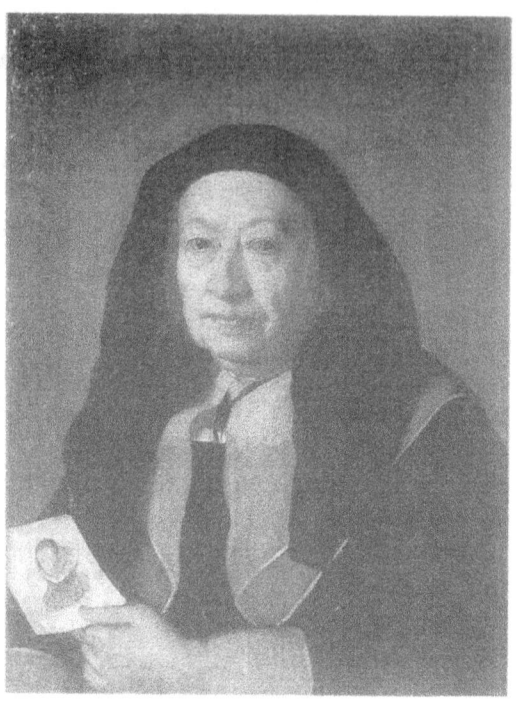

Piceno; Fig. V.8),[38] is probably closer to Garzoni's lost *Self-Portrait* of 1665. It was executed close to the time when she was settling her funerary wishes in her will, and represents her as elderly and dressed in the somber fashion of the time for a woman of advanced age, thus recalling the late portraits of the aging Sofonisba Anguissola. Although portrayed with a tired and wrinkled face, Garzoni's expression is at once serene, gracious and friendly. She presents to the viewer a miniature representation on parchment of a self-portrait of a young woman, suggesting her fame as a miniaturist painter as well as her interest in art from an early age, and probably recalling her first painting, the *Holy Family*, done at the age of 16. As an observer of nature, Garzoni is contrasting two stages of life – youth and old age – but the difference is physical, not spiritual. The inclusion of a second likeness in her self-portrait is calculated. She could have included a botanical drawing, but she preferred instead to create a double portrait, unprecedented in self-images of the seventeenth century in Italy, and anticipating the Venetian painter Rosalba Carriera's double portraiture in the eighteenth century.

Garzoni's and Galizia's wills further document the fact that female painters left money to build funerary monuments in their own honor, and served as patrons of the arts as well as collectors. In order to do these things, they had to have been paid well for their works.[39]

Female painters from England, France, Holland and Portugal responded with the same enthusiasm and inquisitive interest to the portrayal of the self as the Italian painters. Outstanding artists include Josefa de Ayala D'Óbidos (1630–84), Louise Moillon (1615–75) and Clara Peeters (1594–1640), who are all known for their extraordinary still-lifes, while Judith Leyster (1609–60) is noted for her genre scenes and Mary Craddock Beale (1632–99) excelled in portraiture.

Josefa de Ayala D'Óbidos was born in Seville of Spanish parents, Baltasar Gómes Figueira and Catalina de Ayala.[40] In 1634, she moved with her family to Óbidos, in Portugal. After completion of her education at the Augustinian convent of Santa Ana in Coimbra, D'Óbidos trained under her father, a portrait painter, and her maternal uncle Bernabé Ayala, a follower of the Spaniard Francisco de Zurbarán. She was the godchild of the renowned painter Francisco de Herrera the Elder. Óbidos became a member of the Lisbon Academy of Art on the basis of her talent in painting still-lifes and religious and portrait paintings. She was commissioned to do numerous religious paintings, including the altarpiece *The Mystical Marriage of Saint Catherine* for the church of Santa Maria de Óbidos in 1647 (Museu Nacional de Arte Antiga, Lisbon). A recent exhibition at the Museum of Women in the Arts in Washington, DC, brings insight into D'Óbidos's artistic career and accomplishments, demonstrating her celebrity status during the seventeenth and eighteenth centuries.[41] Later sources erroneously describe her work and personality as pious and mystic; recently discovered legal documents also reveal that she was an active member of her community as a landowner. She was also an animal lover with a good sense of humor, naming her cows Elegant, Cherry and Beauty.

Although a self-portrait of Josefa de Ayala D'Óbidos is mentioned in the earlier literature about her no visual records have been found. However, the religious and secular emblematic portraits of *St Catherine of Alexandria* of 1646 and *Wisdom or The Academic Knowledge* of 1653 provide an insight into D'Óbidos's artistic endeavors. *St Catherine of Alexandria* of 1646, an engraving now in a private collection in Lisbon, is signed and dated. D'Óbidos reveals her artistic proficiency and technical skill in etching by the contrast of chiaroscuro lines, cross-hatching and shadowing. Iconographically, D'Óbidos was influenced by the paintings of Francisco Pacheco and prototypes for the popular representation of St Catherine at this time in Catholic countries. According to Jacobus de Voragine, author of the *Legenda Aurea*, Saint Catherine was a philosopher, theologian and scholar whose Christian convictions led her to martyrdom, subsequently becoming the patron saint of education. Voragine says her name comes from *catha*, total, and *ruina*, ruin, meaning that the edifice of pride was destroyed by her humility. Her attributes – the royal crown, the broken wheel with spikes, and the sword and the palm – are symbols of her sainthood.

D'Óbidos's *Wisdom* or *The Academic Knowledge* of 1653, a signed and dated engraving housed in a private collection in Lisbon, may represent a symbolic self-portrait (Fig. V.9), alluding to the artist's intellectual training in the medieval city of Coimbra. It was a separate insert in the *Novos Estatutos de Universidade de Coimbra* (New Statutes for the University of Coimbra), a manuscript of the regulations of the University of Coimbra. D'Óbidos's father had received the prestigious commission, but it was completed by his

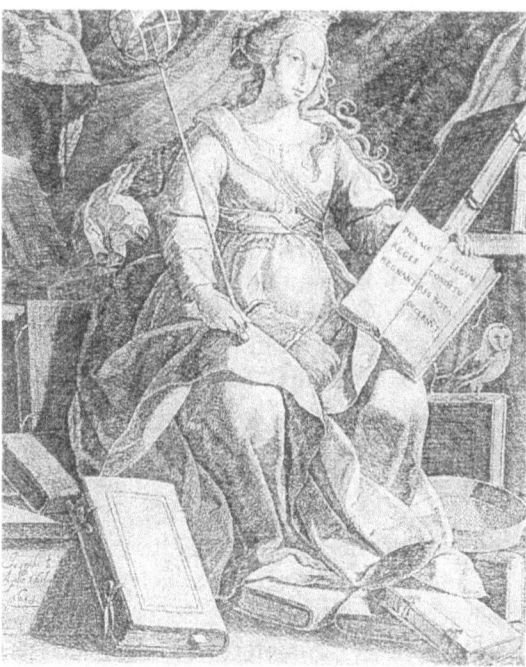

V.9   Josefa de Ayala
D'Óbidos, *Wisdom*, 1653

daughter. The personification of Knowledge or Wisdom is surrounded by the accoutrements associated with humanistic and scientific knowledge, learning and understanding. The figure, D'Óbidos herself, holds an open book with a Latin inscription alluding to governance through reasoning and wisdom: '*Per me reges regnant et legum conditores justa decernūt.*' The numerous attributes of reasoning recall Boethius' description of Wisdom with books and a scepter in *De Consolatione Philosophiae* and Cesare Ripa's of Wisdom (*Sapienza*) printed in the *Iconologia*.[42] Ripa describes and illustrates Wisdom as a crowned female figure, seated and surrounded by books and beams of light. D'Óbidos merges the Christian with the pagan concept of Wisdom: as one of the seven gifts of the Holy Spirit, it is personified by her as *Sapientia*, as indicated by the open book, but an antique symbol of knowledge related to the goddess Minerva, an owl, is placed next to the seated figure. D'Óbidos also replaces the traditional attribute of the scepter or beam of light with an armillary sphere, an astronomical instrument in which the circles of the heavens are represented by rings, including the zodiac belt, which symbolizes the emanation of creativity or the intellect of learned individuals, as well as representing the royal emblem of Dom João IV.[43] The sieve resting among the books implies judgment and prudence in learning.

Louise Moillon, another still-life artist who painted a self-portrait, was born in Paris, and was trained in the art of painting by her father, Nicolas Moillon, a landscape and portrait painter. Her mother was the daughter of a goldsmith, who in 1620 remarried another painter and art dealer, François Garnier. Years later, Moillon was transferred to the atelier of her stepfather to

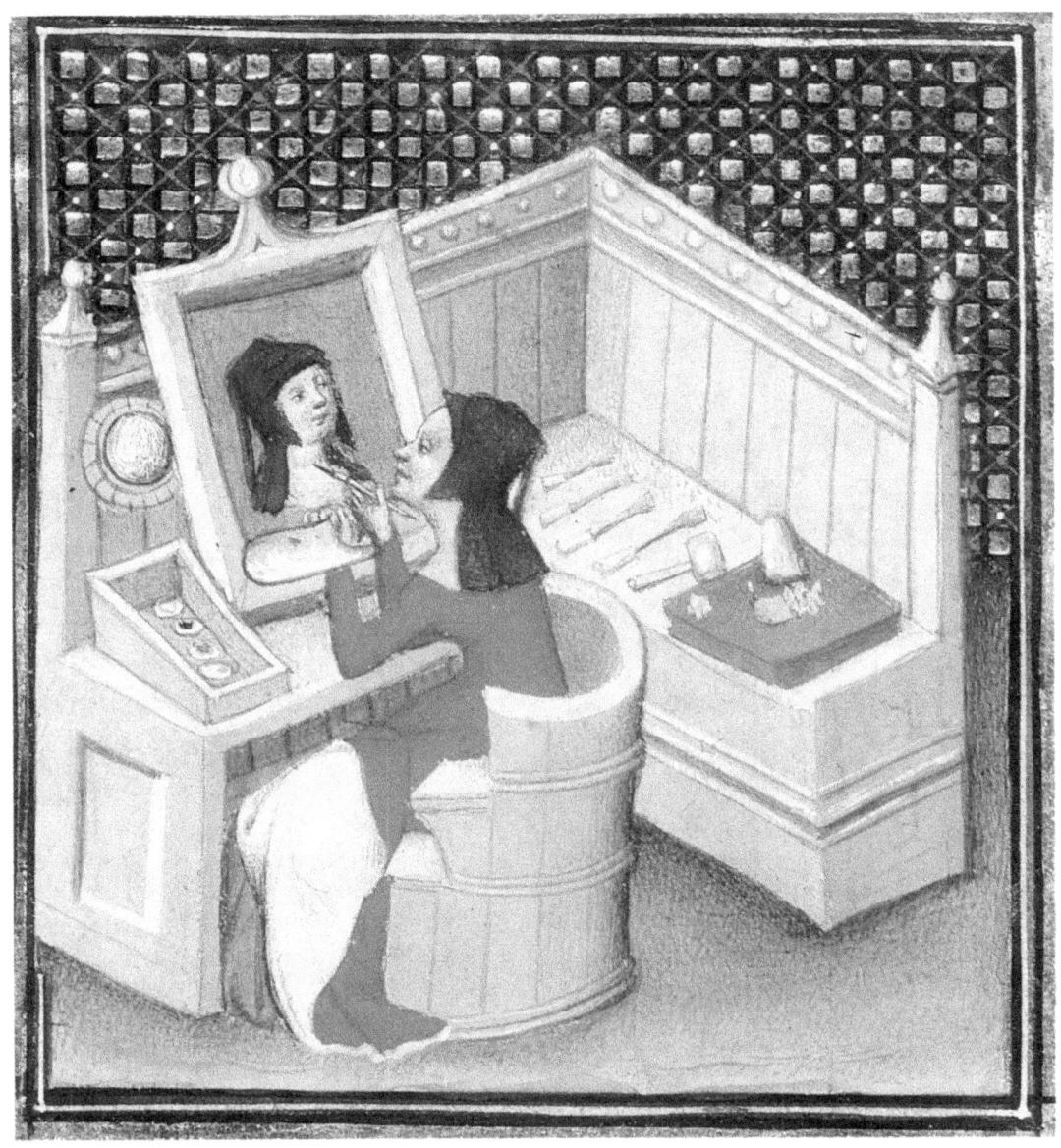

1 Timarete (Thamyris), *Self-Portrait*, in Boccaccio's *Noble and Famous Women*, 1401–2, MS Fr.598, folio 86 recto

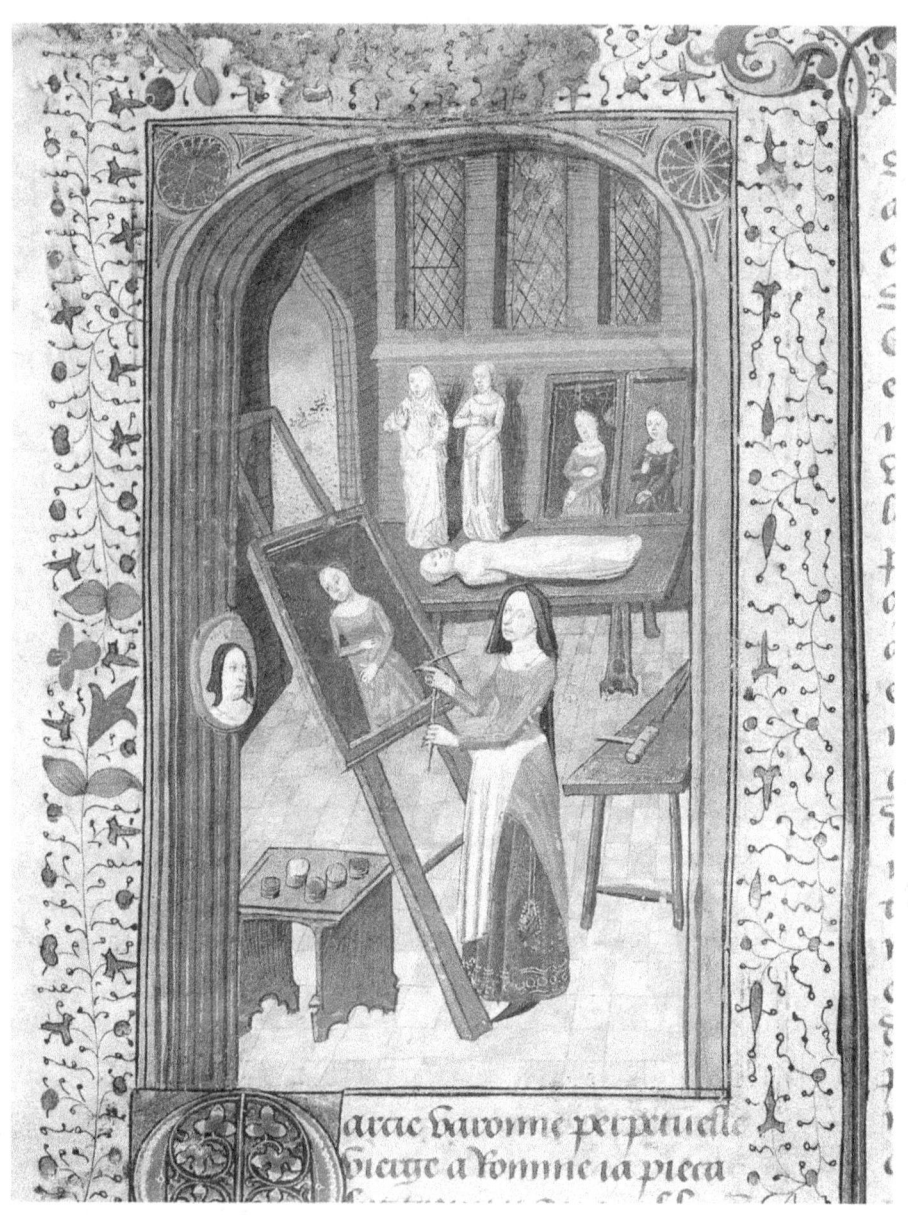

II *Marcia Painting Her Self-Portrait in her Atelier*, in Boccaccio's *Noble and Famous Women*,
c.1470, MS Fr.33, folio 37 verso

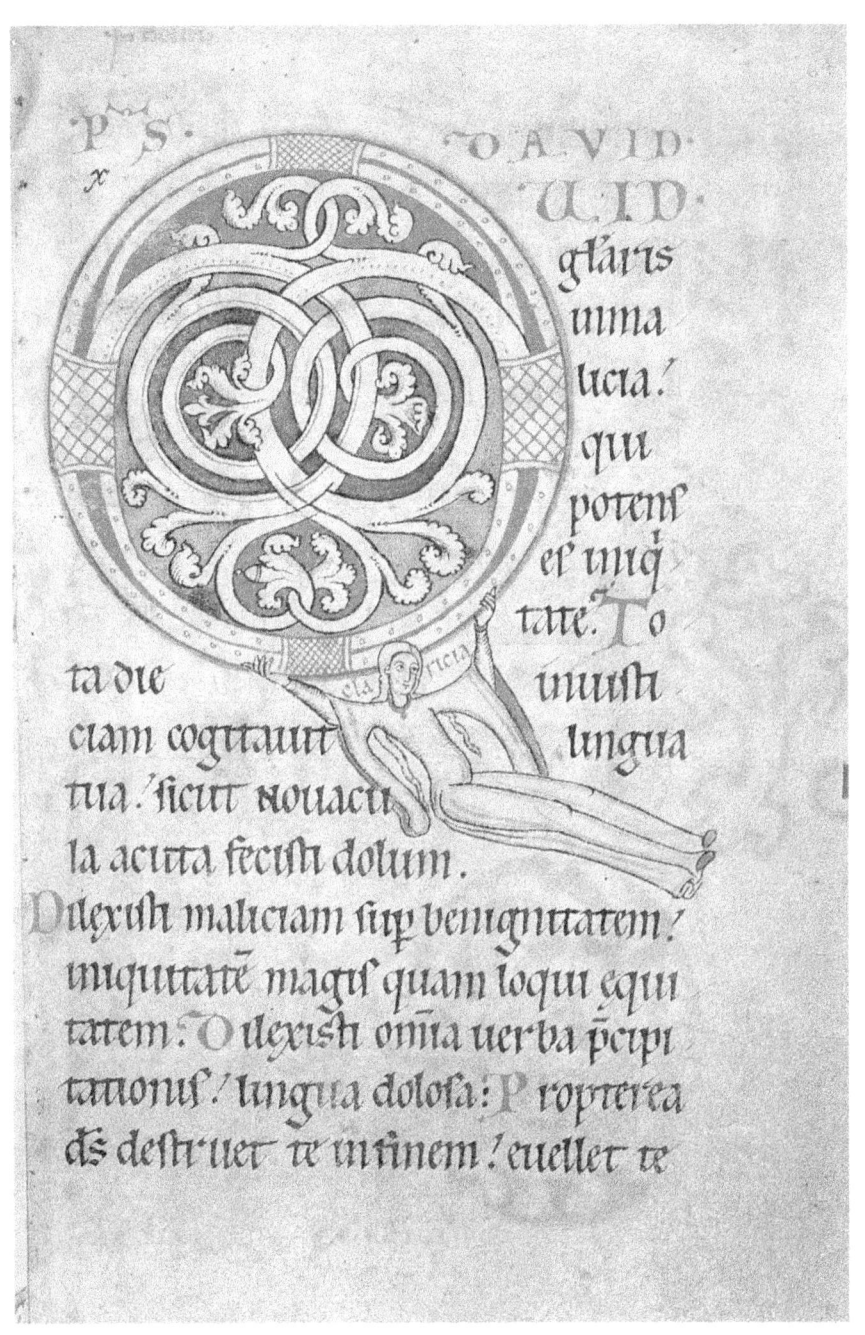

III   Claricia, *Self-Portrait on the Letter Q*, 1200, South German Psalter, W 26, folio 64

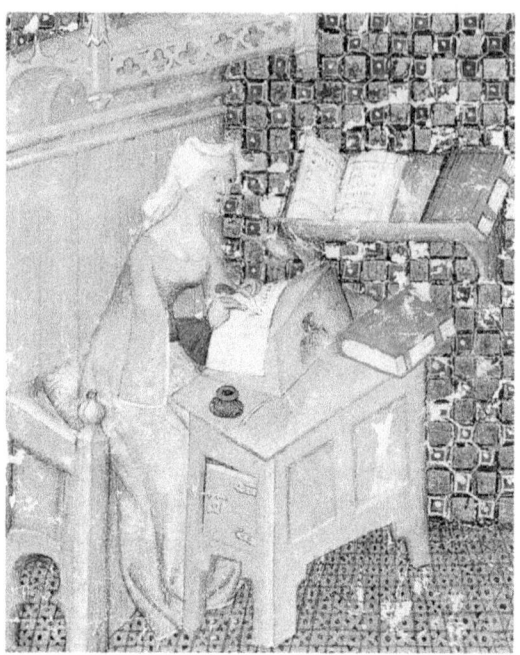

IV   Christine de Pizan, *Self-Portrait in Her Studio*, 1420, in Christine de Pizan's *Le Livre de la mutation de fortune*, Prologue, MS.493/1668, folio 91.232 recto

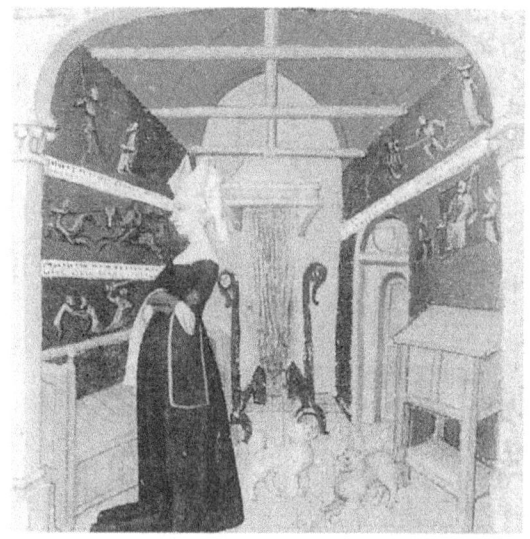

V   *Christine de Pizan Beholds the Paintings in the Salle de Fortune*, 1420, in Christine de Pizan's *Le Livre de la mutation de fortune*, MS Fr.503, folio 127 verso

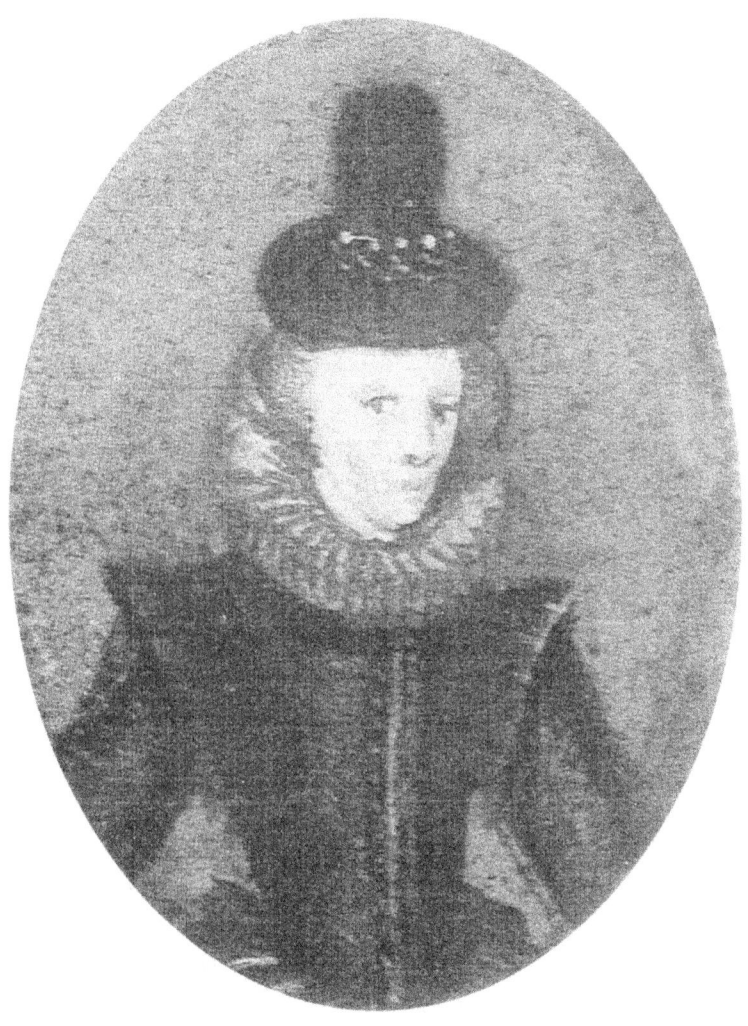

VI   Esther Inglis, *Self-Portrait*, 1615, MS 8874, folio 4 verso

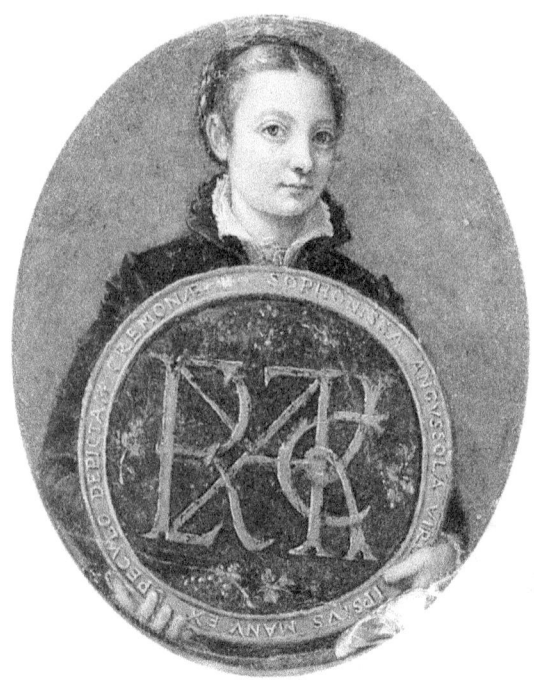

VII   Sofonisba Anguissola, *Self-Portrait*, 1552,
miniature

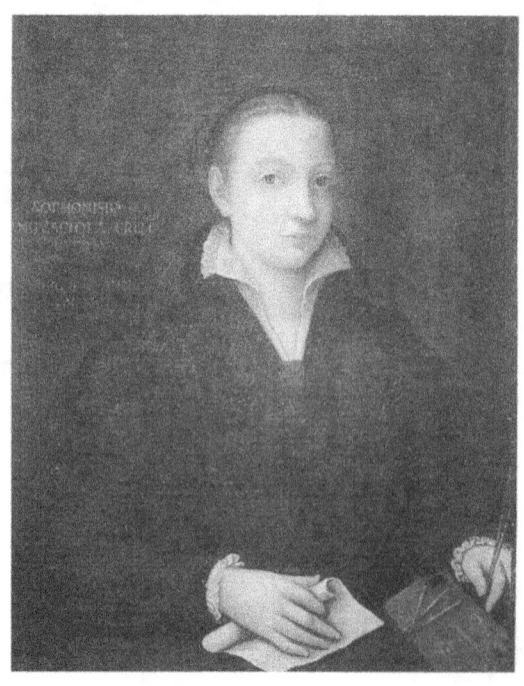

VIII   Sofonisba Anguissola, *Self-Portrait*, 1552–4

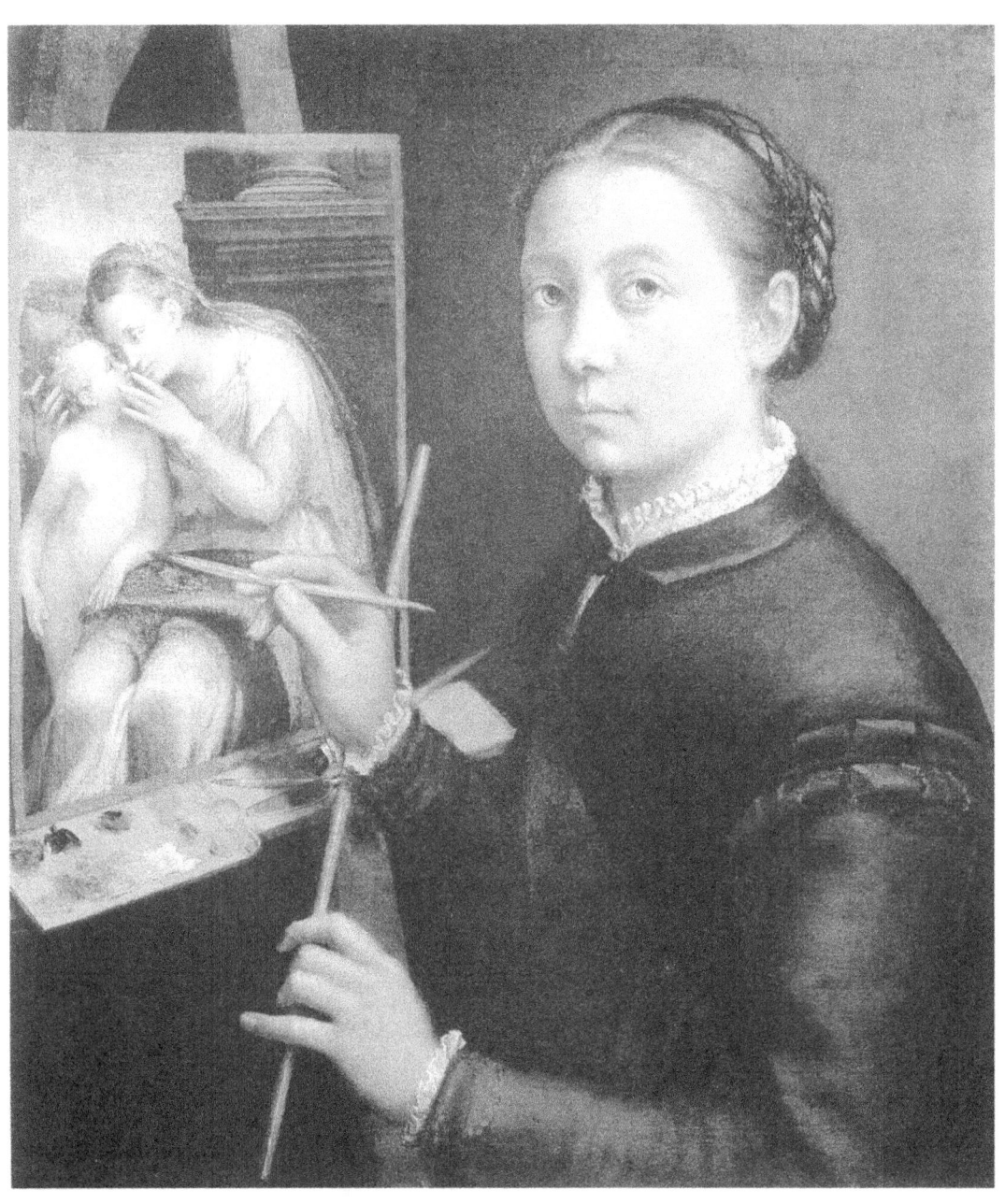

IX   Sofonisba Anguissola, *Self-Portrait at an Easel*, 1556

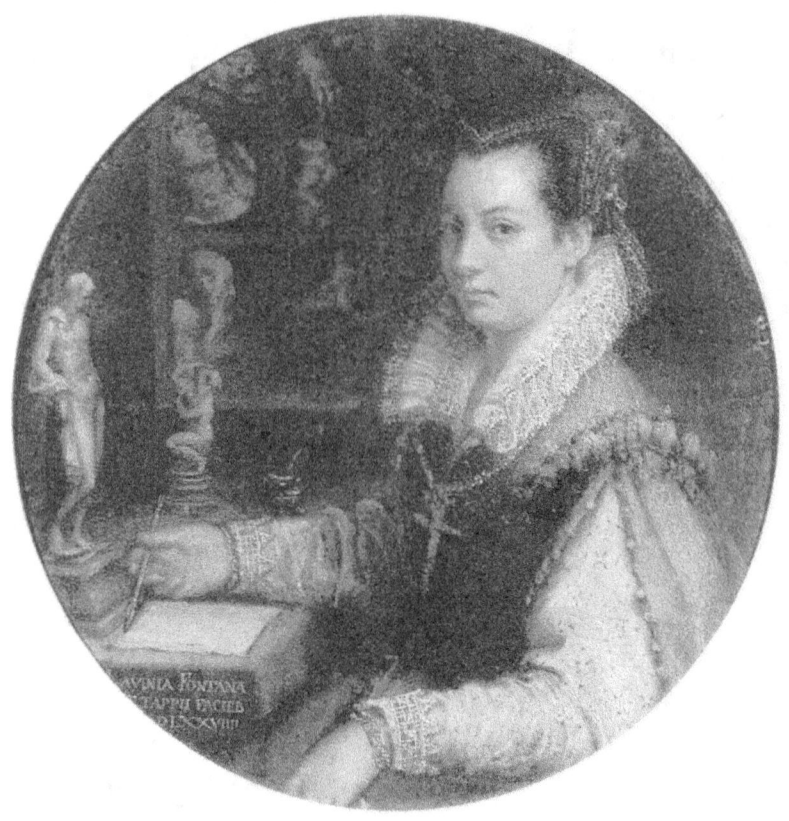

X Lavinia Fontana, *Self-Portrait in Her Study*, 1579,
Florence, Uffizi

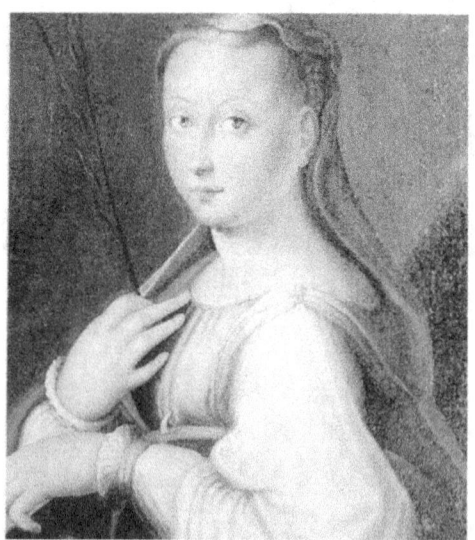

XI Barbara Longhi, *St Catherine of Alexandria*, 1598

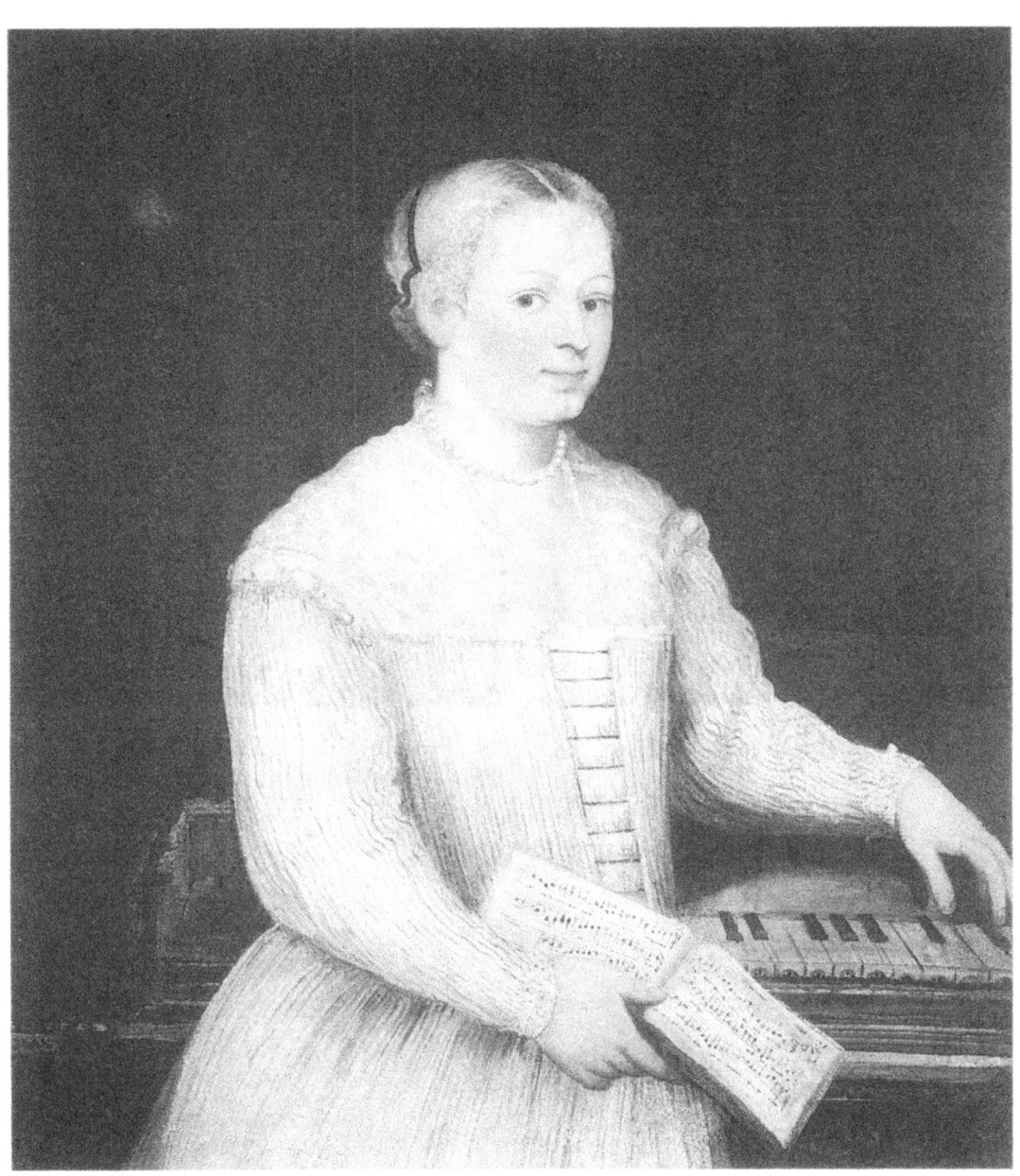

XII   Marietta Robusti, *Self-Portrait*, 1580

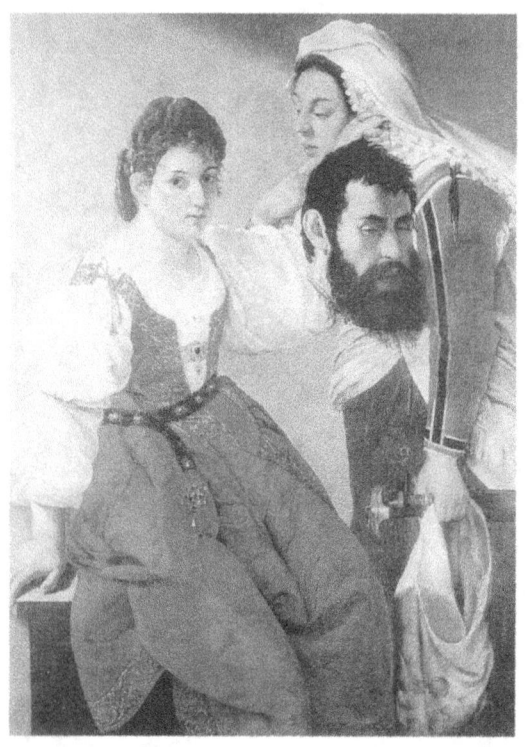

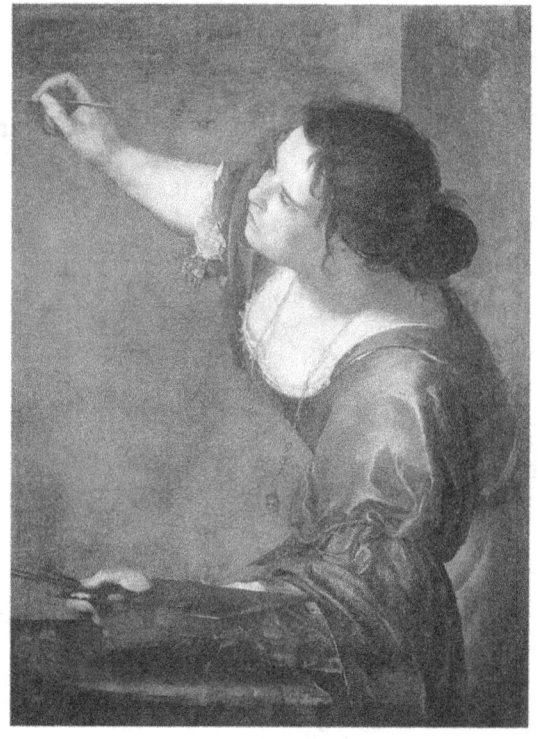

XIII   Artemisia Gentileschi, *Judith and Holofernes*,
1615

XIV   Artemisia Gentileschi, *Self-Portrait as the
Allegory of Painting*, 1630

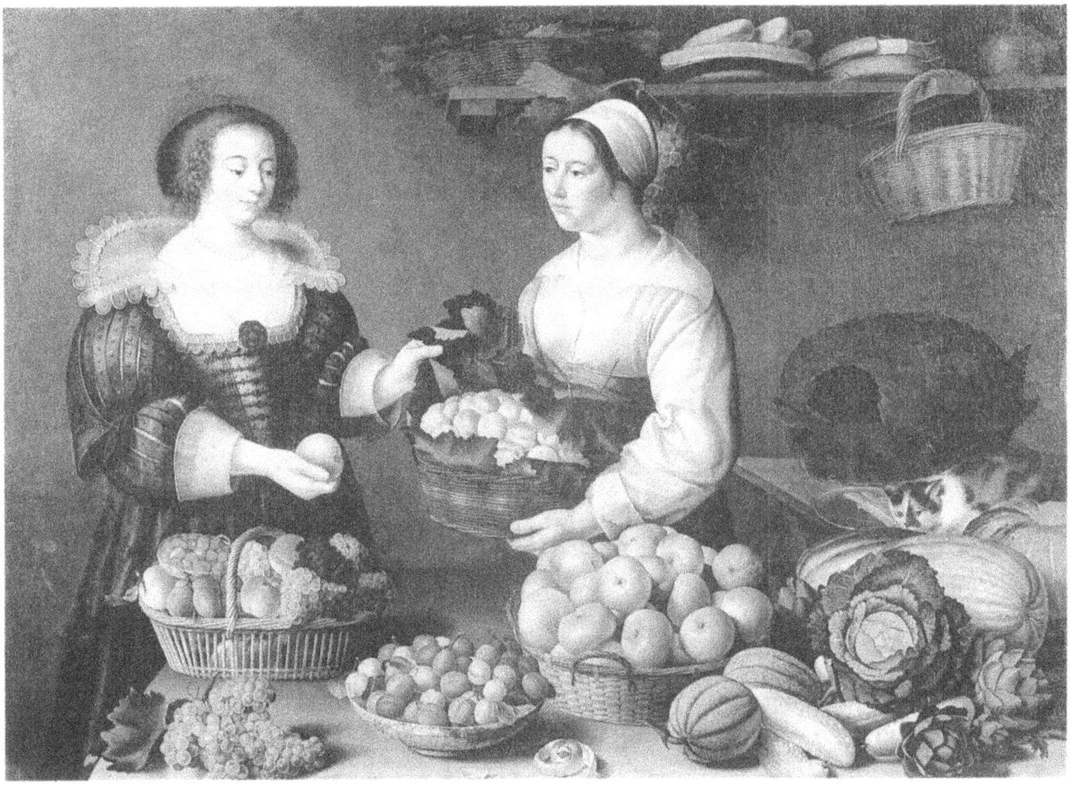

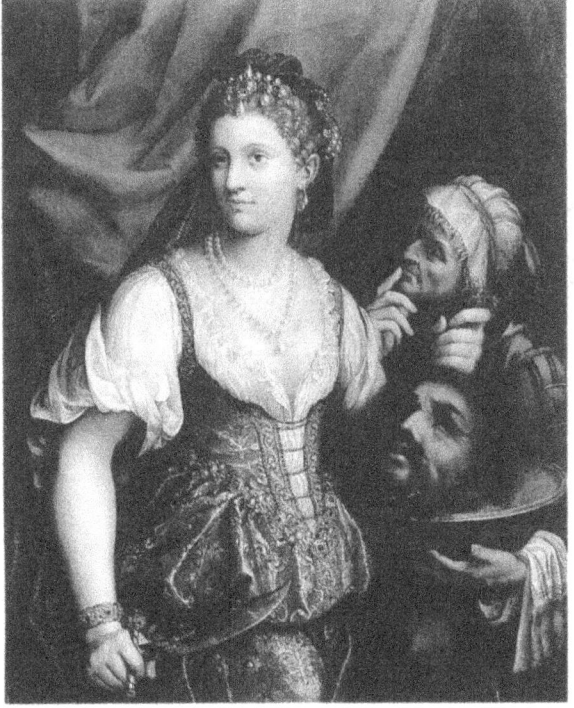

XVI   Louise Moullion, *Self-Portrait with Still Life* (*At the Greengrocer*), 1650

XV   Fede Galizia, *Judith and Holofernes*, 1650

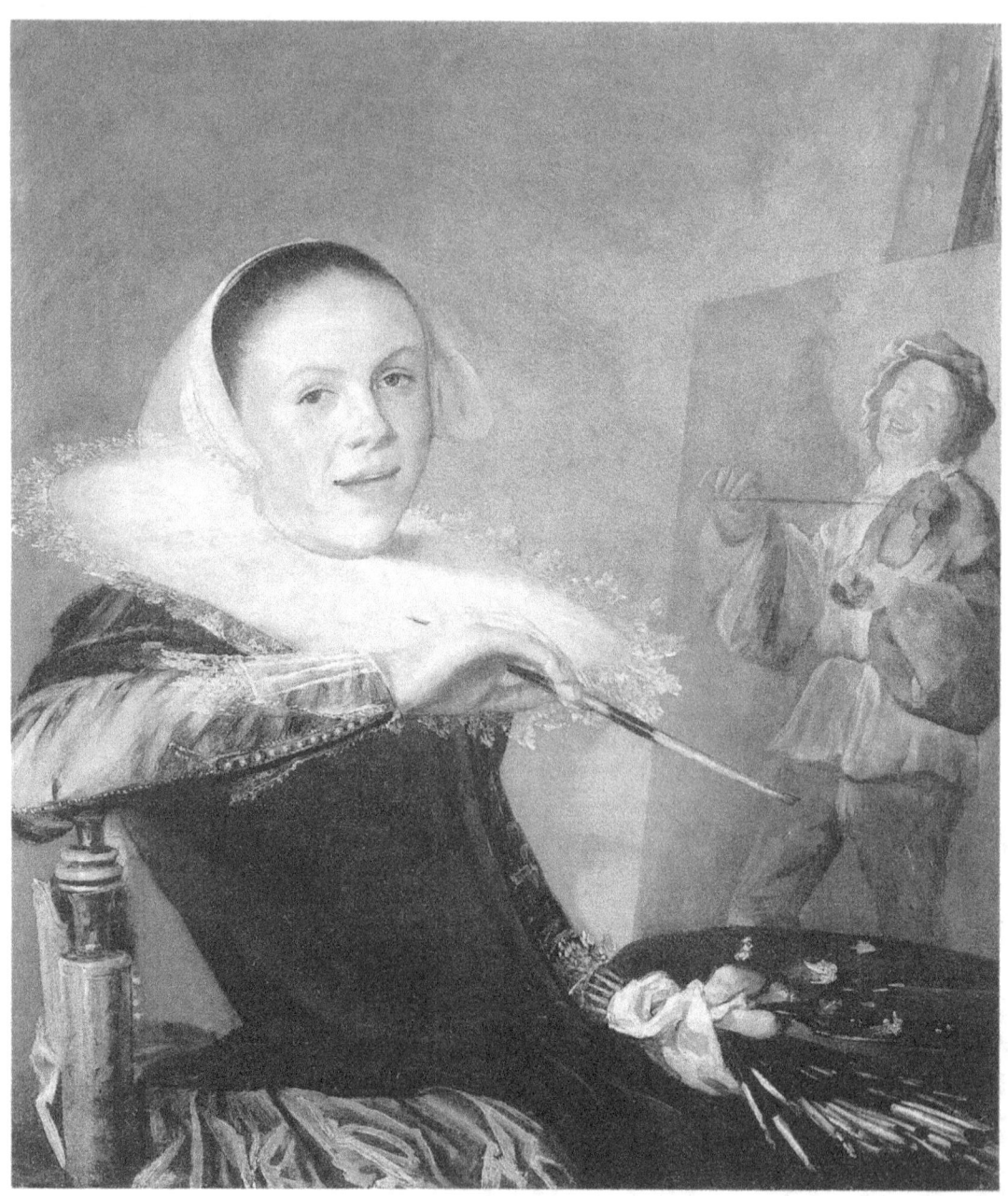

XVII   Judith Leyster, *Self-Portrait*, 1635

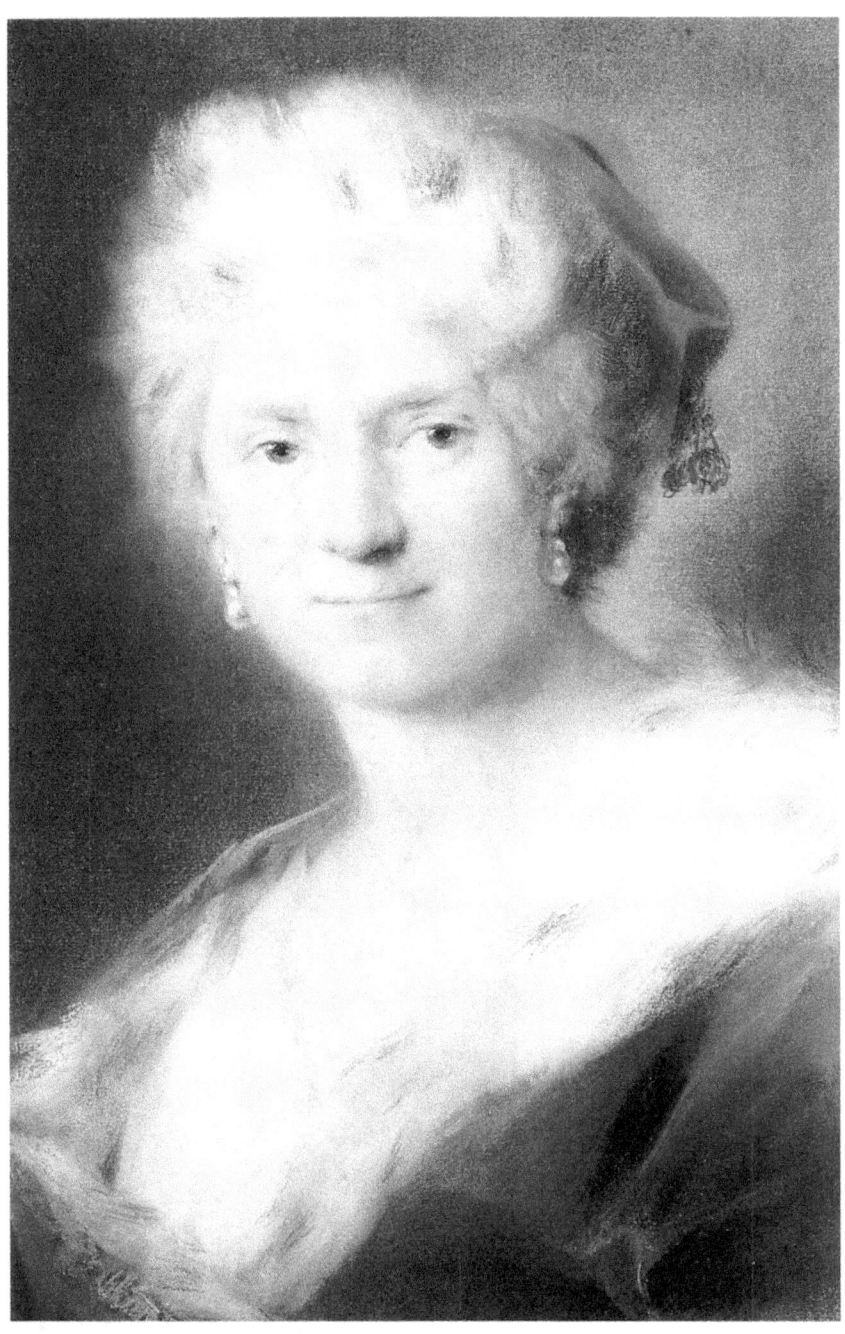

XVIII   Rosalba Carriera, *Self-Portrait as Winter*, 1730–31

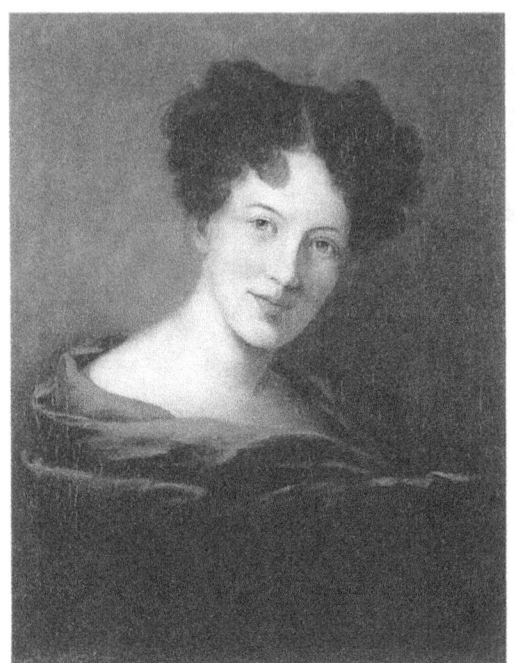

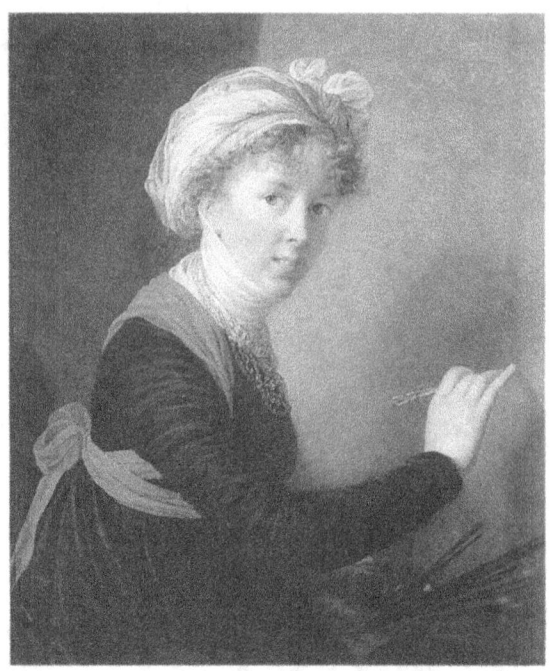

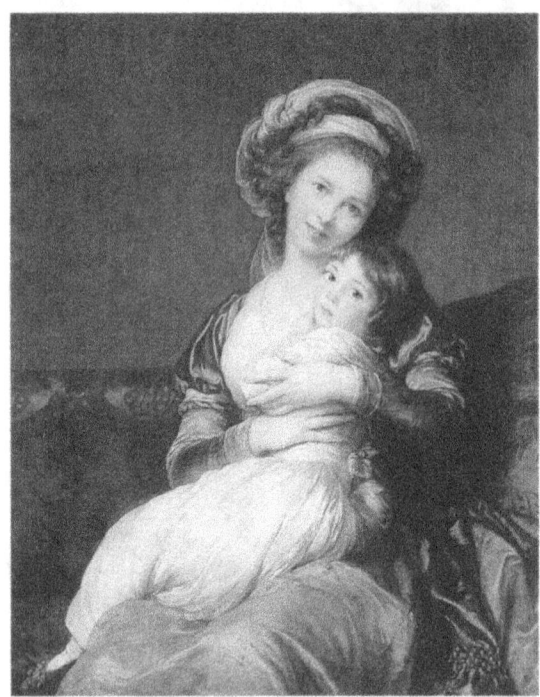

XIX   (top left) Sarah Peale, *Self-Portrait*, 1818
XX   (bottom right) Elisabeth Vigée-Lebrun, *Self-Portrait with Her Daughter*, 1786
XXI   (top right) Elisabeth Vigée-Lebrun, *Self-Portrait*, 1800
XXII   (opposite) Adélaïde Labille-Guiard, *The Artist with Two Female Pupils*, 1785

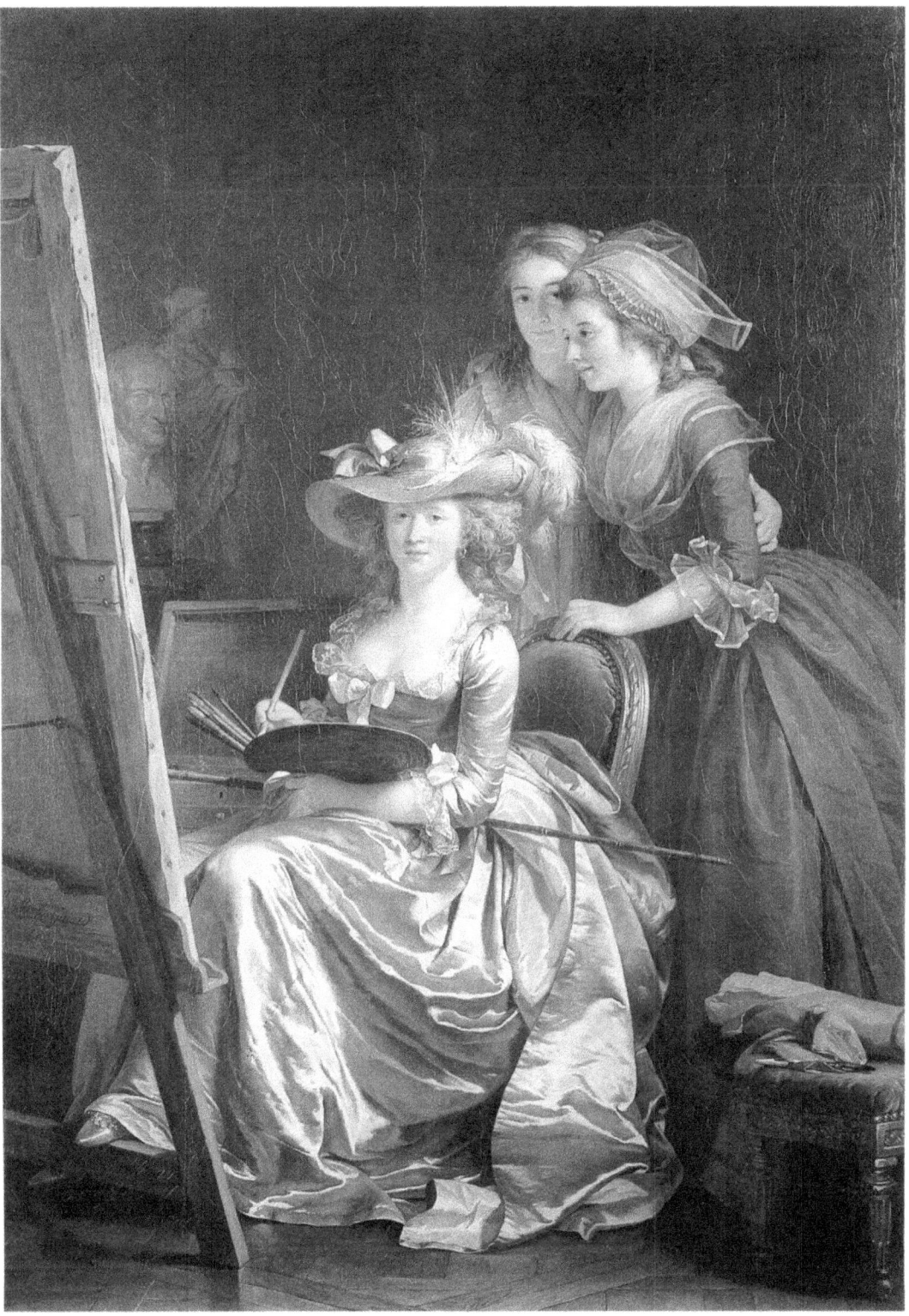

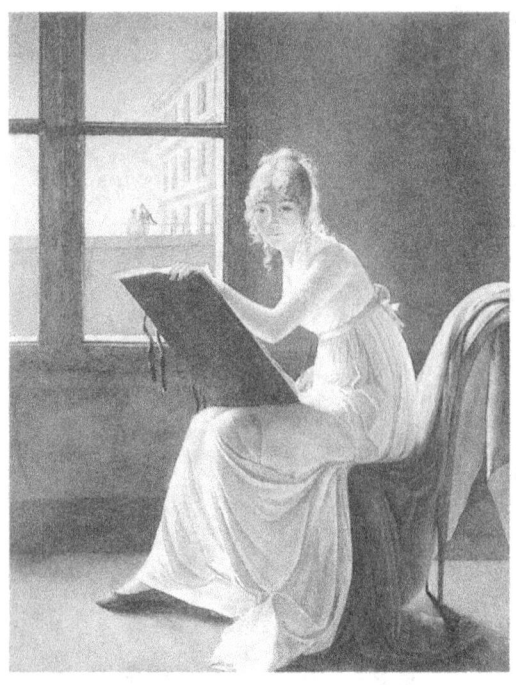

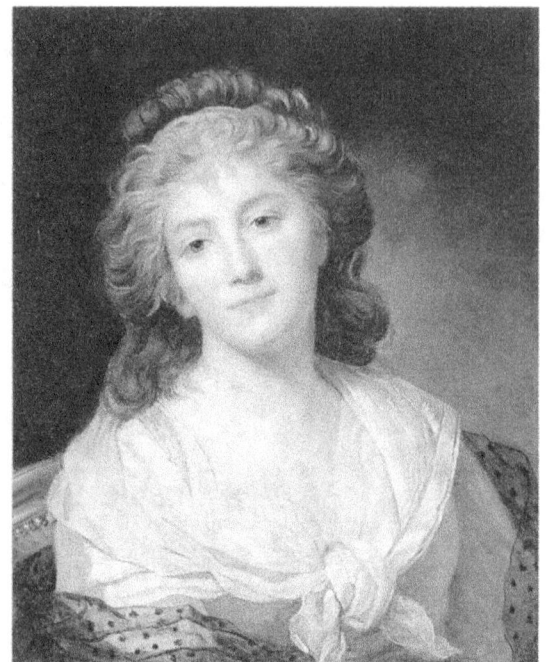

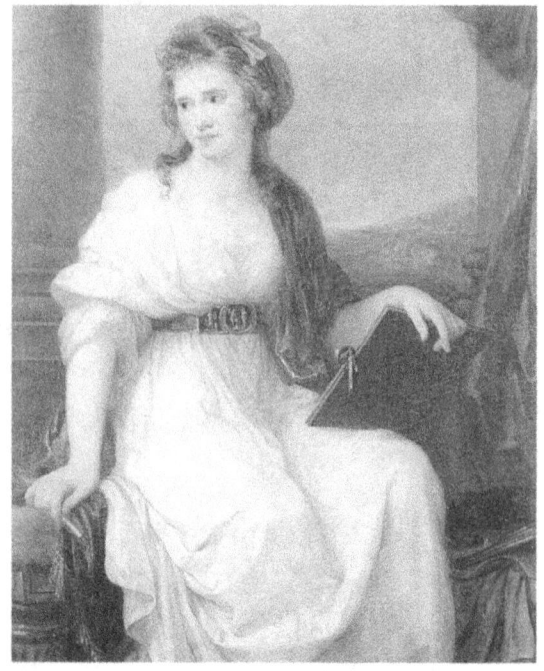

XXIII   *(top left)* Nisa Villers, *Portrait of a Young Artist*, 1799
XXIV   *(top right)* Marie-Geneviève Bouliar, *Self-Portrait*, 1792
XXV   *(bottom right)* Angelica Kauffmann, *Self-Portrait*, 1787

become his assistant and, following her family tradition, she formed a circle of artists working in the Saint-Germain-des-Près area of Paris. During her training, Moillon developed an interest in Dutch and Flemish still-lifes. Although she came from a Protestant family and was married to a Calvinist, Etienne Girardot de Chancout, as her style matured Moillon responded to the mystical messages transmitted by the Spaniard Francisco Zurbarán in his still-life paintings.[44] There are 25 paintings from 1629–82 that are attributed to her.

In *Self-Portrait with Still Life (At the Greengrocer)* of 1650 (Pl. XVI), Moillon reveals an understanding of chiaroscuro, reflective light and compositional decoration. In the forefront of the painting an extraordinary display of fruits and vegetables is presented to the viewer on a table. Behind the table, Moillon serves a noblewoman. The inviting banquet of natural richness presents a dilemma for the participant or buyer. The senses of sight and smell, of touch and taste, are stimulated in the buyer (viewer), who wishes to and does indulge in the sumptuous visual experience and the momentary beauty of the display; however, he or she is unable to select, only visually indulge. Moillon's inclusion of a self-portrait in the natural feast presents an aesthetic moment of suspension, between representation and illusionism. The self-portrait is an image of the self from a reflection and the painted still-life is the artist's portrayal of nature or her imitation of the natural forms. In both instances, the real becomes imaginary and the imaginary natural. The *trompe l'œil* technique, meticulously employed, suggests not only the depiction of different textures, but also an emblematic connotation of several senses, for example a partially peeled lemon alludes to the sense of smell, the noblewoman holding the fruit alludes to touch and the general display of the fruits and vegetables, to sight and taste.[45]

Moillon's *Self-Portrait with Still Life* provides new subject matter as well as a museum of natural history or visual encyclopedia of flowers and fruits. The painting moves away from traditional *vanitas* symbolism to offer a new level of ethical experience, and becomes a representation of the stages of the seasons as well as of life, as also seen in Giuseppe Arcimboldo's *Seasons* of 1573 (Louvre, Paris), Jan Breughel's *Senses* of 1619 (Prado, Madrid) and the engravings of Hendrick Goltzius and Jan Saenredam of *Allegories of the Senses* of 1616–20 (Graphische Sammlung Albertina, Vienna), perhaps an abstract representation as well of the cosmic cycle of life in a individual. Moillon does not present the transitory aspect of life, but rather the suspended instant of being alive.

In Flanders, Clara Peeters broke new ground in the art of portraiture and nature. A recent monograph provides a clear view of the Flemish painter's life, career and artistic merits.[46] From the few discovered documents, it is known that she was baptized in the church of St Walburga in Antwerp on 15 May 1594, and married Henri Joose at the age of 45 on 31 May 1639, in the same church. No signed paintings by this artist have been found from after this date. Even though she did not live long after her marriage, Peeters had probably ceased painting anyway. It was customary with women during the seventeenth century in northern Europe that after marriage their lives focused on domesticity, and any artistic productivity declined or even ceased.[47]

Peeters started painting at the age of 14. From her artistic accomplishments and interest in *vanitas* still-life paintings, it is reasonable to surmise that she trained in the workshop of Osias Beert, the leading still-life painter in Antwerp. The fact that her name has not been found in the records of the artists' guilds in Antwerp and surrounding cities does not diminish her accomplishments as a painter, since there are numerous signed works by her hand.[48] Most of Peeters's 24 surviving works are still-life paintings that demonstrate her technical talent and creative imagination. Her *vanitas* paintings display a combination of precious and ordinary objects, cleverly arranged in such ways as to delight the viewer. Her body of work compares to the exceptional Flemish still-life painters of this period, including George Flegel, Balthasar van der Ast and Artus Claessen.

Peeters's compositions of this kind are 'genre still-lifes', in which she represents Flemish daily domestic objects, as well as rare and expensive objects, such as pewter and Delft dishes, holding a variety of breads or cheeses, to denote her status within the society she inhabited. The arrangement of the compositions establishes a visual and corresponding dialogue among the vertical and circular shapes of the natural forms, as well as a series of geometrical designs, including triangular, elliptical and pyramidal. The *trompe l'œil* is masterful, with light effects enhancing the textural differences between soft and hard surfaces, between translucent and opaque. Peeters's meticulously rendered compositions emerge from somber backgrounds – as is typical of the Baroque illusionistic style. She utilizes objects and food in her compositions, as well as reflecting her image in the metal objects depicted in her paintings.

As with Artemisia Gentileschi's analysis of her first name, Clara Peeters used her initials both to signify herself and to indicate the vehicle of her creativity, the art of painting. The obvious signatures are 'Clara Peeters' and 'Clara P.A.' (Clara Peeters of Antwerp or Painter of Antwerp); others are 'Clara P', the 'P' standing for her last name or the Latin for painter (*pintrix*). Peeters's first name, 'Clara,' from the Latin *claritas*, meaning clarity or lucidity, is alluded to in the reflections and refraction of light obtained in the still-life depictions of metal and glass objects. Still-life paintings revealing the reflections in glasses or metal pitchers include *Dainties*, signed and inscribed 'Clara P.A. 1611', *Pie* of 1611 signed 'Clara Peeters' on the edge of a knife handle (both in the Prado, Madrid) and *Flowers in a Glass Vase* of 1610–15 (private collection, New York).[49]

Peeters's *Self-Portrait with Still-Life* of 1612 (Fig. V.10) is extraordinary in her work because in it she does not disguise herself among the magnificent objects but instead reveals and displays herself as an object – as one of several other precious objects in a still-life. Playing on both the numerous levels of meaning and the physical reflections in glass, metals, jewels and coins, Peeters offers the viewer the opportunity to ponder the transient quality of

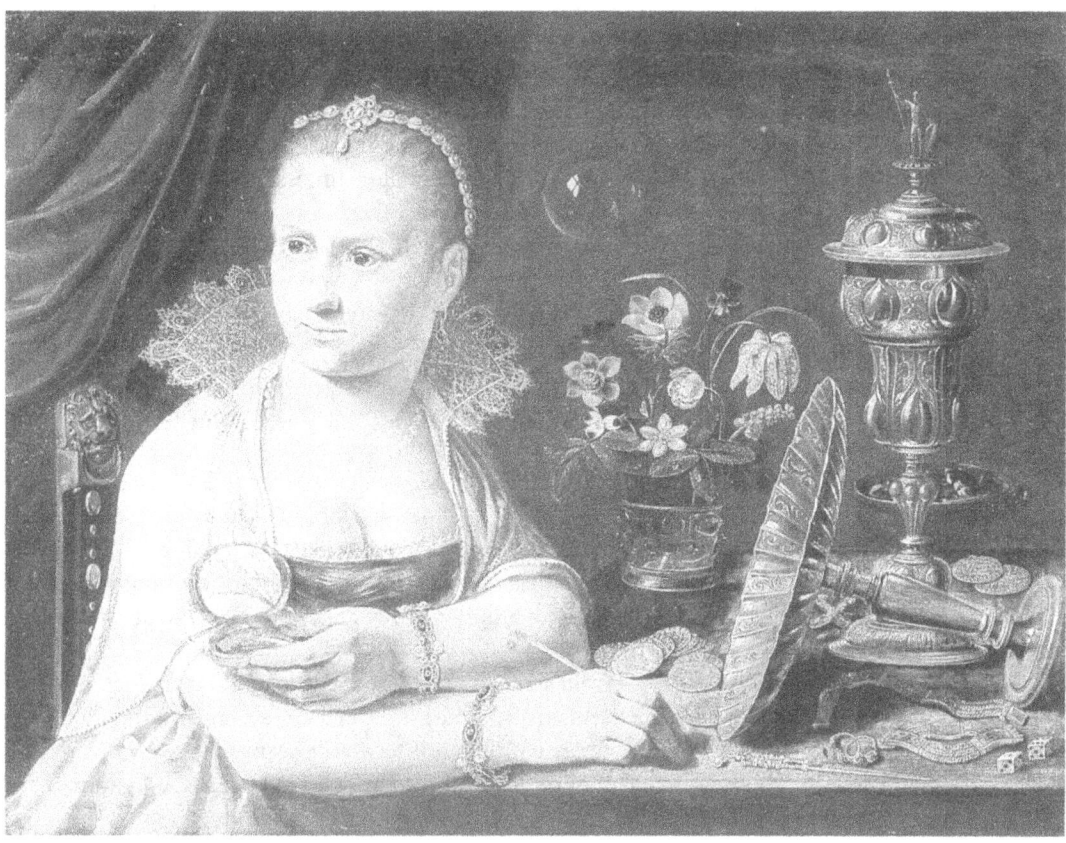

V.10   Clara Peeters, *Self-Portrait with Still-Life*, 1612

life. She holds a magnifying glass close to her chest, inviting the viewer to gaze into the intangible and unreachable, like the painted still-life objects displayed in this picture. The portrait is rendered similarly to the still-life objects, not beautified, but scientifically analyzed. The original and complex compositional arrangement and illusionism created in her paintings, particularly her *Self-Portrait*, makes her one of the forerunners and inventors of the theme of *breakfast* or *banquet* pieces in Flemish painting.

Clara Peeters's counterpart in Holland was Judith Leyster (1609–60). Numerous women who supported themselves as painters and restorers of art are recorded in Dutch inventories, records and documents, as well as by the Haarlem Guild of Saint Luke. With the exception of Judith Leyster and Judith Molenaer, however, their fame did not extend beyond the listing of their names.[50]

Due to a recent exhibition of her paintings at the Worcester Art Museum, in Massachusetts, many works previously attributed to other Dutch artists, including Frans Hals, Gerard van Honthorst and Jan Miense Molenaer (Leyster's husband), have been properly reattributed to her.[51]

In 1630 Leyster became a member of the Haarlem Guild. She also conducted a workshop training art students, thereby showing that she was successful in her field. Unlike other Dutch female painters, who specialized in still-life paintings,[52] Leyster engaged in the art of genre and domestic subjects, such as *The Proposition*, signed and inscribed 'JCS* 1631' (Mauritshuis, the Hague) and *Carousing Couple*, signed and inscribed 'JL* 1630' (Louvre, Paris). She thus broke new ground for Dutch female painters.

Judith Leyster was born in Haarlem on 28 July 1609, at a time when Holland was seeking independence from Spain at the beginning of the Twelve Years' Truce.[53] Her father, Jan Willemsz. Leyster, was a brewer who had taken as his own the name of his brewery, 'Ley-ster' (*lode-star*, meaning leading star). Impressed with this acquired family name, Leyster invented a logo for her signature that included a star. The brewery, a familiar and accessible environment for different types of people, provided Leyster with a repertoire of subjects for her paintings, such as the *Boy with a Wineglass* of 1627–8 (Staatliche Kunsthalle, Karlsruhe), the *Merry Drinkers* of 1629 (Rijksmuseum, Amsterdam) and *The Last Drop* of 1628–9 (John G. Johnson Collection, Philadelphia). In this last painting, Leyster makes an analogy to family achievements with her signature and the image. A signed star monogram on the tankard alludes both to the family's brewery, and to her own artistry as a painter.

In the early 1620s, Leyster was training in the studio of Franz Pietersz de Grebber, a portrait and history painter. Her artistic accomplishments as a teenager were referred to 'as painting with a good, keen sense'.[54] By 1629 she was working in the manner of the brothers Dirk and Frans Hals, and attended their workshops, as well as becoming a friend of their family; on one occasion Leyster participated in a baptismal ceremony for one of Frans Hals's children. Her artistic style has a painterly touch, with broad and loose brushstrokes, creating an impression of the image without outlining or flattening the form, along with patchy treatment of the textures, rich colors and a liveliness of expression. In Dirk Hals's studio, Leyster probably met the painter Jan Miense Molenaer (1610–68), in 1629. Molenaer courted her for years and she finally married him on 1 June 1636. The couple moved to Amsterdam, a center for artists, where they lived for 11 years, had five children and established an art business. Leyster died on 10 February 1660, at the age of 50.

As was customary with women during this era, after Leyster's marriage her life focused on domesticity and childbearing[55] and her husband's artistic career. A family portrait, usually attributed to Leyster's husband, *Family Making Music* of 1636 (Frans Hals Museum, Haarlem), reveals her talented family in an interior setting, a music room. They nearly all hold contemporary musical instruments. Looking at the viewer, Leyster is seated next to the virginal holding a lute, while her husband, without a musical instrument, stands pointing to himself, indicating that he is the head of his household. Other members of her husband's family are seen in the background, where other portraits hang on the wall. The painting is filled with emblematic meanings associated with music and art, and with symbols of the transience of life, represented by a wall clock, blown bubbles, skulls and ancestral portraits.[56]

Leyster's *Self-Portrait* of 1635 (Pl. XVII) illustrates her extraordinary talents.[57] She painted it at the tender age of 21. Dressed elegantly in the high fashion of the time, affirming her success, Leyster reveals herself in her studio, seated in front of an easel and holding a brush and a palette. The canvas on the easel is a copy of one of her early paintings, depicting a laughing fiddler, *Merry Drinkers* of 1629 (private collection in the Netherlands). The painted image of Leyster turns to the viewer as if to converse. As is typical in Baroque paintings, the viewer is drawn into the picture by its figures or objects, in this case Leyster herself.

The illusionism created is at various levels: the viewer gazing at the beautiful painted portraitist, the painted image gazing at the viewer and the painted laughing fiddler gazing at the painter, his creator, as well as at her admirers, the viewers. Leyster interprets the emblematic correspondence between painting and music, a familiar Baroque theme, as we have seen, demonstrating the theory of sister arts, *ut pictura musica*. That is to say, just as painting uses the elements of colors to create an effect, so music uses the sounds of notes to arouse an aesthetic mood, an assimilation of a classical version of a popular humanist theory of art in the seventeenth century. Leyster parallels an implement of her trade, the brush, with that of the fiddler, the bow; her palette of colors with the fiddle and strings; and the visualization of the elements of painting with the aural perception of music.

In fact, Judith Leyster often included musical instruments in her paintings, several of them representing the classical dichotomy between strings and wind instruments, recalling Ovid's tale in the *Metamorphoses* (V, 53–4) of the musical contest between the god Apollo, who played the lyre with divine inspiration, and the satyr Marsyas, who performed with great technical ability, but with lack of inventiveness, on a pipe. This disassociation had also been connected with Pythagoras' concept of cosmic accord and discord between human reason and the emotions. Plato (*Republic*, Book III) associated the pipe with Dionysus, god of wine and revelry, symbolizing the sensuality and passion of the soul, and the stringed lyre with Apollo, god of harmony and reason, with balance and moderation. This discriminatory attitude between musical instruments, their performance and their sounds, which had persisted from classical times, was further enhanced in the seventeenth century. Its symbolism became associated with moral behavior. Calvinism issued a warning in relation to music, since it aroused the passion of the soul and needed to be tempered and modulated through the intellect.[58]

Unlike sixteenth-century female painters such as Sofonisba Anguissola, Lavinia Fontana and Catherina van Hemessen, who portrayed themselves as cultured and educated ladies playing instruments, Leyster, as a product of seventeenth-century Dutch society, portrayed the moral dimension to musical instruments. She portrays herself in the painting not as a musician performing, but rather as a listener to the fiddler. Leyster contrasts the traditional representation of a painter's self-portrait – in the process of painting at an easel – and the new genre subject, merry company, as well as the distinction of portraits from genre paintings. She, as a painter, is able to do both.

When Leyster's *Self-Portrait* was examined through infra-red light, as shown in the catalogue of the Worcester exhibition, it was revealed that the image painted on the easel was originally a portrait of a woman. Perhaps she was attempting to depict another self-portrait on the canvas, as Catherina van Hemessen had done in her *Self-Portrait* of 1546 (Basel). Or perhaps she was attempting to continue the self-portrait tradition of female painters by portraying a 'picture within a picture' of the self. Or maybe she was alluding to the emblematic reference of some of the senses – sight (painting), hearing (music), touch (brush and bow) and smell (color pigments), which were a theme of the period.

Several interpretations have been offered to explain the relation between the two images and the reason why Leyster changed the image from a woman to a man. Some focus on classical references, suggesting Horace's concept *ut pictura poesis*.[59] Others center on the theory of artistic expression, associating the imagery of a painter or a musician with the ancient humors, the sanguine temperament being manifested in the creative artist.[60]

Some art historians rely on the theory of representation as an explanation, discarding classical references and presenting the visual tastes of the time. In this case, Leyster's portrayal of the comic fiddler is a commentary on the possible variations of genre themes, in particular, merry company.[61] Still other scholars emphasize the self-referential theory in which Leyster reuses an image from a painting that has brought her fame and success. It is, in fact, common for painters to quote and repeat motifs they find aesthetically and compositionally pleasing and that comment on their artistic quest.[62] As one Dutch proverb declares, advising the artist on how to add a moral overtone in his or her paintings, *Hoe schilder, hoe wilder* ('The more a painter he becomes, the wilder he is').[63]

Perhaps the emblematic tradition might also assist in interpreting this painting. A key to understanding may be found in Emblem D of Diego Saavedra's *Christelke Saets-vorts*, a popular emblem book first published in Spain in 1640 and in Amsterdam in 1663 (Fig. V.11).[64] An emblem is composed of three parts. One is a caption (or *motto*), as seen in the inscription *Ad Omnia* ('To All Things'). Another part is an image (or *pictura*), as here in the image of an empty canvas on an easel and the hand appearing from the clouds holding a palette and brushes, the attributes of the painter. The third part of an emblem is the description (or *subscriptio*), which explains the meaning of the image and caption. In this case, the written description states, 'like a painter's canvas on which nothing is sketched, the painter can picture anything he likes', alluding to freedom of representation as well as the artist's moral responsibility to society and other young art students for what is portrayed. There are many questions to ponder. Is Leyster's *Self-Portrait* intended to educate the public in the arts? After all, she has stopped painting and has turned to the viewer. Are the viewers supposed to find a moral implication in the two images, the portrait (self-portrait) and the genre scene (merrymaking)? Is this a didactic painting? All these theories may be valid and complement one another as well as helping to explain the painter, the

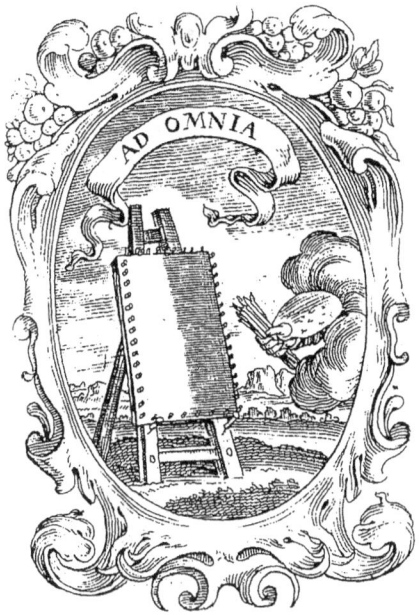

V.11   Diego Saavedra, emblem *On Painting*, 1663, in *Christelyke Saets-vorts*

painting and the painted images. But they also leave the viewer in suspense, since no solution is given to the puzzle.

England, too, produced outstanding female painters during this period, in particular, Mary Craddock Beale (1632–99), who practised religious art and portraiture. She was trained by her father, a clergyman who was an amateur artist. Beale's artistic training is poorly documented, but she likely was also trained by Thomas Flatman, Robert Walker and Thomas Cromwell, and tutored by Sir Peter Lely, who allowed her to copy his large art collection, which included portraits by Anthony van Dyck.[65] Beale established a precedent for other female painters of note in England, by making her living from her art and training painters, including Sarah Curates, in her studio. She provided an intellectual environment in her house in Covent Garden for churchmen, artists and literati, such as Tillotson.[66] In 1651, she married Charles Beale, an obscure painter who took on the domestic role of managing the household, assisting her in the atelier with grinding color pigments, priming canvas and handling commercial accounts and notebooks, while she became the breadwinner. His meticulous notebooks describing his household activities provide great insight into the marital position of painters in England, as well as recording the praise given to his wife's works.[67] The couple had two children, one of whom, Charles Beale, also became a miniaturist portrait-painter, and assisted his mother with her practice. To escape the Great Plague, the family left London in 1665, returning in 1670, where Beale's commissions increased significantly. She painted in various media, including pastels, watercolor and oils, and her works were engraved by contemporary artists.

Beale's *Self-Portrait* of 1666 (Fig. V.12) uses a richly colored and freely

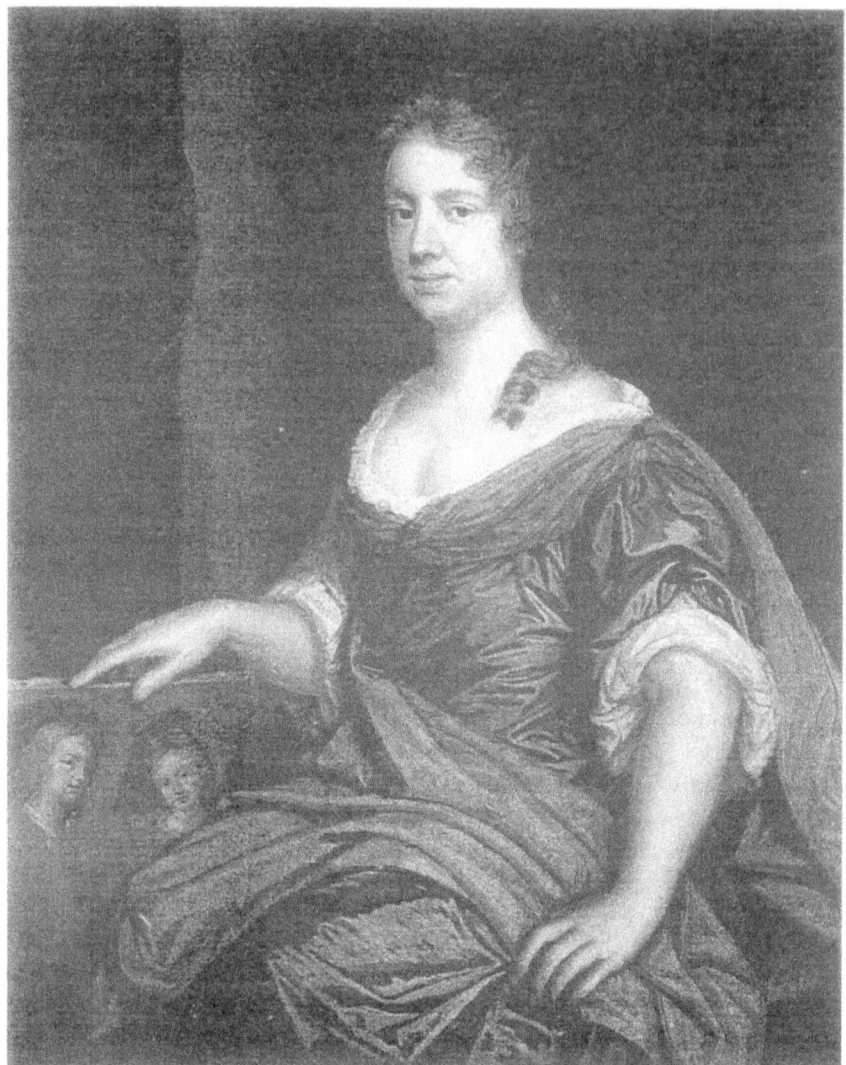

V.12   Mary Beale, *Self-Portrait*, 1666

painted treatment of drapery that displays a strong mastery of her art. It is believed that she learned this technique from Robert Walker, a friend of her clergyman father and the official painter to Oliver Cromwell. The *Self-Portrait* represents the artist in her studio. In the background, her palette hangs on the wall, while in the foreground she is seated comfortably in a chair, dressed in the fashion of the time but with great simplicity, devoid of any embellishment or ornamentation. The composition recalls the portraits of Sir Peter Lely and shows the confidence that Beale had gained from her training, which she passed on to her two sons, who are sketched on an unfinished canvas. Beale painted a portrait of her husband (now in the Manor House Museum in Bury

St Edmunds, Suffolk) as a companion piece to this *Self-Portrait*, to make a family grouping recalling the works of the Flemish Catherina van Hemessen.

These works by Beale are painted essentially in a Flemish Baroque style, one that was to be adapted to the more graceful Rococo by many early eighteenth-century British artists. Although Beale had a brilliant career and was famous in her lifetime, she presents to the viewer her most precious creation, her children, while her palette, the instrument of her fame, hangs obscurely on a wall. The motif of portraying a self-portrait with family members, in particular children, will be a theme elaborated in the eighteenth century by painters such as Elisabeth Vigée-Lebrun as an expression of motherhood, domesticity and joy in living.

Mary Beale established a precedent in supporting herself and her family with her art, anticipating the professionalism of female painters that was to emerge in the eighteenth century. Throughout her career, she painted several self-portraits, experimenting with various techniques and media. These works included the decorative and elegant *Self-Portrait* of 1675–80 (Manor House Museum, Bury St Edmunds, Suffolk) in oils, a classical composition in which she portrays herself as Venus surrounded with the attributes of love: a Cupid, a flaming torch and an urn.

Charles Beale's well-documented record of his wife's work mentions many other self-portraits by his 'Dearest Heart'.[68] A small oil on canvas of 1675 (private collection, London) shows her seated with palette and brushes in hand, and again was painted as a companion piece to a dashing portrait of her husband. A later *Self-Portrait* of 1681 (private collection, London) was painted in oils on bed ticking. Here she wears a loosely draped satin gown and, in true English fashion, pets her small dog. A *Self-Portrait* miniature in watercolor on vellum of 1679 (private collection, London) is also attributed to Beale, although this work may have been painted by her son Charles after one of her self-portraits.

Beale's distinguished career was undoubtedly strongly encouraged by her family. Her father, John Craddock, fully supported his eldest daughter's art education, and her husband and sons, although all artists, tended to the chores of the household while Mary painted from 'dawn until dusk'. Notable aristocrats, including Lord Cavendish and the Earl of Berkeley, flocked to have their likeness captured by 'The Excellent Mrs. Beale'. She, like Sirani, was among the earliest female artists to have women students, opening the way for the many female painters who would have embraced the role of teacher and mentor by the end of the eighteenth century.

As has been shown, the self-portraits of this period typically combine stylistic and psychological illusionism. Physical illusionism was provoked by new technological development of lenses as well as by physical studies on light effects. The psychological confidence or illusion of the self was created meanwhile by the evolving status of the artist, and the painter's role as no longer a mere decorator or artisan. This social evolution did much to assist female painters in being recognized as competitors, providers and teachers.

The eighteenth century: transition, travel and international recognition

Female self-portraits from the eighteenth century demonstrate a tremendous diversity in style, technique and representation. In this period women continued to show themselves as professional painters, allegorical figures and 'learned ladies'. Their new roles, however, included those of teacher, mentor and, most importantly, stylistic and technical innovator. They may show themselves as either beautiful or plain, while demonstrating a new confidence in their roles, not only as successful teachers, but even as mothers, a function they formerly referred to but did not emphasize, perhaps for fear of not being taken seriously as working professionals. Their self-portraits may reflect prosperity or personal pain, which included, for some, blindness, exile, even future suicide. Most of all, their self-portraits show a growing legion of professionally trained, talented and diligent women, fighting to claim their rights as academy members and medal-winners sought out by the wealthiest and most discerning patrons of their age.

The eighteenth century embraced the Age of the Enlightenment, a period characterized by philosophical inquiry and religious skepticism, and which valued gallant entertainments, verbal repartee, charm and wit. Its emergence coincided in France with the death in 1715 of the absolute monarch Louis XIV and the rule of his nephew Philippe, Duke of Orléans, who served as Regent for Louis XV, who was four years old when his great-grandfather died. This Regency period (1715–23) set the tone for an era of moral liberty – some might say debauchery – that was certainly urbane and sophisticated. It ultimately became international in scope and dominated by courtly aristocrats, and by the haute bourgeoisie who emulated them in cities from London to Vienna, from St Petersburg to Naples.

Literature, music and the arts were given much attention. The writings of Richardson in England and Voltaire in France championed the rights of the individual within the framework of a free and open society; this included a number of 'ladies of letters' on the model of the seventeenth-century Madame de Sévigné. Lady Mary Wortley Montagu and Madame de Staël were among many fashionable female authors to gain recognition and even fame.

In terms of art, the first half of the eighteenth century was dominated by the Rococo style, called then the *style moderne*, a reaction to the more serious, dramatic and monumental Baroque period that had preceded it. The Rococo emphasized gracefulness, freedom, gaiety and, most importantly, light – not the strong, serious chiaroscuro lighting of the Baroque age, but a soft, overall lighting, often using pastel colors. This style reflected the prevailing aristocratic spirit of the age, for the ruling classes one in which marriages were arranged, taking lovers was a normal convention, courtship was a game and the greatest fault one could possess was lack of wit, intelligence or taste. Taste being ephemeral, by the mid-century there was a strong reaction to a style that by then had become regarded as decadent, frivolous and shallow. The term 'Rococo' itself was not coined until the Neo-classical style had quite firmly supplanted it in the latter part of the century. It was initially used in a derogatory sense, referring to decorative shell and rockwork (*rocaille*) as a symbol of its over-embellishment as perceived by Neo-classicists such as Jacques-Louis David and his followers. This century also encompassed the early Romantic period, and was pre-eminently the 'age of the portrait'.

One of the most dramatic aspects of the age of Rococo was the leadership role played in some areas of life by women. Two of the most powerful rulers in Europe during the later phases of this period were Catherine the Great of Russia and Maria Theresa of Austria. Powerful consorts, such as Madame de Pompadour, mistress of Louis XV, and Louis XVI's queen, Marie Antoinette, also played strong roles in politics and as patrons of the arts.

In intellectual circles women likewise dominated, as *salonnières*, hostesses at the *salons* they held in their elegant houses. Here the brightest and most talented writers, artists and intellects of the age met to exchange ideas and gossip. Although these gatherings were primarily attended by men, it was the *salonnière* who orchestrated the affairs and often invited select women to participate in lively dialogues and debates. Notable *salonnières* such as Mesdames de Tencin, Geoffrin and du Deffand and Mlle de Lespinasse presided over evenings where the essential aim was an entertaining exchange of ideas. Few topics were off limits and sarcasm was rampant, but it was imperative that those in attendance behave in accordance with the manners of the time. Above all, a participant must not be boring or lacking in style.

It is not surprising that in this stylish atmosphere of enlightened inquiry, involving both men and women, more women would pursue their own professional careers than had previously been seen. This is especially true in the fine arts. The eighteenth century was accordingly the great transitional period for women artists.

The turn-of-the-century Parisian artist Elisabeth Sophie Chéron (1648–1711) paved the way for other talented women of the period. She gained recognition as a portrait painter, but was also one of the few women painters in history to be known specifically for self-portraiture: it was a *Self-*

Portrait that served as her reception piece (*morceau de réception*) to the French Royal Academy in 1672. Chéron was the seventh female member admitted to that august body since its foundation in 1648, and one of only 15 female members in any age. Not unusually, she came from a family of artists. Her father, Henri Chéron, and her younger brother Louis were both painters, as was her sister Marie Anne, who married the well-known portraitist Alexis Simon Belle. As with the majority of her illustrious female predecessors, Chéron thus received her formal training in the family atelier.

Chéron's recommendation for Royal Academy membership came from its powerful first director, Charles Lebrun. Through his position, Lebrun exercised a profound and lasting effect on the arts during the late years of Louis XIV's rule – a period when Paris served as the cultural center of Europe and art patronage was dominated by the court. Chéron catered to this milieu not only by executing numerous portraits of the French aristocracy, but also by producing self-portraits that cast her in the role of muse and inspiration to the society of her time.

It is known that Chéron's self-portraits were numerous, although specific figures are unavailable. The diversity of her approach seen in those currently identified, however, demonstrates that she did not subscribe to a standard formula in representing herself. Her best-known work (Fig. VI.1) shows a compositional approach within its oval frame foreshadowing Ingres's famous *Madame Rivière* painted two centuries later, but displaying Mannerist tendencies. Her left arm is placed in a softly curved position echoing the line of the frame, while her right arm, resting on a parapet, also conforms to the ellipse of the picture plane. The resulting pose is justified by the inclusion of a parchment held in both hands, possibly a reference to Chéron's talents as a poet and engraver, as well as in painting. Her head is tilted gently to the right, and she displays an enigmatic *Mona Lisa*-type smile. The chiaroscuro lighting, the elaborate treatment of the drapery folds and the fluid compositional approach of this self-portrait conform to the prevailing trends of the transitional period from late Baroque to early Rococo. They especially evoke the style of her well-known contemporary François de Troy, as may be seen by comparing this work with his portrait of the Duchesse de la Force (1714, Rouen). A *Self-Portrait* by de Troy (1704, Musée Garinet, Châlons-sur-Marne), however, shows a very different approach. In a manner reflected in other male self-portraits from this period and later, de Troy emphasizes his role as an artist in a very physical way. Not only does he hold an array of brushes and a palette firmly in his left hand, with a maulstick in his right, but he stresses the physicality of art production by his disheveled attire and bold forward-leaning stance against the parapet in front of him. In what was to become a customary contrast of approach between male and female self-portraits of the eighteenth century, Chéron emphasizes her beauty, grace and array of cultural accomplishments, while de Troy focuses on the strength and stamina required of the artist. These qualities were of course required as much, if not more so, in women. But female artists chose not to emphasize this aspect of their profession, in an effort, perhaps, to conform to the more

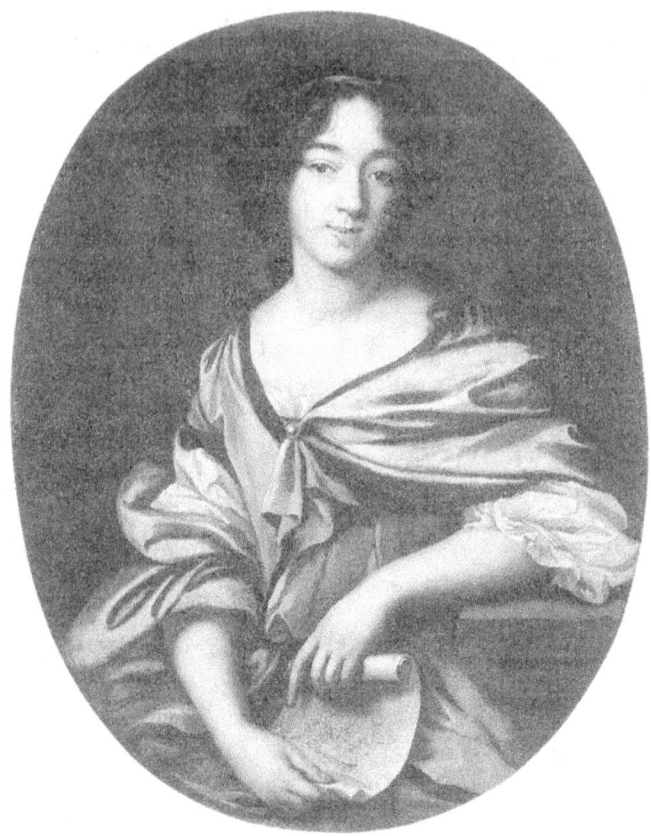

VI.1   Elisabeth Sophie Chéron, *Self-Portrait*, 1672

traditional role of women at the time, since it was one that they dramatically defied by the mere fact of their professional activity. This illusion of effortlessness is reflected in the lines of Chéron's contemporary de Vertron, who wrote of her that 'without effort she would make that [the paint brush] of Apelles tremble'.[1]

Chéron takes a much more realistic and straightforward approach in another *Self-Portrait* (n.d., Musée Magnin, Dijon). Although Germaine Greer suggests that this may be an earlier work than the one just discussed, Chéron's physical features indicate otherwise.[2] In the Dijon *Self-Portrait*, she has dark circles under her eyes and a slight softening of the chin. She also appears fuller figured and much more conservatively dressed. Historically, artists, both male and female, become more willing to abandon vanity as they mature, as we have already seen in the serial self-portraits of Anguissola (see Chapter IV). Chéron again does not include symbolic references to her role as a painter; instead she dramatically holds up a sheet of music indicating her accomplishments in that art. To her contemporaries, Chéron was Erato, the muse of poetry, as well as a talented artist. The Abbé Basquillon said of her that 'nothing save the grace of her brush could equal the excellencies of her pen'.[3] In 1706 Chéron published her own *Livres de dessin…* which included 36 engravings after heads by Raphael.

Why would so many patrons want Chéron's self-portraits, a demand only partially satisfied by engravings after her works? Clearly, the novelty of such a multi-talented and beautiful woman was intriguing. She was also an independent spirit, a fact supported by her decision not to marry until the age of 44, when she became the wife of the King's engineer, Jacques Le Hay. Thus, Chéron was sought after not only as a novelty but, with a number of other women artists, as a commodity to be actually bought and owned, as well as admired. This admiration is reflected in the fact that she was one of the first French painters about whom a monograph was written. This *Eloge funèbre de Madame Le Hay*, by M. Fermelhuis, was published in 1712, the year after her death.[4]

The element of novelty waned as more women established themselves professionally. In fact, the success of artists such as Chéron eventually led to resentment and fear among the male members of many of the academies; in 1706, the French Royal Academy even voted to ban women members altogether. This decision was subsequently modified to allow up to four female members, but it still resulted in the exclusion of many very talented women from one of the most prestigious and influential art organizations of the time.

All rules were abandoned, however, for the recognition of the Venetian artist Rosalba Carriera (1675–1757). Carriera was named the first foreign female member of the French Royal Academy, an honor she received during her stay in Paris in 1720–21. She had been invited to Paris by the wealthy banker Pierre Crozat, with whom she stayed during her visit. Through him, she met the leading French artists of the time, most significantly Antoine Watteau. She was also introduced to important patrons and theorists, including P. J. Mariette, who was to become her lifelong friend.

Crozat was only one of many wealthy and important patrons that Carriera met when they visited her home city. In the eighteenth century Venice was an important site on any traveler's 'grand tour', not only because of its physical beauty and its importance as a leading Italian art center, but because of its notorious entertainments. The Venetian Carnival, which lasted up to six months every year, was a major attraction. Other activities included gambling, prize fights, parades, masquerades, a government lottery and legal prostitution. This festive and decadent atmosphere attracted visitors from throughout the world, many of whom found their way to the commodious house and studio of Carriera on the Grand Canal.

Carriera catered to her sophisticated public by developing an elegant, fresh and spontaneous style in pastels, a medium in which the color pigments are molded into a stick or crayon. She was the first to popularize pastels for finished paintings rather than just for studies or copies. Her innovative technique gained her great fame, and patrons flocked to have their portraits executed or to commission what she called her 'fancy' pieces, often allegorical works featuring a seductive female figure. Her patrons included Maximilian II of Bavaria, Frederick IV, King of Norway and Denmark, and the English parliamentarian and wit Horace Walpole. Her most zealous patron was Augustus III of Saxony and Poland, which was to result in Dresden holding over 150 of her works.

In contrast to the fresh and flattering portraits Carriera did of others, her self-portraits reflect the image of a strong, plain woman and are the most psychologically probing of her works. The Empress Elizabeth of Austria cattily called her ugly, and she certainly lacked the stylish beauty represented later in the century in self-portraits by Elisabeth Vigée-Lebrun and Angelica Kauffmann. Carriera's sociable personality and diligence, however, were highly regarded and in her self-portraits these traits are well reflected.

One of the earliest of these was a miniature in tempera on ivory (1698, private collection, Venice), painted when Carriera was 23 years old. There is no doubt that this miniature is a self-portrait, because she signed the work 'Rosalba Carriera/The Paintress/by herself'; she also included the number 98, undoubtedly a reference to the date.[5] Her satisfaction with this self-image is supported by the fact that she did others, including one now in the collection of the Duke of Portland. Although youthful and fastidiously dressed, she already displays the unflinching inability to flatter herself that would characterize at least eight other self-portraits. In this particular work Carriera, although she holds three paint brushes in her right hand, looks unready for work. It is characteristic that she painted this in miniature for she was recognized as an innovator in small-scale techniques, and it was due to the free and expressive style of such tempera-on-ivory miniature paintings that she first gained recognition. It was the approach she developed in this medium that contributed to her stylistic technique in pastels.

Most of Carriera's self-portraits were executed in the medium of pastel, notably her *Self-Portrait Holding a Portrait of Her Sister* of 1708 (Fig. VI.2), commissioned for the Medici Portrait Gallery of the Uffizi when she was 33 years old. Here she has taken a very controlled, almost realistic approach, in contrast to the impressionistic style typical of many of her pastels. Characteristically of Carriera's work, the color is rich, and she has given special attention to the treatment of lace. (Her mother was a lacemaker, and Carriera's career began by making pattern designs.) She displays considerable control over the chalks, having developed the technique of dragging the flat edge over another surface color. As with her earlier self-portrait, *Self-Portrait Holding a Portrait of Her Sister* shows a fashionable, albeit plain woman. Her pleasant but guileless countenance reflects the written description she left of her temperament in a brief autobiographical note: 'I am not an enemy of pleasure; but I think that one has to enjoy these pleasures with much sobriety and moderation.'[6] Viallet, who has discussed at length all of the female self-portraits in the Uffizi, calls this one of the best.[7]

In her right hand in this portrait Carriera is holding, a *porte-crayon* which she is using to execute the portrait of her sister Giovanna. Rosalba Carriera was very close to both of her sisters, who were also her students. Angela, her

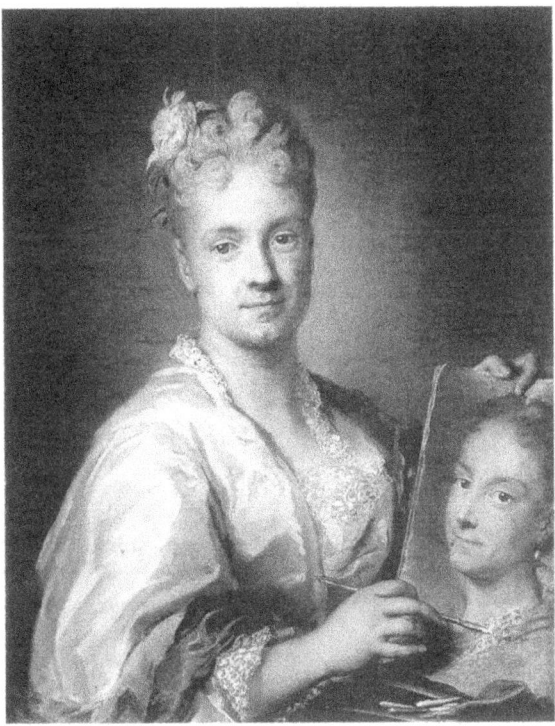

VI.2   Rosalba Carriera, *Self-Portrait Holding a Portrait of Her Sister*, 1708

other sister, married the painter Pellegrini, but Giovanna, like Rosalba, never married. The two lived with their mother in Rosalba's house, where Giovanna served as the assistant to her illustrious sister. Like Anguissola's before her, Carriera's sisters played a strong role in her life and work.

Another *Self-Portrait* by Carriera, indicating a similar age to the Uffizi portrait but with a more reflective facial expression, is found in the Accademia dei Concordia, Rovigno. Malami suggests that this is a portrait of Giovanna, but the facial features are exactly those of Rosalba. Here she is more simply dressed but wears what appears to be a tiara and pearl drop earrings.[8]

A strong and very freely painted *Self-Portrait as Winter* (Pl. XVIII) was executed by Carriera for the Empress of Austria. In keeping with the theme of this work, she wears a velvet tasseled hat, trimmed with fur surrounding the face and echoed in the fur trim of the collar. The artist is recognizable by her familiar features: large round eyes, bulbous nose, thin smiling lips, full jaw and deep dimple in the chin. This work was one of a series depicting the seasons of the year, which was a popular theme with Carriera. Her allegories were often more risqué, sometimes showing youthful beauties exposing their breasts, as seen in her allegory of *Winter* in the Hermitage. She has chosen a more serious and demure approach, however, when using herself as the model.

VI.3   Rosalba Carriera, *Self-Portrait as Tragedy*, 1746

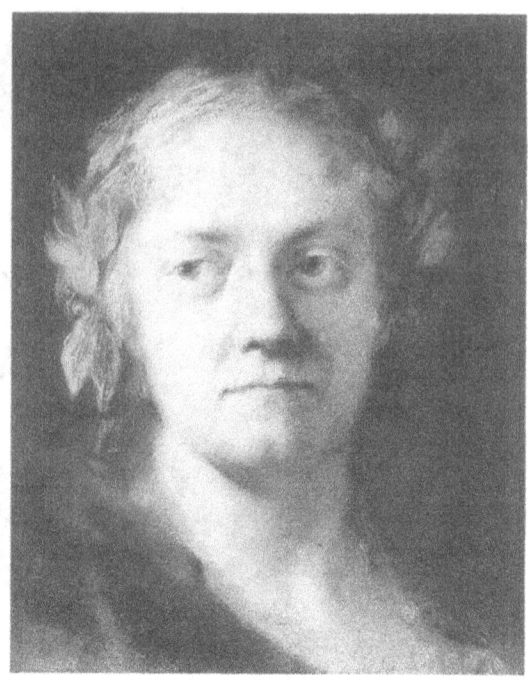

Although Carriera noted that 'no one loves cheerfulness as I do', her self-portraits, particularly her later ones, belie this statement.⁹ She suffered episodes of depression for most of her life, and was particularly plagued by them after the death of her sister Giovanna.

A melancholic spirit pervades the *Self-Portrait* (1744–6, Windsor Castle) painted for one of Carriera's most loyal patrons, her good friend Joseph Smith, the British Consul in Venice. Smith helped to secure many British patrons for Carriera and collected a number of her works, including this *Self-Portrait*, which was purchased by George III in 1762. The confident and mature technique displayed in this pastel shows that she had truly mastered her craft. Her face and physique look much the same as in her earlier works, even though she was now approaching 70. She credited her long life to eating well, walking often and, as already said, pleasure in moderation. The benefits of this are apparent in this *Self-Portrait*.

Approximately two years later Carriera would paint probably her last and most haunting self-portrait (Fig. VI.3), showing her as an allegory of tragedy, as indicated by the laurel wreath in her hair. By this time, cataract problems were seriously impairing her vision. Although she later underwent risky operations to restore her eyesight, she was completely blind for about the last seven years of her life. It is fitting, therefore, that one of her final self-portraits would be symbolic of tragedy. She gave this work to her student and good friend, Felicità Sartori, who accepted a position as painter to Augustus III in Dresden, where she painted self-portraits herself (two were located in the Gemäldegalerie, Dresden, but were destroyed during World War II). Sartori

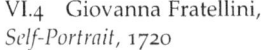

VI.4   Giovanna Fratellini,
Self-Portrait, 1720

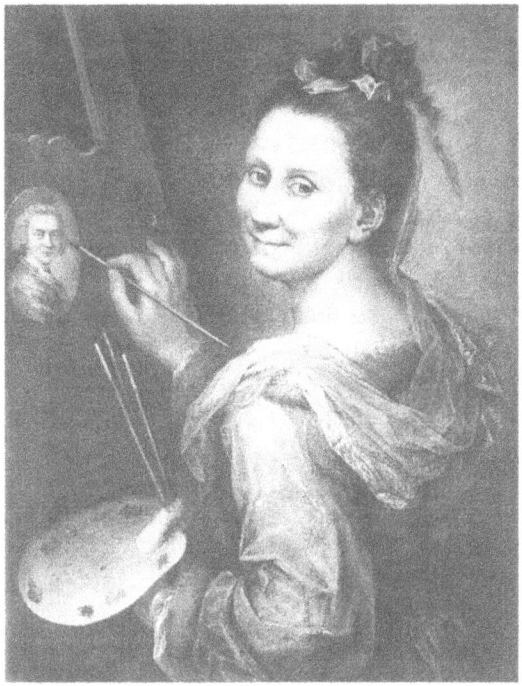

married a courtier named Hoffmann and continued her friendship with
Carriera until her teacher's death in 1757.

Rosalba Carriera was an innovator of the light, graceful Rococo style. Her
bold, fluid use of the pastel medium and her depictions of seductive nymphs
and idealized patrons gained her accolades from all over Europe. She had
more commissions than she could execute and earned a sizable fortune
during her lifetime, which she left to her widowed sister Angela. Carriera's
works have been seen as the embodiment of the early Enlightenment period
– free, fresh, spontaneous and infinitely civilized. She influenced a whole
generation of painters, including the pastelists Quentin de la Tour, Perroneau
and Liotard, other artists whose works are seen as reflecting the spirit of an
age of artifice. Yet her self-portraits, as has been demonstrated, are almost
brutally candid; Michael Levey calls them 'savage'.[10] They are psychologically
penetrating documents of the loneliness, pain, isolation and diligence behind
the sophisticated façade of one of the most celebrated women of the Rococo
age.[11]

Carriera also exerted a profound influence on other Italian women artists.
Her contemporary and chief rival in the pastel medium in Italy was the
Florentine Giovanna Fratellini (1666–1731), 'the Tuscan Rosalba'. Like
Carriera, Fratellini contributed a *Self-Portrait* (Fig. VI.4) to the Medici Portrait
Gallery of the Uffizi. In this work, she is shown actively involved in painting
a miniature portrait of her son Lorenzo, whom she taught to paint, but
who tragically died nine years after this work was executed. The artist seems
not to interrupt her work, while she turns over her shoulder to look at

the viewer. Fratellini appears confident and at ease at her easel, as would befit her recognition as the most celebrated pastelist in Florence after her teacher Domenico Tempesti.[12]

Fortunately, a number of other talented Italian women contributed self-portraits to the Uffizi Gallery during the eighteenth century, otherwise their identities might be lost. They included Lucia Casalini Torelli (1677–1762), Giulia Lama (1681–1747), Violante Beatrice Siries (1710–83), Maria Maddalena Gozzi Baldacci (1718–82), Anna Bacherini Piattoli (1720–88), Chiara Spinelli di Belmonte (1744–1823), Anna Irene Duclos Parenti (b.1754), and Teresa Arizzara (dates unknown).[13] Of this group, Lama and Piattoli are the two most interesting.

Giulia Lama was better known as a philosopher and poet, although she was a pupil of Piazzetta and executed a number of religious paintings for Venetian churches. The pose of her *Self-Portrait* (1725, Uffizi, Florence) is almost identical to that by Torelli painted five years before, but Lama dons a much less elaborate attire and addresses the viewer in a seemingly mocking tone. Greer has quoted the Abbé Conti as saying, 'It is true she is as ugly as she is intelligent, but she speaks with grace and polish, so that one easily pardons her face.'[14] Lama's casual attire and intelligent look render her more modern-looking to our eyes than her contemporaries and perhaps a little better-looking today than she was then perceived to be. Her contemporaries, nonetheless, were very admiring and respectful of Lama, who was the daughter of a mathematician, and in addition to her other talents was a mathematician and scientist herself. It is no wonder that Lama captured in her self-portrait a look of what Moretti calls 'ironic superiority'.[15] Certainly she was an enlightened individual even in this age of enlightenment. She appears to have been an introspective loner, who did not marry and who was often described as living in 'retirement', presumably to commit herself to her many artistic and intellectual interests.[16] These included the daring act of drawing both male and female figures from the nude, making her one of the first women, along with Artemisia Gentileschi, to do so.

Piattoli's self-portraits include a youthful likeness holding palette and brushes (1744), and a pastel where she is embraced by her husband Gaetano (1745–50), donated to the Uffizi in 1941 by Tammero de Marious. The best-known of these is a mature work where she is shown executing a copy in miniature of Andrea del Sarto's *Madonna del Sacco* (1720, Uffizi, Florence). An inscription on the back reads 'Anna Bacherini Piattoli born 1720, aged 56 years'.[17] Although she studied under Violante Siries, her style is more articulate in its detailing and her colors are rich and warm. This work was painted during a difficult time for her, hinted at in her demeanor, since she was recently widowed and experiencing financial problems.

Italy, in the eighteenth century, was not a nation-state, as was France, but was divided into a number of independent territories. Some were duchies, or ruled by the church. A large area of Italy, including the kingdom of Naples and Sicily, was controlled for a time by the Austrian Hapsburgs.

The Hapsburgs, with their capital at Vienna, also served as titular leaders of most of central Europe, by virtue of their election as Holy Roman Emperors or Empresses. The Empire encompassed not only the unified country of Austria, but also a broad array of small territories ruled by representatives, or 'Electors' to the Imperial court. These territories, or electorates, included Bavaria, whose capital was Munich, and Brandenburg, with its center at Berlin. Brandenburg eventually became part of the north German Kingdom of Prussia, one of the most powerful states of the age. Another electorate to take a position of leadership in the eighteenth century was Saxony, whose capital city of Dresden was called 'The Florence on the Elbe' as its rulers became leading art patrons.

It has already been recounted that Augustus III was a major patron of Rosalba Carriera and that her student, Felicità Sartori, who had served as his court painter, died in Dresden. Saxony, however, also produced its own meritorious female artists, including Theresa Concordia von Moron (1725–1806) and the Electress of Saxony, Maria Antonia di Walpurgis (1724–80).

Theresa von Moron, who studied under her father Ismael Mengs, was the sister of the famous early Neo-classicist Anton Raphael Mengs, with whom she traveled to Rome in 1752. She and her sister, Juliane, who later became a nun, both served as court painters to the Elector of Saxony. For Augustus III, Theresa painted copies in miniature of the work of famous artists such as Correggio and received an annual court pension of 300 thalers. She also painted portraits, including a *Self-Portrait* (Fig. VI.5) in pastel which is still in Dresden. This strong and confident work shows the brown-eyed artist wearing a blue dress with a white ruffle and a red-banded cap. A companion to this piece in Dresden is an equally beautiful portrait of her sister. Theresa married Anton von Moron, who was also a painter, and became an important teacher to other women artists living and working in Rome, where she died in 1806.

Maria Antonia di Walpurgis contributed to the history of her times, both politically and culturally, to such a degree that she merited a two-volume monograph by D.C. von Weber, entitled *Maria Antonia di Walpurgis Kurfürstin von Sachesen* (Dresden, 1857); her letters to the Empress Maria Theresa of Austria have also been published (Leipzig, 1908). Walpurgis received attention not only by virtue of her birth and marriage, but also on account of her talents in music, poetry, art, and politics. She was born in Monaco in 1724, the daughter of the Emperor Charles VII and his wife Maria Amalia. She is occasionally referred to as the Electrice of Bavaria but more often as the Electrice of Saxony, following her marriage to the Saxon Prince Frederick Christian in 1747. She became a welcome and witty addition to the Dresden court, but she also traveled widely and was named a member of a number of academies, including the Accademia di San Luca in Rome.

Walpurgis was invited by the Grand Duchess of Tuscany to contribute a self-portrait to the Uffizi, which she did in 1773. This painting emphasizes her role as artist rather than aristocrat, although she does wear a small crown on her head. She also holds a palette and brushes in her hands and regards the

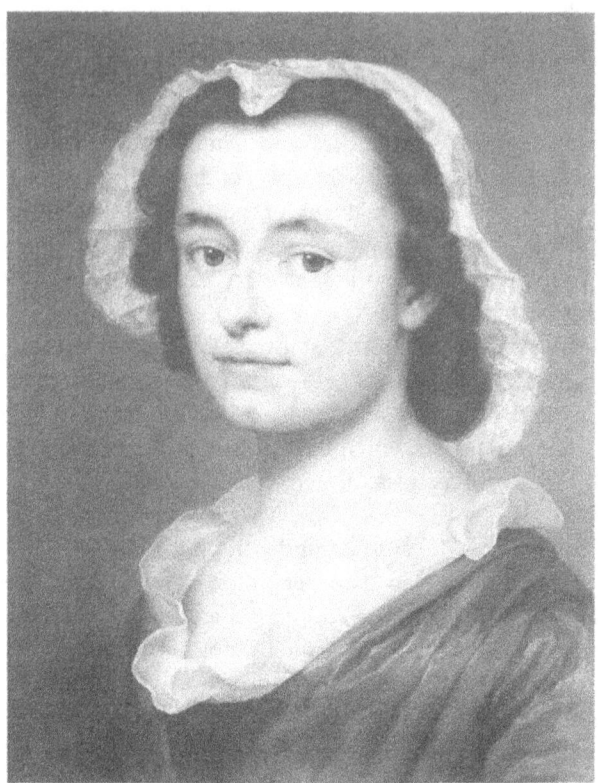

VI.5   Theresa Mengs von Moron, *Self-Portrait*, *c.*1750

viewer with a direct gaze. The regal bearing and undeniable self-assuredness of Walpurgis, however, underscores her aristocratic background. In this painting she wears the type of ruffled dress popular throughout the Rococo period, even though she was a strong supporter of Theresa von Moron's brother, Anton Raphael Mengs, and early Neo-classicism.

Frederick the Great of Prussia created a culturally rich environment at the Prussian court, which included the patronage of women artists. One of the best-known female artists to work for him was the Berlin-born Anna Dorothea Therbusch-Liszewska (1722–82). She executed a portrait of Frederick in 1772, as well as carrying out a number of mythological commissions for him. By the time she appeared at the Prussian court, she had already had an array of noble patrons, including the Duke of Wurttemberg in Stuttgart, for whom she decorated a Hall of Mirrors, and the Elector of Mannheim. She also spent time in Paris where she was made a member of the French Royal Academy, in 1767. Therbusch-Liszewska's success at the French capital was limited, however, due to her matronly, middle-aged appearance and, as Diderot claims, a lack of 'coquetterie'.

However, an absence of coquetry is not apparent in a relatively youthful *Self-Portrait* (n.d., Schloss Grünewald, Berlin) where the blonde-haired, green-

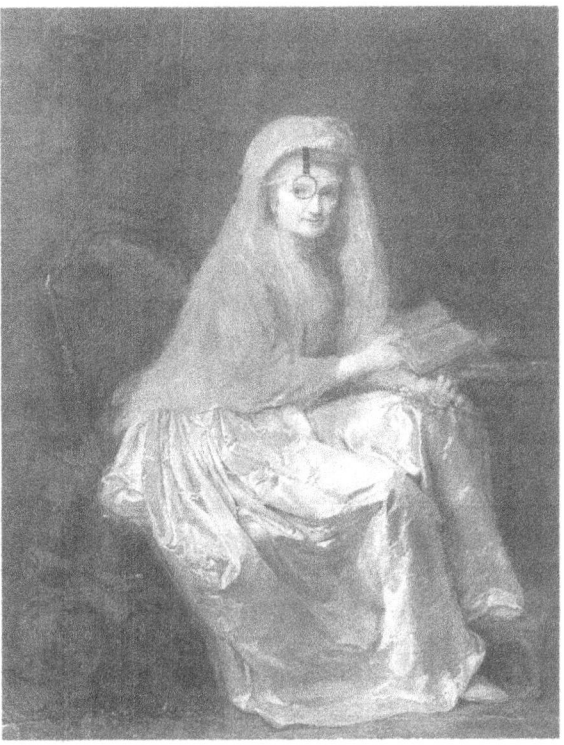

VI.6   Anna Dorothea Therbusch-Liszewska, *Self-Portrait*, 1779

eyed Anna Dorothea flashes a witty, wry look at someone to the viewer's left. Her crossed arms are adorned with green bows, while her palette and brushes sit to her left on the ledge in front of her. A hallmark of her personality was a strong, confident look, and it is duly captured here.

Diderot's comment, however, refers to the middle-aged Therbusch-Liszewska, who arrived in Paris accompanied by a man named Debrosses, believed to be a Prussian spy.[18] This story lends a note of intrigue to an artist who by contemporary accounts was very fearless and forthright. It is certainly a no-nonsense, strong-looking image of herself that is captured in an unfinished *Self-Portrait* of 1779 (Fig. VI.6) in Berlin painted as a pendant to one of her husband. Not only is she completely lacking in coquetry in the painting, but she even wears a monocle. While she was not the first artist to produce a self-portrait wearing spectacles – Chardin had executed some just before she did – it was very unusual for a woman artist to show herself in such an unglamorous way, but it seems that originality and boldness were typical of Therbusch-Liszewska. Marigny commented on her singular ability amongst her sex to paint history and the nude like a man and she was admitted to the Salon of 1767 with a painting of Jupiter and Antiope that was deemed indecent by Cochin and his friends. Diderot, who had supported her admittance, then offered a scathing criticism of the work in his Salon review, calling her again and again the 'L'indigne Prussienne'.[19] This 'unworthy' Prussian ended her Parisian stay pursued by debtors and blaming Diderot for her lack of success. She fled to the Netherlands before returning to Berlin where she died in 1782. Therbusch-Liszewska had a sister named Anna Rosina (1716–83), who also painted a *Self-Portrait* (1782, Provincial Museum, Hanover).

One of the most important female portrait-painters of the eighteenth century was the Scottish-born Catharine Read (1723–78). She was one of the few women artists discussed at length by Horace Walpole when, according to him, he 'scribbled' his *Anecdotes of Painting in England; 1760–1795*. Walpole called her a 'scholar of Rosalba', listing her with the 'Principal Artists' of the period,[20] and she was called by many the 'English Rosalba'.

Read illustrates that Carriera's pastels had a profound impact on British art as well as on the continent, although she was introduced herself to the medium in Paris where she studied with Maurice Quentin de la Tour. She also trained in Rome, where she studied oil painting with Louis Blanchet. Thus, she was well schooled by the time she established her career in London, where she was particularly sought after by fashionable female aristocrats, whom she usually portrayed with Rococo charm and grace, often holding an attribute of their talents (musical instrument, book, or whatever). Her patrons, beautifully dressed in ruffles and lace, smile sweetly and pose prettily in a confidently painted manner that equates with portraits by male contemporaries such as Ramsey and Reynolds.

Read's contemporaries praised her talent. The Abbé Grant stressed that she might have excelled in history painting as well as portraiture had she been given the opportunity to attend life-drawing classes, which were still off limits to women.[21] They were disparaging, however, about her physical appearance. Fanny Burney called her 'most exceedingly ugly' and of a melancholic nature, although she did admit that Read was shrewd and clever. She also commented on her 'strange' manner of dress and inconsistency.[22] How does this contemporary opinion of her looks compare with her own perception of herself? Her *Self-Portrait* in oils (Fig. VI.7) indicates a strong, attractive, if somewhat agitated young woman. She is dressed, not exactly 'strangely,' but in a simple and somewhat disheveled manner. This self-portrait reflects the type of independent spirit that was to lead her to go to India, accompanied by her niece. According to Walpole, she died on her return trip at the Cape of Good Hope.[23]

The English Rococo style was imported rather late into the United States, via a number of American artists who traveled in England. One of these was Charles Willson Peale, whose large extended family of artists was greatly influenced by him. His niece, Sarah Peale (1800–1885), is considered by many to have been the first professional woman painter in America. Typical of American paintings of the eighteenth and early nineteenth centuries, Sarah Peale's works show a keen eye for detailed realism, and usually employ darker tones than those of her English counterparts. This may be found in a

VI.7 Catharine Read, *Self-Portrait*, n.d.

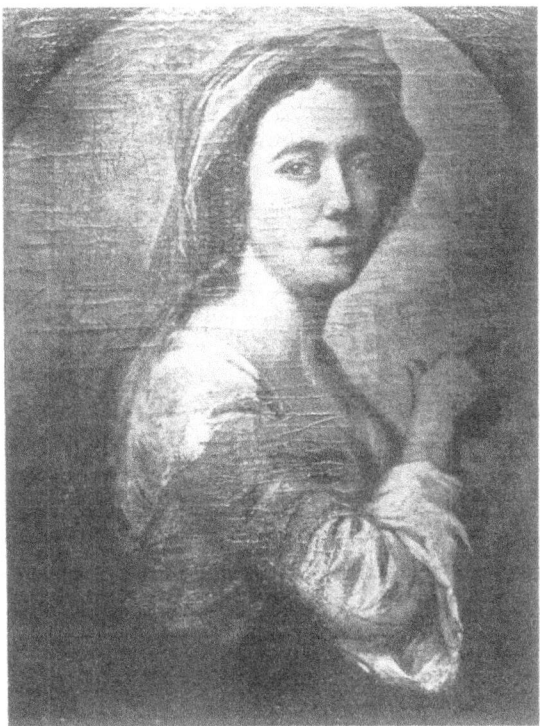

Self-Portrait (Pl. XIX) where one sees a charming, but practical, young woman. She portrays herself as she was described in a contemporary newspaper: as a ladylike, medium-sized brunette of self-dependence and firmness of character. Contemporaries also commented on the great accuracy with which Peale captured the likeness of individual sitters, so it is probable that her *Self-Portrait* is a very faithful rendition, although objectivity may certainly be compromised when artists are depicting themselves.

It is significant that this self-portrait is not a miniature since it was as a miniaturist that Peale's father James and other members of her immediate family were known. Sarah, however, pursued traditional portraiture on canvas at an early age and proceeded to obtain commissions from some of the best-known historical figures of the age. Her career began in Philadelphia where she was born and continued at the Peale Museum in Baltimore, founded by her cousin Rembrandt Peale, and fashioned after his father's museum in Philadelphia. By 1847 Sarah Peale was working in St Louis, where she settled for 30 years. In all of these locations, she supported herself by her art. Daniel Webster, Lafayette, John Tyler and an array of other statesmen posed for her during her long career. She was also known for her fruit and flower still-life paintings, but it was as a portraitist that this unmarried, independent woman became acclaimed.

More directly influenced by the English Rococo were the works of the Connecticut-born Ann Hall (1792–1863), whose portraits were often

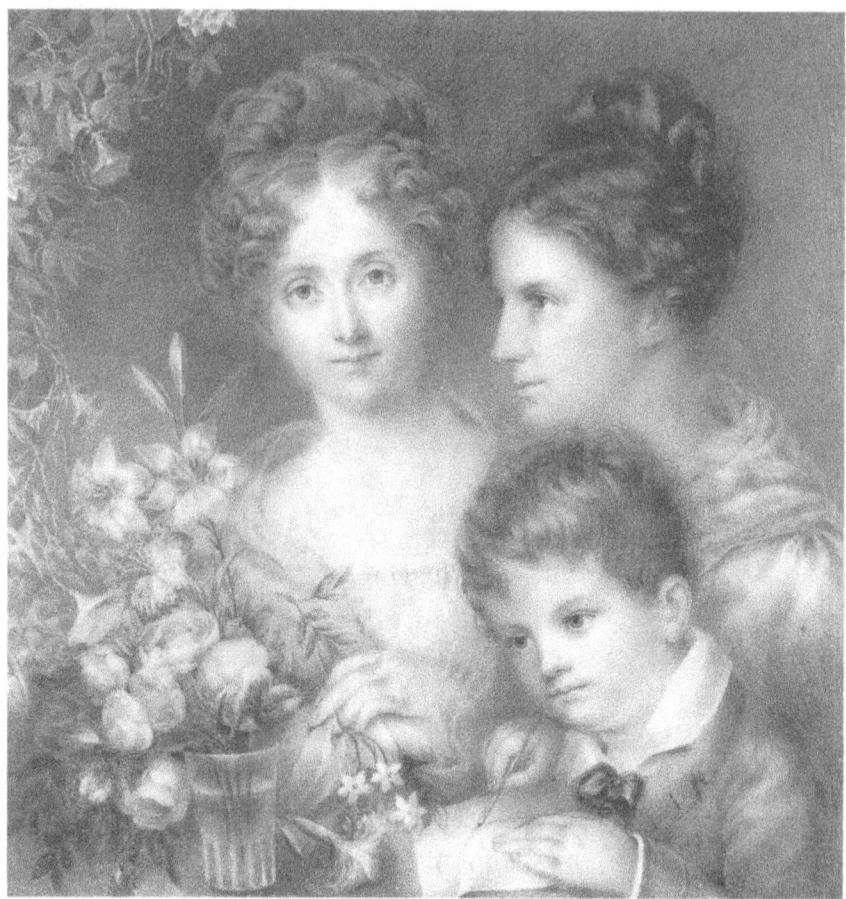

VI.8   Ann Hall, *Ann Hall, Mrs Henry Ward and Henry Hall Ward*, 1828, miniature on ivory

compared to those of Joshua Reynolds and Thomas Lawrence of the English Royal Academy. Hall specialized in miniature painting, as is reflected in a self-portrait she did under the title *Ann Hall, Mrs Henry Ward and Henry Hall Ward* (Fig. VI.8) where she shows a family grouping that includes her sister and young nephew. It is her nephew who is engaged in the art of drawing flowers, while Hall holds a small floral branch in her hand and her sister seemingly stares at an elaborate floral arrangement. The soft pastel colors and quiet intimacy of the figures are characteristic of the Rococo period in England, more than in America. She was, nonetheless, very popular with American patrons, and was formally recognized by her peers when she was made the first woman member of the National Academy of Design in New York in 1827.[24] By the time Hall was executing her Rococo-style miniature paintings in America, the style had long fallen from fashion in Europe.

Marguerite Gérard (1761–1837) was one of the best-known and most personally controversial women painters of the late eighteenth century. The controversy stems from the unusual living arrangements she enjoyed, beginning when she was about 14 years old, in the house of her older sister Marie-Anne and brother-in-law Jean-Honoré Fragonard. The unmarried Marguerite continued to live with them as long as they were alive. The close relationship that Marguerite had with Fragonard, both personally and professionally, led to rumors of a family *ménage à trois*. Whether there is any truth to these rumors remains arguable. On the one hand, Pierre Rosenberg suggests that letters written by Marguerite to her brother-in-law lend 'credence to the idea that she was once his mistress'.[25] Although Marguerite calls Fragonard her '*bon ami*' and '*petit Papa*', there is enough mention of love, friendship and unhappiness without him, for the letters to be at the very least provocative. On the other hand, Ann Sutherland Harris and Linda Nochlin point out that these letters were written when Gérard was over 40 and Fragonard over 70.[26] Their point, it is assumed, is that they were therefore too old for love and passion, a thesis that may be soundly challenged. Jeanne Doin denies that there was contemporary gossip regarding the three and indicates that Marie-Anne was a 'sensible woman'.[27]

Whatever her personal relationship with Fragonard, it is certain that Gérard was encouraged and influenced to become a painter once she joined the couple at their apartment in the Louvre. Works were soon being produced and engraved with the credit given to both Fragonard and Gérard. These included such themes as *The Dear Child* and *Baby's First Steps* – subjects which would characterize the later career of Gérard and were at odds with themes generally associated with Fragonard. Gérard's style and technique were also different than those of Fragonard. She developed a penchant for detailed surfaces and a controlled application of paint which was the opposite of his free, fluid style. In her choice of genre subjects and style she reflects the influence of Dutch painters to such an extent that her work is considered one of the earliest examples of the 'Metsu manner', referring to the Dutch genre painter Gabriel Metsu (1629–67). His paintings such as *A Visit to the Lying-in Chamber* (1661, Metropolitan Museum, New York) show a kinship in both theme and style with the later works of Gérard, such as the meticulously painted and sentimental *Bad News* (1804, Louvre, Paris).

Gérard brings this Dutch-inspired eye for detail to her ambitious *Self-Portrait Painting a Musician* (n.d., Hermitage, St Petersburg), a theme used by the Dutch artist Judith Leyster, as has already been shown. Gérard, however, depicts music as personified by a female rather than by Leyster's male. In Gérard's *Self-Portrait* the artist is at work on a large, precariously tilted canvas, while a model standing to the right of the picture is shown strumming on a guitar. The carefully depicted studio setting includes a small dog to the right of the model and flowers strewn carelessly on the floor. The two figures are fashionably dressed in satin gowns, the beautiful treatment of which is reminiscent of Gerard Terborch, a Dutch Baroque painter like Metsu, known for his attention to texture and drapery. Gérard depicts herself from behind, another hallmark of Terborch, with her head shown in profile, as she observes the model. A pretty brunette with regular features, Gérard was described by her contemporary, Madame Hippolyte Lecomte, as being as tall as her sister but 'possessed of an elegance and a presence besides, while in terms of distinction she was second to none'.[28] It is noteworthy that in a profile portrait of Gérard done by Fragonard (1785, Louvre, Paris), she is shown as having more dramatic features, including a very long nose and full lips. The end result, however, portrays a more striking and beautiful woman than Gérard captures in her own *Self-Portrait Painting a Musician*. Fragonard executed a profile drawing of Gérard at the same time as his own *Self-Portrait*, both of which are done in black chalk on a circular sheet of paper.

Another portrait drawing of Gérard has been identified by Sally Wells-Robertson as a *Self-Portrait* (n.d., Musée des Beaux-Arts, Besançon).[29] In this freely executed bistre wash over black charcoal work, the long nose and full lips captured in the Fragonard profile are dramatically emphasized and framed by large, almond-shaped eyes. Credited to Fragonard in the Rosenberg catalog, this work is certainly a stronger, more confident and more physically attractive execution than the known *Self-Portrait* by Gérard that was copied by her nephew Théophile Fragonard (Bibliothèque Nationale, Paris).[30] In this version, from a work originally done by Gérard in 1814, the style is tighter and more detailed, and the features are less pronounced but also less attractive. This may be explained by the obviously later date of the work copied by Théophile, since the Besançon work shows a youthful Marguerite. It is certain that Gérard's early style was highly influenced by Fragonard and that she did engravings after his work. Accordingly, it is not implausible that the Besançon portrait and the 1814 portrait are both self-portraits.

A *Self-Portrait* drawing by Gérard in black and white chalk on grey paper was included in an important exhibition of eighteenth-century women artists held at the Hôtel des Négociants in Paris in 1926. It portrays the artist in her studio putting flowers into a vase. Once in the collection of Maurice Feuillet, the location of this signed drawing is at present unknown.

Because the two lived and worked together there are many questions of attribution regarding the art of both Gérard and Fragonard. Fragonard's late work *The Lock* clearly reflects the influence of Gérard's more detailed and controlled technique and has been attributed by some to her. Although the style of *The Lock* reflects a more Neo-classical than Dutch manner, the two styles are technically very similar. This subject has been well explored, with regard to Gérard's work, by George Levitine.[31]

Gérard never became a member of the French Royal Academy, because the four places allotted to women had already been filled. Nonetheless, for 25 years she exhibited regularly in the Salon, where she won three medals. This girl from Grasse died a well-known and respected artist in Paris at her apartment on the Rue Neuve-des-Petits-Champs. As Doin reports, she lived there with a dog, a cat and her loyal maid Marie Teissier.[32] Her famous brother-in-law had been dead for 30 years (Fragonard died in 1823), and her sister for 13 years, but she remained very close to the family of their son Alexandre-Evariste, himself a painter, and that of her brother Henri. By the time Gérard died, however, the sentimental messages conveyed in her popular scenes of everyday domestic life were no longer patronized.

The four artists who had secured the coveted places for women at this time at the Royal Academy were Anne Vallayer-Coster (1744–1818), Elisabeth Vigée-Lebrun (1755–1842), Adélaïde Labille-Guiard (1749–1803) and Thérèse Reboul Vien (1735–1805). The first three had long, successful careers, while the fourth was accused so often of having her famous husband paint her works that she ceased exhibiting altogether.[33]

Anne Vallayer-Coster executed a number of self-portraits, including one in colored crayon (1782–3, Versailles) and a lost original known through engravings (1777, Bibliothèque Nationale, Paris).[34] She was best known, however, as a painter of flowers and still-life. Her notable contemporary, Vigée-Lebrun, however, excelled in the theme of the self-portrait.

The long career of Elisabeth Vigée-Lebrun, a French painter and one of the most important women artists in history, maps the transition from a late Rococo sensibility to Neo-classicism and eventually Romanticism. By her own estimate, she executed over 900 works during her 87-year life, which spanned the period 1755–1842. Her works included history paintings as well as landscapes, but the majority were beautifully colored, deftly rendered, idealized likenesses of the most prominent aristocrats of her time.[35]

Vigée-Lebrun's most important patron was the much maligned Queen of France, Marie Antoinette. Vigée-Lebrun painted over 20 portraits of this Austrian-born consort, beginning in 1778 and ending with the artist's own exile from France on the night the king and queen were taken prisoner by a revolutionary mob on 6 October 1789. Two of her best-known portraits of the queen, both located at Versailles, are *Marie Antoinette Holding a Rose* (1784) and *Marie Antoinette with Her Children* (1787). The individual likeness, in the former, with its casual elegance and lush landscape background, is more typical of Vigée-Lebrun's portraits, but the latter was one of her largest and best-known paintings. It was commissioned by the government for propaganda purposes to respond to public hatred for the queen and the view that she was a bad mother. Here Vigée-Lebrun promoted the ideal of a happy family, an image that the artist would later embrace in her own self-portraits.

The elaborate and elegant clothing worn in both of these portraits of Marie Antoinette was not in keeping with the personal taste of the artist. In her published *Souvenirs*, written when she was in her eighties, Vigée-Lebrun states, 'As I detested the female style of dress then in fashion, I bent all my efforts upon rendering it a little more picturesque, and was delighted when, after getting the confidence of my models, I was able to drape them according to my fancy.'[36] One sees this 'fancy' in her most controversial portrait, called *Marie Antoinette en Gaulle* (1783, Collection of Princess von Hessen, Darmstadt), the term used to indicate the queen's softly flowing muslin dress tied high at the waist. The subject also sports a straw hat adorned with feathers and a bow, and again holds her symbol, the rose. This work caused a scandal when exhibited at the Salon of 1783 and the artist was forced to withdraw the picture only a few days after the exhibition opened. Critics protested that the queen looked indecent and unregal but, in fact, the artist was just reflecting a newly emerging, more 'natural' style that Vigée-Lebrun had popularized.

Vigée-Lebrun had far greater freedom when painting her own self-portraits, an enterprise in which she was often engaged. Close to 40 are attributed to her, although many of these were autograph copies of existing originals. This tendency to paint several versions of the same composition was typical of the time and in no way detracts from the importance of the work. Since other artists also made copies of her more admired works, many versions of the same painting may be available for study.

Vigée-Lebrun's self-portraits have met with a wide range of critical response, from the time they were painted to the present day. Her contemporary, Melchior Grimm, called them 'brilliantly graceful', while Michael Levey and Simone de Beauvoir have dubbed them 'narcissistic'. The feminists Rozsika Parker and Griselda Pollock consider them inappropriate representations of a professional woman, while Albert Boime refers to them as both 'spontaneous' and 'superficial'. Mary Sheriff calls them 'skillful artistic performances dependent on the ability to mimic signifying codes, gestures and styles', while Joseph Baillio points out their introduction of a 'more natural' look. However, no one has called Vigée-Lebrun's self-portraits ugly or badly painted, and an examination of her more important self-portraits easily demonstrates why such is the case. They are undoubtedly some of the most beautiful and richly colored visual images ever painted. They also document and reflect the dramatic changes that took place both politically and stylistically during the latter part of the eighteenth century, as will be shown, as well as being a personal evocation of one of the most successful female artists in history.

The great Flemish master Peter Paul Rubens exerted a profound impact on Vigée-Lebrun's color, glazing techniques, compositional approach and use of light. She made copies after his Medici Cycle in the Luxembourg Palace while still a teenager, but was particularly impressed with works she viewed on a 1781 trip to Flanders with her art dealer husband, J.B.P. Lebrun.

Vigée-Lebrun painted two self-portraits under Rubens's influence. The first of these was a *Self-Portrait with Cerise Ribbon* of 1782 (Kimbell Art Museum, Fort Worth), painted when she was 27 years old. Here, she wears a white muslin *robe en Gaulle* with a cherry-red ribbon and bow, a black shawl and a plumed hat – attire similar to that in which the queen posed one year later. The flowing, unpowdered hair favored by the artist, which she says she did herself (her mother was a hairdresser of peasant stock), contributes to what she described as a fresh appearance proper to youth. She also depicts herself as extremely pretty, a fact mentioned by almost every contemporary who commented on her. Her nephew, Justin Tripier Le Franc, described his aunt as blonde, blue-eyed, tall, well-built and with a majestic bearing, a trait she herself particularly admired in Marie Antoinette.[37] Other contemporaries praised her wit, grace and charm – all qualities much appreciated in the Paris of the *Ancien Régime*. This era strongly paralleled the Mannerist period in its courtly sophistication and emphasis on elegant, beautiful forms. It is not surprising, therefore, that Vigée-Lebrun's self-portraits are reminiscent of Lavinia Fontana's approach to the self as a paradigm of female beauty. Certainly, *Self-Portrait with Cerise Ribbon* is just such a painting.

What Vigée-Lebrun has not stressed in this work is her role as an artist, a profession at which she had at this time been working for 12 years, since she began her career at age 15. While still in her teens she earned so much money so quickly that she gained the attention of the law and was threatened with arrest for working without a license. To remedy this situation, she joined the Académie de Saint-Luc in 1774, where she regularly exhibited her works. In 1783, one year after this work was painted, she was made a member of the French Royal Academy. Thus, she was a well-established professional woman by the time she executed this rather sensual, smiling image of herself.

Although Vigée-Lebrun did not include references to her profession in the work just discussed, she did so in a second self-portrait more obviously painted under the influence of Rubens. Called *Self-Portrait with a Straw Hat* (Fig. VI.9) this alludes to Rubens's portrait of Suzanna Luden, *Le Chapeau de Paille*. Vigée-Lebrun notes in her *Souvenirs* that she saw this work in Antwerp and that it 'delighted and inspired me to such a degree that I made a portrait of myself at Brussels, striving to obtain the same effects'.[38] In discussing the reasons she was so impressed by Rubens' work, she emphasized his technical approach, saying, 'The force lies in the two different lights – those of the sun, and of the reflected sunlight...Perhaps one must be a painter in order to appreciate all the power here displayed by Rubens.'[39] Here Vigée-Lebrun has herself emphasized the lights and shadows of the outdoor atmosphere.

Mary Sheriff recently published a provocative and original analysis of Vigée-Lebrun's work generally, and of *Self-Portrait with a Straw Hat* specifically, under the title *The Exceptional Woman* (University of Chicago Press, 1996). Sheriff concludes that in this work Vigée-Lebrun identifies herself as an 'intimate of the Queen, the painter Rubens, his beloved wife (since Vigée-Lebrun thought Susanna Luden was Rubens's wife), a painted figure made by Rubens, a history painter, a hermaphrodite, an inspired artist, an intellectual making a reasoned point (rhetorical gesture), a speaking subject, a beautiful woman, an objectified commodity (sex object), an immodest women/artist pleasuring in Self-display'.[40] Although Vigée-Lebrun would probably jostle the palette and brushes inscribed on her tombstone at the 'hermaphrodite' association (a reference to her talent and success in the male-dominated art world), Sheriff has well captured the abundant sources and references inherent in this self-portrait, a work that the artist said 'added considerably' to her reputation when exhibited in the Salon of 1783.

The High Renaissance painter Raphael stylistically and compositionally inspired the 1786 *Portrait of the Artist with Her Daughter* (Pl. XX). No longer the youthful ingenue or the self-confident professional with palette and brushes in hand, Vigée-Lebrun at this point has become the devoted mother, in keeping with the new age of '*sensibilité*' influenced by Jean-Jacques Rousseau. In the spirit of Raphael's *Madonna of the Chair* the artist embraces her daughter

VI.9   Elisabeth Vigée-Lebrun, *Self-Portrait with a Straw Hat*, 1783

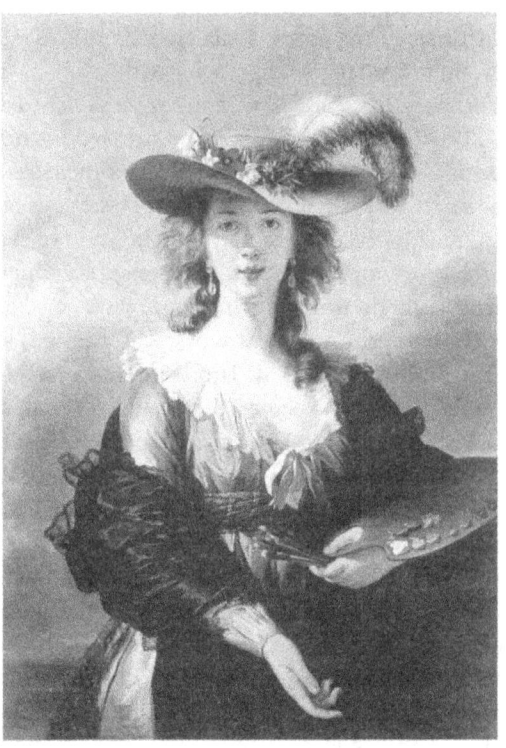

Julie, who was probably named after the heroine of Rousseau's most famous novel, *Emile* (the most widely read novel of the late eighteenth century). It is significant that, in portraying herself as a mother, Vigée-Lebrun has forged new ground in the realm of the female self-portrait. While women artists had a long history of reflecting their roles as stylish and learned ladies or working professionals at their easels with palettes, they had previously eschewed emphasizing motherhood, except in painted references (as seen with Beale and Fratellini), perhaps for fear of not being taken seriously as artists. By this time, however, Vigée-Lebrun was being paid more for her portraits than any other artist, including Gainsborough. The quantity of commissions given to her was fulfilled because she worked all day, every day, with few interruptions. She credited a midday rest she called her 'calm' with giving her the endurance to work as long and hard as she did for so many years. Thus, Vigée-Lebrun had the confidence to reveal herself in the sentimental role of mother without concern for her professional position.

The dry, linear style of the *Portrait of the Artist with Her Daughter*, with its flat application of paint, reflects the nascent Neo-classical movement in France. Vigée-Lebrun would truly embrace this new stylistic trend in yet another depiction of herself with her daughter two years later (Fig. VI.10). This famous work, painted for d'Angiviller, the Director of Royal Buildings, is acknowledged as a dramatic early example of changing taste. Even Levey, who speaks disparagingly of Vigée-Lebrun, credits her with creating a new

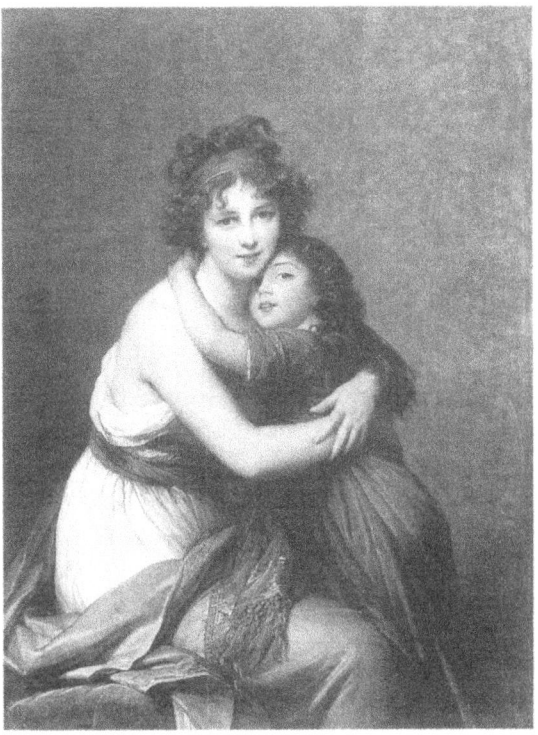

VI.10   Elisabeth Vigée-Lebrun, *Portrait of the Artist with Her Daughter*, 1789

approach to portraiture.[41] J.-L. David's famous *Madame Récamier* painted 11 years later bears a great stylistic similarity to this work. Vigée-Lebrun was well acquainted with David, although the two staunchly disagreed politically. Madame Récamier went into exile due to a falling out with Napoleon and, coincidentally, was at Madame de Staël's when Vigée-Lebrun was painting that famous author's portrait at her château on Lake Geneva.

Vigée-Lebrun spent 12 years in exile following her 1789 flight from Paris. During this time she was welcomed throughout Europe and Russia, where she continued to be deluged with portrait commissions and was made a member of most of the major art academies. In Florence, she was asked to contribute a *Self-Portrait* to the Grand Ducal Gallery of the Uffizi, the Grand Duke at the time being Marie Antoinette's brother. In this work (Fig. VI.11), actually painted in Rome in 1790, she not only emphasizes her role as a professional artist at her easel with brushes and palette in hand, but she underscores her formerly important position as painter to the Queen by showing an unfinished likeness of Marie Antoinette on her easel. When Vigée-Lebrun subsequently executed one of her customary autograph copies of this work, she changed the subject being painted from Marie Antoinette to her daughter, Julie (Ickworth House, Suffolk), perhaps for political reasons, for she longed to return to her home city.

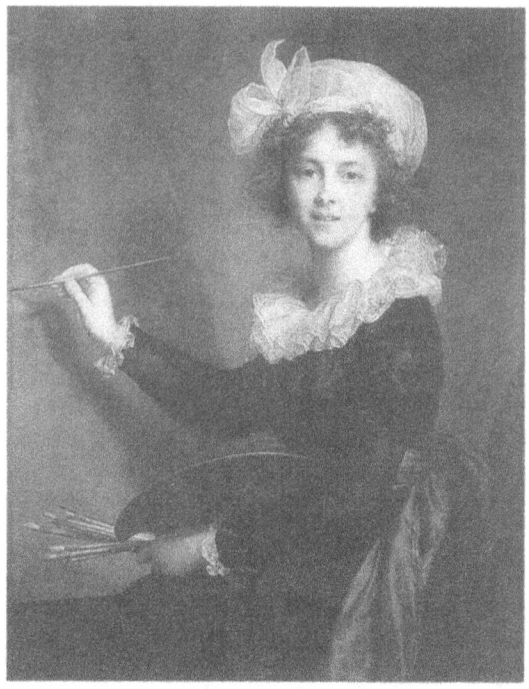

VI.11   Elisabeth Vigée-
Lebrun, *Self-Portrait*, 1790

The easel image was again changed in a print executed by Vigée-Lebrun's
friend Vivant Denon, when she visited him in Venice in 1792. It was now that
of Raphael, a reference to her admiration for the great Renaissance master, but
also signifying the fact that with her Uffizi *Self-Portrait* she would take her
place among the great artists in history, including the Renaissance masters.
Vigée-Lebrun's contemporary Angelica Kauffmann also had a *Self-Portrait* in
the Uffizi, which Vigée-Lebrun praised on her visit there. She later met
Kauffmann in Rome and called her intelligent and knowledgeable. However,
she ruefully adds that she was about 50 (she was 48) and frail, due to being
ruined by the Swedish adventurer whom she had married.[42] Vigée-Lebrun
empathized with Kauffmann's situation, since her own husband was a
gambler and womanizer who had spent all her money. He then divorced her
while she was in exile so his property would not be confiscated. At least in
exile Vigée-Lebrun could keep the fortune she amassed from her work, which
she would later use to buy her ex-husband's property for herself.

Although the Uffizi *Self-Portrait* is the best-known image of herself done by
Vigée-Lebrun in exile, it was not the only one. The first was probably a pastel
(1789–90, private collection) executed during the first year after her flight.
Vigée-Lebrun's choice of medium reflects the early training she had with her
father, Louis Vigée, who was a popular pastel portraitist. She herself was
often called the French Rosalba, reflecting the continued tradition of
comparing almost every female artist of merit, especially those who worked
at all in pastel, to the famous Venetian. Vigée-Lebrun's self-portraits,

however, are very different from the starkly candid works by Rosalba, as may be observed in this pastel self-portrait. It is true that there is a slight hint of melancholy in this work, probably indicating the sadness she felt at being away from her home, but she never suffered the health problems or depression experienced by Carriera. The emphasis is still on capturing a youthful prettiness characteristic of her self-portraits. Even though she was now 35 years old, married to a rogue, a mother, and rumored to be the lover of a number of her patrons, including the former French Minister of Finance Calonne and the dashing Comte de Vaudreuil (rumors she vehemently denied), she has the appearance of an innocent adolescent. Of all of Vigée-Lebrun's self-portraits, this one perhaps best reflects the influence of Jean Baptiste Greuze, who specialized in youthful innocents and whose wife (often his model) looked a little like the artist as here portrayed. When Vigée-Lebrun herself taught students, an enterprise undertaken reluctantly due to the time it took away from her own work, she advised them to pay careful attention to Greuze's heads. *Ma Tête* is, in fact, the title of an earlier work by Vigée-Lebrun (1778), indicating that it may also be a self-portrait, but the figure does not bear a resemblance to the other images of the artist.

Other self-portraits by Vigée-Lebrun after being exiled include one done in Rome for the Accademia di San Luca, of which she was made a member in 1793. Her characteristic casualness is shown in a loosely draped muslin headdress and scarf. Soft and simple, this work was typically copied by her for another patron, in this case, Lord Bristol.

In Russia, Vigée-Lebrun executed a self-portrait graphite drawing in a linear Neo-classical style (Fig. VI.12). Here, she is dressed in 'street clothes', which include an empire-style dress and a fashionable hat tied under her chin, rather than the carefully orchestrated studio attire shown in the *Self-Portrait* of 1790 where she works at her easel. She is again at her easel, however, in a work painted for the Royal Academy at St Petersburg done the same year as the drawing (Pl. XXI). Now 45, she finally displays a slight hint of aging, although only a hint because her neck and chin are covered up to the ears with a collar. Vigée-Lebrun's attire also includes a velvet dress tied under the bodice and a striped scarf wrapped loosely around her head. She is shown interrupted at her easel in the act of executing the preliminary underdrawings for a portrait. Copies of this work also exist, one of which is in the Boston Museum of Fine Arts.

Vigée-Lebrun remained active, both socially and professionally, when she returned to Paris in 1801, having been pardoned by Napoleon on the strength of a petition signed by hundreds of artists to allow her back into France. By now, her stylistic approach reflected a Romantic spirit. She even did a portrait of Lord Byron when she visited England, and made a pilgrimage to the burial site of Jean-Jacques Rousseau in Switzerland. Her heart and soul remained, however, in the France of the *Ancien Régime* as became apparent in her memoirs.

Vigée-Lebrun's contemporary and rival was Adélaïde Labille-Guiard (1749–1803). The two formidable women painters were constantly compared

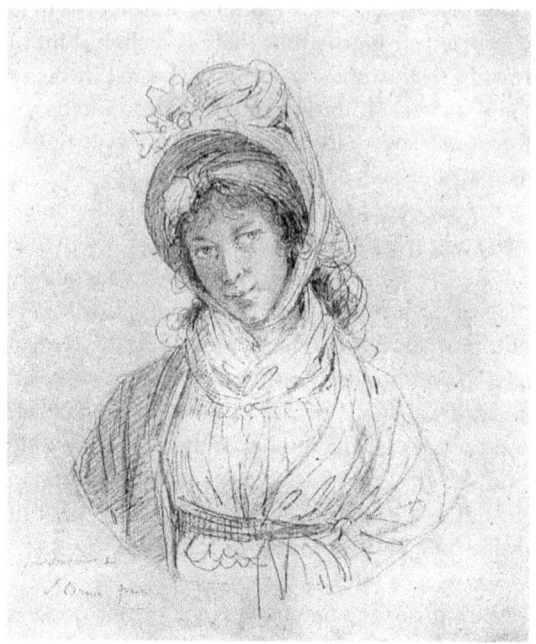

VI.12   Elisabeth Vigée-
Lebrun, *Self-Portrait*, 1800

to each other and often had their works hung next to each other. This was the case in 1782, when they each exhibited self-portraits at the Salon de la Correspondence, an annual exhibition first organized in 1779 by Pahin de la Blancherie and opened at the Hôtel Villayer in Paris in 1781. It was here that Vigée-Lebrun exhibited her *Self-Portrait with a Straw Hat* (Fig. VI.9) next to Labille-Guiard's *Self-Portrait* (1782, private collection, Paris). Pahin de la Blancherie described the positive reception that both of these works received in the *Nouvelles de la république des lettres et des arts*. He said of Vigée-Lebrun's portrait that it perfectly rendered her personal grace and the charm that characterizes her work.[43] As for her rival, the journal of the Salon reported that when Labille-Guiard entered the exhibition hall, the crowd burst into applause due to the amazing likeness of herself in her *Self-Portrait*. This confidently rendered work certainly shows her mastery of the pastel medium, with its bold use of blue and white and emphasis on detail, though the painting shows her seated at her easel holding a palette and brushes. This demonstrates that she also worked in oils. Labille-Guiard's teacher in the use of pastels was the formidable pastelist, Maurice Quentin de la Tour, under whom she studied from 1769 to 1774.

Labille-Guiard's eye for detail was probably due to her early training in miniature, which she studied with François-Elie Vincent, her first known teacher. She executed a *Self-Portrait* in miniature on ivory (private collection, Paris) that shows her working on a miniature painting positioned on a desk in front of her and flanked by a bouquet of flowers. She wears an elaborate dress, a double strand of pearls around her neck and flowers in her well-coiffed hair. As with her later pastel, this work was praised for its remarkable likeness of the artist. It was exhibited in the Salon of the Académie de Saint-Luc in 1774, where again Vigée-Lebrun also exhibited. This Salon was closed soon after (1775) by royal decree as a result of its competition with the French Royal Academy, much to the chagrin of many artists, particularly women who could join and exhibit. It was the closing of the Académie de Saint-Luc that inspired Pahin de la Blancherie to organize the Salon de la Correspondence.

The lives and careers of Labille-Guiard and Vigée-Lebrun continued to run in parallel when in 1783 they were both admitted into the French Royal Academy on the same day. Vigée-Lebrun's membership was opposed by many members due to her husband's occupation as an art dealer since dealers and associates were not allowed to join, but the objections were overcome through the intervention of the Queen. Labille-Guiard, however, was strongly supported and highly admired by her fellow academicians. They praised her seriousness, strength of character and firmness of artistic technique, attributes reflected in her self-portraits. Nonetheless, her life was not without controversy and scandal. In 1769 she had married an accountant, Louis Nicolas Guiard. Their relationship became strained when she began studying oil painting with François André Vincent, the son of her former teacher. In fact, the relationship became the subject of a libellous poem against women published after the Salon of 1783. After a long separation, she obtained a divorce from Guiard.

Labille-Guiard never had children but she forged very strong bonds with her students, two of whom are represented in one of her most beautiful and famous paintings, *The Artist with Two Female Pupils* (Pl. XXII), which was first exhibited at the French Royal Academy Salon of 1785 to wide acclaim. This large and ravishingly painted self-portrait depicts the artist with two of her best students. Marie Gabrielle Capet looks in attentive admiration over the shoulder of her teacher at the unseen work depicted on the easel on which Labille-Guiard gracefully rests her foot. Carreaux de Rosemond rests her arm around the waist of Capet while she, like her teacher, engages the gaze of the viewer.

This scene takes place in the large studio located on the rue de Menars leased by Labille-Guiard after her divorce. It was here that she painted and also ran a popular school for female artists. Rosemond and Capet were only two of the many women who trained with this committed teacher and mentor. At one time she had nine students, all of whom exhibited in the Exposition de la Jeunesse of 1783. Contemporaries called them the Nine Muses, describing them as 'pretty and amiable'.[44] It was due to this group of lovely young women that Labille-Guiard was denied the rooms at the Louvre customarily granted to Academy members. It was felt that the presence of these girls, some as young as 12, in the mostly male-occupied Louvre would lead to problems. Labille-Guiard eventually did gain lodgings in the Louvre in 1795 after the Revolution.

In the left background of the picture one sees two sculptures resting on a parapet. The sculpture furthest back portrays a female figure holding a torch while the other work is a portrait of Labille-Guiard's father executed by the well-known sculptor Pajou, a family friend. It was Labille-Guiard's portrait of Pajou that served as her reception piece when she was admitted to the Royal Academy, and contemporaries noted that the bust was always prominently displayed in her studio.

Labille-Guiard executed a preliminary study for this painting (location unknown) that excludes the two students and many of the other details of the studio setting. It does, however, concentrate on her elaborate satin gown and jaunty straw hat adorned with feathers (reminiscent of Vigée-Lebrun's portrait of 1782), as realized in the finished work. In the final work, the artist holds a palette and brushes as well as the maulstick pictured in the study, and the color of the dress is changed from yellow to a lustrous blue and white, the same colors employed in her pastel *Self-Portrait*.

As was typical of Labille-Guiard, she has devoted much attention to the details of texture and lace and, according to contemporaries, captured an excellent likeness in all three figures represented. Her portraits, generally, are considered to be much more psychologically probing and realistic than the more flattering approach of Vigée-Lebrun. This psychological penetration of her subjects is often credited to her having studied with Quentin de la Tour, who executed his own very lively and original self-portraits, and to her own 'masculine' character. Contemporaries often used words such as 'strong', 'vigorous', 'truthful' and 'clear' to describe her works, but did not at all insinuate that she was not womanly. In fact, she was described as being very elegant, and an inventory at the time of her death listed a number of satin dresses and hats as part of her estate. It is as a mature, confident and elegant professional artist that the 36-year-old Labille-Guiard represents herself in this *Self-Portrait*, in contrast to the youthful, and almost obsequious, students positioned behind her. As Wendy Slatkin has noted, Labille-Guiard's 'proud image' was likely an appeal for patronage from aristocratic patrons with whom she hoped to identify, as she was experiencing financial difficulties at this time.[45]

Above all, Labille-Guiard's *Self-Portrait with Two Female Students* highlights her technical proficiency in the medium of oils and stresses her role as a teacher and mentor to other women artists. As the Metropolitan Museum catalogue entry for this work notes, it served as a propaganda piece for admitting more women to the French Royal Academy. In 1790 Labille-Guiard gave an enthusiastic speech to the Academy against the four-women quota, but was not able to change the rule. However, she was successful in establishing a school to train impoverished girls in commercial art, which was established in 1805 with Prime Minister Talleyrand's help.

Self-Portrait with Two Female Students established Labille-Guiard as a major portrait-painter of the period. As a result of this work, she was given a substantial pension by the Crown and poems were composed in her honor. One read: '*C'est la déesse dans son temple/Qui présente à la fois le précepte et l'exemple*' ('It is the goddess in her temple/Presenting both precept and example'.)[46]

The career that followed this masterpiece included many commissions by the Crown. She was given the official title of Painter to Mesdames, the King's aunts Victoire and Adélaïde (daughters of Louis XV), of whom she did a number of portraits. But, unlike Vigée-Lebrun, she did not remain faithful to the monarchy after the Revolution. Instead, she quickly aligned herself with the new government by executing portraits of many of its leaders, including Robespierre. The Revolution did not come, however, without a personal price. She was ordered by the state to destroy all of the works still owned by her that were commissioned by members of the nobility, including the unfinished *Réception d'un Chevalier de l'Ordre de Saint-Lazare par Monsieur, Grand Maître de l'Ordre*, which was commissioned by the brother of Louis XVI. It must have been difficult for her to destroy this large-scale historical work, as she had hoped it would establish her in the prestigious realm of history painting in the Academy, by this time reorganized as the Institut des Beaux-Arts.

Not until 8 June 1800 did Labille-Guiard marry her painting teacher and long-time lover Vincent. Present at the wedding were her devoted students Marie Gabrielle Capet and Victoire d'Avril. Carreaux de Rosemond had tragically died in 1788, the year of her own marriage. Labille-Guiard's students were like daughters to her, particularly Capet who played an important role in her life. After her teacher's death in 1803, Capet cared for Vincent until he died in 1816 at age 70. Capet herself died two years later.

Marie Gabrielle Capet (1761–1818) became an established artist in her own right, particularly in the field of miniature painting. It was as a miniaturist that Labille-Guiard portrayed her in a portrait of 1798 (private collection). Born in Lyon, Capet was still a teenager when she began studying with Labille-Guiard. By the age of 20 she was exhibiting regularly – first in the Exposition de la Jeunesse (1781 and 1783) and later (1785 and 1786) in the Salon de la Correspondance. In the 1790s she exhibited several miniature portraits at the Salon, including portraits of Labille-Guiard and Vincent. Her largest and most acclaimed work was a portrait, now lost, of Labille-Guiard in the process of painting a portrait of the painter Vien. In this composition, Capet included Vincent, Vincent's student Mérimée, Vien's wife, and a self-portrait showing Capet seated at the side of her teacher and assisting with the palette. This complex imaging of a painter, painting her teacher in the process of painting *her* teacher (also her husband), while including herself in the composition, recalls Anguissola's *Bernardino Campi Painting the Portrait of Sofonisba* (Fig. IV.9). Capet's work was painted as a loving tribute to the woman who taught her how to paint and in whose household she lived even after her teacher's death.[47] Capet left this painting in her will to a M. Boivin. Another independent *Self-Portrait* of Capet, also listed in the will, was inherited by a Mlle Perrier and may be the beautiful portrait once in the collection of Paul Cailleux.

Capet also painted numerous self-portraits in miniature. These three-quarter-view, waist-length works are typically straightforward. They show a serious, unpretentious young woman without reference to her profession or other accomplishments.[48]

Although not as enthusiastic a teacher as Labille-Guiard, Vigée-Lebrun received tribute from a female artist who had presented herself as her student, Marie-Victoire Lemoine (1754–1820).[49] In fact, Lemoine may never have actually studied with her famous contemporary, even though her best-known work is a *Self-Portrait in the Studio of Vigée-Lebrun*, exhibited in the Salon of 1796 under the title *L'Intérieur de l'attelier [sic] de femme, peintre* (Fig. VI.13). This work is dominated by a portrait of Vigée-Lebrun dressed in her characteristic studio attire and holding a palette and maulstick. Lemoine is seen seated, almost crouching, to the left in a diminutive and unnaturalistic proportion to the rest of the painting. She is sketching on a sketchbook positioned in her lap and is facing an unfinished easel painting. The subject of the painting is an historical work, showing a kneeling figure being presented by a priestess to an effigy of the Goddess Athena.[50] The scene takes place in an understated Neo-classical interior and is painted in a dry, uninspired Neo-classical style. Although Lemoine obviously wished to associate herself with Vigée-Lebrun, a comparison of this work with any by Vigée-Lebrun demonstrates why the student did not gain the fame of the teacher. The student–teacher relationship in this case is questionable, since Lemoine was not mentioned as a student by Vigée-Lebrun but she was unquestionably the student of Vigée-Lebrun's good friend, François-Guillaume Menageot. Menageot himself rented an apartment in the house of Vigée-Lebrun and her husband on the rue de Cléry in Paris. He was not only rumored to be one of the many lovers of Vigée-Lebrun but, ridiculously, to have 'touched up' her paintings. The handsome Menageot, painted by Lemoine in 1785 (Versailles), did teach painting techniques to her, but Lemoine's work never took on the power and drama of Menageot's historical compositions, as this *Self-Portrait* demonstrates.

Lemoine painted a more traditional *Self-Portrait* (1780, Musée des Beaux-Arts, Orléans), in which she presents herself as an allegory of painting as Gentileschi did before her. Here, she sits at her easel with a palette and brushes in one hand and a maulstick in the other. She does not engage the gaze of the viewer, but rather looks pensively and reflectively out of the picture. Although painted 16 years prior to her *Self-Portrait with Vigée-Lebrun*, in which both figures are represented as far younger than they actually were at that time, the Orléans *Self-Portrait* shows her as a more mature and sophisticated woman.

Although it is generally regarded as a self-portrait, there is some speculation on other identities of the model for another of Lemoine's works, an *Allegory of Painting*. Possibilities include two of Lemoine's three sisters and a cousin. The family of Charles Lemoine and his wife Marie-Anne Rouselle included not only Marie-Victoire, but Marie-Elisabeth and Marie-Denise, all of whom were artists, and Marie-Geneviève, who was the only daughter not to pursue an artistic career. Their cousin, Jeanne-Elisabeth Gabiou, was also an artist. Thus, there was ample inspiration in the Lemoine household for a female allegory of painting. However, the features of the figure in Marie-Victoire's allegory appear to bear more of a likeness to her than to portraits of

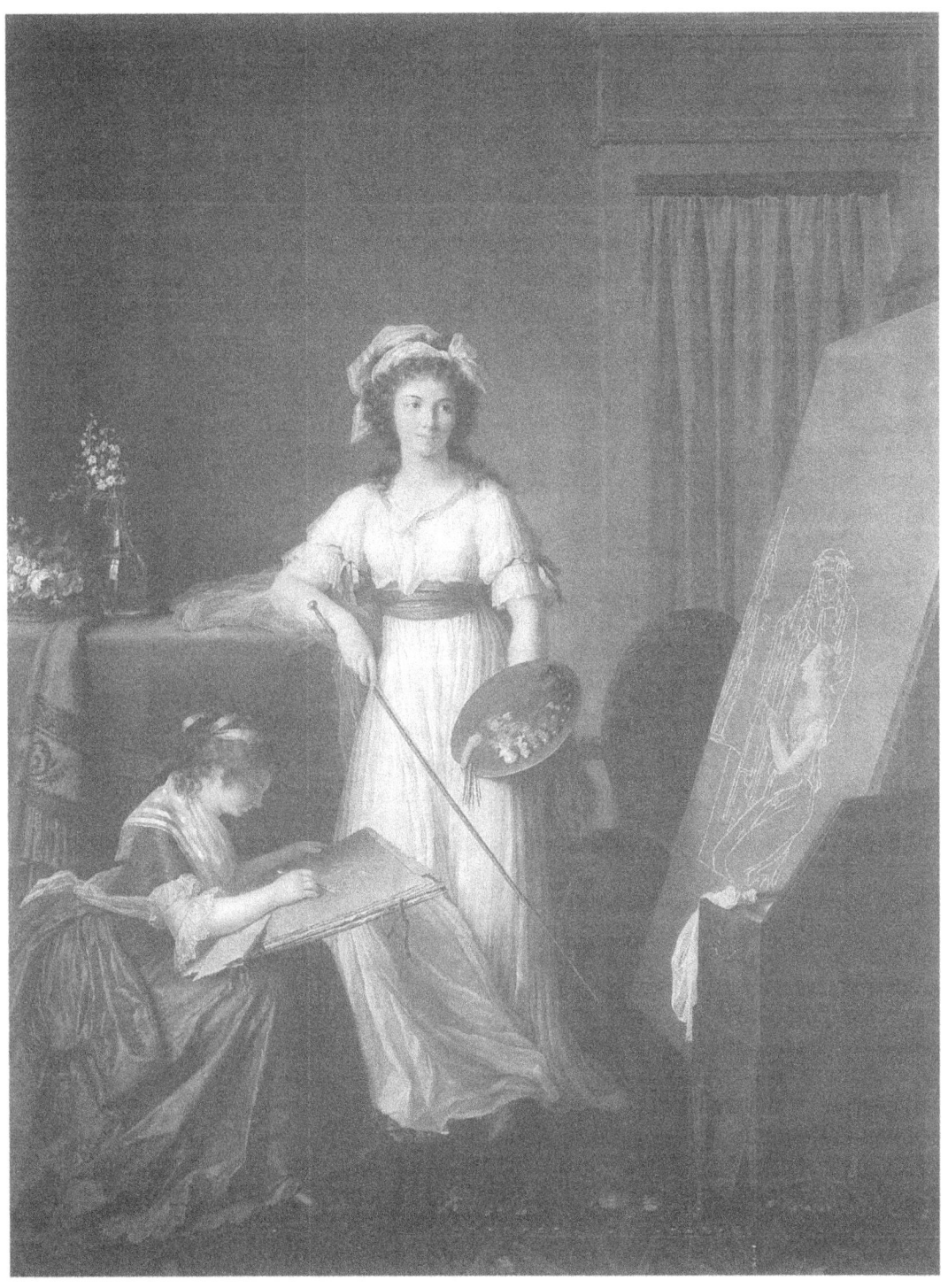

VI.13   Marie-Victoire Lemoine, *Self-Portrait in the Studio of Vigée-Lebrun*, 1796

her family members, although the face does have a relatively long, oval shape. She even holds the palette and brushes in the same manner as seen in the Vigée-Lebrun painting, as well as wearing similar attire, without ruffles, to that of her role model.

If the *Allegory of Painting* by Lemoine was not a self-portrait, neither was it a portrait of her sister Marie-Denise. Marie-Victoire executed a portrait of her sister that shows her with a very round face and almost no chin. The self-portraits painted by Marie-Denise confirm this feature.

Marie-Denise Lemoine (1774–1821) is better known by her married name Nisa Villers, having married the architectural student Michel-Jean-Maximilien Villers in 1794. She studied with the well-known history painter Girodet, and it was as his student that she is recorded at the Salon of 1799 as exhibiting three paintings, including a *Self-Portrait* (now lost). According to a writer in the *Journal de Paris*, she did not do herself justice in this work. He stated, '*Les traits de l'original sont doux & animés, ceux de la copie ont peu d'expression*' ('The features of the original are pretty and lively: those of the copy lack expression'), and continues by asking if she is afraid to flatter herself.[51] If she was afraid to flatter herself, she was not in accord with either her sister or Vigée-Lebrun, both of whom had no difficulty in this regard.

If the now lost *Self-Portrait* was not flattering, Villers may have compensated with two beautiful works, both artistically and figuratively. These include *Study of a Woman after Nature* (Fig. VI.14), exhibited in the Salon of 1802. Although it is often called a portrait of Madame Soustras, Margaret Oppenheimer has pointed out that Soustras modeled for the hands of the figure but not the face, which contemporary viewers suggested was that of Nisa Villers.[52] If this is a self-portrait, it is a very original one. In this work, a veiled woman in an expansive landscape stops to tie her shoe. Her knee is deeply bent as her raised foot rests on a bench in a pose reminiscent of the classical *Sandal Binder*.[53] She has been interrupted by the viewer, whom she regards in an interrogatory way. The woman's features are reminiscent of those of Nisa Villers, as captured in a *Portrait* by her sister, Marie-Victoire, with a soft round face, wide-set eyes, full lips and thick brown hair. An important question to ask is whether these are the features of the famous *Portrait of a Young Artist* (Pl. XXIII) in the Metropolitan Museum, New York. Oppenheimer's argument in favor of this hypothesis is very convincing.

The large and luminous *Portrait of a Young Artist* has a complex history of attribution. Jacques-Louis David was long considered to have painted it, based on the family tradition of the Commandant Hardouin de Grosville, to whom the painting belonged when it appeared in an exhibition of portraits of women and children held in Paris in 1897. The Commandant believed the work to be a portrait of his grandmother, then Mlle Charlotte du Val d'Ognes, an artist herself and pupil of David, although not mentioned as such in a formal list made by Delecluze.[54] Although a number of scholars questioned this attribution on stylistic grounds, it was Charles Sterling's sound challenge that resulted in the work being reattributed, to Constance-Marie Blondelu Charpentier (1767–1849), a well-respected artist at the time this work was

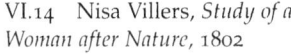
VI.14   Nisa Villers, *Study of a Woman after Nature*, 1802

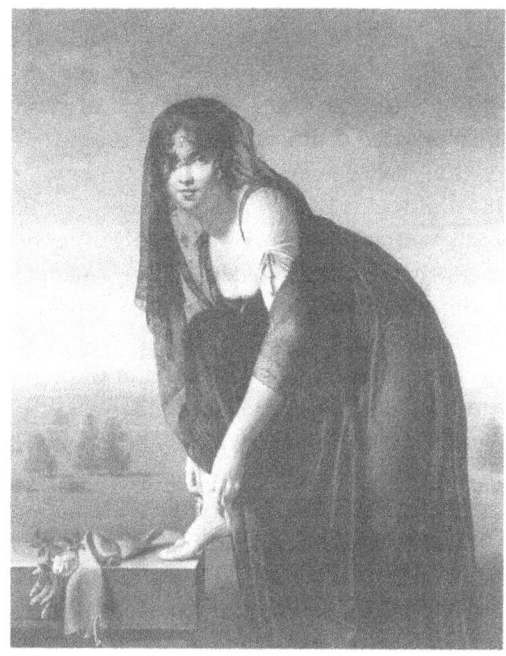

painted. Charpentier was a gold-medal winner and a favorite of important patrons. She exhibited regularly in the Salons between 1795 and 1819, and studied, significantly, with David as well as Gérard, whose own style is similar to the *Portrait of a Young Artist*, especially in terms of its dramatic and translucent lighting. Sterling suggested that a definitive attribution to Charpentier would need far more proof, but that assigning it to a woman was 'an attractive idea'. He states, 'Its poetry, literary rather than plastic, its very evident charms, and its cleverly concealed weaknesses, its ensemble made up from a thousand subtle artifices, all seem to reveal the feminine spirit.'[55] The terms 'weaknesses' and 'artifices' used to support the theory that this was done by a woman seem politically incorrect almost a half century later (and were certainly terms not used when it was credited to David), but the obvious 'charm' and even sweetness of this lovely young artist cannot be denied.

Margaret Oppenheimer recently entered into the debate with another suggestion for an attribution. She credits this work to Nisa Villers and further gives plausible evidence that it may be a self-portrait that Villers first exhibited at the Salon of 1799 and perhaps re-exhibited in 1801, since there is no question that this painting hung in the Salon of 1801, as is evidenced by its inclusion in a drawing of that exhibition by Antoine-Maxine Monsaldey, which was engraved by Devisime.[56] One of the major problems with identification of this work as a self-portrait is the fact that Villers had dark brown hair instead of the blonde locks painstakingly captured in the painting, but this may be due to the radiant light from the rear. It also would not be unheard of for an artist to change the color of a sitter's hair for the sake of artistic merit; David did this rather notoriously in his portrait of Madame

Récamier (Louvre, Paris). The artist pictured also appears younger than Villers would have been at this time. It has been shown, however, that Vigée-Lebrun looked 15 in her self-portraits when she was almost 40, perhaps through artistic license on the part of vanity. As Oppenheimer points out, Villers's basic features, including a small oval face, wide-set eyes and little chin, are reflected in the *Portrait of a Young Artist*. If this was exhibited in 1799 it could hardly have been the 'unflattering' work described by contemporaries, since it is a very beautiful portrait of whomever it represents.

An identity suggested by Sterling but not yet thoroughly pursued is that of Jeanne-Elisabeth Gabiou Chaudet, a cousin to Villers. She exhibited a painting in the Salon of 1801 that included a broken window, such as is seen to the left in the *Portrait of a Young Artist* and through which one views a couple on a terrace.[57] There is a stylistic similarity between this work and paintings by Chaudet such as *Young Girl Eating Cherries* (1812, Musée Marmottan, Paris), most obviously in the treatment of the blonde curls of both figures and the detailing of drapery and scenery.

Another question regarding this work rests with the identity of the artist favored by Sterling. It is known that Mlle Charlotte du Val d'Ognes was an artist herself and, according to family tradition, was taught by David. It is tempting to consider this as a self-portrait by her and then credited to David by the family. The problem with this possibility is that Val d'Ognes is not mentioned in the catalog of the 1801 Salon.

The very personal and engaging feeling observed in this work provides an intuitive, rather than scholarly, reason for wanting to identify it as a self-portrait. Clearly, the debate as to attribution will continue. To date, however, Oppenheimer's suggestion of Nisa Villers as the artist of the *Portrait of a Young Artist* seems the most plausible.

Marie-Guillemine Leroulx-Delaville, the Countess Benoist (1768–1826), was the only one of Vigée-Lebrun's many students whom she identified by name in her *Souvenirs*. Vigée-Lebrun referred to her, however, as Émilie, the name by which Marie-Guillemine became known due to the admiration of the poet Charles-Albert Demoustier. Benoist met Demoustier when she was 16 and he was 25. His enchantment with her resulted in the *Lettres à Émilie sur la mythologie*, which was published in six parts from 1786 to 1798. These poetic letters celebrate the youth, beauty, talent, gaiety and charm of his 'Émilie'. In the dedication to part 3, Demoustier wrote:

> *Cet asile devient pour vous*
> *Le Temple des Vertus, des Talents, de la Gloire*
> *Ah! que j'y tombe à vos genoux*
> *Il deviendra mon oratoire.*[58]

> This place becomes for you a temple of virtue, talent and glory.
> Ah! For me it shall be the chapel where I fall at your feet.

Demoustier's 'Émilie' did not return his affections. By the time the last parts of the poem were published, Leroulx-Delaville had married an aristocratic lawyer from Angers named Pierre-Vincent Benoist. She was also a celebrated artist. Although now known almost exclusively for her beautiful *Portrait of a Negress* (1800, Louvre, Paris), Benoist painted a number of historical and genre scenes. *The Farewell of Psyche, Innocence between Virtue and Vice* and *Sappho* were some of the ambitious themes among her regular exhibits at the Salon.

Benoist began studying with Vigée-Lebrun when she was only 13. Her teacher mentioned that although she was the youngest of her students, she was also very talented. The influence of Vigée-Lebrun on Benoist's early works is apparent, particularly in her self-portraits. An oval-framed *Self-Portrait* (private collection) executed in 1796 shows the young artist in attire and style borrowed directly from her teacher. Looking youthful and sweet – and much like Vigée-Lebrun – Benoist looks down and off the picture plane in a contemplative manner.

Benoist's most famous *Self-Portrait* (private collection) was executed in 1786, when she began studying with David due to renovations being done to Vigée-Lebrun's studio. As Ballot points out, the pose and manner continue to refer to Vigée-Lebrun, but this time have a more Neo-classical style. She also makes reference to her new teacher David, since the painting on which she is working in the *Self-Portrait* is that of Belisarius, a classical theme treated by him.[59] Otherwise, this work is done in the transitional and more painterly Neo-classical style of Vigée-Lebrun. Benoist shows herself dressed in a white tunic, which falls seductively off one shoulder. Her long, flowing hair, ornamented with a headband, seems to move with the action of her energetic turn toward the viewer. Her left hand holds a palette and many brushes, while her right is poised with one brush ready to paint. Called *Self-Portrait in White*, this work was enthusiastically received when first exhibited at the Exposition de la Jeunesse in 1786. It is impossible not to compare it with the self-portraits of Vigée-Lebrun, since the two artists looked and painted so much alike at this time. David did not miss this fact when he did a drawing of the two of them together (private collection). It is very difficult to differentiate which is the student and which the teacher in this work, even though Vigée-Lebrun was 13 years older than Benoist.

From this point on, Benoist's work became sharper, dryer and more linear, reflecting David's influence. This is seen in a self-portrait (now lost) she did in 1801, which was engraved by Delvau. She eventually turned her attention to sentimental genres and became a teacher herself, although little is known of her students and studio. Benoist appears to have abandoned painting during the last decade of her life, perhaps due to the impressive appointments given to her husband, whose own life was full of political intrigue and adventure.

Marie-Geneviève Bouliar (1762–1825) was almost an exact contemporary of the Countess Benoist.[60] The daughter of a tailor and the student of Joseph Duplessis, a well-respected portrait painter of the period, Bouliar's best-known painting is the historical work, *Aspasia* (1794, Museé des Beaux-Arts, Arras), for which she won an award of encouragement at the Salon of 1795. *Aspasia*, depicting the beautiful and intelligent lover of the Greek ruler

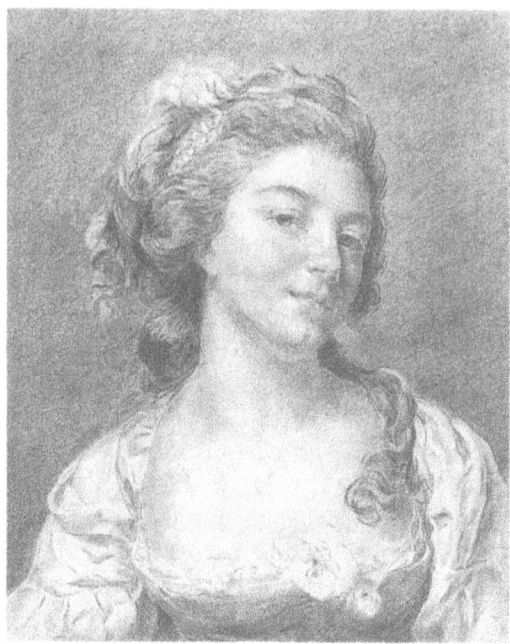

VI.15   Marie-Geneviève Bouliar, *Self-Portrait*, *c*.1800

Pericles, is treated in an early Neo-classical manner, but still retaining a hint of Rococo sweetness.

There is more than a hint of Rococo lushness and charm in the self-portraits Bouliar executed, in both pastels and oils. It is obvious from these works that Vigée-Lebrun, who was only seven years older, had in Bouliar a worthy rival in both beauty and talent. In her *Self-Portrait* of 1792 (Pl. XXIV), Bouliar wears the soft flowing hairstyle and casualness of dress popularized by Vigée-Lebrun, right down to the loosely draped black shawl that appears so often in Vigée-Lebrun portraits. The loosely draped and knotted white muslin shawl also worn by Bouliar in this *Self-Portrait*, and in similar likenesses in Dijon and Angers, may also be seen in many of Vigée-Lebrun's paintings, including her portraits of the Marquis de Grollier and the Countess Potocka. Obviously, this was a popular fashion in this period, but it seems reasonable that Bouliar would be influenced by her famous contemporary, even if she was not directly her student. The two artists are both linked to the works of Greuze, with whom each appears to have received some training.

A pastel *Self-Portrait* (Fig. VI.15) executed by Bouliar is treated in an even freer and more spontaneous manner. Although it is usually dated around 1800, the Rococo style of the dress – with its deep décolletage and rose tucked into the bodice – and more youthful look of the figure indicate that this work may be earlier than the Norton-Simon Museum *Self-Portrait* (Pl. XXIV). Here, Bouliar glances sideways at the viewer in a very coquettish manner. The bodice-length figure boldly dominates the picture plane, and there is a feeling of confidence and strength that seems to belie the coquetry of pose and dress.

In 1825 Bouliar died at the Château d'Arcy in Saône-et-Loire, never having married. Although she had a long career, which included over 40 paintings and drawings exhibited at the Salon, little attention has been devoted to her work.

This is not the case with the remarkable Angelica Kauffmann (1741–1807). The documentation of Kauffmann's life and work was conducted most notably by her friend Giovanini Gherardo De Rossi, who deliberately questioned the artist and noted her career with the intention of recording it for posterity. This he did in 1810, just three years after her death, when he published his *Vita di Angelica Kauffmann* – the artist's first biography. As Wendy Roworth has stressed, this work concentrates on Kauffmann's role as an innovative, highly intelligent and learned painter of historical works.[61] Few women artists managed to achieve success in this, the most highly regarded category of paintings, and Kauffmann became one of the most notable and earliest artists of either sex to paint large-scale historical works in a Neo-classical style. By achieving fame in this manner, she overcame the daunting obstacles to women artists – the prohibition of women from most schools of art and the restrictions against studying from the nude model: even female models had to be clothed when being drawn by women at this time. Thus, the largely self-taught Kauffmann learned anatomy by copying other artists' works, an endeavor in which she was engaged as early as 14 years old.

What formal instruction Kauffmann received came from her father, Joseph Johann Kauffmann. The Kauffmann family was of Tyrolian origin and Angelica was born in Chur (Coire), Switzerland, where her father worked as an artist. Her childhood was primarily spent in Italy, however, since the family moved to Milan (where her mother died in 1757), Parma, and Florence. By 1765, when she arrived in Rome, Kauffmann had already greatly surpassed the success of her father and was recognized as a major talent. She quickly became an integral part of the rising circle of Neo-classicists in the city, which included the great German theorist J.J. Winckelmann, the powerful patron Cardinal Albani and artists such as Batoni, West, Mengs, Piranesi, Hamilton, Dance and a host of others. Kauffmann was lured from this cultured and sophisticated environment in 1766 by Lady Wentworth, the wife of the English ambassador residing in Venice. Kauffmann's brilliant English career included being elected one of the first members of the Royal Academy of Painting and becoming a frequent exhibitor in Academy exhibitions. She eventually returned to Italy with her second husband, Antonio Zucchi, and died in Rome in 1807.

Kauffmann's career involved the execution of many portrait commissions, as well as historical works and an impressively diverse array of self-portraits. These included individual ones typically showing her engaged in the art of painting, allegorical works and paintings with historical themes.

Kauffmann's earliest known *Self-Portrait* (1754, Tiroler Landesmuseum, Innsbruck) was painted when she was just 13 years old. The free and painterly style of this work, as well as the powdered hair and frilly, bowed dress, reflect the influence of the prevailing Rococo taste. Although there is some awkwardness in the treatment of the hands and the chin, this work clearly shows why Kauffmann was considered a child prodigy. Her youthful talents included music as well as art, a reference seen in the sheet of music she holds in the portrait. A devout Catholic all her life, Kauffmann indicated her religious devotion by a cross suspended from a velvet bow around her neck. The pearl earrings and a jeweled tiara seem at odds with her youthful innocence, and show that she was already a fashionable and accomplished young woman.

Although she grew up in Italy, Kauffmann paid homage to her family roots (her father was from Bregenz) by executing a *Self-Portrait in Tyrolian Costume* (1763, Uffizi, Florence). Painted in a darker and more realistic manner than her early Rococo *Self-Portrait*, the work depicts the 22-year-old artist with palette and brushes in hand. This small oil-on-canvas captures a serious and rather rigid young woman dedicated to her work, even though there is a hint of a smile as she turns toward the viewer. Kauffmann gave this work to her friend Cosimo Series the year it was painted (1763), the same year Series donated it to the Uffizi. Kauffmann was not pleased that this youthful work should be the representative of her talent in this major collection of self-portraits and subsequently painted a much more sophisticated painting to replace it.

Kauffmann again alludes to her homeland in the work *Self-Portrait in Vorarlberg Native Dress* (n.d., Museum Ferdinandeum, Innsbruck). This work is probably the least flattering of all her self-portraits. Although she indicates the same wide-set eyes, pronounced nose and thin lips found in other self-images, the end result was usually far more flattering. This may be seen by comparing the Innsbruck portrait with a *Self-Portrait* Kauffmann painted in 1777 for the Accademia di San Luca in Rome (Fig. VI.16), of which she was named a member in 1764. The pose in both paintings is very similar, that is a three-quarter view of the figure which dominates the picture plane in a Renaissance-style triangular composition, but with little attention given to the background. In the Roman work, a copy of an original painted for Reynolds in 1777, Kauffmann wears a Neo-classical-style dress and headpiece rather than the native fashion seen in the Innsbruck portrait, but the stylistic treatment is quite painterly.[62] Her facial features are the same in both works. In fact, her nose is even more pronounced in the Accademia di San Luca work, but the overall effect is more harmonious.

The two best-known and most beautiful independent self-portraits executed by Kauffmann are located in the National Portrait Gallery in London (1770–75) and in the Uffizi, as already noted. In the London work she is holding a sketchbook and a *porte-crayon* in her right hand, while her left gracefully rests on the loosely flowing Neo-classical-style drapery of her bodice. Kauffmann's hair is fashionably piled freely on her head and her strong features have been delineated in a simplified, linear, classical style. The result is the image of a cultured and beautiful young woman, which certainly reflected contemporary opinion. In 1764, Winckelmann described Kauffmann

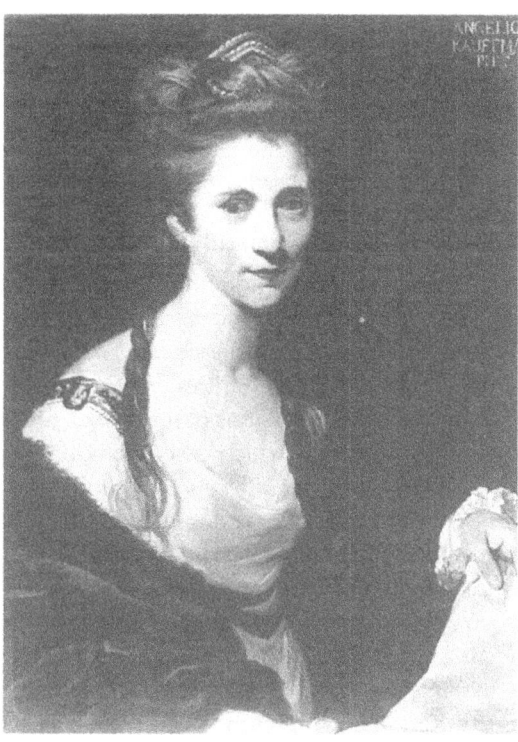

VI.16   Angelica Kauffmann,
Self-Portrait, 1777

as 'a rare person, proficient in German, Italian, English and French and a
beauty and musician as well'.[63] Goethe later called her 'sensitive to all that is
true and beautiful, and incredibly modest'.[64]

Although she may have been socially graceful and modest, Kauffmann's
ego with regard to her talent and work is certainly seen in the *Self-Portrait* (Pl.
XXV) that she contributed to the Uffizi. She again includes a sketchbook and
porte-crayon, but the figure here is almost full-length and placed in an open
loggia against a landscape background. She wears a white muslin, classical-
style dress secured at the bodice with a cameo. As Louise Rice and Ruth
Eisenberg have suggested, the cameo represents a contest between Minerva
and Neptune for control of Athens (Attica). According to legend Neptune
offered the city a horse, while Minerva offered an olive tree. The goddess won
the contest, thereby triumphing over the god. Rice and Eisenberg conclude
that Kauffmann intended the cameo 'as a wry comment on her own
extraordinary success in a profession dominated by men'.[65] The Grand Duke
of Tuscany was sufficiently impressed with her talents to present her with a
large gold medal in thanks for her *Self-Portrait*.

Kauffmann often included allegorical figures in her self-portraits. A
biographically inspired instance of this is *The Artist Hesitating between the Arts
of Music and Painting* (1794, Nostell Priory, Newcastle), where she has
illustrated an event from her youth, as was recounted by De Rossi. He tells of
the difficulty Kauffmann had in deciding between the professions of singing

or painting. Although her family wanted her to follow the less strenuous route of music, she chose painting instead on the advice of a bishop who said painting would bring true, enduring fame while music would be ephemeral.[66] She chose painting, with obvious success, albeit with regret at having to leave music, as her painting makes the viewer aware. She clutches the hand of Music in a gesture of goodbye while she reaches with open palm toward Painting, who is pointing up a rugged hill at the Temple of Glory. Roworth has pointed out that the painting alludes to 'Hercules at the Crossroads' or 'The Dream of Lucian's Career', a popular literary piece that discussed the choice of literature in preference to sculpture for its author, the Greek Lucian.[67] Whatever the source, this ambitious self-portrait, which appears more as a history painting due to the dramatic treatment of the figures, was a favorite of the artist. She subsequently painted two other versions of the work.

Kauffmann executed an earlier self-portrait which also included an allegorical figure. *The Artist in the Character of Design Listening to the Inspiration of Poetry* (1782, Kenwood House, London) includes the familiar features of Kauffmann representing the crucial creative stage in art – the design. It is during this design stage that the artist most ardently seeks the help of inspiration, as represented by Poetry. Poetry physically embraces Design with her right hand as she holds a lyre in her left. Kauffmann, as Design, holds the ever-present *porte-crayon* while looking out at the viewer. In both this work and the self-portrait just discussed, Kauffmann's presence as a female artist seems to serve a dual role as both artist and muse, instead of the traditional depiction of male artist with feminine muse.[68] Kauffmann here assimilates the *ut pictura poesis* tradition.

One of the most complex questions with regard to Kauffmann's self-portraits is that of where she may have included her own features in her historical works. Her suitor, Henry Fuseli, said that all of her heroines were herself, and a look at just some of her historical works seems to support this statement. As Tomory has indicated, this is particularly true in the case of Kauffmann's beautiful *Sappho* (Fig. VI.17), portraying the Greek poet from Lesbos who committed suicide by throwing herself from the Leucadean cliffs into the sea after being rejected by the handsome young Phaon.[69] It is easy to see why Kauffmann would relate to the talented poet Sappho, even without the element of love gone wrong: her first marriage was to the 'Count de Horn', who turned out to be an imposter and in reality a married German named Brandt. Also, Kauffmann's physical features were well suited to her Neo-classical themes: her Sappho has large, wide eyes and a prominent Greco-Roman nose. The full lips of Sappho are the only features at odds with the straightforward self-portraits, in which Kauffmann has thinner, wider lips. Still, the overall impression is strongly that of self-identification.

Zeuxis Selecting Models for His Picture of Helen of Troy (Fig. VI.18) is another historical work that has been identified as containing a self-portrait of Kauffmann.[70] In it, the Greek painter Zeuxis inspects a row of lively models to the viewer's left, while to the far right a female figure framed in front of the

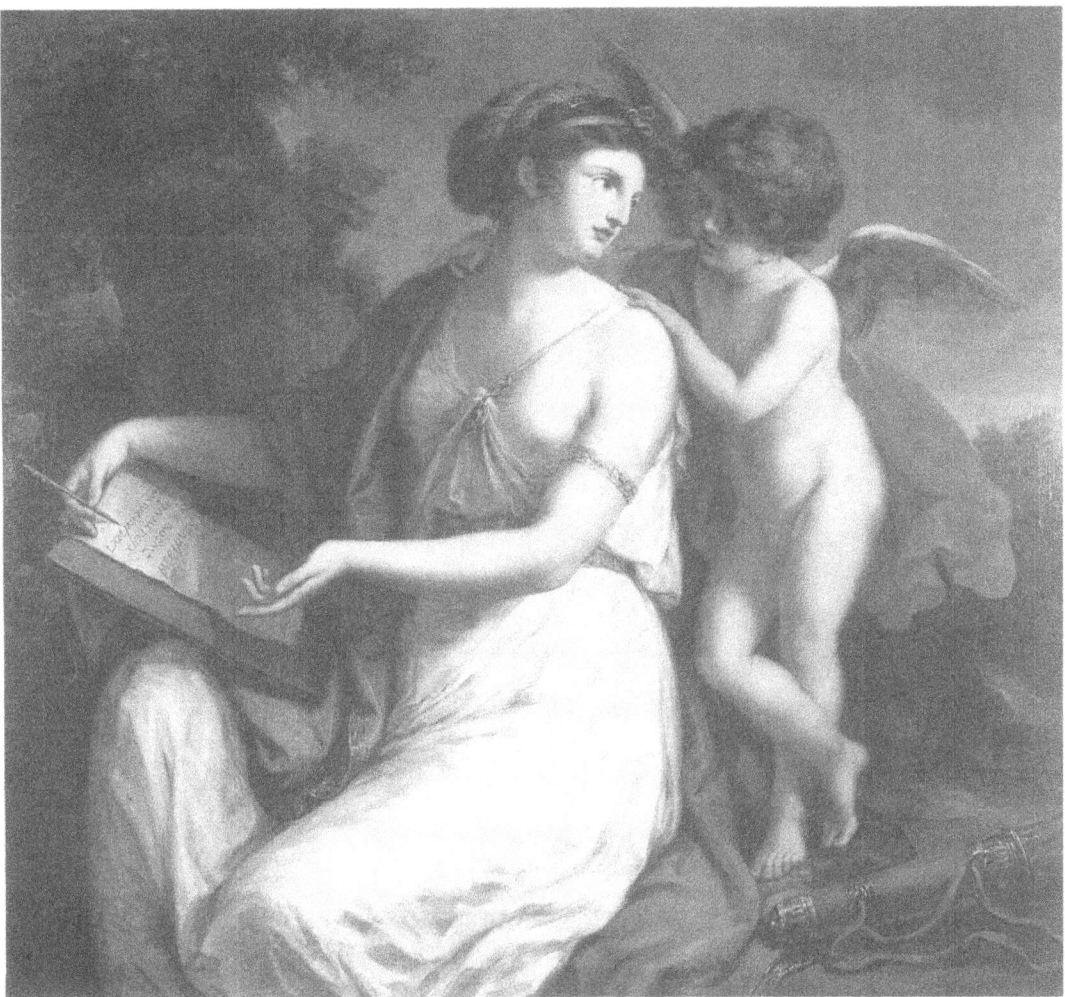

VI.17   Angelica Kauffmann, *Sappho*, 1775

canvas, as if already painted on it, picks up brushes. The features, hairstyle and even dress of this figure are reminiscent of Kauffmann's known self-portraits. Has she here insinuated herself into the painting as both Helen and Zeuxis at once? From what is known of Kauffmann, this certainly seems conceivable. It also displays the type of self-confidence and humor for which she was known. A careful study would undoubtedly reveal many other plausible self-portraits among her heroines, such as those of Hebe, Venus and Cornelia.

Angelica Kauffmann was one of the earliest and most famous Neo-classical painters. Yet her style was seen by many as too 'decorative' and 'soft' during and after her own time. The satirical Dr John Wolcot, who wrote under the name Peter Pindar, included these lines in his *Lyric Odes to Royal Academicians*:

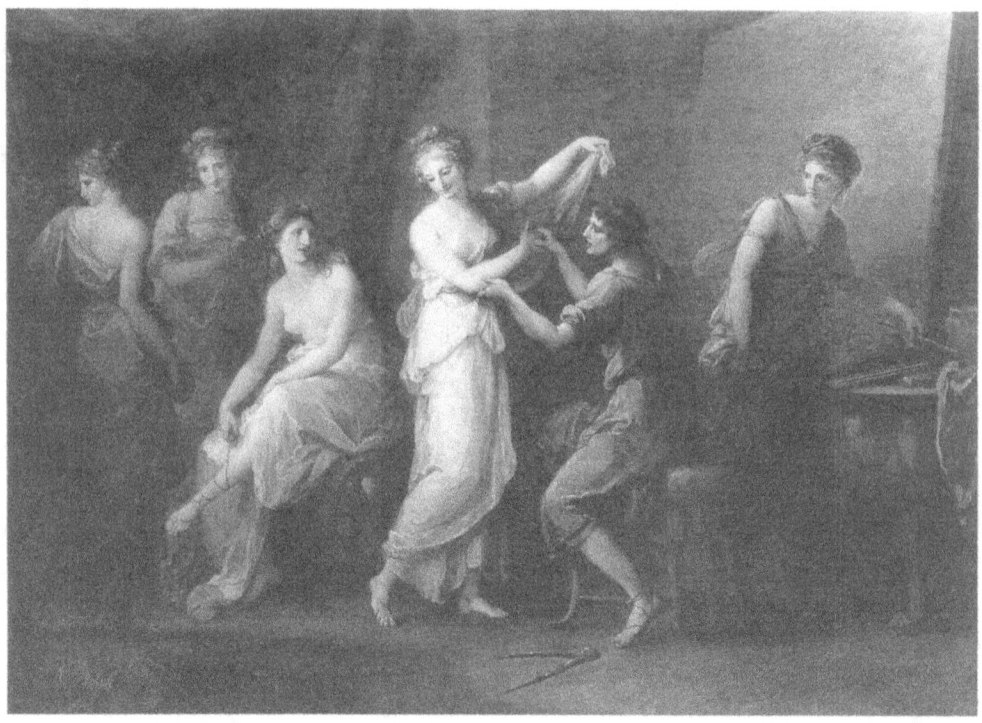

VI.18   Angelica Kauffmann, *Zeuxis Selecting Models for His Picture of Helen of Troy,* c.1764

> Angelica my plaudits gain –
> Her art so sweetly canvas stains! –
> Her dames so Grecian! Give Me such a delight!
> But were she married to such gentle males
> As figure in her painted tales –
> I fear she'd find a stupid wedding night.[71]

It is not surprising that Kauffmann had difficulty with capturing the strength and vigor of the male anatomy, since she was not permitted to study from male nudes. This point was highlighted in a painting by Zoffany, who depicted Kauffmann and Mary Moser, the only two female members of the British Royal Academy, as present only as paintings on the wall during a life-drawing class. For females, Kauffmann always had herself as a model, one on which she appears often to have called.

The British were late in organizing a Royal Academy of Painting and Sculpture. Not until 1768 did Kauffmann and Moser join the initial formation of that organization, which was directed by Kauffmann's good friend, Sir Joshua Reynolds. The inclusion of these two native Swiss women seems not to have concerned British Academicians as they did not, in contrast to the French, formally vote to ban or limit female members. They just never saw fit to admit another woman until 1922.

Mary Moser (1744–1819) and Angelica Kauffmann were good friends, at least until Kauffmann rejected a proposal of marriage from another Swiss artist living in England, Henry Fuseli. Moser appears to have had an unrequited love for Fuseli herself and cooled considerably toward Kauffmann after the latter treated Fuseli coldly. Fuseli took revenge on Kauffmann by going to Italy and becoming a famous artist himself. He later wrote of Kauffmann's heroes that they were 'all the men to whom she thought she could have submitted, though him, perhaps she never found'.[72] It appears that the trio recovered from this romantic intrigue, since they eventually resumed their friendships. Fuseli even voted for Moser to be president of the Royal Academy, instead of the American artist Benjamin West, who won the vote. However, Fuseli's notoriously scathing wit undermines what element of feminism might be perceived in this act. He said 'one old woman was as good as another', and a woman was not allowed as president anyway.[73] Moser appears not to have taken offense at this, probably because she was also renowned for her humor. She was part of a lively circle that included not only Fuseli and Kauffmann, but also the writer and wit Dr Samuel Johnson and the artist Joseph Nollekens.

Moser painted a *Self-Portrait* (n.d., Schaffhausen Museum, Switzerland), formerly attributed to Kauffmann. Suzanne Rosing's entry on Moser, however, in the museum catalog underscores the difference in style between Kauffmann's work and that of Moser. Although Moser wears a classically inspired red cape, the style of this work is more earthy and realistic than Kauffmann's. Moser's realism was particularly apparent in the many paintings of flowers she exhibited at the Royal Academy, the theme for which she is best known. In this *Self-Portrait*, she is engaged in painting a still-life with flowers and fruit. Her personality is conveyed in the rather wry smile directed toward the viewer, who has caught her at her work. Rosing has pointed out that an inscription on the back of the panel declares the work a self-portrait, and a painted-over signature appears to be that of Moser.[74] Moser's family was originally from Schaffhausen but her father, George Michael Moser, also an artist, made his career in England, where he became the first Keeper of the Royal Academy. This appointment must not have hurt Mary's academic acceptance, since she was only 20 when she was elected to membership. Moser exhibited regularly between 1769 and 1792 but her career waned after she was married, to a widower named Captain Lloyd at the age of 53.

Maria Hadfield Cosway (1759–1838) was another foreign-born artist to make her career in England. Although her parents were English, she was born in Leghorn, Italy, where she, like Kauffmann, showed talent in both music and art. It was Kauffmann who encouraged her to go to England to make her career, rather than join a convent as she originally intended. Cosway eventually married the artist Richard Cosway, but she is more notorious for her close relationship with Thomas Jefferson, which lasted the rest of her life after they met in Paris. Jefferson said that Cosway lent 'him her artist's eyes' and the two kept up a correspondence after Jefferson returned to the United States.

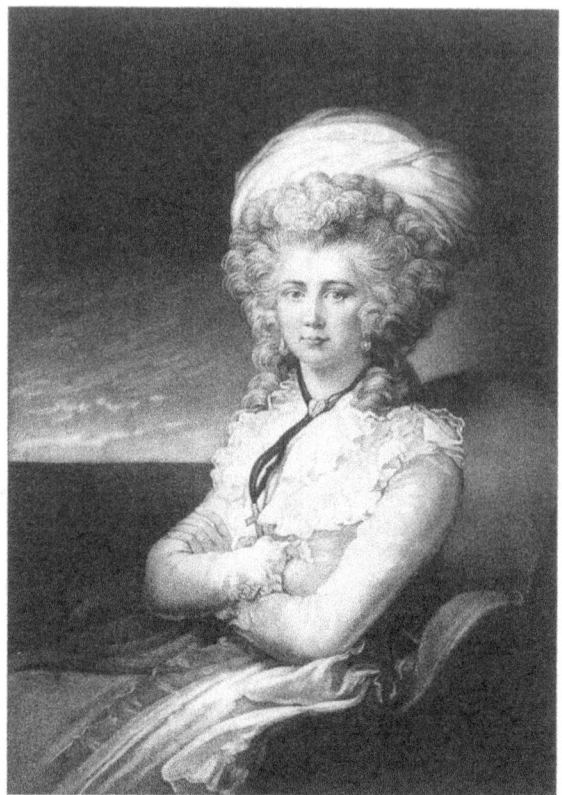

VI.19   Maria Cosway, *Self-Portrait*, 1787, engraving by Valentine Green after original painting now lost

It is as a fashionable but remote woman of the world that Cosway depicts herself in her *Self-Portrait* (now lost, Fig. VI.19). Here her grim expression is reinforced by both of her arms being folded tightly around her waist in a self-protective fashion. Perhaps her body language is a result of her less than ideal marriage to a dandy and Svengali. It is a pose at odds with her reputation as a beautiful and talented hostess in a magnificent residence which the artist Nollekens said had rooms that were 'more like scenes of enchantment penciled by a poet's fancy, than anything perhaps before displayed in a domestic habitation'.[75] This residence was probably more a reflection of her older husband's taste than her own, but there she reigned as a fashionable beauty.

Cosway displays a sense of humor in a portrait set she did of herself and her husband which are now known through mezzotints. They are titled *Richard Cosway as the Macaroni Painter* and *Maria Cosway as the Painter of Macaronis*. The term 'macaroni' referred to the affected young fops of the period, whose posed, pampered and overly refined pomposity were the target of her visual jibes. Cosway's society painter husband was a notorious 'macaroni' and she depicts him as such. He is sitting at his easel painting another 'macaroni' while wearing a high, powdered hairdo and bowed and effeminate attire, and posing in a prissy way. His male model is even more elaborately dressed. In the pendant picture, Maria sits mockingly at her easel with painted 'macaronis' situated both on the easel and behind her. These 'macaronis' are wearing hairstyles that would, in height and elaborateness, rival those of Marie Antoinette. It is refreshing to see this element of levity in Cosway's work, but it seems her true personality is better revealed in the proud and distant *Self-Portrait* previously discussed. It seems Cosway suffered from severe depression much of her lifetime, especially following the birth of her daughter. As Scheerer reports, she left England only three months after her daughter was born (in 1790) to travel throughout Europe, often accompanied by a male companion.[76] She returned only when her daughter was sick (in 1794) and then when the child died, at age six. This cold response to her only child seems unusual for a woman who was very religious and who eventually (in 1812) founded a college for girls in Lodi, Italy, where she settled after her husband died in 1821. Maria herself died there in 1838 and it is at this location that the Fondazione Cosway still serves as a major archive for information about both Maria and Richard Cosway.

By the second decade of the nineteenth century, Romanticism, not Neo-classicism, had become the dominant international style. Characterized by dramatic action, dark tones, painterly technique, craggy landscapes with waterfalls, and brooding themes often derived from literature, the Romantic movement did not attract as many female artists as had the Rococo or Neo-classicism.

Still, many women artists incorporated elements of Romanticism in their works even if they were not primarily associated with the movement. This is evident in the late works of Vigée-Lebrun, as already discussed. It is also true of Constance Mayer (1775–1821).

Mayer was one of the most dramatic women artists associated with Romanticism, in terms of both her life and her work. Like Gérard she was known for domestic genre scenes, but these often included elements of drama and despair, as in her *Unhappy Mother* and *The Poverty Stricken Family*. She was influenced in her work by her teachers Suvée and Greuze, and later by her lover, Pierre Paul Prud'hon, with whom she collaborated on a number of paintings.

Mayer exhibited a *Self-Portrait* (now lost) in the Salon of 1798, but her most famous work is the *Self-Portrait with Her Father* (Fig. VI.20) of 1801. In this work she celebrates the close relationship she had with her father and pays homage to Raphael. Her interest in classicism at this point is reflected in the clarity of the composition, her Grecian hairstyle and the Greco-Roman profile given to her own image. In this work, Mayer looks tall, strong and independent – an independence that was lost when she went to study with Prud'hon in 1805 (they had met in 1802).

The tale of Prud'hon and Mayer is complicated and sad. Mayer was a lively and witty young woman – a spirit captured in a pastel Prud'hon did of her (Louvre, Paris) – when she met him. Prud'hon was married, however, but

VI.20   Constance Mayer,
Self-Portrait with Her Father,
1801

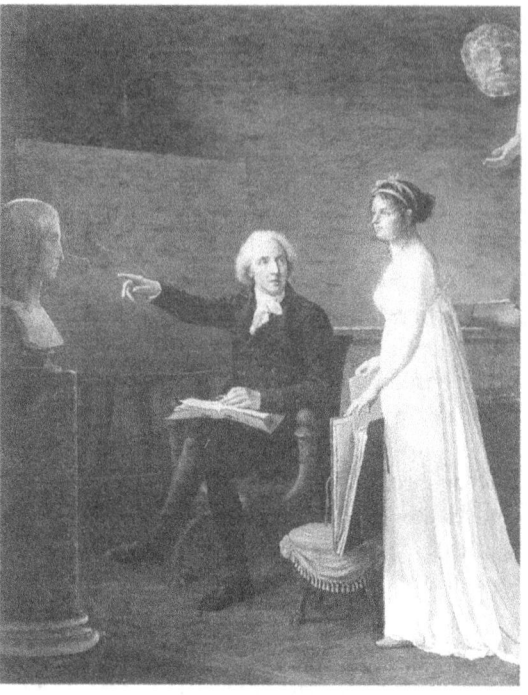

his wife was mentally unbalanced and was eventually put under professional care. Mayer then assumed the role of caretaker to Prud'hon's five children and, apparently, undertook the household and conjugal duties of a wife as well. The two artists also shared professional space in the Sorbonne, where they had adjoining studios. From this point on, many of the paintings by Mayer, including self-portraits, were based on drawings by Prud'hon and, conversely, Prud'hon also appears to have executed works with themes provided by Mayer. This collaborative effort is seen in the romanticized *Dream of Happiness* (Fig. VI.21), for which Prud'hon provided the initial design and also executed a number of individual preliminary studies, perhaps inspired by Greuze's *Allegory of Conjugal Happiness.*[77] The finished work, painted by Mayer, depicts a sleeping mother cradling a small child in her arms, while her handsome, windswept husband embraces them both from behind. They are aboard a boat being rowed by a darkly lit figure of Fortune, who is helped in her task by Cupid. The entire painting is bathed in a dramatic chiaroscuro lighting that virtually obscures the landscape background. Greer has identified the figure of Fortune as a self-portrait of Mayer, which adds a poignant note to this work.[78] Cast in shadow and attended by Love, Fortune looks longingly at the blissfulness of the happy family across from her. By the time Mayer painted this work, her own plans for a happy family life were merely a dream. She was 44 years old and had had no children. Her hopes to marry Prud'hon were dashed when he said he would never marry again and his children turned increasingly against her.

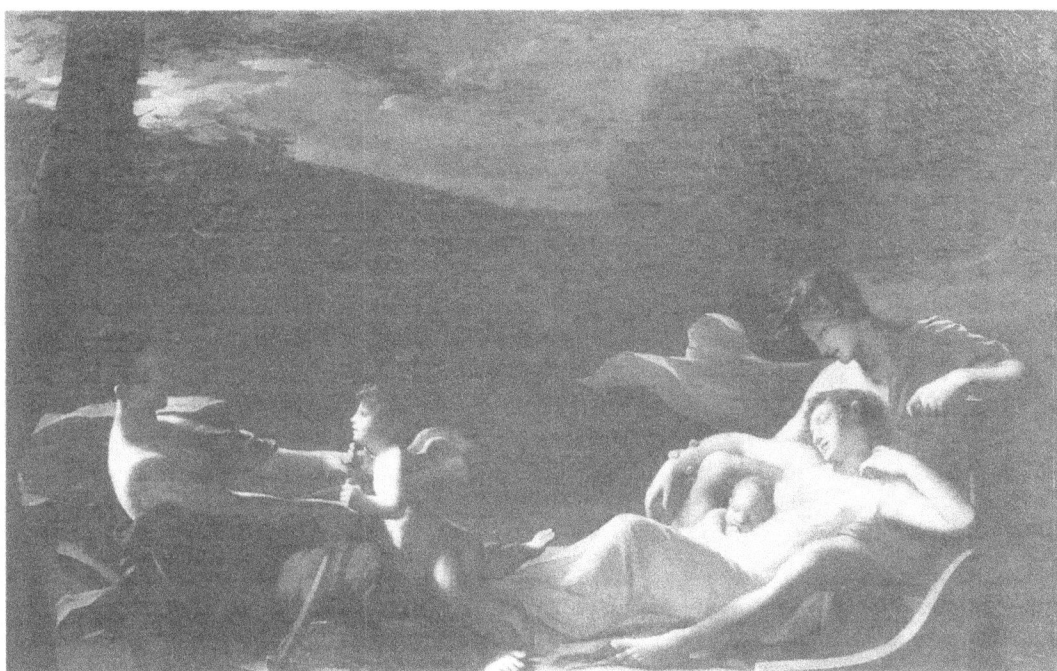

VI.21   Constance Mayer, *Dream of Happiness*, 1819

She grew more and more melancholy during the last years of her life. The final straw seems to have been the eviction of artists from the Sorbonne. Depressed and afraid for the future, Mayer slit her throat with Prud'hon's razor while he worked in his adjoining studio. The devastated Prud'hon then finished her works, organized a retrospective exhibition for her held in 1822 and died himself the next year – a tragically romantic episode in the era of Romanticism.

Although Neo-classicism and Romanticism dominated as stylistic trends until well into the nineteenth century, they began in the mid-eighteenth. They were styles based on an idealized or fantasized conception of nature. This theoretical approach to art changed with the introduction of new technology, which included photography, and the emergence of an industrial economy which created a new political environment.

VII

The nineteenth century: education, exhibitions and new opportunities

There have been so many women artists involved in self-portraiture from the mid-nineteenth century to the present day that a comprehensive survey is impossible. The reason for this increase has to do with expanded opportunities for education and exhibition. Between 1840 and 1870 the number of women in the United States who identified themselves as artists increased fourfold, and between 1870 and 1900 the number of women artists and art teachers grew dramatically faster, from 420 to 11,031.[1] In England there were 278 professional women artists in 1841, and 1,069 in 1871.[2] In France *The Artist* of May 1880 stated that there were 2,150 lady artists, including painters in oil, sculptors, miniaturists, ceramicists, watercolorists and draftsmen in pastel and crayon.[3] This estimate is somewhat at odds with the figures given in *La Gazette des Femmes*, which reported that schools of drawing in Paris had 6,370 women students.[4] The differences may be reconciled by the fact that some of the students were amateurs or non-professional artists, others were learning drawing as one of several teaching skills, and still others may have been studying drawing for industrial design.

By the nineteenth century in both Europe and America, it had become no longer necessary for a woman artist to receive her training from her father, or another male relative. Schools of art in both Europe and America opened their doors to women, and a number of new societies were founded exclusively for female painters. The fact that many other careers were now available to women outside the home reflects the greater independence women had with regard to career choices, whether artistic or otherwise. There were possibilities for both male and female painters. Often artists of either sex would work at another job or profession while striving to establish themselves professionally.

One of the major nineteenth-century artistic movements in England embraced the new role of the woman painter as both a model and an artist.

The Pre-Raphaelite Brotherhood (PRB) was founded in 1848 by seven young artists, including Dante Gabriel Rossetti, out of a belief in the sincerity and simplicity of artists before Raphael, such as Fra Angelico, Benozzo Gozzoli, Andrea Mantegna and Sandro Botticelli. They were also influenced by art critic John Ruskin, who believed in rendering nature exactly as it was, and not idealizing or generalizing, as did the Royal Academy. Pre-Raphaelite artists applied this precept to literary and historical scenes as well, attempting to represent scenes truthfully without glamor or sentimentality.

Although the early Pre-Raphaelite artists were emphatically a brotherhood, women were accepted as equals as the group expanded. These women included Elizabeth Siddal, Georgiana Burne-Jones, Jane Morris and Marie Spartali. Not only did they serve as models, wives, housekeepers and companions, they were also partners on projects – Jane Morris, her sister Bessie and daughter May executed embroideries for William Morris, and Siddal and Rossetti collaborated in producing a painted jewel casket for Jane Morris. However, only Elizabeth Siddal and Marie Spartali painted self-portraits, and although these were not acclaimed in their own time, they have come to be renowned by virtue of Siddal's and Spartali's relationships to the artists of the Brotherhood.

Elizabeth Eleanor Siddal was born 25 July 1829 to a Sheffield-born cutler and his wife, Elizabeth Eleanor Evans. Legend has it that Dante Gabriel Rossetti (1828–82) was drawing in William Holman Hunt's studio when Walter Deverell burst in on his friends extolling his 'find'. Deverell, who had gone with his mother to Mrs Tozzer's shop to help her choose a bonnet, persuaded his mother to ask Siddal to pose for Viola in his painting, *Twelfth Night* (1849–50, Forbes Magazine Collection, New York).

Whatever the truth of her first encounter with the Brotherhood, Siddal soon turned out to be the favorite model for the young Pre-Raphaelite painters, posing for Holman Hunt's *A Converted British Family Sheltering a Christian Missionary* (Ashmolean Museum, Oxford) as well as for his *Valentine Rescuing Sylvia from Proteus* (Manchester Art Gallery, Manchester). Siddal was Millais's *Ophelia* (Tate Gallery, London), posing fully clothed, in a bath tub. She also sat for Rossetti's *The Return of Tibellus to Delia* (c.1851–3, Birmingham City Museum and Art Gallery, Birmingham).

It was bad for a woman's reputation being a milliner's assistant, in trade, but worse being an artist's model. Such models often posed in the nude – a totally scandalous occupation – and frequently conducted liaisons with the artists painting them. In Victorian England especially, it was a taboo occupation, and Rossetti took great care not to have this fact about Siddal divulged by his artist friends or his family. Most models used by the Pre-Raphaelite Brotherhood were in fact quite respectable, as the artists seldom used professionals and prevailed on friends and relatives to sit for them.

Siddal became Rossetti's exclusive model, then his student, and finally, in spite of chronic ill health, his wife, in 1860.

In 1853, she began her first oil, a self-portrait in a tondo frame, in which the subject is shown bust length, facing three-quarters to her left, and looking at the viewer from heavy-lidded eyes (Plate XXVI). The subject has an interesting, albeit not beautiful face, certainly unlike either the one extant photograph (frontispiece of Jan Marsh, *Elizabeth Siddal 1829–1862, Pre-Raphaelite Artist*; the Ruskin Gallery, Sheffield, 1991) or the many idealized portraits of her executed by Dante Gabriel Rossetti. However, William Rossetti described it as 'an absolute likeness'.[5] It also corresponds with his description of her: 'tall, finely formed, with a lofty neck, and regular yet somewhat uncommon features, greenish-blue unsparkling eyes, large perfect eyelids, brilliant complexion, and a lavish heavy wealth of coppery hair'. It seems to say, 'My mind and my feelings are my own, and no outsider is expected to pry into them.'[6]

Part of Siddal's reserve may have stemmed from her awareness of her lower-class status and from fears of committing *faux pas*, although it may also have denoted self-possession and self-knowledge. In its own way, this self-portrait is a truthful mirroring of Siddal's features, not a romantic illusion or self-serving flattery. It is, in addition, a testimony to the fact that she seems to have had more art training than her brief apprenticeship to Rossetti would indicate.

Siddal's self-portrait also conforms stylistically to the ideals of Pre-Raphaelite painting in that it depicts its subject truthfully and realistically, with a nearly photographic concentration on the minute details of features, costume and background. Following the critic John Ruskin's dictate to observe and copy nature faithfully, Siddal's *Self-Portrait* presents an image of heightened realism without artifice or pretense.

In 1855, when Ruskin first viewed Siddal's drawings, he purchased them all immediately and proposed paying her an annual allowance in return for first choice of her works. Of this event, Rossetti wrote, 'He declared that they were far better than mine, or almost anyone's and seemed wild with delight at getting them.'[7] Unfortunately, with the allowance came Ruskin's advice, catching Siddal between two powerful masters determined to dominate her life. She became so ill that in 1857 she found it necessary to relinquish Ruskin's allowance and the accompanying control.

Ruskin's patronage of Siddal is one of the fairly rare examples of patronage of women artists in the nineteenth century. Although portraits of others were still desired by patrons, self-portraits by female artists do not appear to have been commissioned in any number during the nineteenth century, unlike the earlier self-portrait commissions of Sofonisba Anguissola and her contemporary female artists. This had the effect of changing the nature of female artists' self-representation – rather than depicting beautiful, accomplished gentlewomen, women's self-portraits became more of a personal record or an exercise in creating likeness.

In 1861 Siddal was delivered of a stillborn baby girl, an event of much sorrow to both her and Rossetti. She began to rely more heavily on that Victorian cure-all, laudanum, to ease her pain and illness. It was a particularly unreliable drug, as its opium content varied from dose to dose. On 10 February 1862, Rossetti returned home to find his wife unconscious, either from an accidental overdose or possibly a suicide attempt. In spite of her husband summoning four physicians, she could not be revived, and on the morning of 11 February 1862 Siddal died.

Siddal's brief life became the subject of legend, but the possibilities of her art were never realized. She was the first woman to show with the Pre-Raphaelite artists, in an exhibition at 4 Fitzroy Square in 1857, but it was not until 1991 that a retrospective of her art was held, at the Ruskin Gallery in Sheffield, having been organized by Jan Marsh and Janet Barnes, the keeper of the Gallery. During her life, Siddal produced over 100 drawings and paintings, a number of which are now known only by their titles or by their photographs from glass negatives in the Ashmolean Museum. What other works might she have produced if she had lived longer? It is impossible, of course, to say. But both Ruskin and Rossetti were convinced of her genius and originality, and Charles Eliot Norton, one of the first art historians, owned one of her works. Siddal came a long way, from milliner's assistant and artists' model in a rigidly class-conscious society censorious of her occupations and origins, but it was at a very high price – perhaps that of her very life.

Although the original Pre-Raphaelite Brotherhood is usually dated to 1848–57, Pre-Raphaelitism as a style and as an aesthetic philosophy continued into the twentieth century, with a second and a third generation of Pre-Raphaelite artists. Marie Spartali Stillman (1844–1927) was a second-generation Pre-Raphaelite artist who also painted self-portraits. She was born in Tottenham, Middlesex, one of two daughters of Michael Spartali, a Greek merchant and consul-general for Greece from 1866 to 1882. Both Marie and her sister Christine were esteemed great beauties and were asked by various artists to sit for them. Marie sat for Ford Madox Brown, for Val Prinsep and, in 1869, for Rossetti for three chalk heads for his painting *Dante's Dream on the Anniversary of the Death of Beatrice* (Walker Art Gallery, Liverpool) as well as for the painting itself in 1871. She also modeled for Rossetti's *The Vision of Fiammetta* (private collection). It is important to note, however, that Spartali debuted as an artist before she did any modeling, for artists who were her friends, and also that her own painting, *The Last Sight of Fiammetta*, shown in London and Manchester in 1876, predated Rossetti's *Vision* by 18 months.

In 1871 Spartali married a friend of Dante Gabriel Rossetti's, the American journalist William J. Stillman. Stillman had begun his career as a painter, but was discouraged by Ruskin's meddling and constant advice, although he remained a firm supporter of Ruskin's ideas. Since Stillman was a widower with three children, little wealth and no job, he was not considered to be an ideal mate in the eyes of Spartali's family. The marriage proved a happy one, though, and Spartali continued her career as a painter, sending works to exhibitions in London, even from Florence (1877 to 1886) and from Rome, where the Stillmans lived from 1886 until their return to England in 1898. After her husband's death in 1901, Spartali resided with her stepdaughter Lisa, a portrait painter, and her daughter Effie, a sculptor.

The Delaware Art Museum owns Spartali's 1871 *Self-Portrait* (Figure VII.1), a charcoal drawing on paper that depicts a half-length figure leaning on a

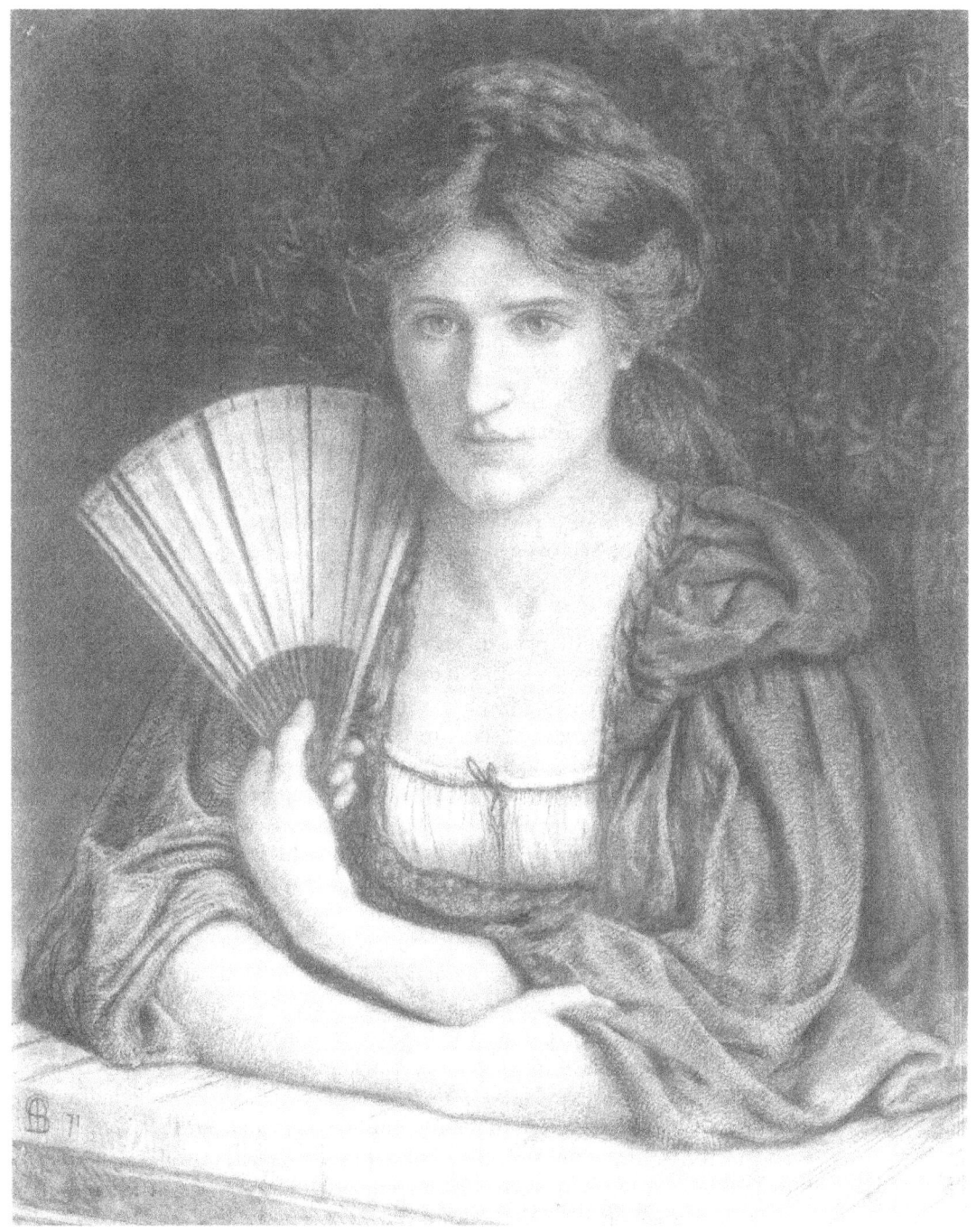

VII.1   Marie Spartali Stillman, *Self-Portrait*, 1871

parapet, dressed in Renaissance costume and holding a fan. The background is of a patterned fabric, and Spartali's monogram on the parapet at bottom left imitates Rossetti's monogram signing device. It was Rossetti who, using Venetian prototypes, created this type of half-length portrait in *Bocca Baciata* (1859, Museum of Fine Arts, Boston) and subsequent works. In her *Self-Portrait*, as in many of her representations of women, Spartali exhibits a pensive and inward-looking expression of seriousness, even wistfulness. It is noteworthy that the Greek iconography of her earlier work does not appear, perhaps because her parents and other Greek relatives were adamantly opposed to her marriage to Stillman. She chose independence and the right to be an artist rather than someone's ornament. She continued on this career path for 60 years until her death in 1927. The greatest tribute to her art came from Henry James in his review of an 1875 watercolor exhibition at the National Academy of Design, New York, which included works by Winslow Homer and John LaFarge. James wrote, 'The most interesting things, however, were not American. These consisted of four elaborately finished pictures by Mrs. Spartali Stillman. This lady is a really profound colorist, but the principal charm of her work is the intellectual charm – that thing which, when it exists, always seems more precious than other merits, and indeed makes us say that it is the only thing in a work of art which is deeply valuable.'[8]

The careers of Pre-Raphaelite artists Elizabeth Siddal and Marie Spartali raise a number of issues relevant to the life of a female artist in the nineteenth century. One in particular was the ever-present burden of being a female in a male-dominated art world, one that excluded women from the most prestigious art schools, denied them privileges such as the drawing and painting of male nudes, prevented them from joining art clubs and withheld the advantages of belonging to the best professional societies. Female artists were also subject to the prevalent philosophy which held that a woman's place was in the domestic sphere, especially after marriage, in the education of her children and the governance of the household. Henrietta Ward, an artist married to an artist, so testified: 'In my young days most people would have agreed…that a wife and mother had no right to be a practitioner in paint, and I think in most households it would have been rendered impossible by the husband's and relations' combined antagonism to the idea.'[9]

Pre-Raphaelite artists, however, held much more egalitarian notions about women's careers. Dante Gabriel Rossetti, for example, wrote indignantly in 1860 to his friend William Allingham about his wife, Elizabeth Siddal, 'Indeed and of course my wife *does* draw still. Her last designs would I am sure delight you…I feel surer every time she works that she has real genius.'[10] (Rossetti's mention of Siddal's 'genius' here is especially significant, as the Romantics exalted genius, and usually viewed its possession as an exclusively male attribute.) Rossetti's real esteem for his wife's art was not idle words. In a letter dated 22 November 1860 to Allingham, he wrote, 'We have got one of our rooms completely hung round with Lizzie's drawings which I would like to show you.'[11]

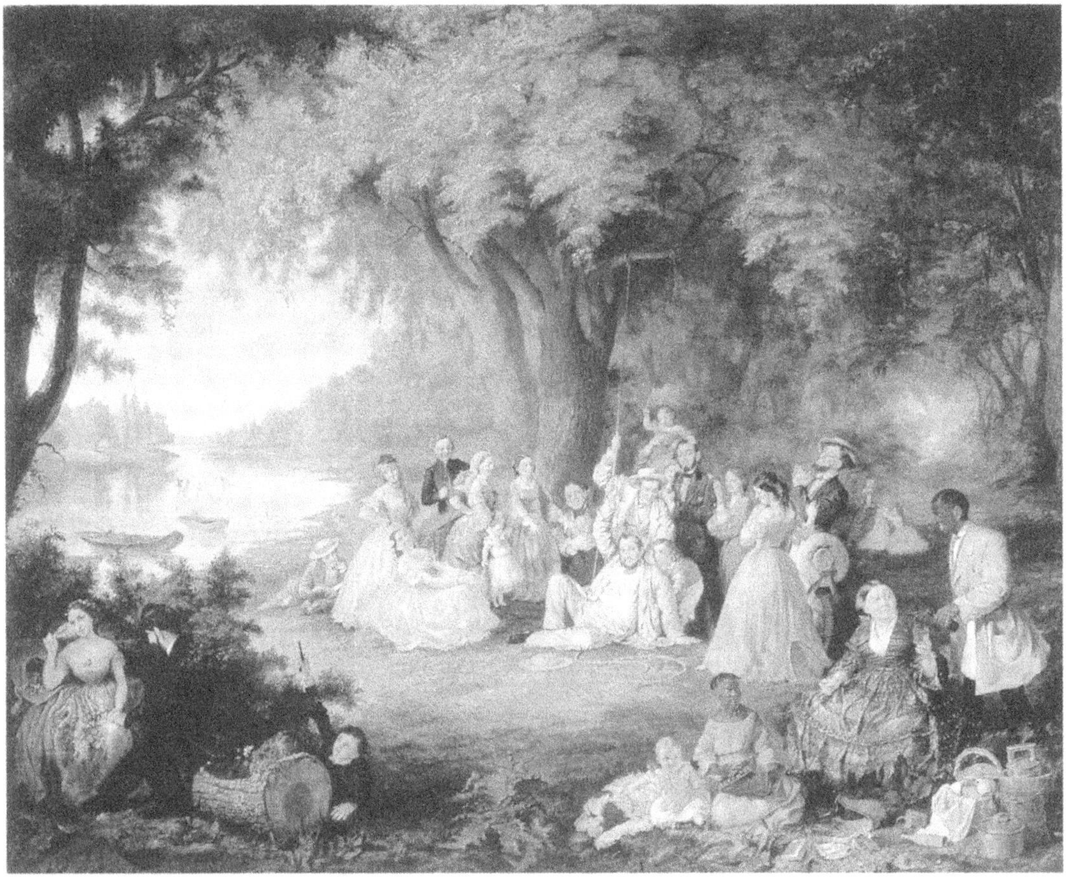

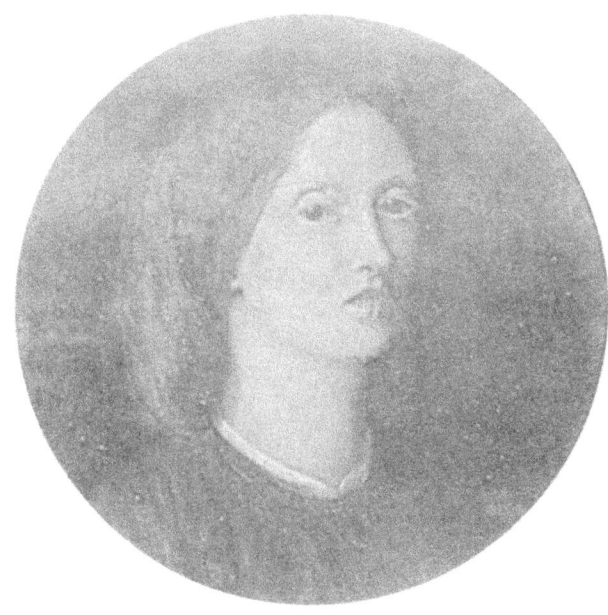

XXVIII   Lilly Martin Spencer, *The Artist and Her Family at a Fourth of July Picnic*, c.1864

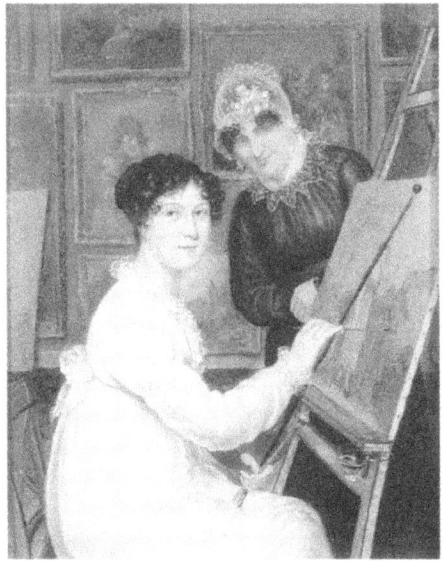

XXVII   Rolinda Sharples, *The Artist and Her Mother*, c.1825

XXVI   Elizabeth Siddal, *Self-Portrait*, 1854

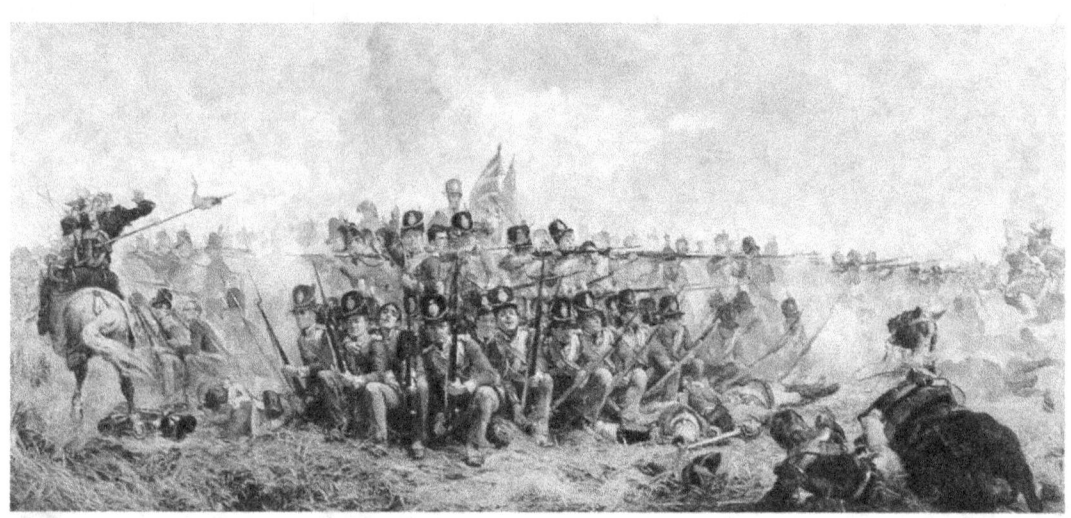

XXIX   *(top)* Elizabeth
Thompson (Lady Butler),
*The 28th Regiment at
Quatre Bras, 1815*, 1875
XXX   *(right)* Berthe
Morisot, *Self-Portrait*,
c.1885

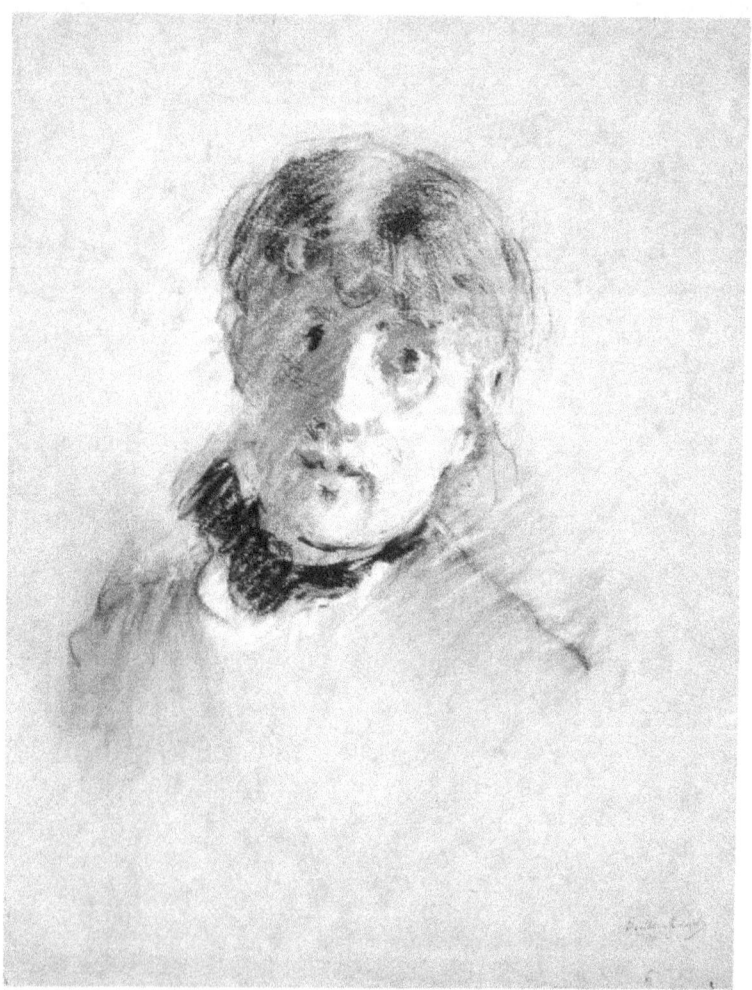

XXXI Mary
Cassatt, *Self-
Portrait*, c.1880

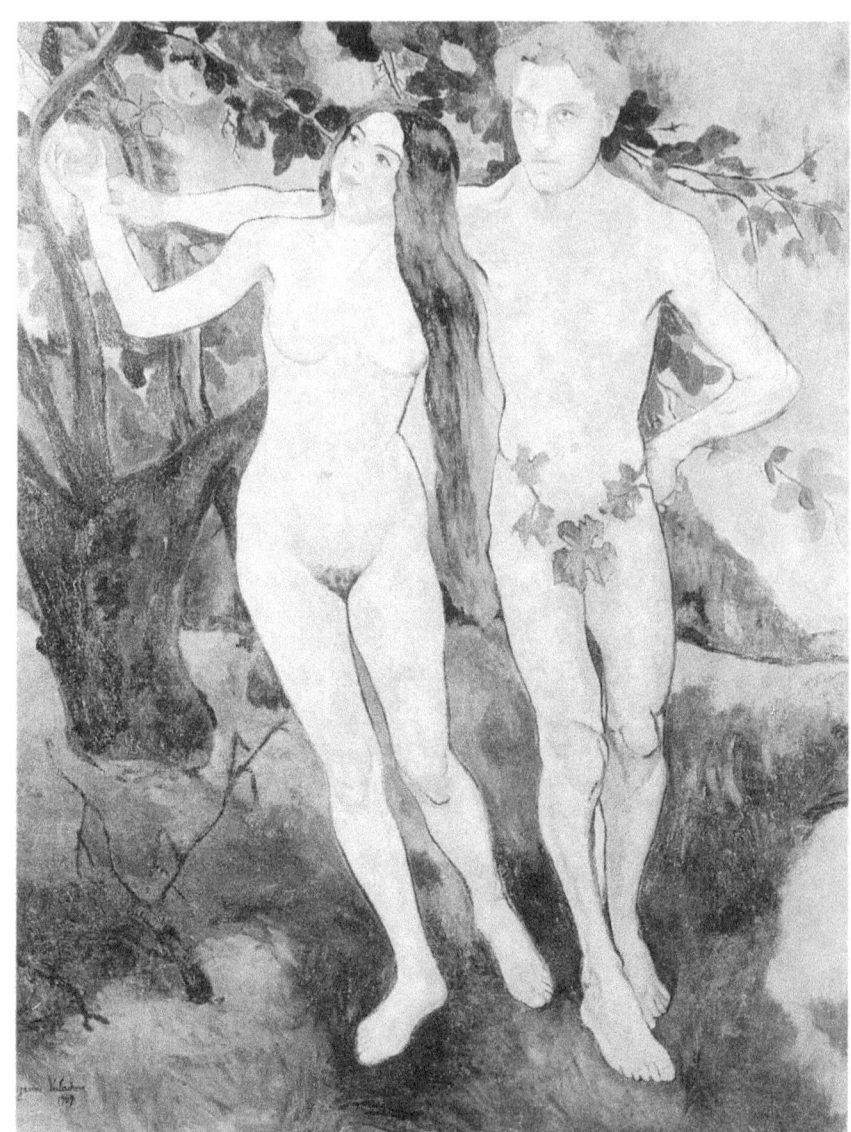

XXXII   Suzanne
Valadon, *Adam and
Eve*, 1909
XXXIII   *(opposite)*
Gwen John, *Self-
Portrait*, 1902

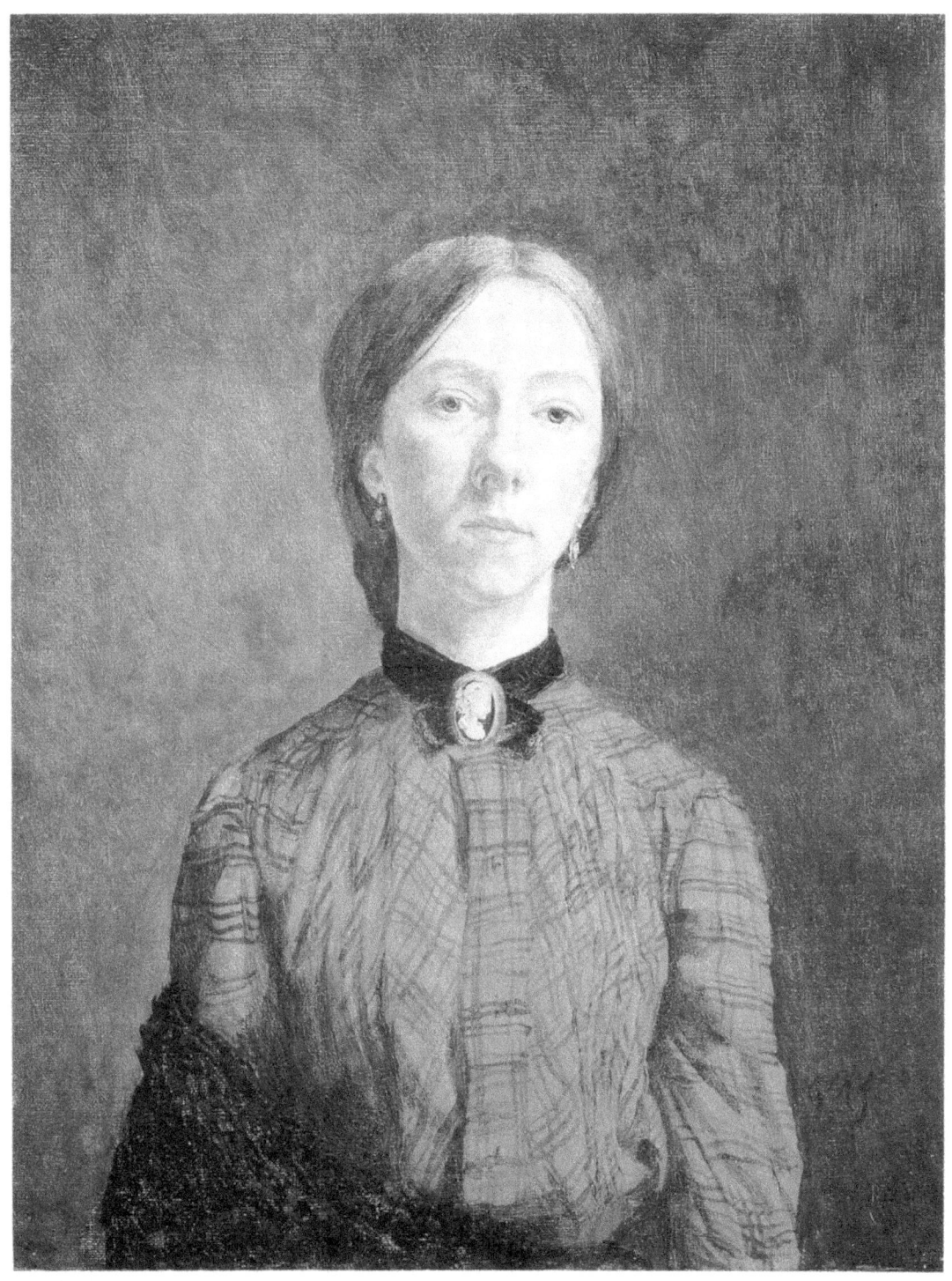

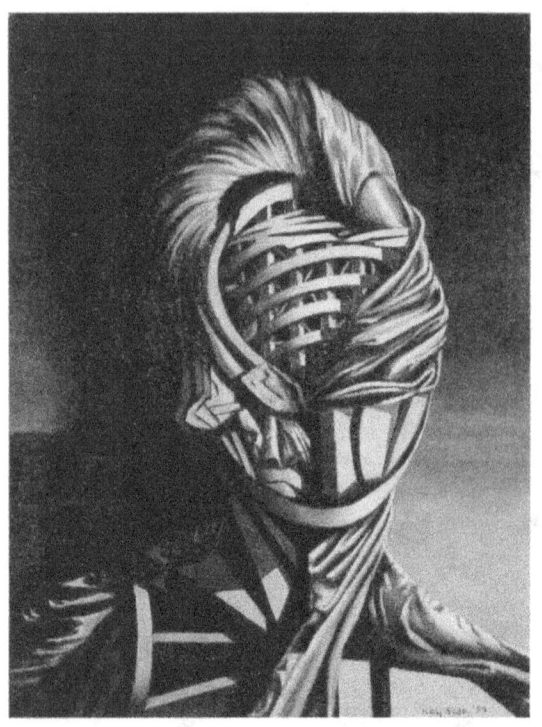

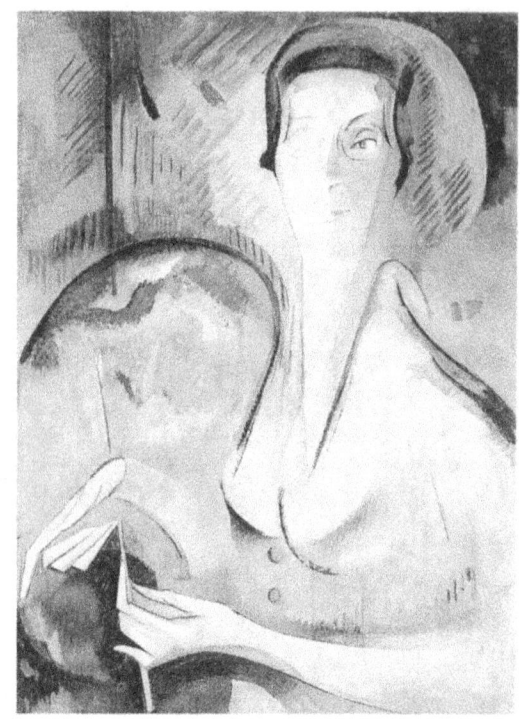

XXXV   *(top right)* Alice Bailly, *Self-Portrait*, 1917
XXXVI   *(top left)* Kay Sage, *Small Portrait*, 1950
XXXVIII   *(bottom)* Remedios Varo, *Exploration of the Sources of the Orinoco River*, 1959

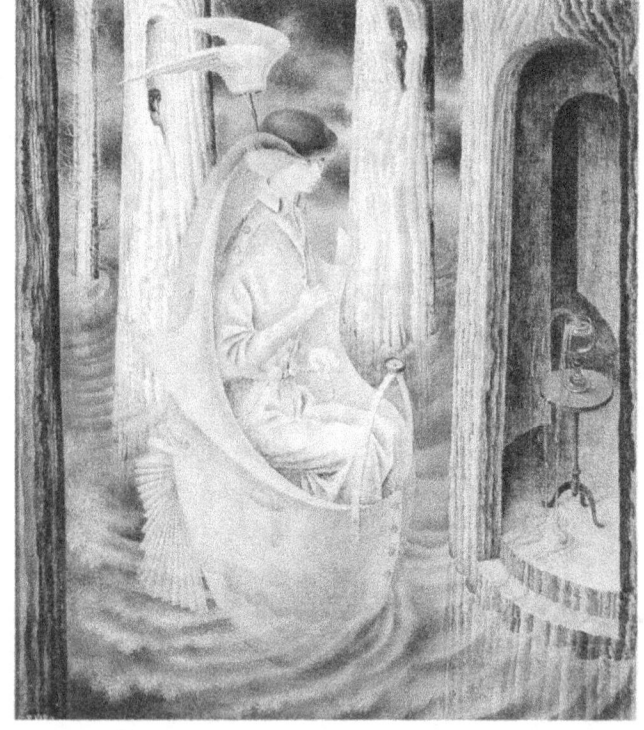

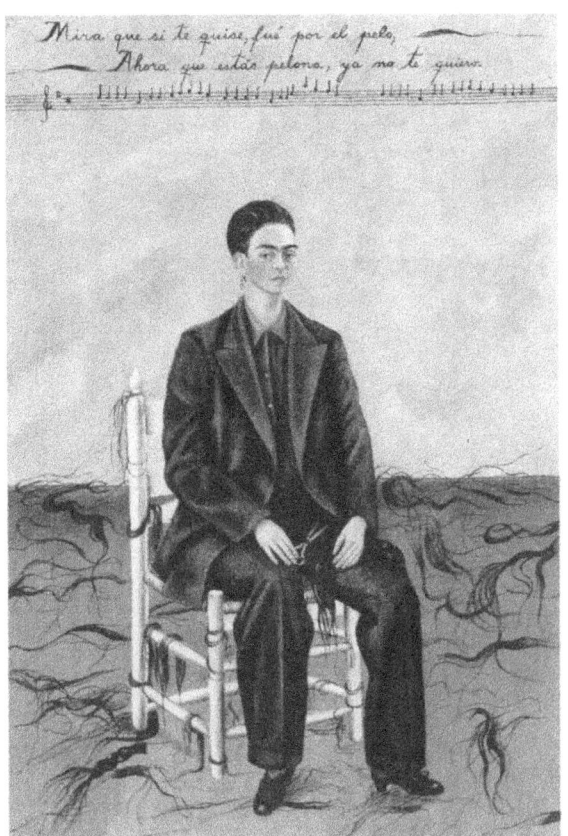

XXXVII *(top)* Frida Kahlo, *Self-Portrait with Cropped Hair*, 1940
XXXIV *(bottom)* Paula Modersohn-Becker, *Self-Portrait*, 1906

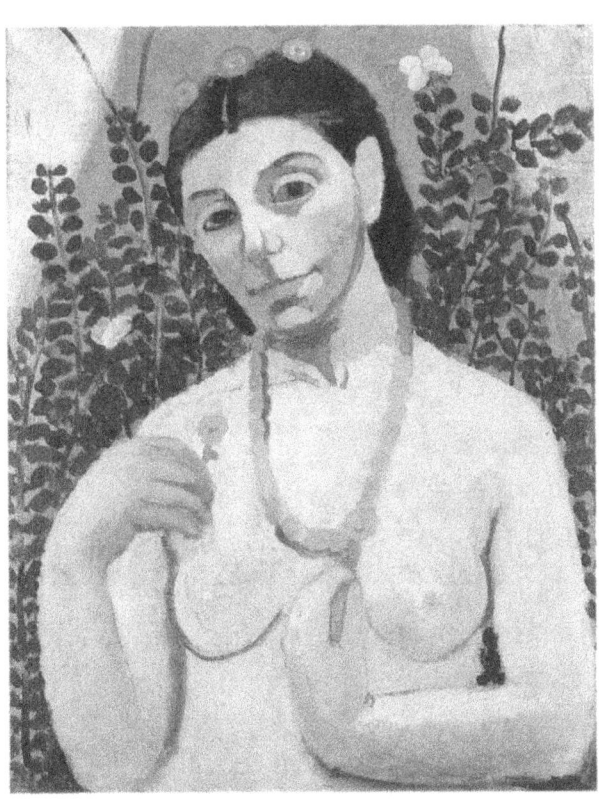

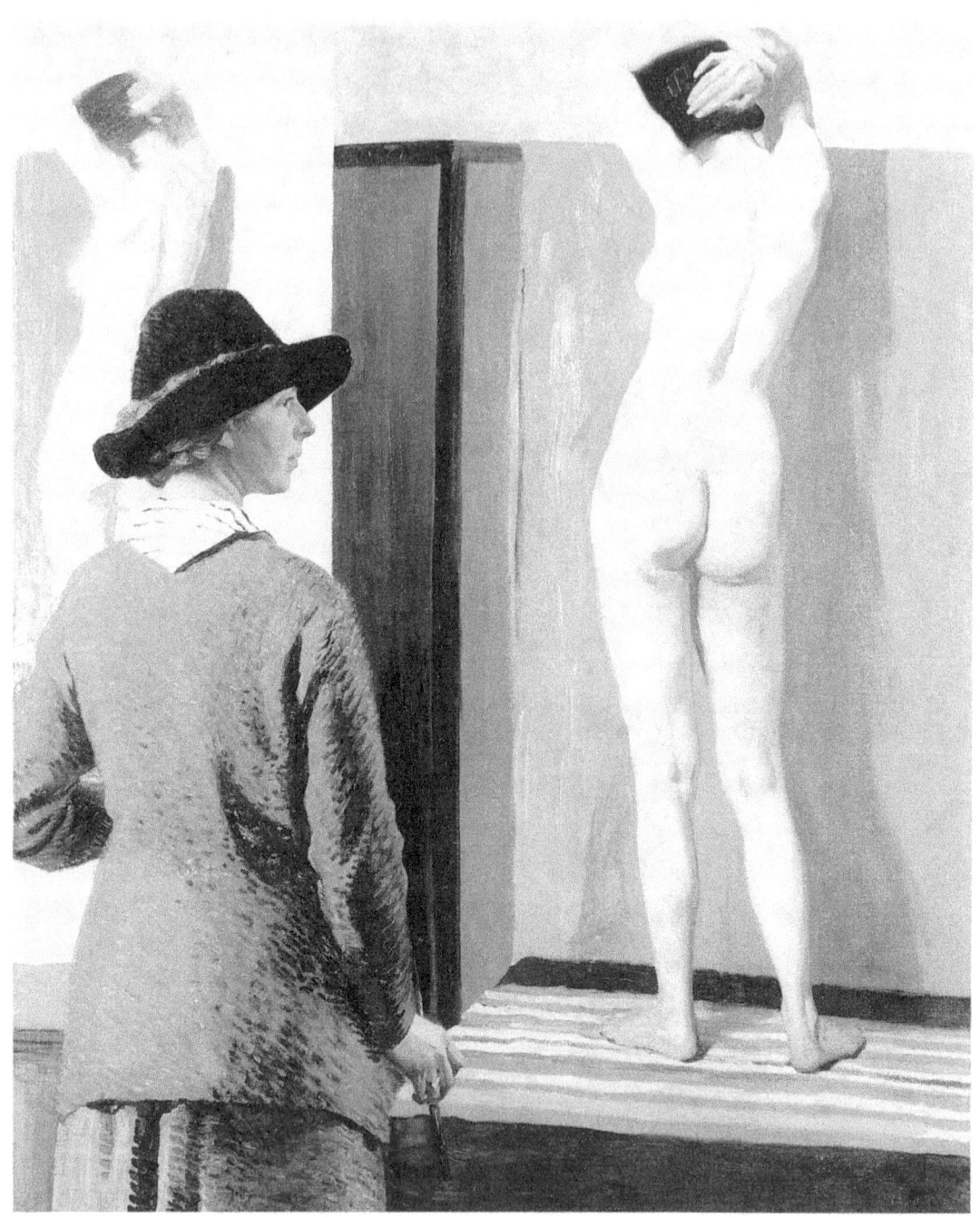

XXXIX   Laura Knight, *Self-Portrait with Nude Model*, 1913

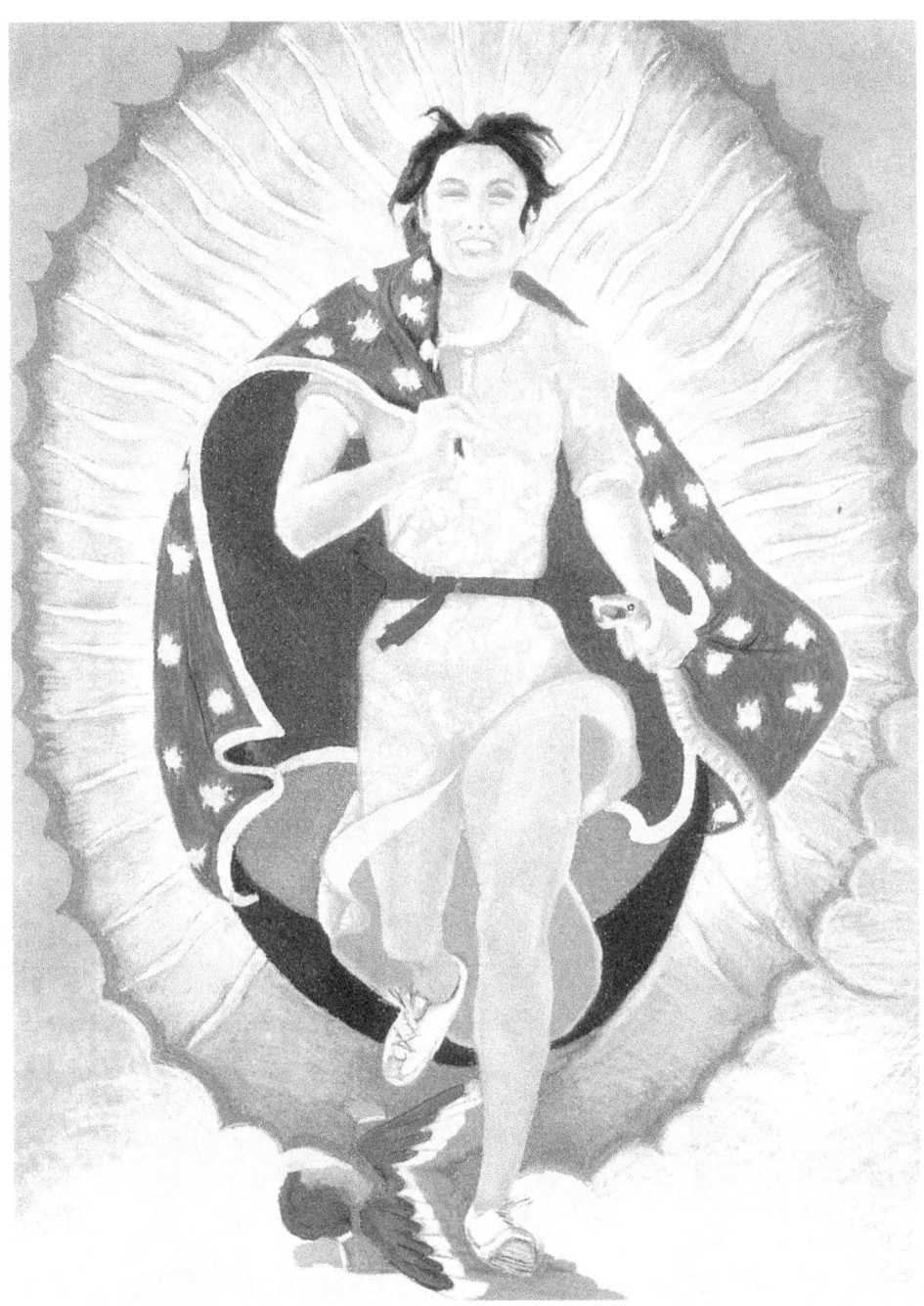

XL   Yolanda Lopez, *The Artist as Virgin of Guadalupe*, 1978

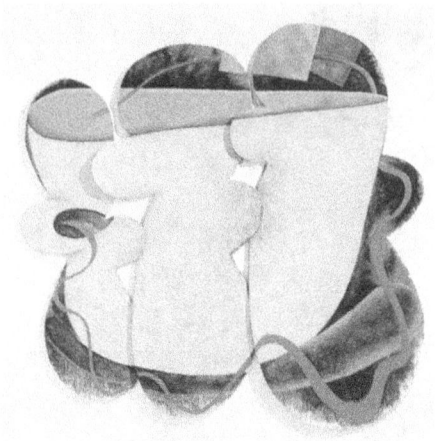

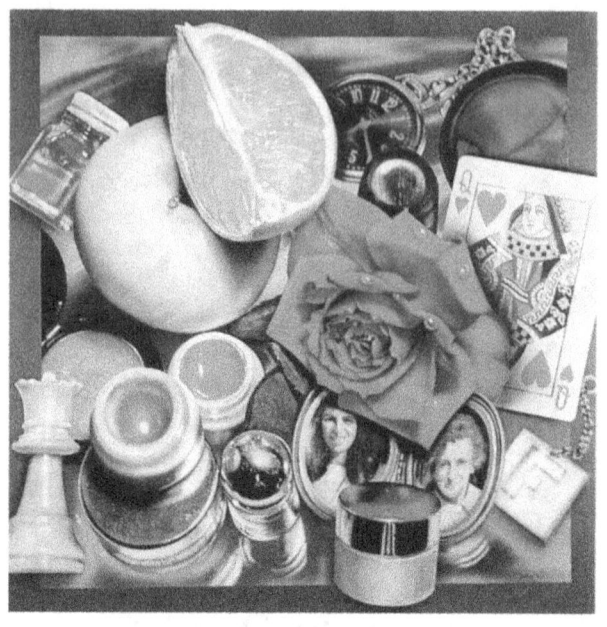

XLI   *(bottom)* Jaune Quick-To-See Smith, *The Red Mean: Self-Portrait*, 1992
XLII   *(above right)* Audrey Flack, *Queen*, 1975-6
XLIII   *(above left)* Elizabeth Murray, *Sail Baby*, 1983

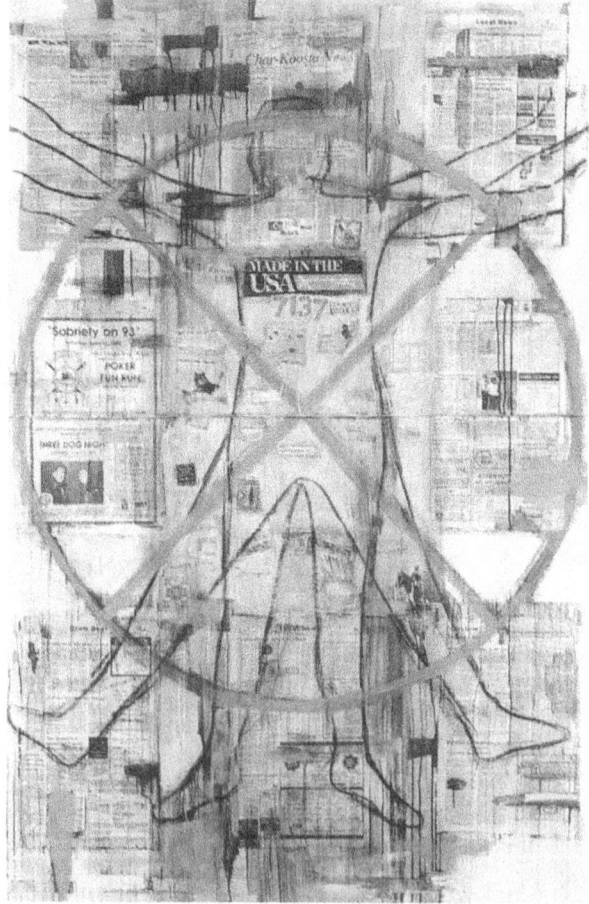

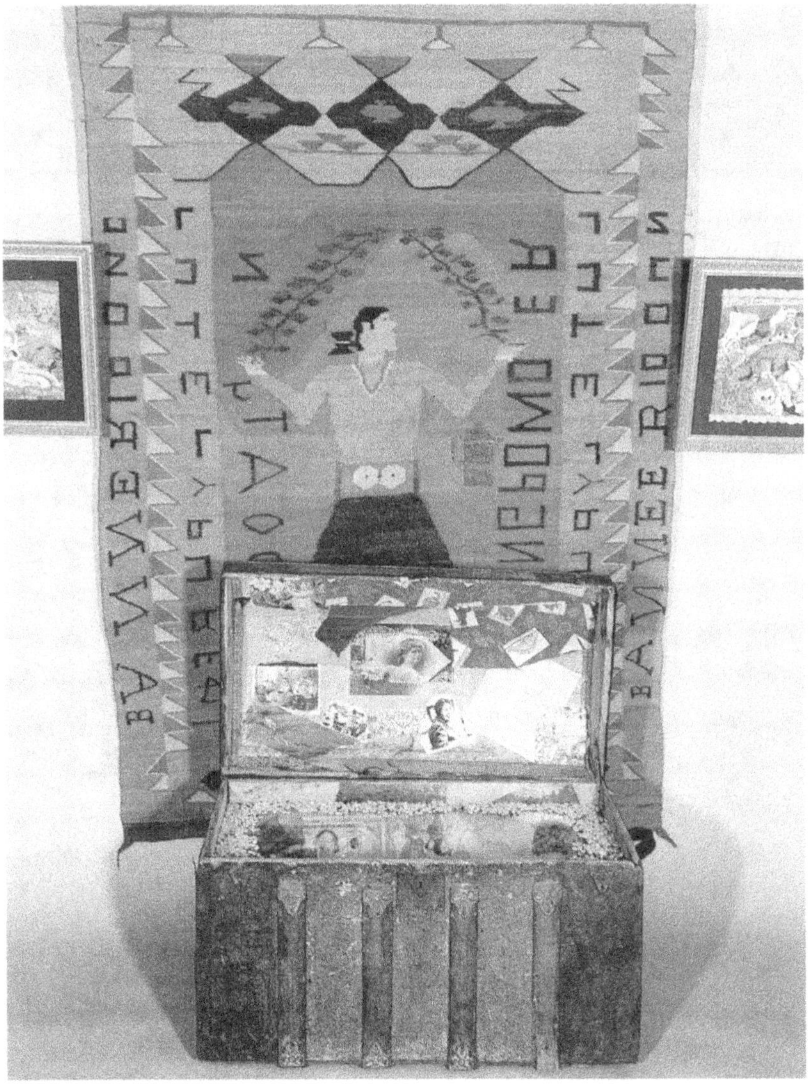

XLV *(top)* Ana
Mendieta, *Body Tracks*,
1982
XLIV *(left)* Melanie
Yazzie, *Raggedy Ann*,
1994

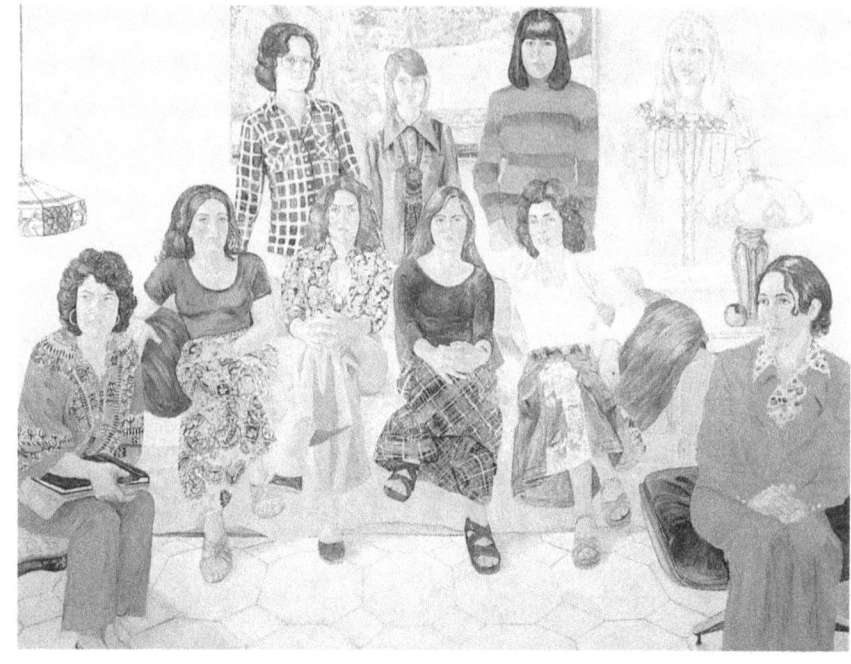

XLVIA Sylvia Sleigh, *Artists of the SoHo 20 Gallery*, 1974

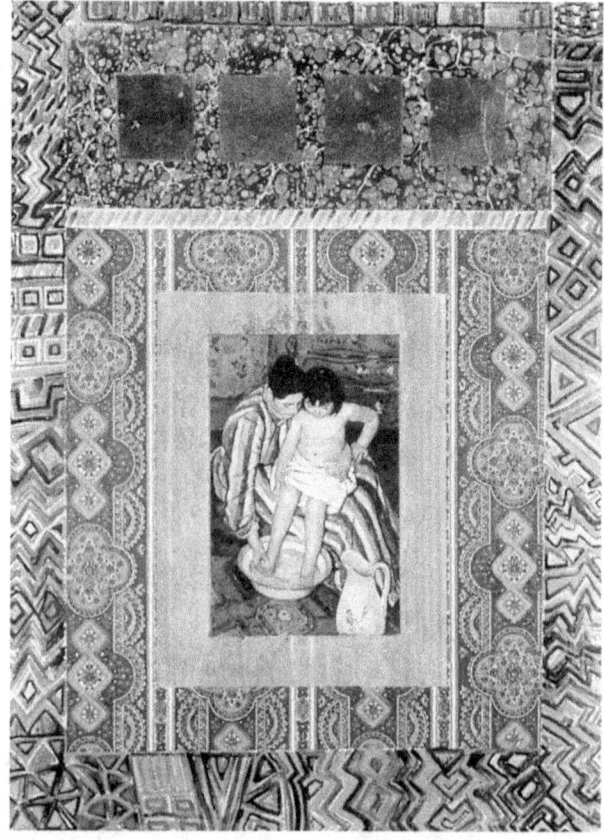

XLVII Miriam Schapiro, *Collaboration Series: Mary Cassatt and Me*, 1976

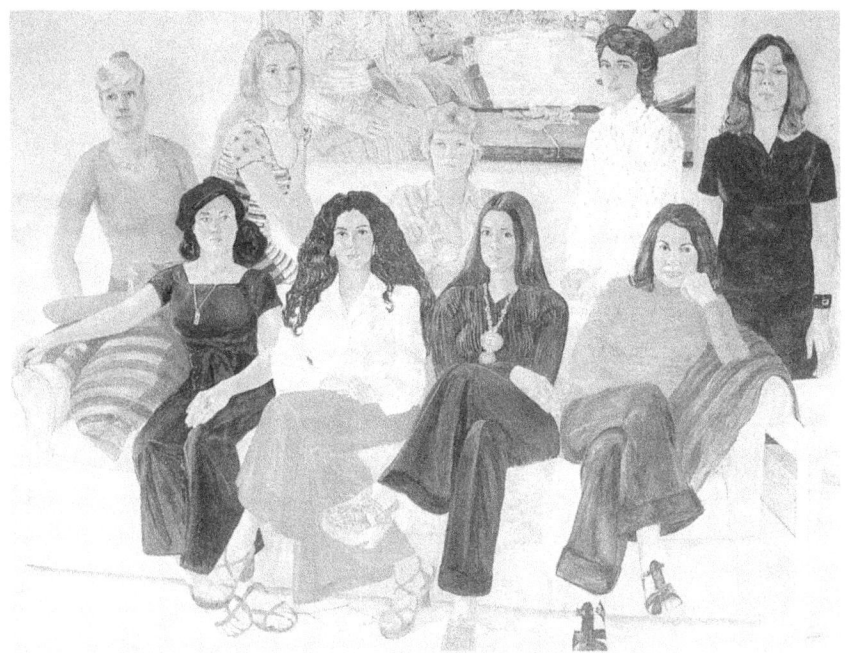

XLVIB Sylvia
Sleigh, *Artists of the
SoHo 20 Gallery*,
1974

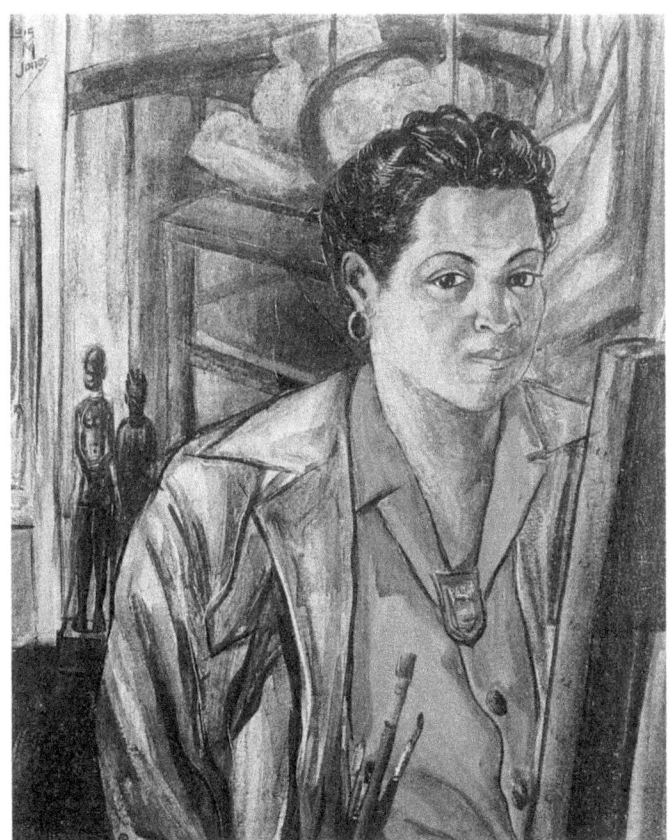

XLVIII Lois
Mailou Jones, *Self-
Portrait*, 1940

L   Howardena Pindell, *Autobiography:*
Water/Ancestors/Middle Passage/Family Ghosts,
1988

LI   Emma Amos, *Will You Forget Me?*, 1991

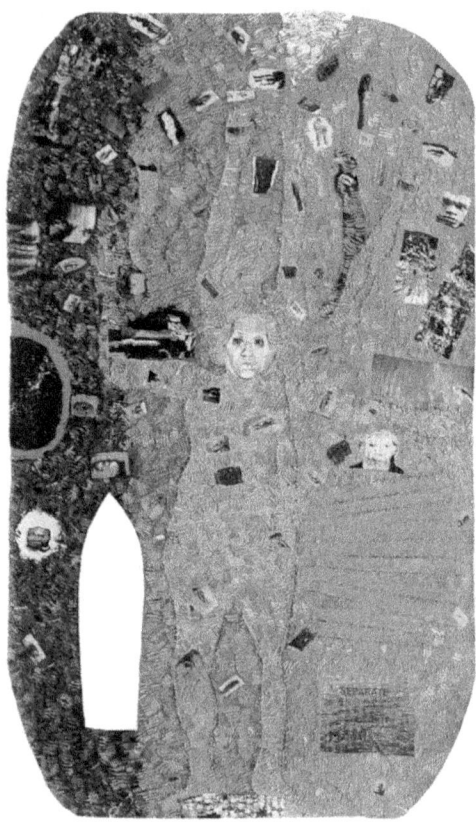

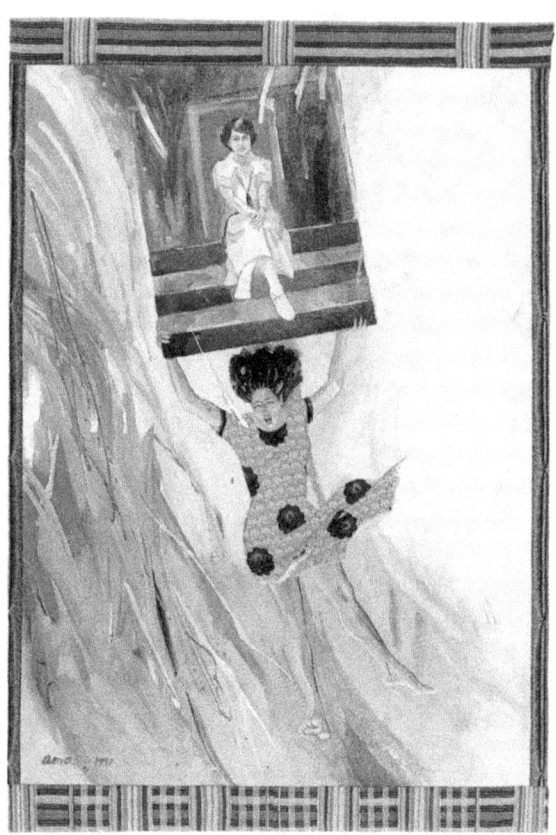

XLIX   *(opposite)*
Paula Rego,
Joseph's Dream,
1990

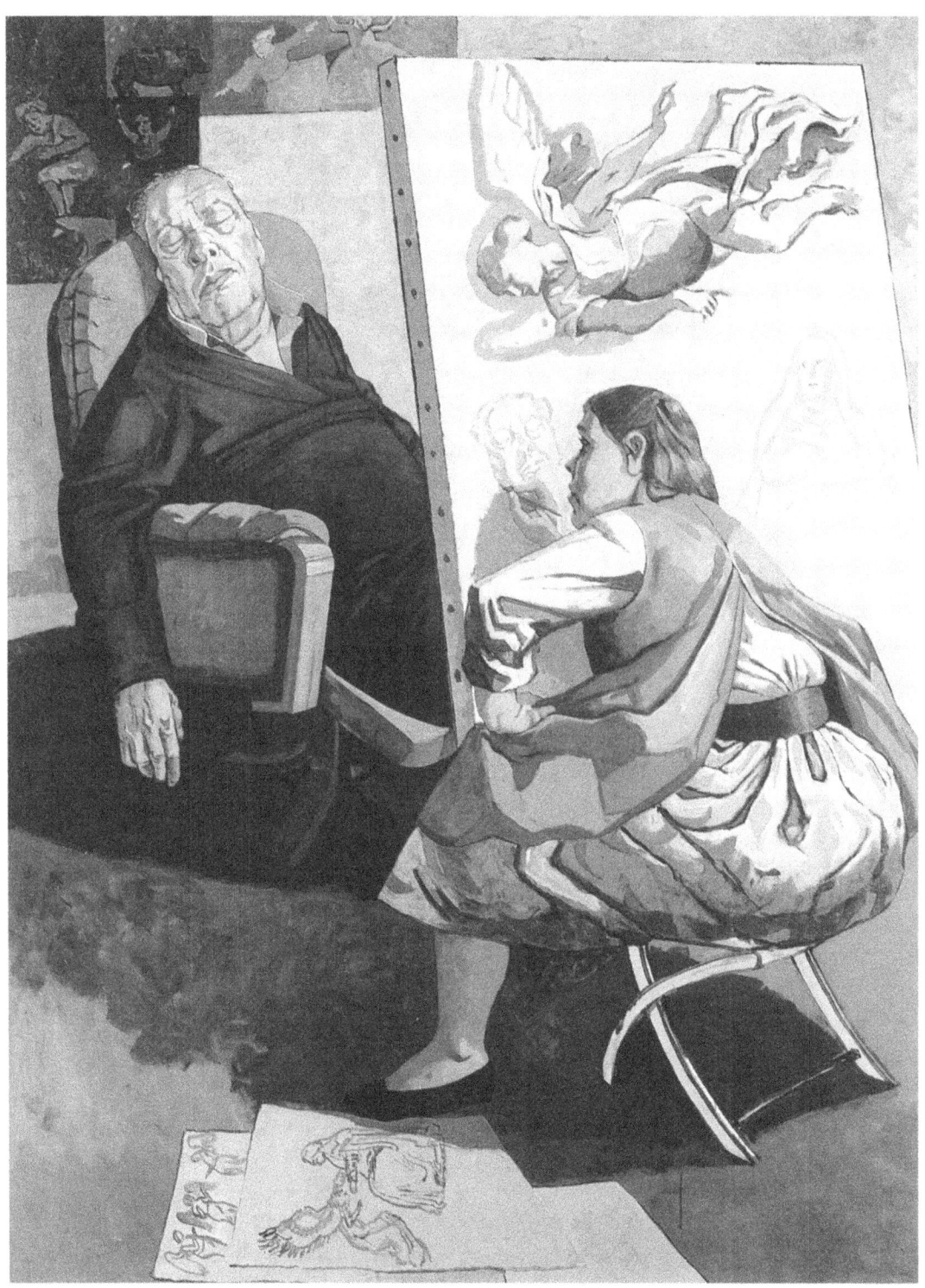

LII   Alice Neel,
Self-Portrait, 1980

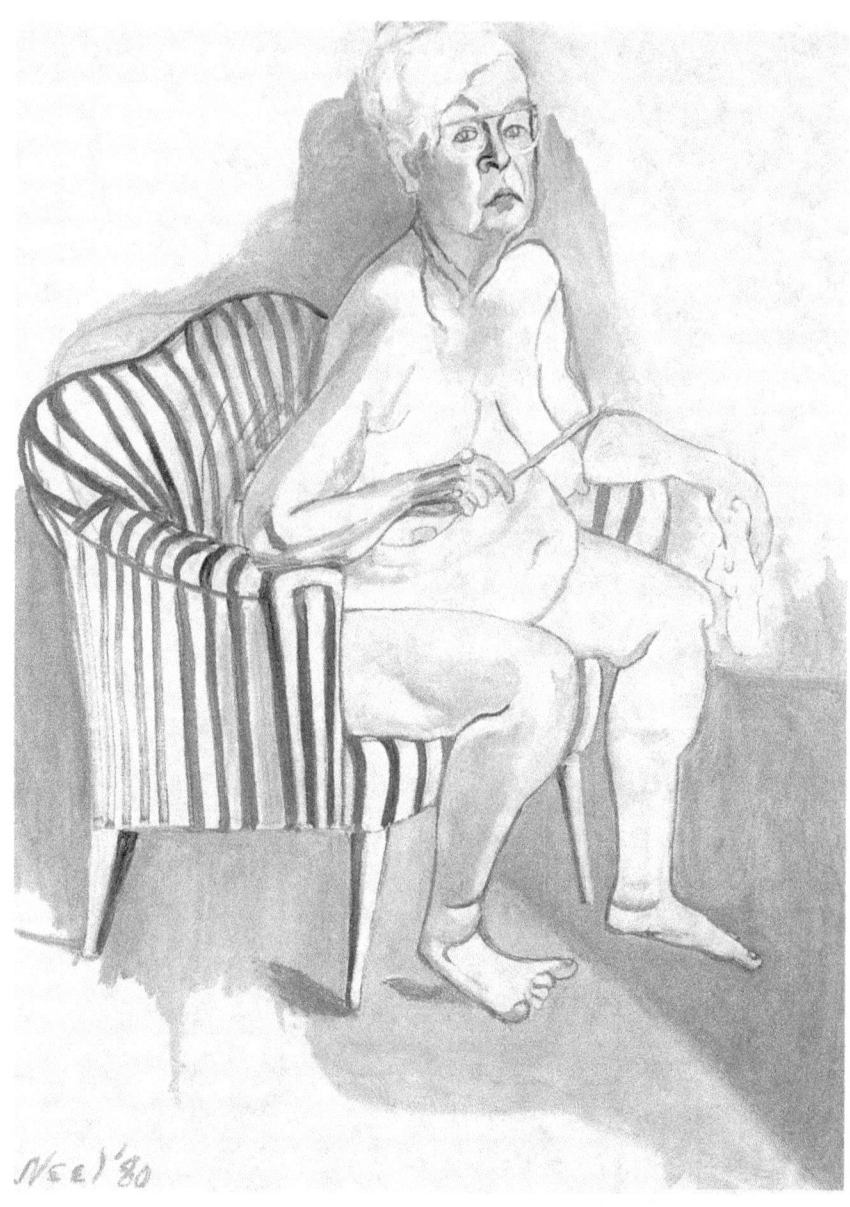

Another aspect illustrated by Siddal's and Spartali's art careers is the change in educational possibilities for female artists in the nineteenth century. Both of them studied with male artists – Siddal with Rossetti and Spartali with Ford Maddox Brown – thus replicating the relationship of Sofonisba Anguissola with Bernardino Campi and Elisabetta Sirani's with Guido Reni. Siddal was able to attend the Sheffield School of Art because it admitted women, an innovation at that time.

One of the most interesting of American artist families in which women played a decisive role was the Sharples family, which included James and Ellen, their daughter Rolinda (c.1793–1838) and their sons Felix and James Junior. The sons joined the family enterprise at the respective ages of 17 and 15, and Rolinda even younger, at age 13. The father, whose specialty was pastel portraits, established his practice in England, but ventured to the United States around 1794, in search of a market with less competition. The family lived and worked in both Philadelphia and New York and traveled in New England as itinerant portrait-painters. Partially because of the uncertainty of James's practice, his wife Ellen became a copyist of his works. She also began educating her daughter in art. Rolinda's success at portrait painting, executing large multi-figured history paintings in oils as well as pastel and oil portraits, led her to become a professional artist. When James developed heart disease and died in New York in 1811, Ellen, Rolinda and James Junior moved to Clifton in England, to resume their family portrait business.

Rolinda became very successful, exhibiting at the Royal Academy in 1820, 1822 and 1824 and eight times at the Society of British Artists. Unfortunately, her career was cut short in 1838, when she died of breast cancer at the age of 45.

Rolinda's most unusual painting is a double portrait of *The Artist and Her Mother* (Pl. XXVII). This work may be unique, certainly it is extremely rare, in being a self-portrait of the artist with his or her mother, and is particularly unusual in that the mother is also a practicing artist and instructor of the daughter in art. There are, of course, self-portraits of female artists and their daughters, including the well-known ones by Elisabeth Vigée-Lebrun in the Louvre. There are also self-portraits that show a mother who is an artist instructing her young daughter in art, such as an 1885 painting by Berthe Morisot (private collection), as well as a drypoint of the same subject by Morisot in 1889, but in the latter case the daughter is not a mature, practicing artist. Similarly, there are self-portraits of female artists with their pupils, such as Adélaïde Labille-Guiard's painting discussed earlier, but neither pupil is the artist's daughter, nor are they shown painting a portrait, as does Rolinda Sharples. This is a portrait of two individuals earning their own incomes as artists after their male provider has died. Ellen Sharples, the mother, who had not been trained as a professional artist as a young woman, firmly believed that women should learn a skill in order to support themselves and their families should illness, death or loss of fortune strike the family.

In *The Artist and Her Mother*, this belief is actualized. The artist, Rolinda, is depicted in the foreground, looking at the viewer while seated before a canvas which is being painted. She wears a charming white muslin frock with lace, which accentuates her presence but which she may not have actually worn to paint, much like Adélaïde Labille-Guiard's elegant outfit in her self-portrait. In Rolinda's left hand she is holding brushes and a maulstick, while touching the canvas with a brush in her right hand. Her mother stands on the right of the canvas, wearing a lace cap and black dress, the traditional garb of widows. She looks over at Rolinda's canvas, thus suggesting her tutelage and support as well as the cooperative nature of the studio. The background wall is covered with paintings so closely hung that there is little space left between the gilded frames. Another detail, in the left background, is part of an easel with a canvas on it, suggesting that Ellen Sharples shares the studio with her daughter. The composition is set in a diagonal from the lower left bottom to the upper right top of the canvas, which includes Rolinda, her mother and the slanting easel holding a painting – almost an allegory of the artist's world.

Despite a move away from the older family workshop organization of art production, there were a number of well-known artist families functioning during the nineteenth century. These included productive female artists such as the Bonheurs, Manets and Pissarros in France; the Wards, Boyces, Madox Browns, Hayllars, Sandyses, Solomons, Morrises, De Morgans and Stillmans in England; and the Peales and Stuarts in America. The female artist was occasionally the financial head of the family, examples of whom were Evelyn De Morgan and Louise Jopling. Such was the situation also for Lilly Martin Spencer (1822–1902), which eventually encouraged a very original self-portrait. Spencer was precocious, holding her first exhibition in Marietta, Ohio in 1841. She moved to Cincinnati that same year in order to enhance her training in art, studying with John Insco Williams, a Cincinnati portrait-painter. In 1844 she married Benjamin Rush Spencer, who gave up his job in the cloth trade to take on domestic duties, while Lilly became the principal breadwinner of the family. And quite a family it was, with 13 children, seven of whom survived. It is small wonder that so many of Spencer's paintings have children in them – they were always available as models.

The situation of being a househusband is graphically depicted in Spencer's painting, *The Young Husband's First Marketing* (1854, collection of Mr and Mrs Edward Abrahams, New York). Here a dandy passing by laughs at the husband, whose fowl are falling out of his market basket. It was this type of painting of scenes of everyday life which made Spencer famous. As Susan Fisher Sterling points out, 'the newly prosperous middle class in nineteenth-century America expressed a strong preference for scenes of everyday life. Genre painting dominated the art market, and Lilly Martin Spencer was one of its most acclaimed practitioners.'[12] Another trait in Spencer's painting endeared her to the American public, as she wrote on 11 July 1847, 'I mean to try to make my painting have a tendency towards moral improvement.'[13]

Spencer had already executed a fine single-figure *Self-Portrait* (c.1842, the Ohio Historical Society), but *The Artist and Her Family at a Fourth of July Picnic* (Pl. XXVIII) is original as a self-portrait, being part of a group portrait which is also a genre scene. Spencer shows herself as the 'blind man' in a game of 'blind man's bluff' on the left in front of a tree, while in the central position her husband is on the ground, his weight having broken the swing he was on. Everyone watching is enjoying his downfall. In the guise of producing a conventional picture of a family outing, Spencer has actually created a subversive painting. The usually upright and commanding paterfamilias, typically given the central primary position in a composition, is actually supine on the ground, his mishap brought on by his own foolishness. He is a figure of mockery, not of respect or dominance. The painter has also shown herself, whose vision as an artist is the family's economic mainstay, as blind and feeling her way.

This painting, which took a year to produce, is one of Spencer's most elaborate productions, containing at least two dozen figures, the accoutrements of a picnic and an extensive background.[14] It justified the labor it entailed, since it came to be engraved by Samuel Hollyer and J. Rogers for *Demarest's Monthly Magazine* in 1865 and for M. Peters and P. and J. Levy in New York in 1866. Being at the time possibly the most elaborate work ever engraved in the United States, it was bound to appeal to America's work ethic as well as to the era's artistic aspirations.

This painted self-portrait, in showing a conventional family portrait, is a good summation of Spencer's artistic production even though her own family was unconventional by nineteenth-century standards. It also represents a typical Spencer subject – a sentimental and amusing genre scene which would sell and which would also provide additional income through the sale of engravings. It also underlines how Spencer could not afford the luxury of experimenting in art because she had to please an audience in order to live and support her family, both a great anxiety and a limitation.

One of the significant innovations of the nineteenth century was the advent of government-funded schools of design, which admitted women.

As mentioned in Chapter VI, academies exerted a major role in training professional artists, although in the nineteenth century these institutions often limited the number of women they admitted. The practice of female students training in the ateliers of individual artists, both male and female – seen so dramatically in the eighteenth century with, for example, Labille-Guiard, Vigée-Lebrun, David and the Countess Benoist – continued into the nineteenth century. In 1881, May Alcott wrote that Chaplin, Barrias, Carolus-Duran, Cabanel, Bougereau, Robert-Fleury, Lefebvre and Luminais all taught female pupils.[15] This made Paris a magnet for women artists, many of whom painted self-portraits. They included Mary Cassatt and Cecilia Beaux from the United States, Paula Modersohn-Becker from Germany and Gwen John from England.

One of the most popular ateliers to include women was the Académie Julian, founded in 1868 by Rudolf Julian. Here too, however, female painters experienced discrimination – classes for men and women were segregated and women paid 700 francs a year for education, whereas men paid only 400 francs,[16] a distinction common among French ateliers. However, the highest form of art education, at the École des Beaux-Arts, was not open to women students until 1897, and even then, male students hounded women out of the school with cries of '*À bas les femmes!*' ('Down with women!').[17] It was not until 1900 that women in France could receive state-funded art education equal to that of men.

One of the problems associated with women's art education was the fear of the effect of mixed classes on the students. This question so upset the architect J.-L.-C. Garnier at a meeting addressing the issue that he responded to Guillaume's advocacy of the mixed class as follows: 'Had I seen a nice feminine face next to my easel, to hell with my drawing! Oh, Guillaume! You are not a man!' Guillaume supposedly riposted, 'Oh, Garnier! You are not an artist!'[18]

Another delicate question for women was the prerequisite of having knowledge of human anatomy and drawing from the 'undraped figure', especially that of the male. In France the opposition to this appears to have abated by 1874, since at the École des Dessins pour les Jeunes Filles prizes were awarded to women for drawing from the nude.[19] However, in America, sculptor Harriet Hosmer was debarred from anatomy study in any college in New England because of being a woman. In Germany, the situation was even worse. Beata Bonus Jeep, a classmate and friend of Käthe Kollwitz, wrote that instruction in anatomy in 1885 at the Women's School of Art 'consisted...of a box full of bones passed among the students. The women were never told which bones were which or how they fit together in a skeleton.'[20]

Anatomy aside, drawing from the live undraped model was felt to violate the delicacy of female art students. Drawing from the undraped female was not as great a problem: the first Ladies Life Drawing Class using a nude female model was established at the Pennsylvania Academy of Art in 1868, and both in England and in France women art students banded together to hire life models outside the conventional curriculum of the art schools. In 1893 English female art students were allowed to study the male nude, but not using a fully naked model, as the Annual Report from the Council of the Royal Academy to the General Assembly of Academicians makes clear: 'It shall be optional for Visitors [i.e., instructing Academicians] in the painting school to set the male model undraped, except around the loins, to the class of female students, the drapery to be worn by the model to consist of ordinary bathing drawers, and a cloth of light material nine feet long by three feet wide which shall be wound round the loins over the drawers, passed between the legs and tucked in over the waist-band, and finally a thick leather strap shall be fastened around the loins in order to insure that the cloth keep its place.'[21] In spite of these precautions, some nineteenth-century women artists did paint the nude, such as Anna Lea Merritt and Henrietta Rae, who showed their work in the 1885 Royal Academy exhibition and were roundly censured by the press for their daring.

The ostensible issue behind the barriers placed in the way of women artists studying the male nude may have been a concern for the modesty of the delicate female, but there were in addition two unnamed ones: a fear of competition and the threat to male power. A prerequisite for painting Neo-classical compositions of battle scenes and mythology was a thorough knowledge of both the male and female nude. Women artists, being excluded from this knowledge, were not able to paint the basic vocabulary of these scenes and so were relegated to the lesser types of works in the hierarchy of painting, namely portraits, landscapes and still-lifes.

Male nudity also suggested male vulnerability in a setting where the artists were clothed and the model unclothed, or as Lynda Nead has pointed out, 'the juxtaposition of the natural model and the clothed artist is a usefully blatant visualization of the power relations that are traditionally embodied in the life class'.[22] Knowledge of the nude body, male or female, became an exercise in control and power, with access only easily available to the dominant gender.

Partially as a result of these prohibitions, women artists decided to organize their own societies and hold yearly exhibitions. The Society of Female Artists was established in London in 1856, and its first exhibition opened 1 June 1857 with 358 works by 159 artists in a gallery in Oxford Street. This exhibition was the first in England, France or America organized by women to show works of painting and sculpture only by women. The society's second exhibition was held at the Egyptian Gallery and showed works by 582 members. Although generally reviews of this exhibition were patronizing, *The Englishwomen's Journal*, just founded by Barbara Leigh Smith Bodichon and Bessie Parks, commented on the criticism of the exhibition: '*The Athenaeum* says we must not look for a Michael Angelo among the ladies, but we cannot say that we discern much trace of a Michael Angelesque genius in the English School at large just now!'[23]

Societies of female artists were also formed in other countries, and included the Verein der Kunstlerinnen in Berlin (1868) and the Union des Femmes Peintres et Sculpteurs, founded in Paris by Madame Léon Bertaux. The Union's first exhibition took place in January 1882, and by 1896 it had 450 members. Its exhibitions at the Palais des Champs-Elysées, were non-hierarchical in nature and showed a wide range of oil paintings, watercolors, drawings, miniatures, sculptures, fans, faience and porcelain, and included self-portraits.

Elizabeth Thompson, later to become Lady Butler (1846–1933), was the most successful painter of military scenes in nineteenth-century Britain and one of the female artists who earned the most patronage. In 1869, she executed a *Self-Portrait* (Fig. VII.2), inscribed 'Mimi Thompson' (her nickname). This self-representation shows the head of a rather serious young woman in a frontal pose, the right half of the face in the light, the left half in shadow. She did not depict herself as an artist, in contrast with an earlier three-quarter-length *Self-Portrait* of 1866 (private collection, London) where she is seated before an easel with a number of soldiers on the canvas. The *Self-Portrait* of 1869 depicts a more thoughtful and introspective interpretation of the self – reflecting Thompson's austere background. She was born in Lausanne, Switzerland, the daughter of James Thompson, a gentleman of independent means, and Christine Weller Johnson, a pianist and artist. Both

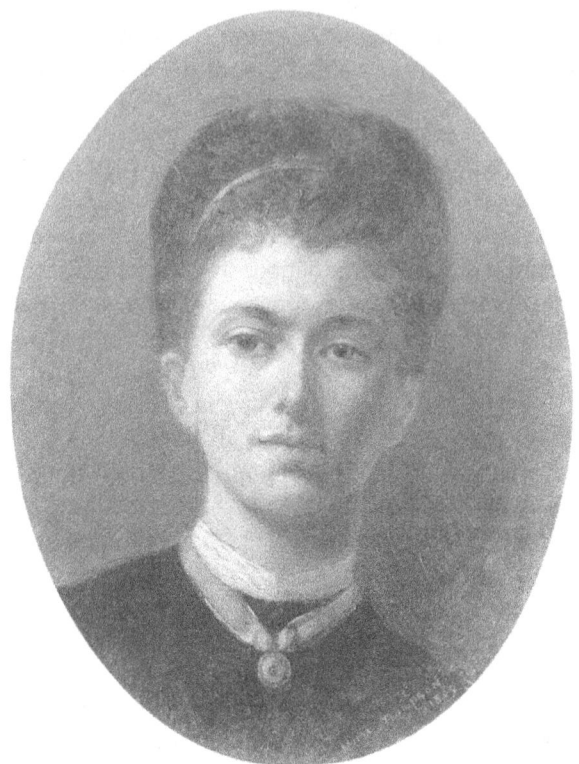

VII.2   Elizabeth Thompson (Lady Butler), *Self-Portrait*, 1869

she and her sister Alice were educated by their father.

'I think that, having no boys to bring up, he tried to put all the tuition suitable to boys and girls into us', Lady Butler observed later in life.[24] As an eldest daughter with no brother, Butler may have filled the role of son to some extent. The family summered in England and wintered in Italy, where Thompson's parents would hold musical evenings, with Christine playing the piano and singing. Thompson once lamented, 'I cried my heart out when, through the open windows, I could hear my mother's light soprano drowned by the strong tenor of some Italian friend in a duett [sic]... It seemed typical of her extinction, and I felt a rage against that tenor.'[25]

The incident typified significant strands in the formation of Thompson's character: an education on masculine principles and a rage against the 'extinction' of the dearest woman in her life, her mother, and the pattern of domination of women by males. At least some of these may provide a partial explanation as to why a young woman with no military men or military painters in her life took on this subject – so atypical of women artists – as her primary theme.

In 1872, Charles Galloway commissioned Thompson to paint *The Roll Call*, which was exhibited (number 142) at the 1874 Royal Academy exhibition under its official title, *Calling the Roll after an Engagement, Crimea*. In it, Thompson strove for verisimilitude, acquiring uniforms and equipment of soldiers along with reading written accounts and interviewing veterans who had been present. The long horizontal painting, measuring 91 x 182.9 cm, represents a powerful view of the Grenadier Guards. It most likely portrays the aftermath of the battle of Inkerman, 5 November 1854. The Grenadier Guards' third battalion lost 104 officers and men killed and 130 wounded, with barely 200 men responding to the roll call.[26]

On varnishing day, 28 April 1874, Thompson found her work given the best place and surrounded by academicians waiting to congratulate her. It was the painting of the year, thus solidifying her reputation.[27]

Thompson began her next major battle painting in 1874, *The 28th Regiment at Quatre Bras, 1815* (Pl. XXIX). She spared nothing in its execution, getting two troopers to ride full tilt at her to achieve the feeling of what the troops withstood at Quatre Bras. To depict the setting accurately she also bought part of an appropriate rye field at Henley similar to the scene of the battle. This painting too was a major success, at the Royal Academy exhibition of 1875.

One of the most important effects of *Quatre Bras* was that it changed John Ruskin's opinion of female artists forever – as he wrote in *Academy Notes* in 1875: 'I never approached a picture with more iniquitous prejudice against it than I did Miss Thompson's, partly because I had always thought no woman could paint, and secondly, because I thought that what the public made such a fuss about must be good for nothing. But it is amazing work this; no doubt of it, and the first fine Pre-Raphaelite picture of battle we have had.'[28] (Ruskin had the habit of calling anything he liked Pre-Raphaelite. But, in a footnote, he explained that he referred to Thompson as seeing things as they really were because she painted them with correct detail and a fidelity to truth that was a characteristic of Pre-Raphaelites.)

On the basis of her painting triumphs, Thompson was nominated for Royal Academy membership in 1879, the only woman in the nineteenth century to reach such eminence. But she lost to Hubert Herkomer by a small margin, causing the Academy to breathe a sigh of relief. Yet the pre-eminent French battle-painter Meissonier said at the end of his life, 'England really has only one military painter – a woman.'[29]

Not all women artists were as successful as Thompson in getting their works exhibited and purchased. The plight of the female artist without the male protection of a husband, father or brother is revealed in Emily Mary Osborn's putative self-portrait, *Nameless and Friendless*, shown at the Royal Academy in 1857 and engraved for the *Art Journal* in 1864 (Fig. VII.3). The painting depicts a young woman dressed in black mourning clothes with a young boy, also in black, carrying an artist's portfolio at the center of the composition, with a man behind a desk on the right, presumably a gallery owner, looking at a small painting with a skeptical expression. Since the woman appears too young to be the mother of the boy by her side, it may be presumed that he is her brother and both are in mourning for their father, the mainstay of economic support for the family. Both the young woman and the

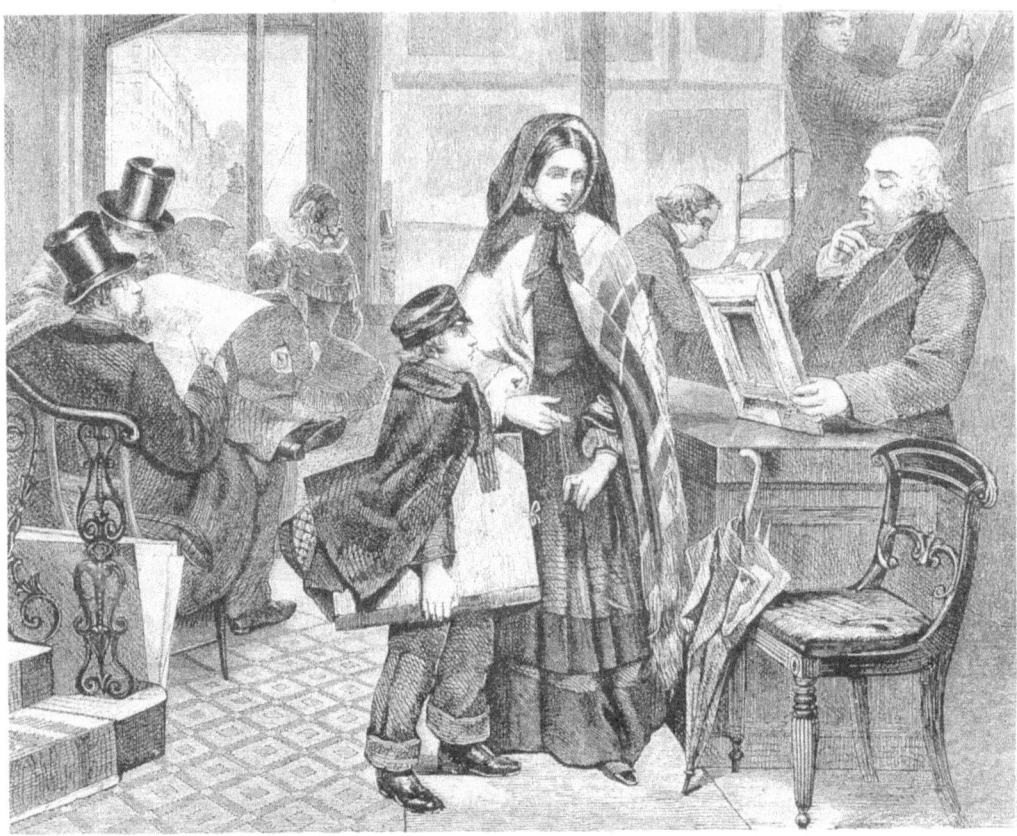

Engraved by]   NAMELESS AND FRIENDLESS.   [J. Cooper.

VII.3   Emily Mary Osborn, *Nameless and Friendless*, engraving (detail), J. Cooper, *Art Journal*, 1864

boy look apprehensive as they wait for the critical evaluation of the painting. The artwork offered for sale could be one executed by the demised father, but the review in the *Art Journal* (new series) volume III of 1857, p. 170, interpreted it thus: 'A poor girl has painted a picture, which she offers for sale to a dealer, who, from the speaking expression of his features, is disposed to deprecate the work. It is a wet, dismal day, and she has walked far to dispose of it; and now awaits in trembling the decision of a man who is become rich by the labours of others.'

Nameless and Friendless has been interpreted by a number of commentators as a self-portrait of the artist, whereas others view it as a generic representation of the nineteenth-century woman artist's plight – powerless in a society where men held all the keys to acceptance and success. It also has been noted that the time of the painting, 1857, was the date of the first exhibition of the Society of Female Artists, which offered a new venue for the exhibition and sale of the work of female artists.

If *Nameless and Friendless* is a self-portrait, it is, indeed, very much at odds with the actual facts of Osborn's career as an artist. Between 1851, when she began exhibiting at the Royal Academy, and 1884 she submitted 43 works to the Academy along with exhibiting at the Society of British Artists, the Dudley Gallery, the Paris Salon, the Grosvenor Gallery, the Crystal Palace and the New Gallery. Moreover, she numbered Queen Victoria among her patrons. Osborn, who never married and seems to have supported herself entirely with her art, was a respected professional artist and scarcely nameless or friendless.

A crucial factor influencing nineteenth-century portraiture and one of its subsets, self-portraiture, was the invention of photography, in 1839 – as a reproducible print by William Henry Fox Talbot in England and as a single-impression daguerreotype by Louis-Jacques Mandé Daguerre in France. This had a significant impact on the market for portraits, since it eliminated long sittings and was much less expensive and time-consuming. However, it also brought the shock of visual truth rather than a flattering representation of the sitter. Some customers, in fact, could not believe that the talbotype or daguerreotype actually represented them. In creating painted self-portraits, photographs could be very helpful by presenting the artist from new angles such as profile or back views to augment or replace frontal mirror images.

However, it was not photography but rather the retinal image or what was actually experienced by the eye that became the basis of a new style of painting in France known as Impressionism. If anything, Impressionism was anti-photographic since it was based on the individual artist's perception of what was observed under various conditions of light at varying times of the day and seasons of the year, filtered through the temperament and feelings of the artist. Rather than presenting a sharp photographic image, outlines were blurry and indistinct under bright light or submerged in shadows of a deeper hue of the dominant color.

Impressionist artists held a series of exhibitions of their work in Paris between 1874 and 1886, the first group exhibition in France without a jury and not held under government auspices. One of the artists who exhibited at all the exhibitions – except for the fourth one in 1879 due to the birth of her only child – was Berthe Morisot (1841–95). Her father, a civil servant, was moved to several posts in her childhood, and around 1852 the family settled in Paris with their daughters Yves, Edmé and Berthe and a younger son, Tiburce. Berthe's art education began when her mother decided to arrange art lessons for the girls from a local painter, Geoffrey-Alphonse Chocaine, a rather dull Neo-classical artist. The lectures of their next teacher, Joseph Guichard, enthused the young ladies, as did their visits to the Louvre. It was Guichard who cautioned Madame Morisot that Berthe and her sister Edmé were so talented that they would become professional artists and confound bourgeois expectations of a proper life.

Morisot had her first paintings accepted in the Salon of 1864; none of these, however, have survived. Her mother fulfilled Guichard's prophecy by becoming worried about whether Berthe, so engrossed in her art, would ever get married, the proper goal of a well-brought-up young woman. Berthe's older sisters married, Yves in 1866 and Edmé in 1869, but this did not push Berthe into following their example. About this time Morisot met the Manet family, posing for Edouard Manet's *The Balcony* in 1868 (Paris, Musée d'Orsay), where she is the seated figure on the far left. She sat for him again in 1870 in *Le Repos* (*Portrait of Berthe Morisot*) (Fig. VII.4), a painting criticized at the time for the lounging attitude of the young subject. In c.1871–2 Morisot created one of her own masterpieces, *On the Balcony* (private collection). It depicts a graceful woman in black seen in profile while looking over an ironwork balcony, along with a little girl in a pinafore seen from the back standing on the right beside her, against a cityscape of the Seine in Paris. The freely brushed figures and atmospheric view may have been an inspiration for a subsequent work by Manet, *The Railroad* or *Gare Saint-Lazare* of 1873 (National Gallery of Art, Washington, DC). One of the interesting transfers are the red and white flowers in an urn, upper right in Morisot's painting, which show up on the black hat of Manet's model, Victorine Meurent – perhaps a subtle homage.

In 1874, the year of the first Impressionist exhibition, Morisot married Eugène Manet, Edouard's younger brother and also a painter, although never as well known as either his wife or his brother. Their daughter Julie, born in 1878, is featured in a number of Morisot's portraits and self-portraits. In one of the latter, *Self-Portrait with Julie*, an oil of 1885 (private collection, Paris), she paints the loving relationship of mother and daughter, as Vigée-Lebrun had done before her with her daughter, coincidentally also named Julie. In her drypoint *Self-Portrait with Julie*, Morisot is both artist and mother, drawing as Julie looks on closely. In an 1885 pastel *Self-Portrait* (Pl. XXX), it is difficult to believe that it is the same woman as she seems much older, her face drawn, her eyes anxious, with none of the beauty evident in photographs or portraits of her by other artists, such as *Le Repos*. Morisot's *Self-Portrait* is, in contrast, very much an Impressionist portrait in its sketchiness, blurred lines, the fall of light and its immediacy. It appears as a perceived mirror image, caught in a brief period of awareness, the artist striving to capture an impression in one passing moment in time.

The 1997 *catalogue raisonné* of Morisot's paintings by Alain Clairet, Delphine Montalent and Yves Rouart[30] lists five self-portraits in oil, not including the 1885 pastel found in the Chicago Art Institute. The first, number 127, was executed in 1883; 169 and 170 were painted in 1885; and the last two, 219 and 220, date to 1887. Of these, only number 169, *Portrait de Berthe Morisot* (1885), shows Morisot alone; the four others portray the artist in the company of her daughter, Julie, thus testifying to the important role of motherhood in Morisot's life and her strong bonding with her daughter – so strong, in fact, that it is part of her self-image.

The image of woman as mother found easy acceptance in the nineteenth century. The image of woman as artist, as shown in Morisot's unaccompanied self-portrait in which she holds a brush and palette in the lower left of the painting and faces the viewer directly, was less conventionally acceptable.

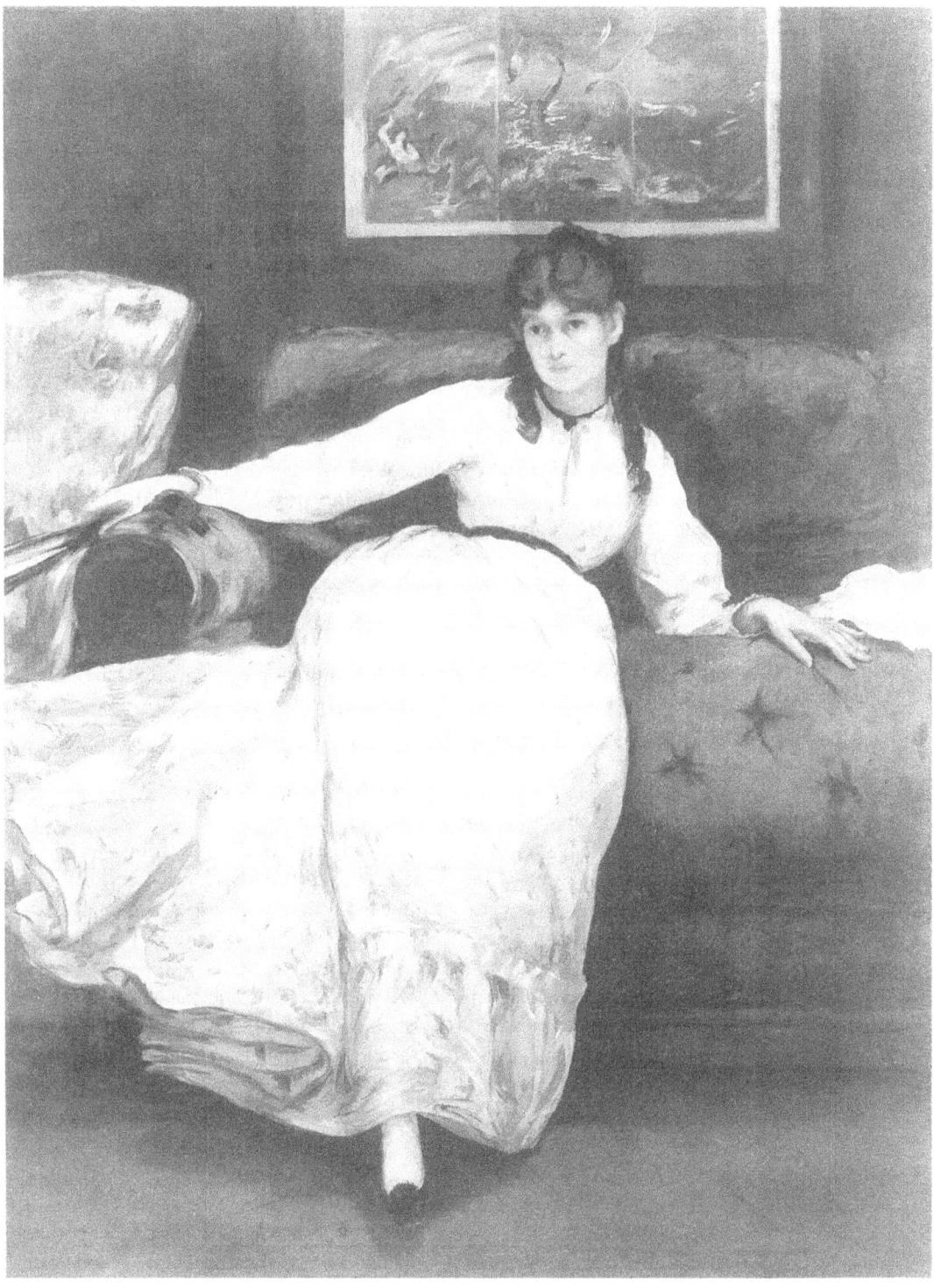

VII.4   Edouard Manet, *Le Repos* (*Portrait of Berthe Morisot*), 1870

This is pointed out by Delphine Montalent in the Morisot *catalogue raisonné*: 'There has been much discussion about women in the Impressionist movement and of their difficulty in having acceptance as Impressionist painters. Considered as minors, absolved of all responsibility by the French *Code Civil*, women living in the mid-nineteenth century were seldom acknowledged as equals to men, but those who wished to become professional painters found recognition even more difficult.'[31] However, Morisot clearly perceived herself as equal to her male Impressionist colleagues, as evidenced when she wrote in 1890, 'I don't think there has ever been a man treating a woman as equal to equal and that's all I have asked – because I know I'm as good as they are.'[32]

The year 1892 was a professional triumph for Morisot, with an exhibition of her work at Boussod and Valadon, private dealers in Paris, but it was also a time of tragedy as her husband died that year. In 1894, the French government purchased Morisot's *Young Woman in a Ball Gown* (c.1876, Musée d'Orsay, Paris), a symphony in shimmering colors and light, confirming her professional status and merit. Morisot's hour of triumph was short-lived, though; she contracted pulmonary congestion, possibly as a result of nursing her daughter, and died on 22 March 1895, only 54 years old.

During her lifetime, Morisot painted 608 oils and pastels, 238 watercolors, 8 drypoints and 1 colored lithograph[33] – an extraordinary record for a woman of the *haute bourgeoisie*, called on to be a gracious hostess, a supervisor of a household, a sympathetic wife and a devoted mother, one whose only studio was the dining room, where she hid her painting implements on the arrival of company. She was also a staunch member of the Impressionist group, helping organize its exhibitions and entertaining its members.

The American artist Mary Cassatt (1844–1926), the other major female painter in the Impressionist group, was three years junior to Morisot, and lived for 21 years after Morisot's premature death. As with Morisot, Cassatt came from an upper-class background and, although unmarried, also had obligations to her family. She nursed her sister Lydia until her death of Bright's disease, and took care of both her parents, who came to live with her in Paris in their senior years. In spite of these responsibilities, which were expected of a woman in the nineteenth century, Cassatt, like Morisot, was amazingly productive, creating an oeuvre of 614 oils and pastels, 220 prints and 74 watercolors. Only two self-portraits, however, are at present known.[34]

Cassatt came to the Impressionist group late, invited by Degas to exhibit in the Fourth Exhibition of 1879. She continued with the group through its last exhibition in 1886. Like Morisot, her works had been accepted at the Salon, and, again like Morisot, she remained faithful to the group, not returning to the Salon exhibitions or even private galleries, as some of the men did, until after the last Impressionist exhibition. Both women were good friends of Degas. Though often described as a misogynist, Degas encouraged female artists, created opportunities for them and admired their art. At the same time, though, he would make jibes about Cassatt's paintings, as when he remarked while standing in front of one of her works, 'I will not admit a woman can draw like that!'[35] Cassatt exhibited *Girl Arranging Her Hair* (National Gallery of Art, Washington, DC) in the concluding Impressionist exhibition, a painting which took an ugly, undistinguished model in a banal situation and redeemed the work with her composition and drawing. When Degas saw it, he wrote to Cassatt, 'What drawing! What style!' and added it to his collection.[36]

Cassatt has often been characterized as a painter of the mother and child theme, but in reality only a quarter of her works deal with this subject. She painted portraits, many of which were of her extended family as well as women together, group scenes and portraits of children. Unlike much nineteenth-century art, Cassatt's approach to her subjects was totally unsentimental. She showed relationships, characteristic attitudes and gestures, and endowed her paintings with immediacy and life.

Around 1880, at the age of 36, Cassatt did a small watercolor self-portrait (Pl. XXXI). This work shows the artist three-quarter-length in a dark dress, wearing a sketchily painted pink and yellow hat, seated before an easel or drawing board, and outlined against a yellow-ochre background. She looks at the viewer directly, obviously in the process of drawing her own image. It is full of life, color and immediacy. The artist is depicted at her vocation, very much both a woman and an artist. Although not a beautiful woman, Cassatt was a distinctive and distinguished one. Her *Self-Portrait* projects the feeling that she has found her vocation and begun to live.

The term 'Post-Impressionism' was coined by the British art critic and painter Roger Fry (1866–1934), who organized two Post-Impressionist exhibitions between 1910 and 1912 in London, using the title to denote the diverse art movements which followed Impressionism. He emphasized the supremacy of form over narrative painting, a theme that would later have important consequences for abstract art and formal design.

One of the artists who created a link between nineteenth- and twentieth-century self-portraiture was the Post-Impressionist painter Suzanne Valadon (1865–1938). A less likely candidate for an artist would be difficult to find. She was the illegitimate daughter of Madeleine Valadon, a sewing maid in Bessines-sur-Gartemps. As a small child, she was taken to Paris, where her mother worked as a cleaning woman. Enrolled as a day student at the convent of St Jean de Montmartre, she learned to read, write and do arithmetic, leaving when she was about 11 years of age.

Valadon had a number of early occupations, including being an *equestrienne* at the Cirque Moher until she had a fall and had to seek out other work. She became an artists' model from age 15 to 28, a long career for a model of that day, especially one who posed in the nude as well as clothed. Artists for whom she posed included Pierre Puvis de Chavannes, Auguste Renoir (she was the model for *The Dance in the Country*) and Henri de Toulouse-Lautrec. On Toulouse-Lautrec's advice, Valadon took a portfolio of her drawings for Degas to criticize. He told her, 'You are one of us', and he became her mentor, encouraging her in her career, calling her 'terrible Maria' because of the stark truth of her images, and buying her work.[37] Degas insisted that she enter five of her drawings in the Société Nationale des

Beaux-Arts Salon in 1894, her first formal exhibition. The odds were against a self-taught artist without Beaux-Arts training, whose subject matter of plain adolescent girls and worn old women was not alluring. Nonetheless, she became an instant success. In 1897 art dealer Ambroise Vollard gave her a solo exhibition, and in addition she exhibited at Lebarc and later Berthe Weil.

Valadon's first extant work is a pastel *Self-Portrait* of 1883 (Musée National d'Art Moderne, Paris) in which she portrays herself at bust length off-center to the left, looking at the mirror, which is also the viewer. Her glance is measured, direct and somewhat withdrawn, slightly suspicious of what she sees.

In 1896 Valadon married wealthy broker Paul Mousis, and moved her mother and her own illegitimate son, Maurice Utrillo, into her new quarters. In 1909, she met André Utter, a friend of her son's, and despite the difference of 21 years in age, they became lovers. She subsequently divorced Mousis and moved back to Paris and a studio at 12 rue Cortet. That year, she began to paint in oils at Utter's urgings. One of her first such paintings was a self-portrait with Utter called *Adam and Eve* (Pl. XXXII), which was exhibited at the Salon d'Automne. It was the first painting by a woman to show a male and a female nude together. Originally, both figures were portrayed in full frontal nudity, but when the painting was exhibited at the 1920 Salon des Indépendants, Valadon was asked to paint tactful greenery over Adam's genitalia, which she did.[38] There was no objection to Eve's nudity. Here, there is an obvious fear of the vulnerability represented by nudity, not for the female, who is supposed to be vulnerable, but for the male, who cannot be seen in this unprotected way.

This, of course, is not what the painting depicts. In reality, it embodies two equal lovers lost in the newness of love, Adam and Eve in paradise at the beginning of their relationship. The figures are set in a verdant landscape, defined by sinuous linear outlines and modeling similar to Valadon's earlier pastel technique. The color is simplified and forceful; the work is so accomplished, in fact, that it is difficult to believe that it is one of her first efforts in oils. In its expressionistic content and primitivist reference to a lost Eden it relates to some of Gauguin's Tahitian works and the expressive side of Post-Impressionism.

Valadon was a pioneer in a number of areas of art. She presented an image of childhood, awkward and diffident, at odds with the nineteenth-century cult of the happy family and its often sentimental portrayal. Her paintings exhibit bold, almost Fauvist colors, as well as incisive line. Her portrayal of the male nude is unconventional and original, being a totally novel view in which both male and female figures are treated as equals, without resorting to coquetry or timidity.

In 1938 Valadon succumbed to a heart attack. She left an oeuvre of 478 paintings, 273 drawings and 31 etchings, including a number of self-portraits of devastating honesty. She was called an artist's artist, and was admired by Toulouse-Lautrec, Degas and others who purchased her work. She was the Eve of the new century's painting – unorthodox, unconventional and unforgettable.

The career of the American artist Cecilia Beaux (1855–1942), as with that of

Valadon, is divided between the nineteenth and the twentieth centuries. Unlike Valadon, though, Beaux cannot be easily categorized in any one style, possibly because she mainly painted portraits, including self-portraits, throughout her career, earning her living as a portraitist. Her choice of this field raises an interesting issue – the change in the status of portrait-painting at the conclusion of the nineteenth century and particularly in the twentieth century. The list of the most respected artists of the nineteenth century contains few artists whose major expression in art was painting portraits. Whistler and Sargent may be cited, but they painted other subjects in addition to portraits, such as Whistler's nocturnes and compositions and Sargent's architectural and landscape renderings. The most esteemed nineteenth-century portraits were not commissioned, but studies of friends and family, such as those of Cassatt, Degas and Cézanne.

Beaux was born in Philadelphia in 1885, the youngest daughter of a silk manufacturer who had come to the United States from Provence. Her mother died 12 days after Beaux's birth, and she and her sister Etta were brought up by their maternal grandmother and aunts. Beaux started art lessons at age 16 and made a career in teaching and decorative work, sporadically attending the Pennsylvania Academy of Art and then studying in Paris at the Académies Julian and Colarossi in 1888 and 1889. When she returned to Philadelphia in 1889, she made her reputation painting elegant portraits of the city's elite, later moving on to New York and summering north in Gloucester, Massachusetts.

Beaux's *Self-Portrait Number 3* of 1894 (Fig. VII.5) exemplifies the qualities that made her a pre-eminent portrait-painter of her time: bravura brushstrokes, vibrant color against a dark background and a faithful, yet flattering likeness of the sitter, with subtle modulations of light and shade to highlight facial features. This self-portrait was created to fulfill the conditions of her election as an associate member of the National Academy of Design. It is bust-length, whereas most of her portraits are three-quarter- or full-length renderings of the sitter.

Beaux was equally successful in portraying men and women, showing the men as distinguished, the women usually beautiful and elegantly dressed. Her style has been compared to the portraiture of Whistler, Sargent and Boldini, and she was certainly the most successful woman portrait-painter of the late nineteenth and early twentieth centuries. Beaux painted the rich, the famous and the academically distinguished in their outward splendor, but often left the viewer pondering the inner life of her sitters – their full personhood rather than just their outward personae. Her *Self-Portrait* of 1894 presents a similar external view of the 39-year-old sitter who is not categorized as an artist or identified in any particular way. The sitter would be likely to be recognized on the street, but one would not know what she was thinking or feeling.

Unlike the great prestige accorded to earlier professional portrait-painters, such as Anguissola, Fontana, Gentileschi and Vigée-Lebrun, the admired artists of the nineteenth and twentieth centuries were not painters of commissioned portraits. There appears to have been a shift of taste away from capturing likeness into other areas. The move to abstraction in early

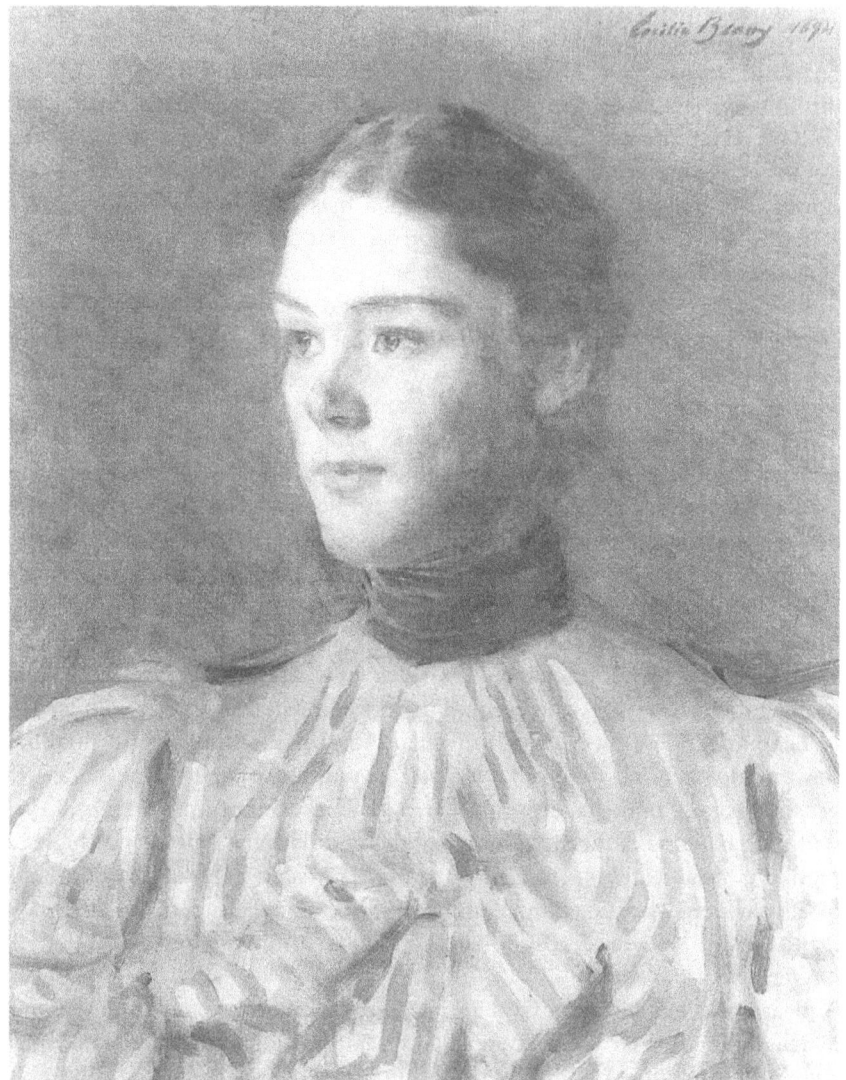

VII.5   Cecilia Beaux, *Self-Portrait Number 3*, 1894

twentieth-century art may be a partial explanation. The ease and popularity of photographic portraiture and its less strenuous demands on sitters is undoubtedly another. Still another factor for the shift from past portraiture to nineteenth-century representations could be that in order to be a successful portrait-painter, the artist had to be able to paint the sitter in his or her best light, in other words, to flatter the sitter, make the inelegant elegant, and the commonplace beautiful. By the close of the nineteenth century, and certainly during the twentieth, truth and originality rather than beauty and elegance became the virtues most admired and sought after in art – aspects which are not generally acceptable in commissioned portraits.

The symbolic self: women painters' quest for identity in the twentieth century

Because of its valorization of novelty and originality, the twentieth century has been a time of constantly evolving new styles in art, with one following another in rapid succession as if they were tied to the increasing speed of communication and technological innovation. At the same time, new styles and older ones have co-existed and overlapped; for instance, Pre-Raphaelitism and Post-Impressionism were practiced at the same time as Fauvism, German Expressionism and Cubism.

One of the problems with dealing with self-portraiture in the twentieth century is that there is a general lack of portraiture and figuration in the century's avant-garde art. Abstraction, the dominant mode, does not encourage self-representation or recognizable self-portraits. Although there are abstract works specifically called self-portraits by their creators, in general abstraction by its nature discourages the conveying of literal images. Similarly, female painters whose chosen subject-matter excludes figurative representations, such as landscape, still-life, abstract collages or flower painting, are less likely to produce self-portraits.

Nevertheless, this century has produced serial self-portraits, often extending over the artist's whole history, especially in the works of Käthe Kollwitz, Paula Modersohn-Becker and Frida Kahlo. The serial self-portrait can be seen as a continuation of the Romantic ideal of the painter embarking on a spiritual journey, a heroic feat in which the artist becomes a surrogate for humanity, but in the twentieth century women's self-portraiture becomes more personal, more of a quest for self-knowledge than a superhuman saga undertaken in an heroic persona. The journey is more inward than outward and is introspective and imaginative in its identifications of the artist with the seer, the goddess or the witness, as seen in Gwen John's and Vanessa Bell's self-portraits.

Gwen John (1876–1939) represents a Post-Impressionistic approach to self-portraiture with her muted palette and quiet scenes. In many ways she was just as unorthodox as Valadon since her introverted and reclusive temperament led her to depict life in shadows and tonal harmonies, subtle and subdued. John is a study in contradictions: a proper and intensely private young woman, she modeled in the nude to earn a living in Paris in 1904, met the sculptor Auguste Rodin (1840–1917) and was his lover as well as his model from 1904 to 1914. Having previously been financially independent, John accepted an allowance from the collector John Quinn from 1913 until his death in 1924 in return for giving him first choice of her works. Although she described herself as 'a little piece of suffering and desire',[1] she fashioned for herself a life of solitude and contemplation with very rare human interruptions.

John was born in 1876 in Haverford, Wales, one of four children of a solicitor. From 1895 to 1898 she studied in London at the Slade School of Art, where her younger brother Augustus had preceded her by one year. In 1898 she went to Paris to study with Whistler at his Académie Carmen, where the emphasis was on painting rather than draftsmanship, which she had already studied at the Slade. From Whistler she learned subdued and subtle color and tonal values. Whistler said that he did not teach art but rather the scientific application of paint and brushes, much like the scientific Post-Impressionism of Cézanne. In keeping with this, John's notes reveal careful recording of color values – 'road 32, roof 13–23, grass 25, black coats 33'.[2]

With a friend, Dorelia McNeill, John decided to take a walking trip to Rome from where they were staying in Bordeaux, but it took so long that they stayed in Toulouse in the autumn of 1903. Of this sojourn McNeill wrote, 'I do remember some very lighthearted evenings over a bottle of wine and a bowl of soup. She appreciated the good food and wine to be had in that part of France, though we mostly lived on stolen grapes and bread.'[3]

John and McNeill moved to Paris and lived at 19 boulevard Edgar Quinet in Montparnasse. To earn a living, they modeled for various male artists, though John reputedly felt ashamed of this expedient.[4] She modeled for a number of women artists as well.

John exhibited her paintings on an irregular basis at the New English Art Club from 1900 to 1911 and in Paris at the Salon des Tuileries exhibitions from 1923 on. In 1926 she had a very successful exhibition at the Chenil Galleries with 44 paintings and drawings and four albums of drawings. With the proceeds she bought a house on the rue Babie, where she lived with her cats until her death in 1939. Writing to her brother Augustus about her lifestyle, she said, 'I told you in a letter long ago that I am happy. When illness or death do not interfere I am. Not many people can say as much...If to "return to life" is to live as I did in London, *merci monsieur*. There are people like plants who cannot flourish in the cold, and I want to flourish.'[5]

In the beginning of her career, John did two self-portraits. The earlier one, a standing three-quarter-length figure in front of an easel on the right, gazes at the viewer with hand on hip, a feminine version of the 'swagger portrait' of a Renaissance condottiere or a nineteenth-century type in the manner of

Sargent (1899–1900; National Portrait Gallery, London). A slightly later *Self-Portrait* (Pl. XXXIII) shows the same steady gaze in a half-length portrait against a dark background, but the mood is more subdued. The artist is wearing a red blouse, the brightest color ever to appear in her work, with a black velvet ribbon around her neck, fastened in front with a cameo brooch. In this work she used a technique of slowly building up delicate layers and glazes of color, possibly having learned this method from her friend Augustus McEvoy's study of Old Master techniques. She submitted the work to an exhibition of former Slade students organized by Professor Fred Brown, who immediately bought it himself and kept it until his death. It is a brilliant work, quiet but self-assured. John later changed her technique to more subtle color harmonies and an impasto of chalky paint applied to the canvas in abbreviated strokes. In her works she shows the awkwardness of an adolescent model, quiet sunny corners of a room, women reading or contemplating in similar poses; they manifest a very individual vocabulary and a very individual life.

While Gwen John lived a solitary life, Vanessa Bell (1879–1961) seems always to have been surrounded by people: her family, her friends, her lovers and her children. She was the first child of Leslie Stephen and Julia Duckworth and seemed fated to run a household and create some order out of chaos. Three more children were born in the next four years: Julian in 1880, Virginia in 1882 and Adrian in 1883. They lived in a house overcrowded with Victorian furniture, made especially gloomy in 1895 with Julia's death, which left Stephen a heartbroken widower. Although Vanessa was supposed to become hostess and household manager after her mother's death, she managed to study from 1896 to 1900 with Sir Arthur Cope and to attend the Royal Academy Schools from 1901 to 1904, where she was a student of Sargent. Stephen died in 1904, and after a holiday abroad Vanessa moved with her brothers and sister to 46 Gordon Square in London's Bloomsbury. In the autumn of 1906 the Stephen family traveled to Greece but Vanessa fell ill while her brother Julian, known to the family as Thoby, contracted typhoid and died at the age of 26, a devastating loss for Vanessa. When Thoby's best friend Clive Bell proposed to Vanessa (for the third time), she accepted, and after their marriage in 1907, Clive Bell moved into 46 Gordon Square and her brother Adrian and sister Virginia moved to 29 Fitzroy Square nearby.

This was the era of the formation of the Bloomsbury group of artists and writers: Virginia and Adrian Stephen, Vanessa and Clive Bell, Lytton Strachey and his sister Marjorie and Gwen Darwin. Later members included E. M. Forster, John Maynard Keynes, Duncan Grant, Desmond and Molly MacCarthy and Roger Fry.

Clive and Vanessa's first child, Julian, was born in February 1908, their second, Quentin, in August 1910. The addition of children to their society troubled Clive as they took attention away from him. The Bloomsbury group was very free-wheeling in its love relationships. They were determined to break with Victorian conventions and their stultifying atmosphere, and they did so with a vengeance. Clive, who continued to be married to Vanessa, had a flirtation with her sister Virginia and a long-lasting sexual liaison with a mistress, Mrs Ravens-Hill. Vanessa fell in love with Roger Fry on a trip to Turkey in 1911 when she fell ill and Fry nursed her back to health. Later she had a long relationship with the artist Duncan Grant, who also had homosexual lovers. Grant fathered Vanessa's third child, Angelica, born in 1918, although the fiction that Clive Bell was her father was maintained by the whole group. Angelica herself was to marry Bunny Garnett, a former lover of her father Duncan Grant. Fry was only partly ironic when he remarked, 'It really is an almost ideal family based on adultery and mutual tolerance...'[6]

To display the work of women artists who were normally excluded from exhibitions, Vanessa Bell instituted the Friday Club. Her own first exhibition took place there in 1905. The greatest artistic influence on her work was the first Post-Impressionist exhibition in London in 1910, which showed paintings by Monet, Gauguin, Cézanne and contemporaries Picasso, Matisse, Derain, Rouault and Denis. The brilliant coloring of the Fauves, or 'wild beasts', who caused a sensation at the 1905 Paris Salon, was particularly important. The leader of the group, Henri Matisse (1869–1954), influenced her work in 1911–1912. Bell's portrait of Lytton Strachey (1911, Anthony d'Offay Gallery, London) uses Fauvist techniques in the handling of the paint in small distinct strokes and the use of patterned material on the sofa. In October 1912, Fry's second Post-Impressionist exhibition included four paintings by Bell.

From 1913 to 1915 Bell painted simplified forms and often flattened them. This can be clearly seen in her *Self-Portrait* (Fig. VIII.1). Although the half-length figure is recognizably the artist, she downplays the beauty that is evident in photographs of her. Bell concentrates on large areas of flattened form and strong colour, with the colored hatchings on the side of her nose reminiscent of Picasso's technique at this time, especially in his primitivist studies. Here, she appears as a strong woman able to manage both a complex household and a career, which she did very ably.

Bell's complete honesty and openness of spirit can be seen in a letter of 10 March 1920 to her friend Madge Vaughan, who was considering renting Bell's house at Charleston, but was somewhat put off by Bell's unorthodox life-style. 'Why on earth should my moral character have anything to do with the question of your taking Charleston or not? I suppose you don't always inquire into your landlords' characters...As for gossip about me, as to which of course I have not been left in ignorance, I must admit it that it seems to me incredibly impertinent of you to ask me to satisfy your curiosity about it.'[7]

Looking at her 1915 self-portrait, one can well believe that Bell wrote these dismissive and principled words. At the same time, it must be said that however much Bell also identified with the working class, her career was made possible by an independent income, as was that of her husband. She did not have to resort to painting pleasing pictures in order to live, or cater to public taste in order to sell her work, as did many other artists.

The two female painters Paula Modersohn-Becker and Käthe Kollwitz are representatives of German Expressionism, although neither is typical of its style. Modersohn-Becker was a forerunner of the movement, while Kollwitz

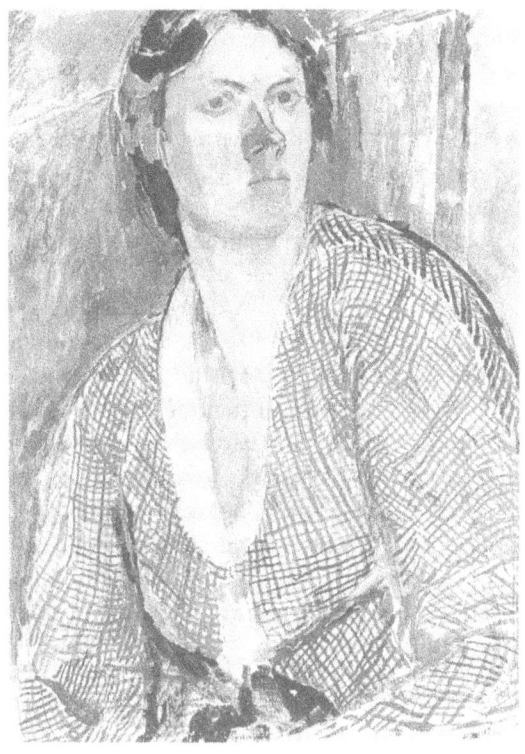

VIII.1   Vanessa Bell, *Self-Portrait*, *c*.1915

has often been classified as an independent Expressionist as she did not belong to either of the main formations of German Expressionism, *Die Brücke* (The Bridge) or *Der Blau Reiter* (The Blue Rider). These movements were comprised entirely of male artists. Unlike them, neither Modersohn-Becker nor Kollwitz deformed their figures for expressionistic emphasis nor did they use much of the Christian imagery derived from medieval art favored by those groups. They were also not influenced as directly by African or Oceanic tribal art. *Die Brücke* and *Der Blau Reiter* were interested in disseminating their work in multiples such as woodcuts or etchings, and both Modersohn-Becker and Kollwitz made prints, especially Kollwitz. The interest in nature and the use of large simplified forms close to the picture plane pioneered by Modersohn-Becker is also found in the work of a number of later German Expressionist artists.

Paula Becker was born in Dresden in 1876. Her parents urged her to enroll in a two-year teacher training course to be able to support herself, but she wanted to study art. They reluctantly sent her to the Berlin School for Women Artists from 1896 to 1898, after which she settled in the artists' colony at Worpswede and studied with Fritz Mackenson. The founders of Worpswede rejected city life and believed in living in small communities and in contact with nature. Their main subjects were landscape and genre scenes with peasants. Modersohn-Becker made good friends in the colony, such as Clara Westhoft, but she felt the limitations of the group and went to Paris, studying at the Académie Colarossi in 1900 and 1903 and at the Académie Julian in 1905, with anatomy studies at the École des Beaux-Arts during her four visits there.

In 1901, she married the widower Otto Modersohn whom she had also met at Worpswede, partially to escape being a teacher or governess, as her parents were reluctant to finance her career any further. Unfortunately, the marriage did not meet her expectations, as she wrote in her diary in March 1902: 'It is my experience that marriage does not make one happier. It destroys the illusion that has been the essence of one's previous existence, that there existed something like a soul-mate. The feeling of not being understood is heightened in marriage by the fact that one's entire life beforehand had the aim of finding a being who would understand one.'[8] She added, 'I couldn't stand it any longer and I'll probably never be able to stand it again either. It was all too confining for me and not what – and always less of what I needed.'[9] The 'it' was married life and the narrow provincialism of the Worpswede colony, both of which she escaped when she went on a final trip to Paris in 1906. Her husband did not want her to leave, then he wanted to join her in Paris. She resisted, but in a letter of that year she had to ask him for a monthly allowance of 120 marks so she could live, since in German law all of the wife's money belonged to her husband.

In Paris Modersohn-Becker was exposed to the art of Vincent Van Gogh, Paul Gauguin and Paul Cézanne, and the paintings in the Louvre. The primitivism and vibrant colors of Gauguin can be seen in her *Self-Portrait* (1906; Pl. XXXIV), in which she shows herself nude to the waist, with flowers in her hair and hands, against a screen of green branches. She presents herself as a nature goddess or Flora, goddess of spring, with a strong physicality in the simplified forms, thick impasto paint and direct gaze. This painting relates to other fertility images of 1906, such as *Mother and Child Lying Nude* (Ludwig Roselius collection, Bremen) or her *Self-Portrait on Her Sixth Wedding Anniversary* (Ludwig Roselius collection, Bremen), in which she shows herself pregnant, although she did not actually become pregnant until sometime later. These works relate in turn to her earlier Worpswede paintings of peasant mothers, old women and candid views of children depicted frontally and close to the picture plane.

Otto Modersohn eventually joined her in Paris after pleading with her to come back to Worpswede, and when they left in April 1907 she was pregnant. On 2 November she gave birth to a daughter, Mathilde. Less than three weeks later she died of a heart attack caused by an embolism. In her brief, intense life, she created over 400 paintings and more than 1,000 works on paper. Unrecognized except by a few friends during her lifetime, knowledge and appreciation of her work has gained her a position of importance, especially as a precursor of German Expressionism. Like Kollwitz, Modersohn-Becker showed the poor, the dispossessed and those rejected by society, and, like Kollwitz, a significant part of her work concentrated on the representation of women, including themselves, unsentimentalized and enduring.

While Modersohn-Becker's work is identified with rural life, Kollwitz showed the urban proletariat, in scenes which carry social comment. Born in Königsberg in 1867 as Käthe Schmidt, she studied there with the engraver Rudolf Maurer and painter Emil Neide, because the Königsberg Academy of Art did not admit women. She later went to Berlin to enroll in the Women's School of Art of the Berlin Academy, followed by the Women's School of Art at the Munich Academy. In 1891 she married Dr Karl Kollwitz and lived at 25 Weissenburg Street in Berlin where he had a worker's clinic as a health insurance physician. Their first son Hans was born there in 1892, their second son Peter in 1896. However, Kollwitz did not abandon her career as an artist, doing her first etchings in 1891 and exhibiting with the Berlin Secession in 1893.

When the Nazis came to power in 1933, Kollwitz was expelled from her studio because of her political and anti-war sentiments, and forced to resign her teaching position. Her works, like that of other German Expressionist artists, were taken from museums, and art galleries were forbidden to exhibit them. She and her husband were threatened with deportation to a concentration camp, and both always carried lethal poison with them to take their own lives in this eventuality. It is no wonder that Kollwitz's last great drawing and print cycle was entitled *Tod* or *Death*. Modeled on the medieval Dance of Death, it shows the skeletal figure of Death coming to different classes of people, including children, mothers and outcasts. In the last representation, *The Call of Death* (Fig. VIII.2) a skeletal arm reaches out to touch the shoulder of a seated figure whose features are Kollwitz's own.

This is the next to last self-portrait in a series she made from 1885 to 1938. Usually showing the face alone in a number of expressive poses, Kollwitz executed a large number of self-portraits in drawings, etchings, woodcuts, lithographs and sculptures. Like Rembrandt's self-portraits, these seem to be a representation not just of the artist but of all humanity. Through the self-portraits, suffering and aging are graphically portrayed, and at the end of her life she welcomes the call of death.

The first decade of the twentieth century spawned a number of avant-garde movements. Of these Cubism was perhaps the most radical, developed by two young artists, the Spaniard Pablo Picasso (1881–1973) and the Frenchman Georges Braque (1882–1963). Marie Laurencin (1883–1956) introduced Braque to Guillaume Apollinaire (1880–1918), who in turn introduced him to Picasso.

Laurencin became identified as the woman painter of the Cubist group, and she commemorated this connection in a group portrait of 1908, *Group of Artists* (sometimes called *Apollinaire and his Friends*, Fig. VIII.3). This oil painting shows Picasso in profile on the far left, holding his dog Frika, Laurencin standing between him and the seated Apollinaire, who is in the center of the composition, with Picasso's mistress Fernande Olivier in a coy pose on the far right. In the depiction of herself, Laurencin has placed the right half of her face in shadow, suggesting both a full-face and a profile simultaneously, a technique Picasso used in later paintings. Her features have been regularized and abstracted in the pale oval of her face, a very

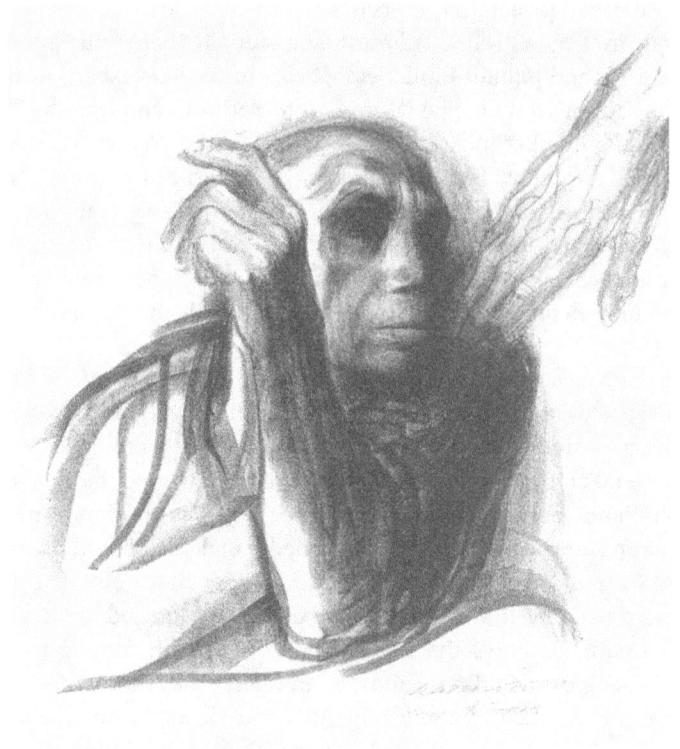

VIII.2   Käthe Kollwitz, *The Call of Death*, 1934–5

commanding representation. Laurencin said of her interest in portraiture, 'I love portraits. To me a portrait is like a voyage: it has to me the attraction of a new experience. When I make a portrait, I feel as though I were traveling through another person.'[10]

Although Apollinaire associated Laurencin with the 'scientific' Cubism of Picasso, Braque, Gleizes and Gris in his book *The Cubist Painters*, her work is not Cubist in theory or execution. She does not employ their limited palette of grays, tans, greens and muted blues, nor does she abstract the object, landscape or figure into divided and intersecting planes. It was her friendship with the artists of Cubism that placed her in their camp, rather than her style. At the same time, her portrait *Group of Artists* of 1908 launched her career as a professional artist, as it was bought by Gertrude Stein (1874–1946), the redoubtable poet and collector of avant-garde art.

The Swiss painter Alice Bailly (1872–1938) was also connected with Cubism. After studying art in Geneva and Munich, she decided to go to Paris to study the latest movements. Bailly became part of the international art scene there and was influenced by Gauguin, Cézanne and the new movements of Fauvism and Cubism. In 1910 she met Raoul Dufy and André

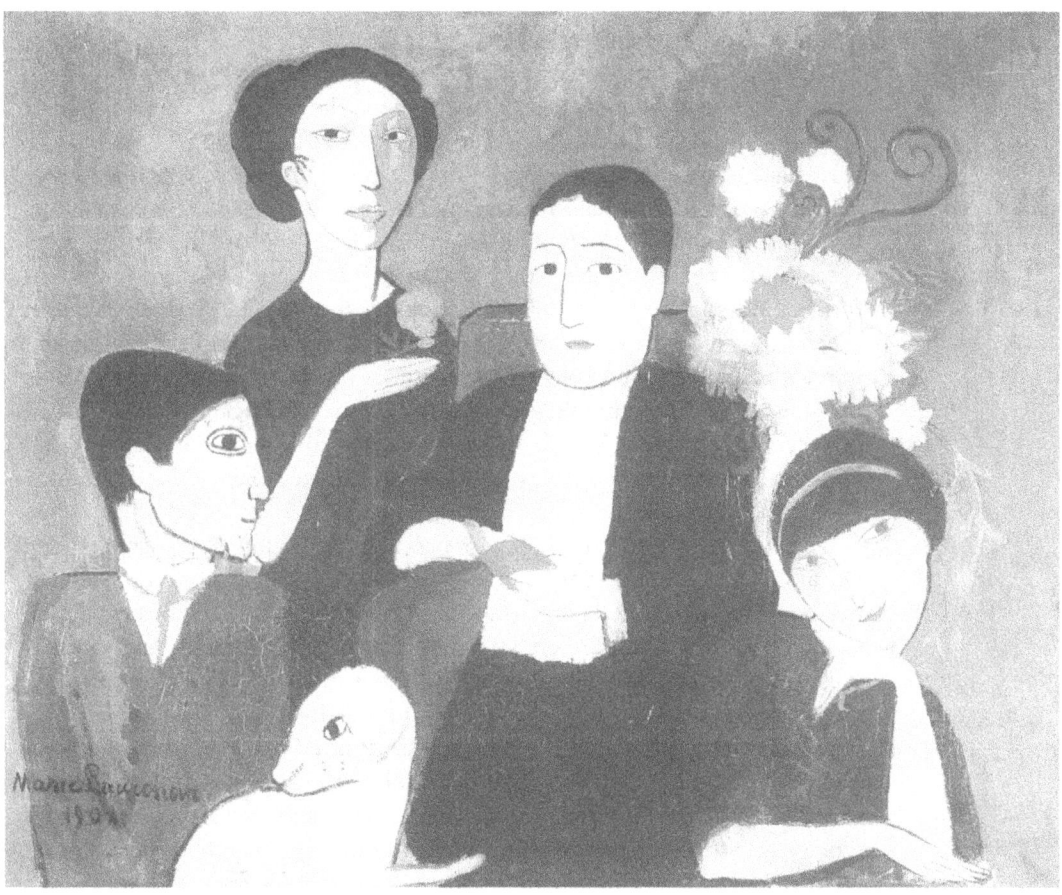

VIII.3   Marie Laurencin, *Group of Artists*, 1908

Lhote, both young Cubist-influenced artists, and moved her art away from Fauvist brilliantly colored canvases to the formal structures of Cubism.

Bailly's 1917 *Self-Portrait* (Pl. XXXV) shows the influence of Cubism very clearly in its flattening of forms, intersecting planes and combined frontal-profile view. Although the face and figure are rendered in the subdued palette of Cubism, the bright hues of the background show the influence of Fauvism. She depicts herself in the acts of painting and of seeing herself, constructing both her own image and the painting itself. It is a complex image of form and color, sharp planes intersecting with curvilinear rhythmic lines.

When World War I broke out in 1914, Bailly returned to Switzerland, becoming involved in the beginning of the Dada movement in Zurich, a movement that revolted against the senseless slaughter of war. It took its name from a word chosen at random from a dictionary, 'Dada' meaning hobbyhorse in French and 'yes, yes' in Russian. Bailly knew the poet Tristan Tzara, and the painter Francis Picabia was also a friend. Eventually, she returned to Lausanne where she received a commission to do large murals in the foyer of Lausanne's theater, but the strain of the massive task brought on her death from tuberculosis in 1938.

Dadaism with its emphasis on nonsense and irrational behavior was the basis for a longer-lived successor, Surrealism. The term 'surrealist' was first used in Apollinaire's play, *Les Mamelles de Tirésias*, which he labeled 'a surrealist drama' in 1917.[11] The so-called 'pope' of Surrealism, the writer André Breton, defined Surrealism in his 1924 *Manifesto of Surrealism* as: 'Psychic automatism in its pure state, by which one proposes to express verbally, by means of the written word, or in any other manner, the actual functioning of thought. Dictated by thought, in the absence of any control exercised by reason, exempt from any aesthetic or moral concern.'[12] Interested in the illogical, the subconscious and the importance of dreams, especially as promulgated by Sigmund Freud (1856–1939), the original Surrealists included both writers and painters. Like Cubism, it was an international movement, involving artists from France, Spain, Germany, Austria, Switzerland, America and Mexico.

The Surrealists took their notion of beauty from a quote by the poet Isidore Ducasse, the 'Comte de Lautréamont', as 'the chance encounter of a sewing machine and an umbrella on a dissection table'.[13] 'Beauty will be convulsive or it will not be', stated Breton.[14] Bizarre creations and illogical juxtapositions were the essence of Surrealism, and the source of creativity was the subconscious and the world of memory and the dream.

It has often been stated that Surrealists admired the 'child muse' role of women, but did not treat them as equally talented colleagues. However, some of the most interesting self-portraits of the twentieth century were done by women artists associated with the Surrealist movement. Perhaps the defiance of rules and the encouragement of creativity from new sources gave them a license to explore and delineate their inner beings, as seen in the self-portraits of Romaine Brooks and Kay Sage.

Romaine Brooks (1874–1970) was not associated directly with the Surrealist group in France, but both her life and her art are distinctly surrealist. The daughter of an unbalanced, wealthy mother, Ella Waterman Goddard, and a father who left the family shortly after her birth, Brooks was cast in the role of caretaker of her brother, St Mar, whose behavior became increasingly abnormal and finally ended in his mental illness and death. It was not until she was 21 that she was able to live a life of her own, on a small allowance. She studied art at the Scuola Nazionale in Rome during the day, where she was the only woman student, and at the Circolo Artistico in the evening. As a woman alone in Italy, she was subject to harassment by male artists. In 1899 she went to Capri to paint and became part of a colony of artists and writers. After her mother's death she wedded John Ellingham Brooks in a marriage of convenience and then bought her freedom from him with an annual allowance to him of three hundred pounds. She traveled to St Ives in Cornwall in 1904 and developed a style of painting based on a severely limited palette of black, white and a range of gray hues.

Brooks then moved to Paris, living on the Right Bank, and had her first exhibition at the Durand Gallery in 1910, exhibiting 13 paintings, all dating from 1905 and all of women. The exhibition was an immediate success, and was followed by an equally successful show at the Goupil Galleries in 1911. Critic Louis Vauxcelles said that after Mary Cassatt and Cecilia Beaux, Brooks would be the only American artist to remember.[15] Apollinaire praised the somber elegance of her works but noted that, beside strength, she painted with great sadness.[16] Brooks's friend, the dilettante Robert de Montesquiou, called her a 'Thief of Souls' because her portraits captured the inner essence of their subjects. Although she painted portraits of male subjects, such as her writer friends Gabriele d'Annunzio (1912, Musée National d'Art Moderne, Paris) and the Surrealist poet Jean Cocteau (1914, Musée National d'Art Moderne, Paris), her primary models were women, either as nudes, such as the dancer Ida Rubinstein in *The Crossing* (c.1911, National Collection of Fine Arts, Washington, DC), or as society leaders, such as her lover of 40 years, Natalie Barney as *L'Amazone* (1920, Musée du Petit Palais, Paris). The image of the Amazon, a nineteenth-century term for women riders, is echoed in Brooks's dramatic *Self-Portrait* (Fig. VIII.4), in which she presents herself in a black riding habit. Here, however, the image of the attractive horse-tamer presented earlier by Courbet, Manet and Renoir has been subverted into an icon, a forbidding and isolated figure, a re-cycling of a concept in a counter-discourse, in this case a lesbian context. The main figure is in black, shown in three-quarter length against a gray sky and dominating the picture space. It conveys a sense of isolation and loss, the black of the riding habit also taking on the connotation of mourning.

In Brooks's *Self-Portrait* the presence of the artist dominates the canvas. Just the opposite effect is evident in Kay Sage's *Small Portrait* (1950, Frances Lehman Loeb Art Center, Vassar College, Poughkeepsie, NY) in which the scaffolding of the head appears to enclose nothingness, and to be a portrait of the absence of the artist, a hollow woman who is the visual counterpart of T. S. Eliot's poem *The Hollow Men* of 1925.

The Surrealist painter Kay Sage (1898–1963) was born in Albany, New York, and lived in Italy where she married Prince Ranieri di San Faustino in 1925, and studied briefly at the Scuola Libera delle Belle Arte in Rome. In 1937, she moved to Paris where she joined the Surrealist group around André Breton and met the artist Yves Tanguy. With the onset of World War II in 1939, she left Paris for New York, and helped many of the Surrealist group come to the United States, including Tanguy, whom Sage married in 1940. Her *Small Portrait* of 1950 has been identified by a number of commentators as a self-portrait (Pl. XXXVI). The structure of the head is typical of Sage's work in the 1940s and 1950s, but here it seems locked, to keep inner secrets from revealing themselves. In a 1959 book of poetry, *Faut dire c'qui est* (Paris: Debresse Poésie), she included a poem entitled 'Tears' which contains the words, 'Ended are the tears/the tears that one cries –/they have dug a hole/inside.' The *Small Portrait* reveals Sage's development in the creation of a fantastic and nightmarish figure dredged from the subconscious and the dream.

When André Breton visited Mexico in 1938 to deliver some lectures and meet Leon Trotsky, he stayed with the Mexican muralist painter Diego Rivera

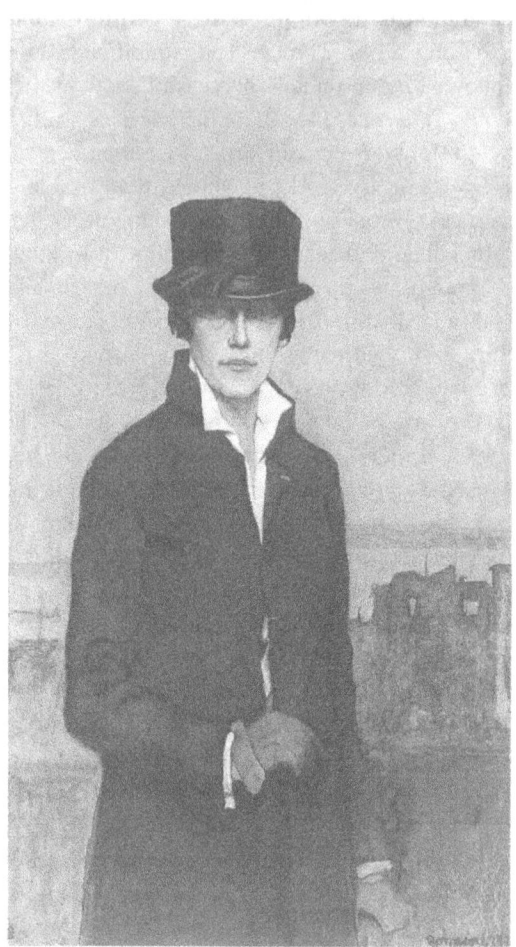

VIII.4   Romaine Brooks, *Self-Portrait*, 1923

(1886–1957) and his wife Frida Kahlo (1907–54), also an artist. Breton admired Kahlo and her paintings, which he pronounced to be 'pure surreality'. Although often using dreams and memories, Kahlo's work is more a record of actual events in her troubled life, transformed into stark images of pain and loss. The effects of a streetcar collision when she was 15 years old which broke her spine, crushed her pelvis and fractured her foot gave her constant pain, and she endured this condition through 35 operations and several miscarriages until her death in 1954.

In 1940 Rivera and Kahlo were divorced, although they later remarried. Kahlo's *Self-Portrait with Cropped Hair* (Pl. XXXVII) is a defiant record of this separation. Kahlo sits in a chair, wearing one of her husband's suits which envelops her, with her shorn hair surrounding her on the floor. Above her is a song in Spanish, which translated reads, 'You see, if I loved you, it was for your hair. Now that you've cut it off, I don't love you any more.' There are obviously a number of sub-texts in this representation. Kahlo is protesting against the stereotyping of femininity in which love depends on an expendable attribute – luxuriant hair – rather than on the person herself. Wearing her ex-husband's oversized suit, she seems to be saying, 'Do I have to be a man to succeed as an artist, whether this role is appropriate to me or not?' The scissors held between her legs may be a reference to the Freudian idea of the female as a castrated male, one filled with penis-envy because of its 'absence' in her anatomy. (Kahlo had read Freud and her painting *The Birth of Moses* is a response to Freud's analysis of Moses's birth.) *Self-Portrait with Cropped Hair* is not the most Surrealist of Kahlo's paintings, but it does fit Breton's definition of her as 'a ribbon around a bomb'.[17]

This self-portrait is one of a series of self-representations. Early portraits, such as *Self-Portrait with a Necklace* (1933; Jacques and Natasha Gelman collection, Mexico City) are mirror images of the young artist. Later she combines her face with symbolic animals, as in *Fulang-Chang and Me* (1937, Museum of Modern Art, New York) and *Self-Portrait* (1940, University of Texas, Austin), in which the monkey is both a pet and a symbolic reference to an untamed or lustful love of life. Many of Kahlo's self-portraits refer to real or imagined episodes in her life, such as *Henry Ford Hospital* (1932; Dolores Olmedo collection, Mexico City), which represents a miscarriage, or *The Broken Column* (1944; also Dolores Olmedo collection, Mexico City), which depicts Kahlo in an iron brace to support her broken spine, her body covered with nails to indicate her pain. Kahlo's husband appears in a significant number of her self-portraits, such as *Frida and Diego Rivera* (1931; Museum of Modern Art, San Francisco), which celebrates their first marriage, *Self-Portrait as a Tehuana* (1943; Jacques and Natasha Gelman collection, Mexico City), in which the image of Rivera's face is inscribed on Kahlo's brow, and *Diego and I* (1949; S. A. Williams collection, Wilmette, Il), a close-up of Kahlo's head in which an image of Rivera is again represented on her forehead. In this portrait Rivera has a mystical third eye, symbolic of the superhuman or divine. In Kahlo's diary, written during the last ten years of her life, she expressed the same idea in words, 'You are here, intangible, and you are all the universe which I shape into the space of my room.'[18] Theirs was a turbulent relationship, but one which endured despite infidelities, deceptions and illness.

A late work, *Self-Portrait with the Portrait of Doctor Farill* (1951; Eugenia Farill collection, Mexico City), shows Kahlo in a wheelchair next to an easel that holds a portrait of the doctor who saved her life; it is a secular *ex-voto* in which Dr Farill takes the place of a holy image. The artist holds a palette in her left hand, her brushes in her right. On the palette is her heart, the expressive source of her art. Kahlo's representations grew from Mexican, Pre-Columbian and European sources, an art in which fantasy and reality mingle, and dreams and memories – the material of Surrealism – are often present.

Like Kahlo, Remedios Varo (1908–63) is the protagonist in almost all of her paintings but, unlike Kahlo, Varo does not always show experiences from her own life, but instead travels in worlds of fantasy. She is easily identifiable by her heart-shaped face, thick mane of hair and aquiline nose, features which turn up in the main female figures in her paintings. Varo was born in Angeles, a town north of Barcelona, as her father, a hydraulic engineer, was probably working on a project there. The family traveled throughout Spain and North Africa during Varo's childhood, following her father's work. Her father had her copy his drawings and diagrams, an exacting craft which may have fueled her interest in science and in representing fantastic machines. After travels in Casablanca and Tangier, the Varo family settled in Madrid where Varo was sent to a strict Catholic convent. She was able to escape this confinement by studying art at the Academia de San Fernando in Madrid and by marrying a student there, Gerardo Lizarrago, in 1931 when she was 21.

On the eve of the Spanish Civil War, Varo and her husband left for a year in Paris. In 1932 they returned to Spain to live in Barcelona, where Varo met the Surrealist poet Benjamin Peret, one of André Breton's closest friends. When Peret returned to Paris in 1937, Varo joined him there, divorcing Lizarrago about this time. The move put her in exile, as Franco sealed the Spanish borders in 1939 to all who had Republican allegiances.

As Peret's companion, Varo was accepted into the Surrealist group, but both she and Peret had to work at odd jobs to live. In spite of this, she loved life in Paris but was forced to leave with Peret with the advent of World War II. Peret could not flee to the United States as he was denied entry because of his liberal political record. Finally, in 1941, with the help of the American Rescue Committee, Varo and Peret went to Mexico. They lived in Mexico with a group of Surrealist exiles, among them the artist Leonora Carrington who became a close friend of Varo's.

In 1947 Varo separated from Peret who returned to France while she remained in Mexico City. In late 1947 she went to Venezuela to visit her brother Rodrigo, who was serving as chief of epidemiology at the Ministry of Public Health. Varo remained in Venezuela until 1959 and took a trip exploring the Orinoco river. It is this trip which she documents in her self-portrait *Exploration of the Sources of the Orinoco River* (Pl. XXXVIII). Here, she shows herself in a fantastic boat navigating through a flooded forest to a hollow tree where water pours out of a goblet on a table. A number of meanings are suggested in this image: her actual experience in the flooded area of the Orinoco river, the sense or non-sense of a magical and illogical source for the river, a boat propelled by wings and a paddle wheel, the possible memory of similar trips with her father, the androgynous character of the explorer and the representation of water, a symbol of female creativity. According to Janet Kaplan, the goblet from which the water flows may be a representation of the Holy Grail and the exploration of the river's source is 'a metaphor for the spiritual quest'.[19]

There is also something humorous in the source of a mighty river flowing from a dinner goblet, and a number of Varo's paintings show a sly sense of the ridiculous, such as her *Still Life Reviving* (1963; Beatrice Varo de Cano collection, Valencia), which has fruit rotating in the air, *Hairy Locomotion* (1960; private collection), in which three learned gentlemen with their heads in the clouds navigate using their moustaches as handlebars and their long beards as wheels, and *Woman Leaving the Psychoanalyst* (1961; private collection), which shows a cloaked female figure dropping a bearded head into a well, presumably the image of her father, or possibly the psychoanalyst himself.

Varo had the first exhibition of her works at Galería Diana in Mexico City in 1956. It was so well received that she was invited to have a solo show at the gallery the following year. This too elicited enthusiastic reviews and purchases. Her second solo exhibition in 1962, at the Galería Juan Martín in Mexico, established her as an important and self-supporting artist. In 1953 she married Walter Gruen, who encouraged her in her career. On 8 October 1963 she suffered a heart attack and died unexpectedly, cut off in the prime of her career. She has been hailed as one of the greatest painters in Mexican history, and the 1971 retrospective of her work at the Museo de Arte Moderno, in Mexico City, drew the museum's largest audience ever, surpassing even those for Rivera and Siqueiros.

Varo does not exemplify the truism that it takes much longer to be recognized as a woman artist. Often recognition only occurs after the artist's death, or occasionally, as in the cases of Alice Neel and Louise Nevelson, in her lifetime provided that she has lived long enough. The Surrealist artist Meret Oppenheim (1913–85), on the other hand, is both an exception and an example of the rule. She experienced instant success while young with the exhibition of her 'sculpture' *Breakfast in Fur*, more popularly known as *The Furred Teacup*, in 1936. It was exhibited at the Galerie Charles Ratton in Paris and bought by Alfred Barr for the collection of the Museum of Modern Art, New York. However, no major exhibition of her work was held until 1989, at the Institute of Contemporary Art in London, and then 1996, at the Guggenheim Museum in New York. The Guggenheim exhibition was ironically entitled *Beyond the Teacup*, indicating that Oppenheim had created much more art than the public was aware of, art which included self-portraiture.

Born in Berlin-Charlottenberg in 1913, Oppenheim spent much of her early childhood in Switzerland with her grandparents in order to escape the dangers of World War I. Interested in art at an early age, she went to Paris in 1932. In 1933 she met the sculptor Alberto Giacometti who visited her studio with Hans Arp and invited her to exhibit at the Surrealist exhibition at the Salon des Surindépendants. Oppenheim contributed to several Surrealist exhibitions, was part of the group that met with André Breton at the Café de la Place Blanche and posed for several photographs by Man Ray, some in the nude, in 1933–4. In 1937 she began to spend time in Switzerland where she experienced long bouts of depression from which she did not completely emerge until she started working again as an artist in the 1950s. Of this period she said, 'I felt as if millennia of discrimination against women were resting on my shoulders, as if embodied in my feelings of inferiority.'[20]

One of the most intriguing elements of Oppenheim's work is a series of self-portraits, beginning with a *Grimacing Self-Portrait* in India ink, and continuing with a *Future Self-Portrait as an old Woman* (1938) and a conventional realistic head, the *Self-Portrait* of November 1943 (Kunstmuseum, Bern). Her 1964 self-portrait, *X-Ray of M. O.'s Skull*, shows the bony structure of the skull underneath a profile photograph, in a twist of Surrealist black humor. This concept is also present in an etching by the Belgian artist James Ensor (1860–1949), *My Portrait in 1960* of 1886, in which he represents himself as a reclining skeleton.

In 1966 Oppenheim did a symbolic self-portrait entitled *Self-Portrait and Curriculum Vitae since the Year 60,000 BC* (Fig. VIII.5). In the drawing, a primitive dwelling is shown with a shaft of light piercing the darkness in the center. The roof is a representation of a landscape, and above it is a mystic crown of flowers and leaves resting on a triangular base. The artist wrote of this work,

> My feet stand in a cavern on stones smoothed by many steps. The bear meat tastes good. Flowing around my stomach is a warm ocean current. I stand in lagoons. I notice the reddish walls of a city. Torso and arms are decked in an armor of tightly overlapping leather scales. In my hands I hold a white marble turtle. Thoughts are locked in my head as in a beehive. Later I write them down. Writing burned up when the library of Alexandria went up in flames. The black snake with its white head is in the museum in Paris. Then it burns down too. All the thoughts there have ever been roll around the earth in a huge mindscape. The earth splits, the mindsphere bursts, its thoughts are scattered in the universe where they continue to live on other stars.[21]

Here is a world, possibly revealed to Oppenheim in a dream, in which the artist becomes a mythic being, perhaps the Great Mother, existing from the beginning to the end of the world.

Oppenheim claimed she was not a feminist and would not exhibit in all-women exhibitions. She felt that art had no gender, but nonetheless, she observed men's devaluation of women; as she said in her acceptance speech of an award from the city of Basel in 1975, '"Women should not think." Is male self-esteem really so vulnerable? "Intellectual achievements by women are embarrassing." So, they have to be repressed and forgotten as quickly as possible. Ideas? Every genuinely new idea is by nature aggressive, and aggression, as a trait, is diametrically opposed to the image of femininity imprinted in the minds of men and projected onto women.'[22]

Dame Laura Knight's (1877–1970) approach to self-portraiture was as a realist, not a Surrealist. She was the first woman accepted into the Royal Academy in England since its foundation members, Angelica Kauffmann and Mary Moser, and was not connected to any radical group in the arts. She was born Laura Johnson in Derbyshire, England in 1877, and attended the South Kensington School of Art from 1894 to 1895 on a Prince of Wales Scholarship. In 1903 she married a fellow artist, Harold Knight, and in 1906 they went to live at the art colony in Newlyn in Cornwall. Her reputation was established when a painting of hers, *The Beach* (1908), was sold at the Royal Academy exhibition. In 1911 she began doing paintings of dancers.

After World War I, Knight and her husband moved back to London where she executed her first circus paintings. In 1929, she was made Dame Commander of the Civil Division of the British Empire. Knight was seemingly no rebel, yet in 1965 she wrote, 'Even today, a female artist is

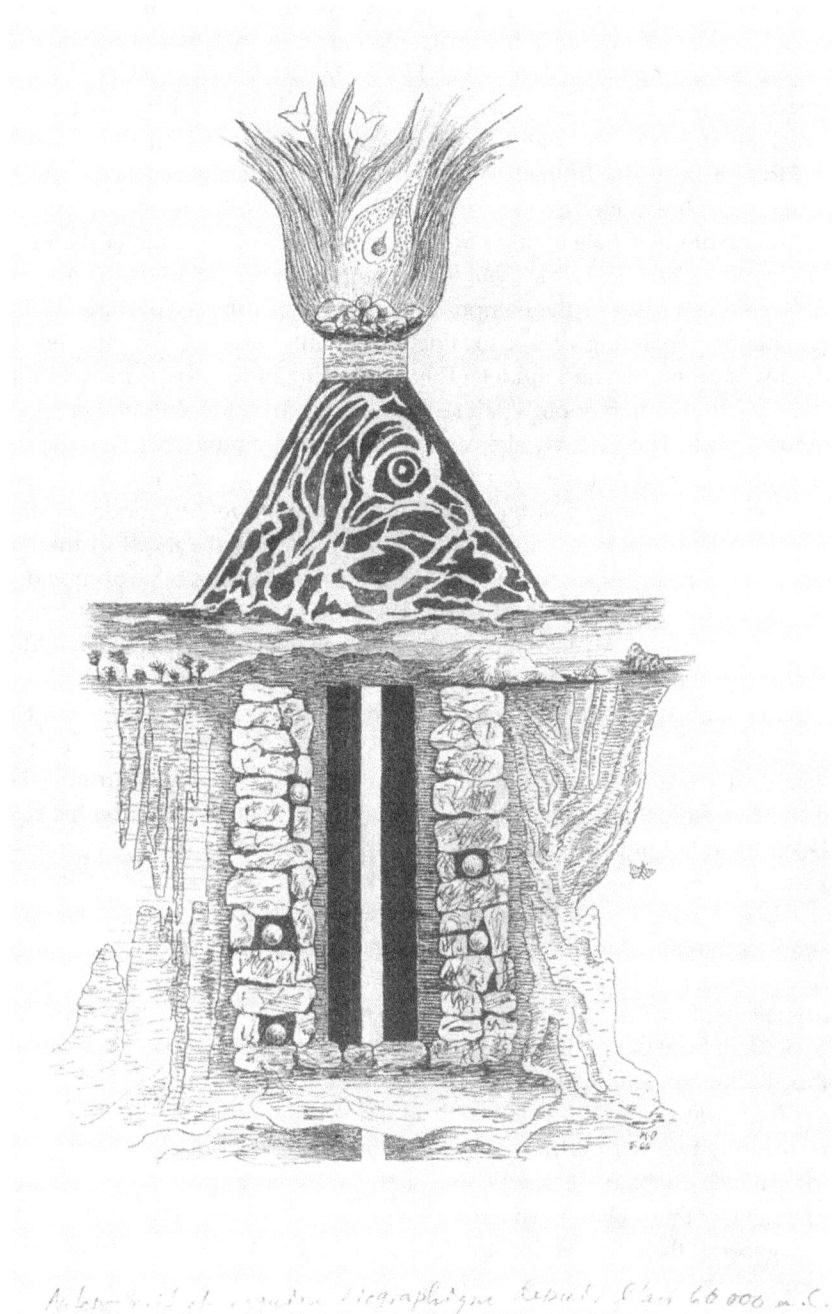

VIII.5   Meret Oppenheim, *Self-Portrait and Curriculum Vitae since the Year 60,000 BC*, 1966

considered more or less of a freak, and may either be undervalued or over-praised, and by sole virtue of her rarity and her sex be of better press value.'[23]

In her *Self-Portrait with Nude Model* (Pl. XXXIX), Knight shows herself in the foreground left, three-quarter-length, with a brush in her hand, her head turned in profile to the right, looking at the nude model on the model's platform on the right. In this self-portrait she emphatically proclaims she is the artist, not the model, a role to which females were often relegated. Such a declaration of the female identity of the artist with a woman painter painting a nude model had never been made before in the work of a woman artist.[24] The severe geometry of the composition underscores the seriousness of the occupation of painting and also, not incidentally, sets off the curvilinear outlines of both artist and model. (The typecasting of women as models still exists, as the contemporary painter Rita Donagh expressed in her 1994 painting, *Slade*. The first day she came to fill her appointment as a teacher at the Slade School of Art, she was automatically led to the Life Room because any woman who worked at the school was presumed to be a model for the life class.[25] This experience testifies to a continuation of the mode of the life class in the nineteenth century where the power relations of male dominance and control over the female body were re-enacted.) In Knight's *Self-Portrait* it is a female artist who has seized the position of control and defied the encoding of the artist's body as inevitably male.

In this context it is interesting to compare Knight's self-portrait with a male artist's self-portrait of the same era, such as the *Self-Portrait in Tuxedo* by Max Beckmann (1884–1950) (Fig. VIII.6). Beckmann aggressively confronts the viewer in a frontal pose close to the picture plane, his right hand on his hip, his left hand holding a cigarette. He dominates the picture space, in contrast to Knight, who views herself from the back and shares equal space with the model. Beckmann concentrates on the masculine power of his persona. The same dominating frontal view is consistent with a number of Beckmann's self-portraits. Even in a double self-portrait of Beckmann and his wife Quappi (1941; Stedelijk Museum, Amsterdam), he stands close to the picture plane on the right, in front of her, and filling two-thirds of the picture space. The theme of the Beckmann self-portraits is not self-definition, as in Knight's *Self-Portrait with Nude Model*, but a bid for control and self-importance. The difference between the two self-portraits is striking, both in stylistic and psychological terms, and perhaps underscores an essential difference in the way men and women view themselves even as late as the twentieth century.

In general, the twentieth century presented a break with representational modes of the past, so there are relatively few traditional self-portraits of twentieth-century artists. Instead, influenced by such movements as Cubism, Expressionism or Surrealism, painters have either created a stylized fractured view, as in Bailly's *Self-Portrait*, or presented the material of Surrealism, such as dreams, memories and the fantastic, as seen in works by Kahlo, Varo and Sage. The female image has been transformed from the gracefulness of Anguissola, Fontana, Vigée-Lebrun and Labille-Guiard, into representations of age, pain and emptiness. Truth no longer necessarily means beauty. Now,

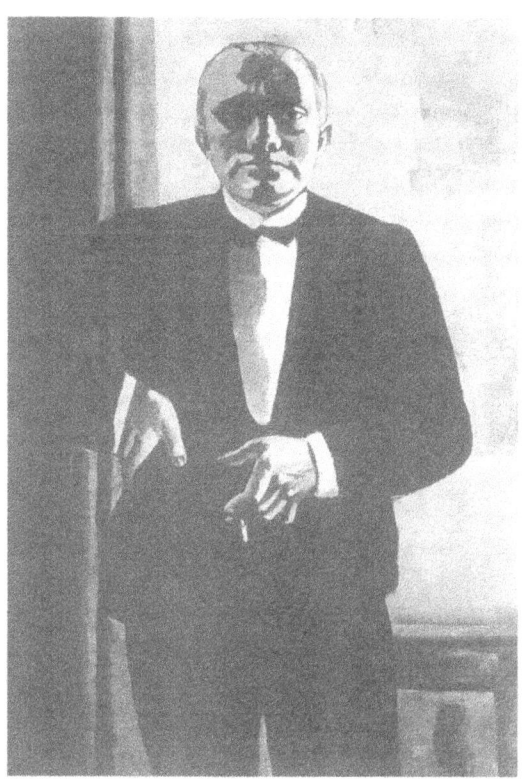

VIII.6   Max Beckmann, *Self-Portrait in Tuxedo*, 1924

at the end of the twentieth century, self-representation signifies and incorporates psychological and spiritual self-identity. Psychologically, the female self-portrait manifests a search for an understanding of the painter's emotional experience, while spiritually, the self-portrait also reveals a search into the complex labyrinth of the mind. Still further transformations and interpretations of the self-portrait were to come in the Post-Modern age.

Contemporary art: journey to the inner self

The Post-Modernist era has encouraged great variety in materials, stylistic references and unorthodox presentations. Unlike the preceding Modernist period, which set narrow parameters for the avant-garde, Post-Modernism has been characterized by variety in types of expression and by an openness to diversity. According to Charles Jencks,[1] the term 'Post-Modernism' was apparently first used by the Spanish writer Federico De Onis in his *Antología de la poesía española e hispanoamericana* in 1934 to describe a reaction to Modernism. This developed into an attack on the orthodoxies and elitism of Modernism and an endorsement in the arts of the 1970s counter-culture values of experimentation, multiculturalism and inclusion. The deconstruction of Eurocentrism and of dominance by white male preferences, as well as the revaluing of ethnic, non-white and women's art, has led to a greater receptivity of all manifestations of art. As opposed to the rigid Modernist standards of pure form in painting and in steel-and-glass Bauhaus-style architecture, and of the imperatives of abstraction, Post-Modernist art is eclectic, recycling and enriching work with artistic and architectural references from the past. It includes narrative, conceptual, feminist, gay and lesbian art, featuring personal histories, political statements and non-traditional materials. This has encouraged multicultural and pluralist art, and has allowed women artists more visibility.

The expansion of the definition of art which is characteristic of contemporary art has made possible the inclusion of whole new genres, many of which have grown out of women's traditional art forms, such as weaving, quilt-making, stitching, and installations with domestic furnishings and props. Ideas of what constitutes a self-portrait are evolving and changing, moving away from narrow forms of likeness to realms of imaginative reconstruction. In many of these areas, women are in the vanguard of the discourse. The mirror image takes on a meaning beyond likeness, in the territory of exploration of self and psyche. In works such as Howardena Pindell's *Autobiography* series, the viewer is included in the artist's experiences, history, fears, dreams and hopes. The female self-portrait is no longer a mask but rather a revelation, a sharing of the dark journeys of the spirit and the courage of the quest. The material of expression too, as well as the recognizable reproduction of the artist's features, is changing. Paint, drawing and sculpture are only some of the options. The Post-Modern artist has a range of expressive possibilities, which also include assemblage, installation, collage, performance art, video, photography, film, and fiber art.

One of the most important manifestations of the Post-Modernists' rejection of narrow standards of judgment and a hierarchical system of values has been the inclusion of formerly marginalized groups. In the United States this has been especially so of African-American, Afro-Caribbean, Latino, Native American, Asian-American, and lesbian and gay artists. Unlike earlier eras when artists of color were automatically excluded from exhibitions, the participation of a widespread variety of groups is encouraged, both within larger exhibitions and themed exhibitions, and as significant groups of interest in themselves. It is still an uphill battle, though, for the minority woman artist who is doubly disadvantaged by gender and ethnic background. As Michele Wallace has written, 'Although her work isn't often seen, the black female artist is alive and making art – despite her double dose of oppression. Being neither white nor male, she satisfies neither of the prerequisites for recognition of an artist in this country.'[2] The situation has improved in the 25 years since this statement was made, especially with the efforts of women's art groups such as the Women's Caucus for Arts, who insist on including minority artists on all panels, awards and literature, but there is still a long way to go.

Even with these disadvantages, during the 1970s female art began to be more evident. Calvin Tompkins later wrote, 'At a certain time during the 1970s, it suddenly occurred to me that half of the interesting new artists in America were women. This was such a startling realization – nothing like it had ever happened in the history of art...'.[3] New areas were opening up for women's art. One of these was public art, art on a large scale in public spaces. The first women's mural collective, Las Mujeres Muralistas in San Francisco, made stunning public murals in 1974 which married the traditions of Mexican muralists with contemporary events and social concerns. Judy Chicago and Miriam Schapiro started the Feminist Art Program in 1971 at the California Institute for the Arts, and the cooperative exhibition, Womanhouse, opened to the public in 1972. New organizations for women artists and art historians were founded, such as the aforementioned Women's Caucus for Art in 1972, and new public art forums, including *The Feminist Art Journal, Women Artists News* and *Woman's Art Journal*.

Two exhibitions brought knowledge of famous women artists of the past to the public's notice: *Old Mistresses* at the Baltimore Museum of Art in 1972 and *Women Artists 1550–1950*, which began its touring schedule in 1976 at the Los Angeles County Museum of Art. *The Dinner Party* by Judy Chicago and over 400 assistants was created during 1974–9 with special plates and 999 tiles with names in gold to commemorate the contributions of women to world history. It toured the United States. A similar collaborative project, the Sister

Chapel, opened at P. S. 1 in Queens in New York in January 1978. In 1982 Maya Lin, a 21-year-old undergraduate architecture student at Yale University, won the commission to create the Vietnam Veterans' Memorial in Washington, DC, one of the most successful public monuments in America's history. When asked if her work had a particular female orientation, Lin replied, 'In a world of phallic memorials that rise upwards, it certainly does. I didn't set out to conquer the earth, or overpower it, the way Western man usually does. I don't think I've made a passive piece, but neither is it a memorial to the idea of war.'[4]

A new area that women artists entered was that of art using formerly devalued forms, such as quilts, ceramics, masks and cloth hangings, not associated with 'high art'. Faith Ringgold (b.1930) began using cloth in her art in 1973 with her first soft sculpture in her *Family of Woman* masks. In Australia, Heather Dorrough used cloth in her 1983 series of 30 self-portrait hangings of life-sized pieces of organza, screen-printed with photographic images of herself both clothed and nude. Dorrough said, 'The fabric is a collaborator. Fabric, material and thread are infinitely familiar…With it I am able to express my "femaleness" more forcefully than by using canvas and oil paint.'[5]

As did the art world in general, the self-portrait entered new realms and new types of expression, one of which was the self-portrait in the guise of an updated religious or mythological figure. A dramatic example of this mode is Yolanda Lopez's *The Artist as Virgin of Guadalupe* (Pl. XL) from the *Guadalupe Triptych* which includes her mother and grandmother on either side of this central image. In this work the Chicana artist creates a new active and contemporary context for the Virgin Mary. Lopez holds a snake, which connects her with the mythology of both the Great Goddess and the symbol of Mexico. In this self-portrait the artist proclaims her allegiance to her Mexican roots and also to the contemporary world as she strides forward in her running gear.

Cuban American artist Ana Mendieta (1948–85) paid homage to the mythic Earth Mother in her *Silueta* series (1973–80). In this she imprinted or photographed her own body as the goddess in caves, on river banks, on beaches and in flower silhouettes.[6] Like Mendieta, Mary Beth Edelson identified herself with the Great Goddess in performance rituals, as did New York artist Betsy Damon. Susan Schwalb's silverpoint drawings of orchids made during the 1970s, and her small Goddess altars, connect the modern with the mythic in different varieties of homage. Cynthia Mailman's nine-feet-tall *God* (self-portrait) (1977, private collection, New York) from the Sister Chapel made the identification with a feminine deity overwhelmingly clear.

Another artist identifying with a mythic and tribal heritage is Jaune Quick-To-See Smith (b.1940). Her *The Red Mean: Self-Portrait* (Pl. XLI), a 90 x 60-inch oil, mixed media and collage on canvas, is a large red painting with a center circle containing an X, like a sighting area on a rifle. A faceless figure is outlined inside the circle. Where its heart should be, the image reads 'Made in the USA' and below it '7137', the artist's enrollment number as required of a

Native American. Smith says the painting 'is a powerful statement of identity…The medicine wheel here is a measure of perfect proportion akin to the classical Greek idea of the Golden Mean. Three vertical sections represent the body, mind and spirit.'[7] With its aggressive brushstrokes and drips, *The Red Mean* has evident connections with Abstract Expressionism and the pictographs used by Robert Rauschenberg. This is also a two-way street, as the Abstract Expressionists drew on Native-American art for their work, using totem poles, masks and sand painting.

Smith describes the elements in her work as 'Pictogram forms from Europe, the Amur, the Americas; color from bead work, parfleches, the landscape; paint application from Cobra art, New York Expressionism, primitive art; composition from Kandinsky, Klee or Byzantine art provide some of the sources. Study of wild horse ranges, western plants and animals or ancient sites feed my imagination and dreams.'[8] The title, *The Red Mean*, is an obvious elision of 'The Red Man' nomenclature given to Native Americans and the Golden Mean of Greek art and Renaissance standards. *The Red Mean: Self-Portrait* is also a prime example of a self-portrait in which identity resides in forms other than a reproduction of the artist's facial features, an identity which is a witness to the life experience, tribal heritage, iconic vocabulary and emotional makeup of the artist. Smith's self-portrait is a representation of the spiritual and inner life of its creator, a sign of the journey and quest of the artist.

Smith comes from a heritage of Flathead, French-Cree and Shoshone tribes and is an enrolled member of the Confederated Salish and Kootenai Nation. When she was born on a reservation in Montana, only one in ten Native-American babies survived, due to lack of medical care, malnutrition and inadequate housing. She is proud of her Native American background and says, 'White people think they have a long history because they've been here 500 years. My people have been in that one place for 12,000 years.'[9] Smith's painting is an affirmation of her tribal roots and the heritage of her ancestors. Her painting is in some sense a disguised self-portrait. The viewer would not know it was a self-portrait unless the artist clearly identified it as such.

In *Queen* (Pl. XLII), Audrey Flack (b.1931), a Photo-Realist or Super Realist artist, presents the viewer with a disguised self-portrait in which her presence is not immediately evident. The acrylic painting takes its name from the Queen of Hearts card on the right and is a tribute to Flack's mother, who is pictured right, in the locket frame under a rose and next to a key chain with the initial 'F'. Flack herself, as a young girl, appears on the left side of the locket frame, frowning slightly but with a fixed smile. The rose, the makeup, the orange slices given to Flack by her mother, all indicate Flack's associations with her mother. But *Queen* has another meaning, as indicated by the card and the chess piece of a queen: the fact that her mother, like all members of the Flack family, was a lover of games of both skill and chance. Flack wrote of her family, 'Like Dostoevski, my family gambled – not casually, but with a passion. For many years I sought to understand the nature and meaning of gambling. Gamblers use cards and dare to challenge the fates…the gods…the ultimate authority. Only a very few win. In their game of life almost all gamblers are losers.'[10]

Although she has painted realistic self-portraits, Flack enjoys teasing the viewer with disguised self-images. She also painted a self-portrait in at least two other gambling paintings, *Gambler's Cabaret* (1976; private collection) and *Wheel of Fortune (Vanitas)* (1977; private collection). The last-named work comes from a series of *vanitas* paintings, an important category in her art, where she connects the ancient tradition of the *vanitas*, a reminder of mortality and the vanity of worldly things, to contemporary painting techniques.

The *vanitas* series also includes archetypes seen as female deities, as in Marilyn Monroe in *Marilyn (Vanitas)* (1977; University of Arizona Art Museum, Tucson), and Flack has developed this idea into sculptures of a number of updated goddesses, such as *Egyptian Rocket Goddess* (presented in an exhibition at the Louis Meisel Gallery in New York in 1991). These extraordinary figures evolve from both the nineteenth-century sculpture tradition and Flack's Super Realist painting style. Some of the figures, which can be as large as 12 feet high, may also be projections of herself or mythic self-portraits.

A disguised self-portrait can appear in a seemingly totally abstract painting. Such is the case in several of Elizabeth Murray's (b.1940) paintings, including *Sail Baby* (Pl. XLIII) and *More Than You Know* (1983; Edward Broida Trust, Los Angeles). As is typical of twentieth-century art, the iconography is a personal one, not based on universally recognized symbols or references. Of *Sail Baby* Murray said, '*Sail Baby* is about my family. It's about myself and my brother and my sister and, I think, it's also about my own three children, even though Daisy wasn't born yet. It's about childhood and using yellow.' The painting is made up of three shaped canvases, 126 x 135 inches, and suggests three figures of slightly different sizes in a row. The contours of each figure are similar, which implies the common features of a family, and they appear to be propelled in one direction. The composition creates both flattened and illusionistic space, with the overlapping of forms and the illusionistic 'hole' into which a green ribbon disappears. The repetition of shapes may also signal that the associations of Murray's brother and sister are now being replicated in the artist's own family. It has been remarked that artists have a pipeline open to their childhood and create from their associations of the past, often from subconscious sources. Murray's work would seem to bear this out; she says, 'The subconscious is what you paint about.'[12] The compressed-shaped canvas, *More Than You Know*, has both autobiographical elements, in that it shows the chairs and kitchen table where she had her last talks with her dying mother, and art-historical references, in the form of a skull that alludes to Munch's *The Cry*.

A type of self-portrait closely allied with the disguised portrait is the surrogate self-portrait in which another figure, symbol or object takes the place of the artist. Paula Rego (b.1935), a Portuguese-British artist, adopts an animal symbol as a humorous surrogate for herself in her *Pregnant Rabbit Tells*

Her Parents (1982; private collection). The painting depicts an episode in her own life. She became pregnant by her future husband, Victor Willing, when they were both students at the Slade School of Art, and gave birth to her first child, Caroline, in January 1956. Since Victor was married to another woman at the time, communicating news of the pregnancy was awkward to say the least, and Rego conveys this in the stance and drooping ears of a rabbit, an obvious symbol of fertility.

Melanie Yazzie, a Navaho artist, executed a poignant surrogate self-portrait, *Raggedy Ann* (Pl. XLIV), in which she identified herself with a doll. She said, 'When I was in grade school ... I had a Raggedy Ann doll that I felt represented me. She was a rag doll going through life's adventures – confronting different monsters and obstacles, but always moving forward. The trunks in *Raggedy Ann* are to some extent who I am and what I am about. I used these trunks to carry my things to boarding school. Inside the trunks are keepsakes and things I have collected around my home and they remind me of my family. I value my mother and grandmothers for what they have taught me and this piece speaks about our relationship.'[13]

Theresa Harlan, the guest curator of the exhibition in which *Raggedy Ann* was shown, *Watchful Eyes: Native American Women Artists*, said, 'Melanie Yazzie's *Raggedy Ann* installation is essentially a self-portrait. In the work she narrates how she developed self-definition amid various sources of information, what she identifies with and what she values as important. Yazzie held on to her memories of her mother, grandmother and home wherever she traveled by taking trunks with her containing such things as corn, silver spoons and newspaper clippings ... Yazzie shows us that the simple and ordinary can articulate the complexity of how she defines and speaks for herself.'[14]

Raggedy Ann also testifies to the mixed heritage of contemporary Native Americans, as Yazzie identifies with an Anglo doll and her story as well as native artifacts and reminders of her Navaho roots. Yazzie, born in 1966 on Ganado Navaho Nation reservation, currently teaches at the Institute of American Indian Arts in Santa Fe, New Mexico. She received a BA in 1990 from Arizona State University at Tempe and Master of Fine Arts in printmaking from the University of Colorado at Boulder. Her witness in *Raggedy Ann* to Native American history is an important contribution to the continuation of that history.

Like Yazzie, the Cuban-American artist Ana Mendieta (1948–85) lived within two cultures. Born in Cuba in 1948, she was sent by her parents with her sister Racquel to the United States in 1961 to escape the Castro takeover. Her art echoes this traumatic break with her motherland, an art of exile and return. She attended art school at the University of Iowa, graduating with an MA in painting in 1972, followed by a MFA in multi-media and video art in 1977. She was already creating works in video and photographs that documented her art in three countries: Mexico, where she spent many summers in the 1970s; Cuba, to which she returned in the 1980s; and the United States. In 1985, at the age of 36, she met a tragic death falling from a window of a 34th-floor apartment in Greenwich Village where she and her husband, the sculptor Carl Andre, lived. Andre was tried for her murder but was found not guilty.

Mendieta's painting, *Body Tracks* (Pl. XLV) was created as a performance at Franklin Furnace, New York in 1982. Smearing her arms with blood and red tempera paint, she marked the side panels of a triptych with both arms and hands in a V formation, and the central panel with vertical right and left arms and hands reaching up. Seen together they seem like a cry on an altar of sacrifice. The tracks her body made stand for herself and her art. The traces of her arms and hands are surrogate forms which represent the whole in eloquent witness. In this work the medium of paint and blood testifies to the performance in which it was created, thus combining two types of self-representation in one work. In this way it is similar to the performances at beaches, creeks, groves, firework displays, deserted monasteries and other sites which bear traces of the artist's presence and which are documented in photography and on videotape. In Mendieta's work there is a sense of the body, a physicality and an imprint of the self even though the original sites and performances are ephemeral.

An interesting variation on the theme of self-portraiture is when the artist includes herself as a member of a group, with a significant other or others with whom she identifies and who help define her status as an artist, family member or partner. Although this type of self-portrait has been done in the past in the teacher–student paintings of Anguissola and Labille-Guiard, the mother–daughter representations of Vigée-Lebrun, Sharples and Morisot, and the husband-and-wife representations of Kahlo, contemporary artists have been particularly creative in their use of this model.

Such identification can be seen in Sylvia Sleigh's (b. *c*.1935) *Artists of the SoHo 20 Gallery* (Pl. XLVI), a diptych in which the artist appears in the right panel as the standing figure on the group's far left. This cooperative gallery offered space to women artists who were often denied exhibitions, not because of the quality of their work but because of their gender.

Sleigh had experienced discrimination against women artists in England. Born in Wales and raised in Brighton, she attended the Brighton School of Art against her father's wishes, but the faculty discouraged her so she ceased painting altogether. Hoping to earn a living as a commercial artist, she discovered that British publications and firms did not hire women for such work. She continued to paint anyway. At an evening art history class at the National Gallery in London, she met art historian Lawrence Alloway; after their marriage they moved to the United States. She had her first solo show in New York in 1963 and later exhibited at the Hemingway Gallery in 1970. There she met artists Nancy Spero and May Stevens, who involved her in the women's art movement.

Partially as a result of the support she received from women artists, Sleigh created a series that reversed the usual artist–model relationship of male painter and female nude model. Typical of this is *Philip Golub Reclining* (1972; private collection, New York) which shows a male nude from the back lying on a sofa, his face appearing in a mirror which also reveals Sleigh painting the work, fully clothed, in the background. Her most daring innovation was *The Turkish Bath* (1973; private collection), in which five male art critics are shown nude, an obvious reversal of Ingres's *The Turkish Bath* (1864; Louvre, Paris). Nudity implies vulnerability and often availability, and male nudity has been avoided by male artists, who have often gone to great lengths not to show full-frontal male nudity by making use of tactful drapery, greenery or weapons, for example. Sleigh's painting therefore breaks a number of taboos. Her male nudes are also individualized and are actual portraits of her sitters, not generic nudes. She is not the first woman artist to show male frontal nudity (witness Suzanne Valadon and Alice Neel), but her realistic depiction includes a sensuality seldom seen in such portrayals, with as much delight in male attractiveness as male artists have taken in their female models.

A very different kind of group portrait that includes a self-portrait has been created by Miriam Schapiro (b.1923), in *Collaboration Series: Mary Cassatt and Me* (Pl. XLVII). This is one of a group of 'collaboration' self-portraits in which Schapiro identifies with women artists of the past, including Vigée-Lebrun, Morisot, Kahlo and various Soviet painters. The painting is subversive in several ways: first, the identification with a female rather than a male inspiration, a foremother rather than a forefather; then, the use of cloth, a non-high-art material and the joining of a high-art painting with a patchwork cloth border. The stress on cooperation and collaboration is also evident as a contradiction of the 'solitary genius' persona of the male artist fighting against the world. In reproducing Cassatt's painting Schapiro pays homage to a significant woman artist and her accomplishments and also testifies to a feminine history of art, as celebrated in the Ann Harris and Linda Nochlin exhibition *Women Artists 1550–1950* of 1976, which inspired her.

The Chinese-American artist Hung Liu (b.1948), who came to America in 1984, has a different type of group identification, that of an immigrant. In *Golden Gate* (Fig. IX.1), her own face represents every immigrant woman who has come to the United States in search of a better life, and the hopes embodied in this search. This is a self-portrait of dignity, in spite of the lowly status often assigned to Asian and other immigrants. The 'Golden Gate' title identifies a specific port of entry, San Francisco, where the artist now lives and works.

Liu's immigrant is doubly disadvantaged, being both a foreigner and a woman. Allison Arieff wrote, 'Just as Liu's paintings examine how the concept of femininity is socially constructed, they also explore how the West has constructed "The Orient" by giving it an inferior cultural status.'[15] Another Liu painting, which is also a self-portrait, is *Resident Alien* (1988; private collection). Made from a US Department of Justice Immigration and Naturalization Service green card, it shows a 'mug shot' of Liu, her fingerprint, resident alien number and the name 'Fortune Cookie', a slang term for a Chinese woman.

Born in the city of Chang Chung, China, in 1948, Liu was raised essentially by her mother since her father, a former officer in Chiang Kai Shek's army,

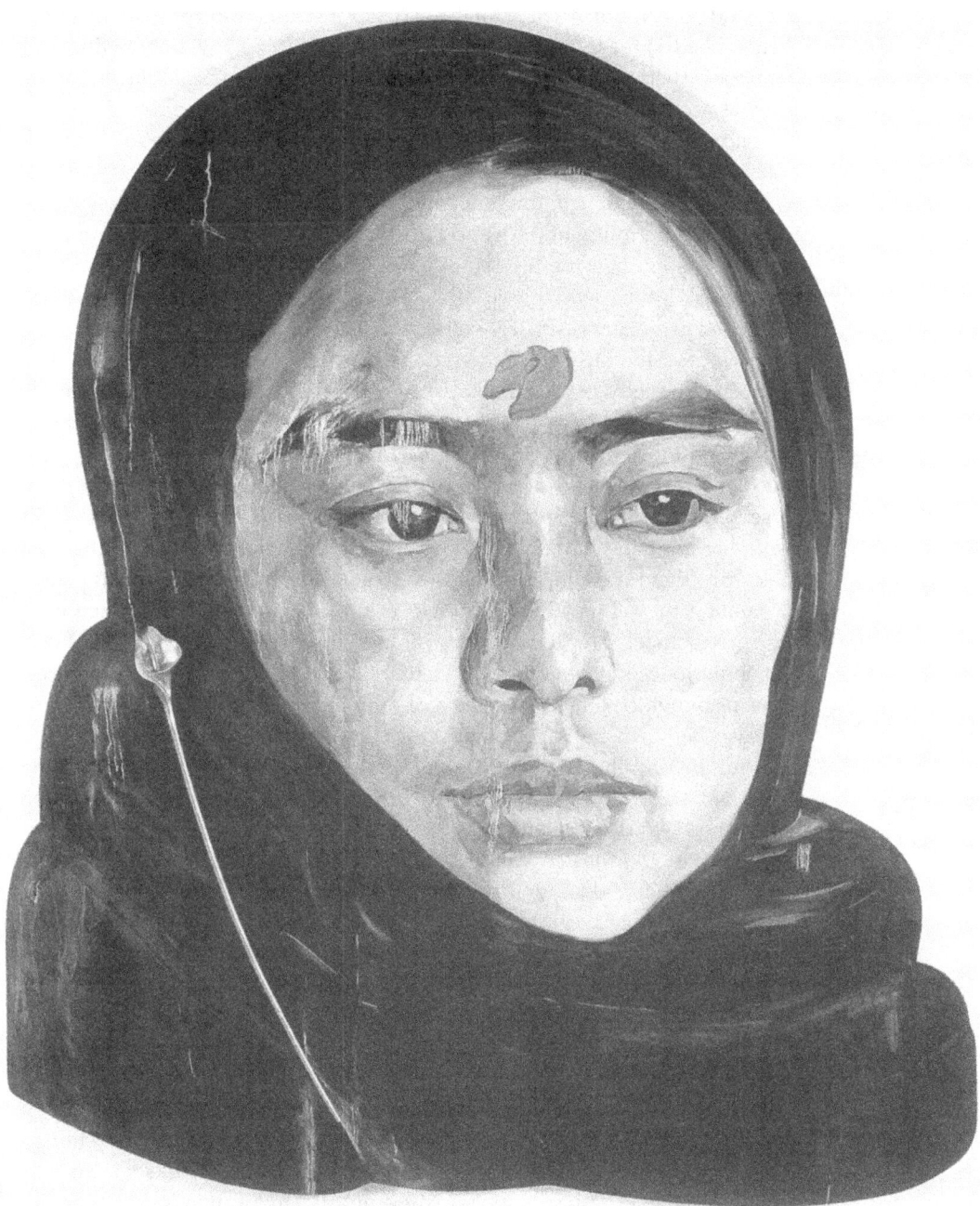

IX.1   Hung Liu, *Golden Gate*, 1994

was captured and jailed when she was only six months old. When Liu was 18 and looking forward to college, the Cultural Revolution began. She was labeled an 'intellectual' and sent to a military farm for re-education and hard labor. She entered Beijing's Teachers College in 1972 with her laborer's status, and studied art, but it was seen only as an instrument of propaganda. She then applied to the Central Academy of Fine Arts in Beijing, only to find that here, too, artists were supposed to be propagandists in a Social Realist style. Liu was accepted for graduate school at the University of California in 1981, but had to wait four years to get a passport to leave China to go to a country which had 'degenerate art'.

Liu's first major commission after graduate school was a site-specific installation and mural at the Capp Street Project Art Gallery in San Francisco in 1988. She studied the history of Chinese immigration to San Francisco's Chinatown. Liu now teaches at Mills College as an associate professor of art, is married to an American, Jeff Kelley, and has a son, Ling Chen, whose name means 'above the dust'. Liu's own name means 'rainbow', an arc in the sky between two pieces of land, perhaps an inspired foreshadowing of her role as an artist and her identity as a person.

Lois Mailou Jones's (b.1905) *Self-Portrait* (Pl. XLVIII) presents the typical self-identification of an artist. Here the painter shows herself half-length, close to the picture plane and off-center to the right, her brushes by her right hand, her left hand hidden by the easel at the right side of the painting. She looks directly at the viewer with a steady gaze, the mirror of her own glance in painting the self-portrait. The vivid color of her red dress, accented by a blue-green smock over it, draws the viewer's eyes to the artist immediately.

Behind Jones in the background left are two African carved wood figures, a means by which Jones proclaims not only her interest in African tribal art, but also her own heritage as an African-American. There is a chair on a platform behind the artist's head and Jones employs the white cloth on the chair and the chair's curvilinear arm, which forms a nimbus around the artist's head, to draw attention to her head and possibly provide a modern equivalent of Old Master paintings' halos or hats.

Jones has had a distinguished career as a painter. As a young woman she won four consecutive scholarships to the drawing classes at the Boston Museum of Fine Arts. While still a student she was employed to assist in design, costume and masks for the Ted Shawn School of Dance, a pioneer of modern dance. Jones's first academic position was creating and heading an art department at the Palmer Memorial Institute, a junior college in Sedalia, North Carolina. In 1930 she moved to the art department of Howard University in Washington, DC, where she taught and later headed the department until her retirement. In 1937–8 Jones received a fellowship to study at the Académie Julian in Paris. Among important works she created there, *Les Fétiches* (1938; National Museum of American Art, Washington, DC), an oil painting of African masks and carvings, testifies to the interest in African art which she acquired in Paris and which she continued in her self-portrait of 1940.

Jones exhibited widely in the United States at a time when works by African-Americans were not accepted in exhibitions by using the device of sending rather than taking her art to the exhibitions, or having it brought in by white friends. Her marriage to Louis Vergniaud Pierre-Noel, a graphic-design artist and a Haitian citizen, introduced new artistic elements as they traveled and she came under the influence of Haitian art. Another element, African art and design, entered her paintings in 1970 when she visited 11 African countries on a research grant. Her African journey resulted in some of the strongest work of her career, vibrant in color and tribal motifs. Here again an ancestral heritage became an important contribution to an artist's work and sense of identity.

An emphasis on the artist's role can also be seen in Paula Rego's self-portrait in *Joseph's Dream* (Pl. XLIX), Rego was appointed in 1990 as the first artist associate at the National Gallery in London, the only mandate for the position being to create works inspired by paintings in the collection. *Joseph's Dream* is loosely based on Philippe de Champaigne's *Vision of St Joseph* of 1638, which takes its subject from Matthew 1:18–25. In this passage, Joseph is told by an angel to take his pregnant fiancée Mary as his wife because the child she is to bear has been conceived by the Holy Ghost. However, in Rego's self-portrait, the artist seated in the foreground is the center of the painting, and the figure of Joseph is older than the young man of Champaigne's painting; one of Rego's favorite models, he is sleeping in an armchair. Rego has transformed the older painting, seen sketched on the artist's canvas, into a classic 'artist and model' rendering, its real subject being the vocation of the painter. The twist of female artist and male model is consciously introduced by Rego; she has underlined the situation of active artist and passive model in her statement, 'I want to do a girl drawing a man very much, because this role reversal is interesting. She's getting power from doing this you see.'[16]

The hidden self-portrait is the direct opposite of the artist publicizing her central role in a painting. In the hidden self-portrait, the artist does not appear directly, but instead hides behind or within a composition. Howardena Pindell, an African-American artist born in 1943, disguises her declarations of self in abstract or semi-abstract works, which nevertheless reveal her history and experiences. *Autobiography: Water/Ancestors/Middle Passage/Family Ghosts* (Pl. L), for example, refers to the notorious slave voyages from Africa to America which some of Pindell's ancestors had taken. Her *Autobiography Series* depicts some of the experiences of her life in paintings on hand-sewn canvas and collaged works on paper. *Autobiography: Earth/Eyes/Injuries* (1987; collection of William and Gloria Johnson, Woodlands, Tex) portrays a car accident in 1979, an event that turned out to be a crisis in the artist's career. Pindell was trapped in her car while onlookers refused to rescue her because they were afraid the car would explode. The eyes in the painting represent the experience of being watched by the onlookers. Another painting, '*Who Do You Think You Are? One of Us?*' (1991; private collection), relates to the racism and prejudice constantly encountered by African-Americans.[17]

Pindell says of her *Autobiography: Water/Ancestors/Middle Passage/Family* Ghosts, 'My ancestral background is a vast stew. The painting symbolizes this mixture and the fact that Africans kidnapped and held hostage in this country were massively tortured and sexually abused by their captors, who drew up laws to prevent those they had enslaved from protecting themselves. The text of one of the laws is included in the painting...An image of a ship with enslaved Africans during the Middle Passage is located on the lower left. Eyes throughout the painting represent witnesses, even if silence was the only testimony permitted...The head of the African woman in the upper center represents the one African woman from whom all human life is traced by scientists.'[18] The blue color representing the sea is the ground on which the events and texts are painted and collaged. The artist's face and figure outline appear in the center of the canvas, engulfed and almost drowning in the sea of associations. The massive size of the painting, 118 x 71 inches, seems to invite the viewer into its space, as both collaborator and victim.

The jeopardy of the position of the African-American woman artist is expressed also in Emma Amos's poignant self-portrait, *Will You Forget Me?* (Pl. LI). Amos began her *Falling Series*, which includes her self-portrait, in 1988. It is a metaphor for the precarious position of both women and minority groups, and also a protest against the disappearance of the social safety net under the Reagan administration. In *Will You Forget Me?* Amos shows herself falling through space holding on to a large photograph of her mother, almost as a parachute to break her fall. The painting has a border of African fabric, both as a framing device and as a testimony to Amos's African heritage.

In another series, *Changing the Subject*, Amos challenges the canon which glorifies white male artists and ignores women, African-Americans, Native Americans, Chicanos, Latinos and Asian-American artists. One of the paintings, *Which Way is Up, George Baseless?* (1991; private collection) ridicules the upside-down figures of German Neo-Expressionist painter Georg Baselitz. Other paintings in the series take on Penck, Fetting, Immendorf and other artists privileged by the establishment.

The painful awareness of the minority status of African-American women artists in American culture was voiced by Amos in an interview with bell hooks, 'I think that I've had to learn that success is not going to come the way it came to the blue chip artists, and that only a small number are really successful in the marketplace, anyway. And it's not going to be me, and if so, it's going to be a late splurge on the order of what happened to Alice Neel, Elizabeth Catlett or Faith Ringgold...I'm doing exactly what I always wanted to do and that's kept me going.' For Amos and Pindell, the slogan of the woman's movement, 'The personal is political', is revealed as eminently true in their self-portraits.

In Native American artist Kay WalkingStick's (b.1935) series of self-portraits, *I Can't Make It Without You* (Fig. IX.2), the occasion for making the self-portraits was a personal grief, the unexpected death of her husband of 30 years at the age of 54. 'I had lost my mentor. I felt that I'd died with him – I wasn't sure that I was here either,' she said.[20] In making this series of charcoal drawings she was able to express these feelings and begin a healing process. She felt her husband's spirit urging to start work again.

The format of WalkingStick's drawings is similar to her acrylic, wax and oil landscape diptychs in which one side presents a realistic view of the terrain while the other shows abstract forms. She says of this work, 'One portion has

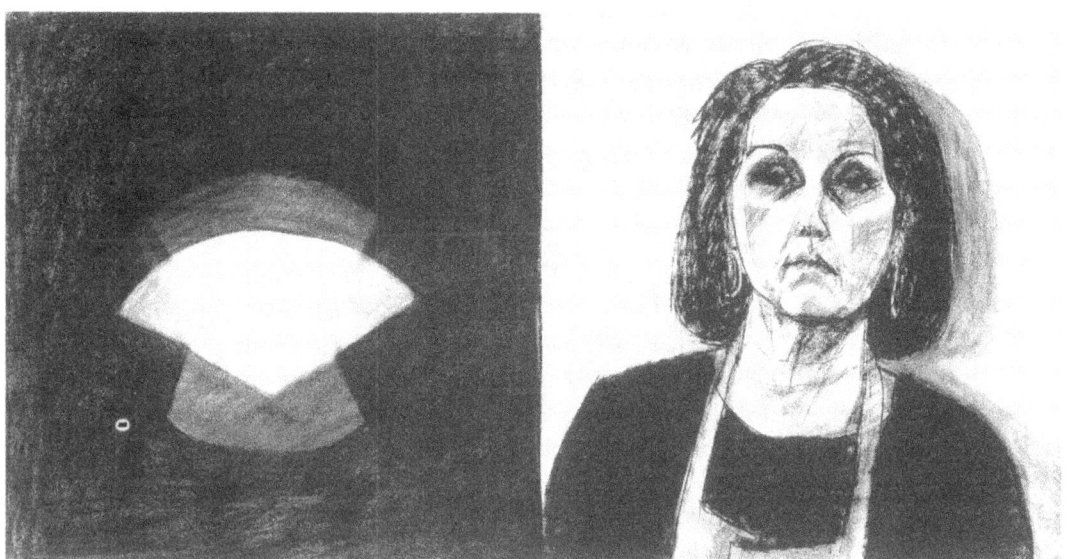

IX.2   Kay WalkingStick, *I Can't Make it Without You Number 2*, 1989

to do with the momentary, fleeting memory and the other the more spiritual, long-term memory…They are not landscapes but paintings about my view of the earth and its sacred quality.'[21]

The duality of the works also testifies to WalkingStick's own background as daughter of a Cherokee father and a white mother. She expressed this Native American heritage in *Messages to Papa* in 1974: 'At about the time I went to graduate school, I realized that it was necessary for me to come to terms with my own genetic heritage. I made a tipi and called it *Messages to Papa*. I had never known my Cherokee father. Of course, the Cherokees don't build tipis, but the tipi is a sort of symbol of the Native American to non-Native Americans. And I hung messages in Cherokee on the inside of the tipi…I sat inside it hanging those messages from string. When I finished it, I really loved it…and I did think it was a serious work of art as well, not just a ritual act.'[22]

In *I Can't Make It Without You*, a realistic portrait of WalkingStick's head and shoulders, is on the right of the composition, while on the left there is an abstract symbol against a dark background. The symbol has a dual form – a horizontal white fan intersects a vertical darker form, possibly expressing the intersection of two lives, the darker one in the background receding away from the picture plane. The image is one of loss and recovery: loss of husband, mentor and companion, recovery in the very act of confronting the loss in the work of art.

A number of twentieth-century women's self-portraits adhere to traditional practice by creating realistic representations of the artist. One of these is by Alice Neel (1900–1984), a nude *Self-Portrait* (Pl. LII). At the age of

80 Neel was no 'sweet old lady'. She was a feisty proto-feminist who said, 'All insults, all attacks, all downgrading and exploitation of women should be fought by all women. To permit a psychiatrist to say you suffer from "penis envy" is like singing "Old Black Joe" to a Black Panther.'[23] Although Neel did landscapes and still-lifes during her career, she is mainly known for her extraordinary portraits. She liked to persuade her sitters to pose in the nude so she could tell the whole truth of a person stripped of the accoutrements of power or the lure of costume.

The question might be asked, 'Why did Neel wait until she was 80 to do a nude self-portrait?' When younger, she always felt that her pretty, soft looks did not express her character and were not strong enough to be interesting. By her eightieth year, she may have decided that her looks were distinctive enough to merit a self-portrait. And, of course, there was the aspect of breaking a taboo against showing older people nude, because the nude is supposed to be a vision of beauty, not age. The *Self-Portrait*, defiant of conventions, presents a magnificent view of an artist who always told the truth as she saw it, in a distinctive, original style, and had to wait 40 years before her paintings were recognized. It reverses the nineteenth-century cult of the ideal figure and the power dynamics of the life class. Here the artist is in control of the representation of her own body and is not afraid of showing an image of aging, a less than ideal form and reality, not beauty.

Just as Neel's 1980 *Self-Portrait* is a realistic portrait with a twist, so the French artist Annette Messager's (b.1943) *How My Friends Would Do My Portrait* (Fig. IX.3) is a new type of self-portrait, the self-portrait as putatively created by others. A wall installation of 62 ink drawings on paper and 55 gelatin silver prints, the images exemplify the two titles Messager gives herself – Annette Messager, Artist, and Annette Messager, Collector. Her works are a combination of artwork, photography, stuffed animals and constructed shapes, an art of *bricolage* and odd collections of things. Her tone is usually ironic, as in *How My Friends Would Do My Portrait*, an acknowledgment that no two people see a friend in exactly the same way, and that self-images often contain other persons' views of us. Not only that, but our views of ourselves can be changed, rearranged, puttered around with, as with the assemblages of articles.

'My work speaks out about me as a woman. At the beginning, my work was almost like a diary. I was young and didn't know what to do with my life. I was almost like a reporter – what it was to be a woman at that moment', Messager said in 1997.[24] Daughter of an architect who loved painting more than his career, Messager studied art at the École des Arts Décoratifs in Paris. At that time, she won a trip around the world with a photograph her mother had entered in a contest sponsored by Kodak. During the trip, she bought a camera in Hong Kong and her many photographs are now a key element in her art. If Messager didn't know exactly what she wanted to do, she knew what she didn't want to do – and that was to create grandiose canvases or Pop Art images, as these seemed to her part of an all-male history of art. Since then, she has created her own highly individual vocabulary, from stuffed

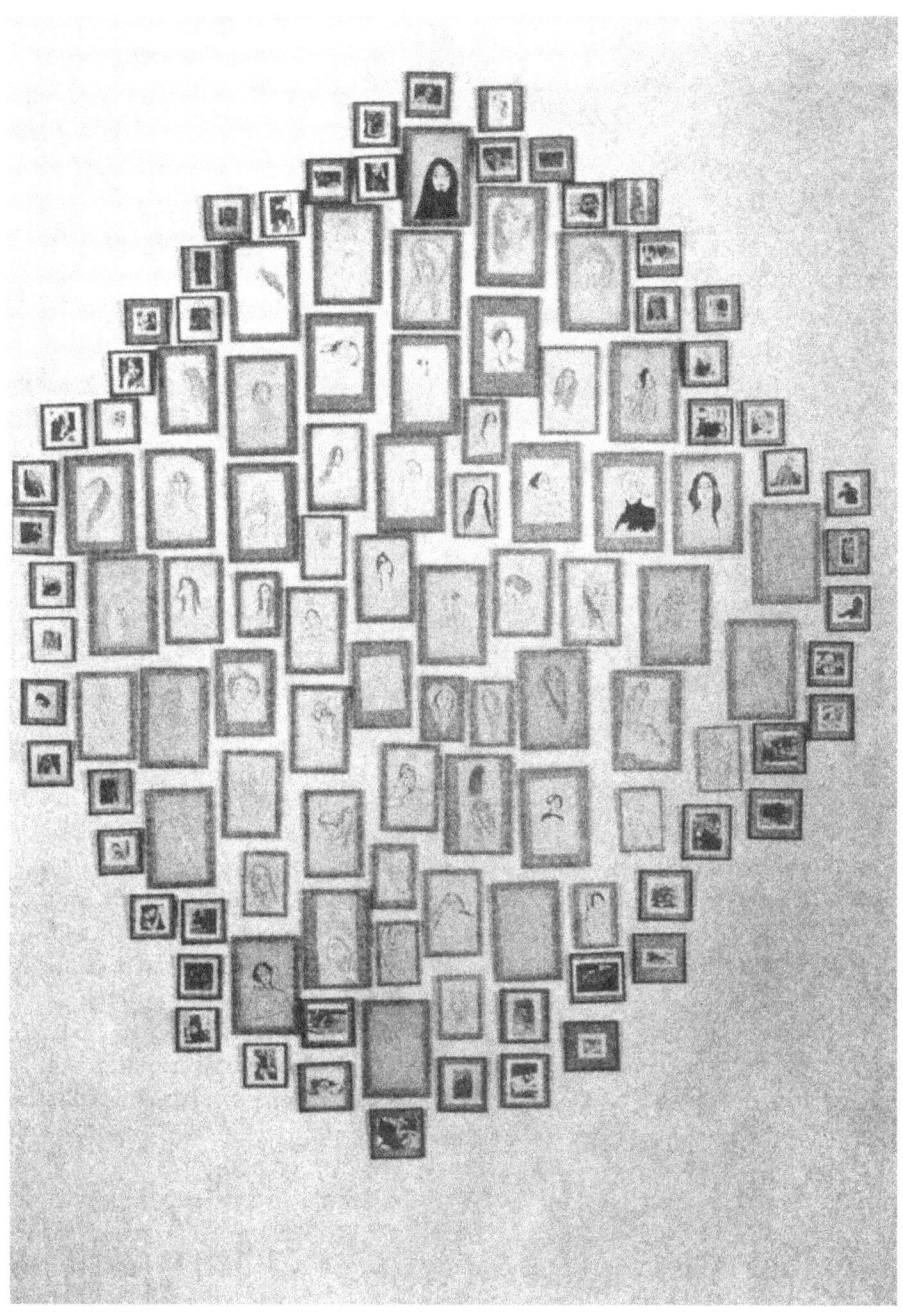

IX.3   Annette Messager, *How My Friends Would Do My Portrait*, 1972

animals, body organs made of cloth, chimeras and a group of fantasy figures impaled on pikes; hers is a world of imagination which testifies to the reality of our deepest wishes, fears and psychological makeup.

A self-portrait, whether the artist wishes it or not, reveals certain

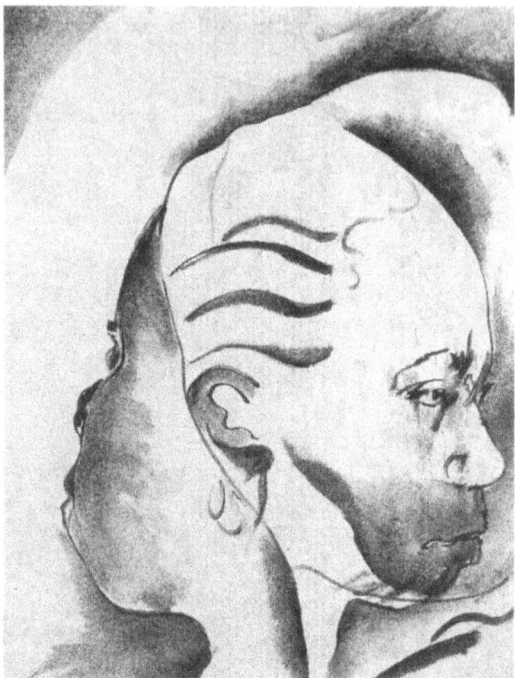

IX.4   Therese Musoke, *Self-Portrait Number 1*, 1985

orientations, beliefs or circumstances of its maker's life. This is very vividly illustrated in the African artist Therese Musoke's *Self-Portrait Number 1* (Fig. IX.4), where a Janus-like head faces in opposite directions.

Therese Musoke was born in Kampala, Uganda, in 1945. Her father was a Sasa tribal chief who had converted to Roman Catholicism. He sent his 17 surviving children to the Catholic Mission, to receive their first education in two traditions, African tribalism and European culture. Most of the Musoke children went on to universities and into different careers in Kenya, England, Germany and the United States. Therese attended Trinity College, a secondary school in Uganda, then went to the Margaret Trowell School of Fine Art, Kampala, where she learned the European traditions of painting and the fine arts. In 1965 she had a one-person exhibition at the Uganda Museum of Art, a significant beginning for a 20-year-old artist. She continued her postgraduate study in art at the Royal College of Art in London and at the University of Pennsylvania. Returning to Kenya, Musoke persuaded Gallery Watatu to give her a solo show in 1974, the first of many successful ones there.

There are several interpretations of Musoke's *Self-Portrait Number 1* that are possible. One may be a representation of the ambivalence of the artist, both looking out and looking in. Another may refer to times past and future, or to the two-faced tradition of African tribal masks. At a deeper level, the self-portrait seems to signify the artist's experience with the two realities of her existence, her African essence and her European education and painting style. The image embodies the duality of living in two worlds, with both its opportunities and its drawbacks. It is also a realistic representation of the artist's features and a visualization of her psychic state.

New York artist Anita Steckel uses her self-portraits to dramatize the issues of the feminist revolt against masculine values and judgments on art and society. As Ruth Iskin points out, 'Steckel utilizes collage for its political potential. In addition, collage provides Steckel with a means of addressing and using available (male) traditions of culture while giving them a feminist twist – allowing her to introduce her own point of view of those traditions while using them.'[25]

A case in point is Steckel's *Last Supper* (1962–73; private collection), an obvious parody of Leonardo da Vinci's *Last Supper*, in which a collaged group of formally dressed Victorians sits at a table where a giant female nude has been served for their delectation, implying that it is women who have nourished a patriarchal society and whose bodies are at the service of men. In *Mona Lisa* (1973; private collection) Steckel painted a collage portrait of Mona Lisa in giant size, holding a paintbrush in front of the New York skyline, recalling the liberties Marcel Duchamp took with this image by adding a moustache and titling it *L.H.O.O.Q.* (1919; private collection, New York). Arlene Raven commented, 'The hairy-lipped Mona Lisa remained the sole twentieth-century representation of this woman until New York artist Anita Steckel presented a monumental mixed-media *Mona Lisa* (1973) as an American artist, placing an empowering brush in her hand and positioning her smack up against the Manhattan skyline.'[26]

The New York skyline also plays a key role in Steckel's imaginative self-portrait, *Giant Woman on New York* (Fig. IX.5). In this work a huge female nude figure, with the artist's collaged features, holding a poised paintbrush, straddles the Empire State Building, riding and controlling what was for many years the tallest building in Manhattan and the world. This is an audacious portrait fantasizing about the power of women over New York and its art world. Since art historian and critic Arlene Raven selected this work as the key (and only) painting to represent a 20-year period of women's art for the Twentieth Anniversary Issue of *Ms Magazine* and also for the anthology *New Feminist Art Criticism*, it has become an important icon of feminist art and aspiration. There is always a danger that a work with heavy ideological implications can lapse into propaganda, but Steckel uses humor and imagination to give her work both depth and layers of meaning.

Not all feminist self-portraits are so triumphant. Juanita McNeely's *A Delicate Balance* (Fig. IX.6) shows the artist in a precarious position, walking a tightrope with a baby tied to her waist, attempting to work on a painting behind her, a representation that would be amusing if it were not so poignant and true to life. The painting is based on McNeely's seeing a woman on the street dressed in rags, bleeding and crooning or muttering to a doll she held.[27] The vision haunted McNeely and she turned it into a self-portrait showing the artist striving desperately to meet the demands of motherhood while practicing her vocation as an artist.

The contemporary self-portrait by a woman painter takes many forms, from the totally abstract to detailed realism, and from outward mask to inner

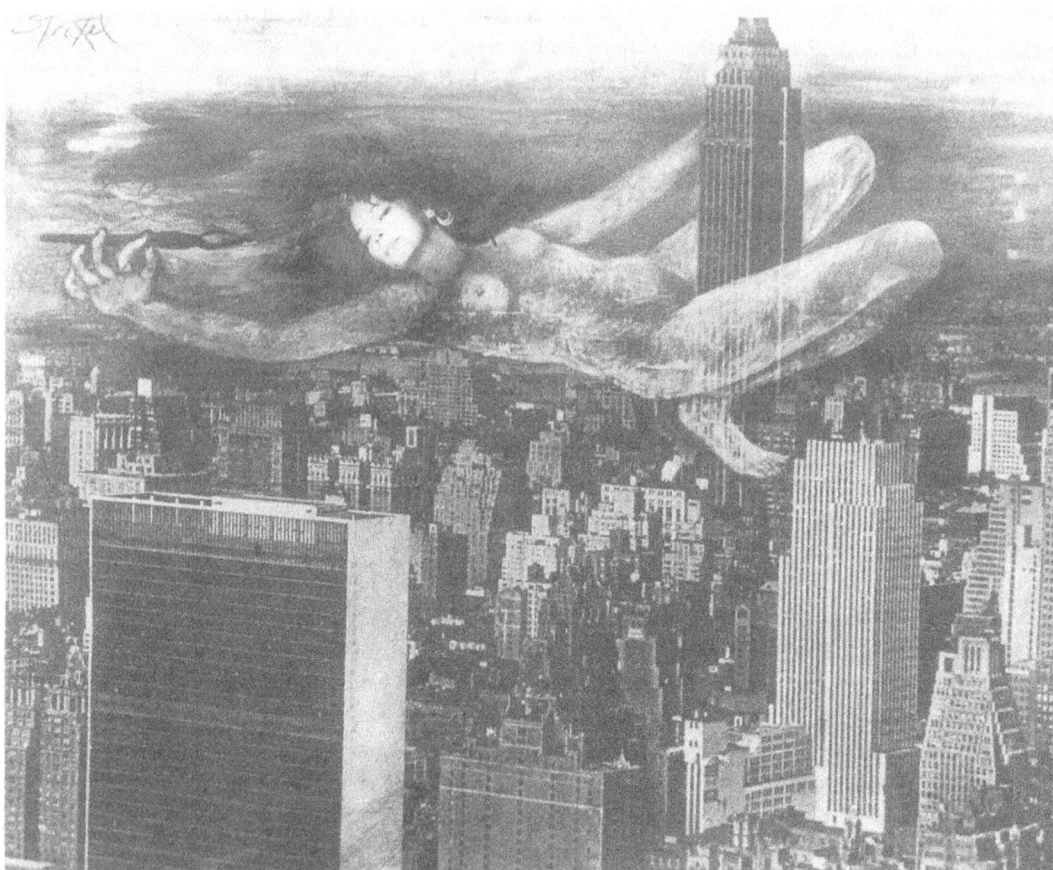

IX.5   Anita Steckel, *Giant Woman on New York*, 1973

emotions. Representations range from mirror image to symbolic surrogates and from fantasy to despair. Contemporary female painters have created multifarious vehicles for their self-expression and self-portrayal that have enriched our understanding of both art and women. They have expressed images of vulnerability and of power and the entire spectrum between.

Women have employed self-portraiture in the Post-Modern age to present issues of concern to them and to become instruments of advocacy, unlike female artists' self-portraits of the past. In so doing some contemporary women painters have included references to history, and especially the history of art, in their self-representations. This can be seen in Schapiro's *Collaboration* series, Murray's inclusion of Munch's *The Cry* in *More Than You Know,* and Rego's use of Philippe de Champaigne's *Vision of St Joseph* in her *Joseph's Dream.* Other artists such as Jones, Mendieta, Smith and Lopez have referred to their ethnic heritage through the representation of artifacts or cultural symbols in their self-portraits. In all these manifestations contemporary

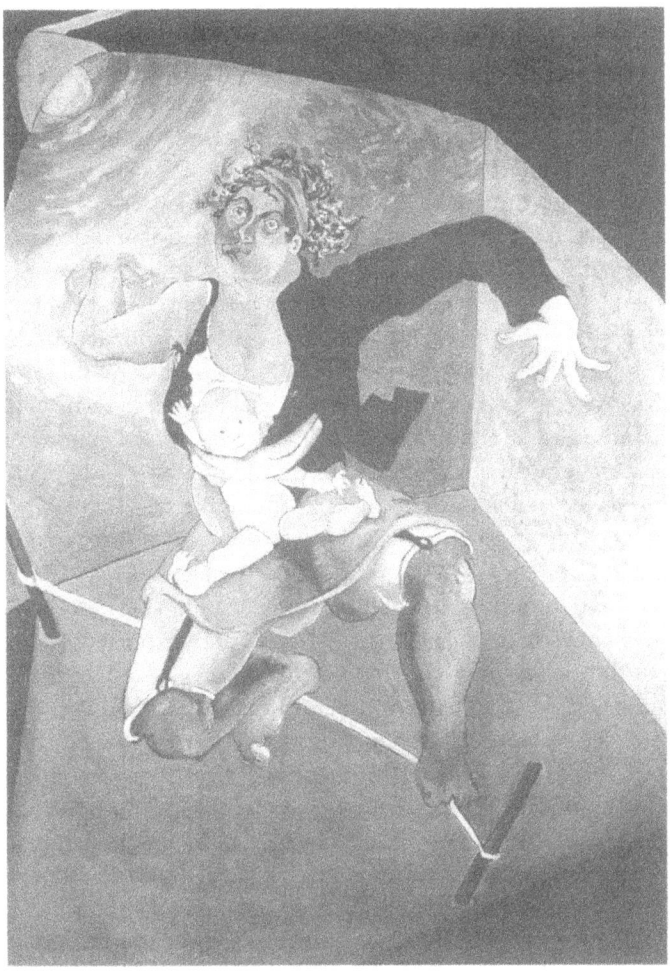

IX.6   Juanita McNeely, *A Delicate Balance*, 1973

women painters have gone beyond conventional self-representation and have stretched the boundaries of our understanding of self-portraiture.

One of the questions to be asked about twentieth-century self-portraits by women is what is the source or cause of their departure from earlier norms of self-portraiture which portrayed the artist in a mirror image or as seen by the viewer, and in a traditional role: that of artist, cultured woman, teacher or mother? Why this flight from traditional representation, why this invention of new paradigms for female self-representation, why this avoidance or reinterpretation of past models?

One of the reasons obviously lies in the change in modes of representation in the early twentieth century in general, such as in Fauvism, Expressionism, Cubism, non-objective art, and, in particular, Surrealism. New psychological analysis of the self has been important here. One of the most potent of these influences is Freudian psychology and in the twentieth century (like men) women have no longer lived in the rational terrain of Victorian certainties and the imperatives of moral behavior and accountability.

The irrational, the spontaneous, the unpremeditated were glorified in Surrealism over the rational and intentional and were viewed as *desiderata*. What appeared on the surface and in accepted behavior was undermined by unconscious urges and desires. As a result of these new perceptions of reality, women painters have turned their gaze from traditional modes of representation to create an irrational world based on dreams, memories and desires. Chance became glorified and has been used extensively by some painters. The inner world rather than the outer façade became the locus of self-representation.

For women painters, this often meant giving up traditional expectations of the female role. They could expand their self-images beyond those of dutiful daughters, loving wives and mothers, housekeepers, even women of education and culture. Painters such as Remedios Varo, Leonor Fini, Frida Kahlo and Meret Oppenheim could see themselves in new and fantastic roles, as sphinx, monster, witch, seer, goddess, earth mother, destroyer, *femme fatale* and a number of other undomesticated images. Surrealist theory undermined traditional female identifications and gave both male and female artists new areas of association and representation of the feminine. These images, like Surrealism itself, were transgressive, subversive and disturbing, exposing the dark side of the psyche to view.

In a similar fashion, the later twentieth-century questionings of feminism have produced new and threatening images of women. They have exposed new aspects of the concept of womanhood that have previously been relegated to the private sphere, such as the blood rites of menstruation, the details of miscarriage, the agony of birthing, the pain of operations, the terror of aging, and many other once unmentionable topics. Feminist theory has drawn on myths and early matriarchal societies and a return to goddess imagery. Images of women in general, and in self-portraiture in particular, have assumed these new representations of the feminine, which have broken with accepted images and rituals. The personal has not only become political, it has become embodied in the personae of self-representation. The female image has become a role model and an inspiration.

As part of the major psychological and political transformations taking place in the world, feminism has encouraged female painters to break with previous models in art. Often, as seen in self-portraits from the end of the century, the inner life and personal fantasies have supplanted representations of more traditional subjects. In contemporary women's self-portraits, ideals of beauty have been deconstructed in favor of representations of inner truth, which have often been chaotic and threatening. There is a cost, but also a promise – in their self-portraits, women painters have revealed their inner psyche as well as their outer image. As a consequence, contemporary self-portraiture, both male and female, aims to depict the individual *élan vital* inspired by personal convictions and social allegiances rather than conventional models of the self. As illustrated, these new approaches to the self coexist with traditional representations, thus providing a broad range of experiences for self-imaging.

X

Conclusion

This book has sought to detail the accomplishments, skills and originality of female self-portrait painters from classical antiquity to contemporary times. In each period of history, from the fifth century BC onward, records of outstanding female self-portraiture abound. Such works represent the genre both in taste and style, fulfilling the elements demanded by it: veracity, mastering the medium, and the universal connection between the observed and the observer.

These self-portraits present the experience of being female, while often incorporating the constraints that a male-dominated society imposed on that experience. Questions have been raised and answered. What makes the painted female self-portrait different from male self-portraits, in both concept and actuality? When comparing such portraits, we find a number of similarities in the works of both male and female artists, such as the artist shown as a painter, the artist depicted with spouse, family, parent or child, the artist as an aristocrat or with an enhanced persona, the artist in the presence of illustrious personages. Contrasting the differences between female and male self-portraits, however, reveals different creative innovations. One of these is the artist's impersonification of allegorical figures, such as Painting or Poetry, these being always represented as a woman.[1] For example, in the seventeenth century, Artemisia Gentileschi's *Self-portrait as the Allegory of Painting* (Pl. XIV), or *La Pittura*, depicts the self as both woman and personification. A male artist could show himself with the personification of a female figure as Painting but only a female artist could actually assume that personification. Another example of the female painter's assumption of a female allegorical figure, which is also a self-portrait, is Angelica Kauffmann's self-portrait, *The Artist in the Character of Design Listening to the Inspiration of Poetry*, where the self-image of the female painter and the female personification of poetry are one and the same.

One innovative type of self-portrait, uniquely female, is that in which the artist shows herself with a female teacher, as in Rolinda Sharples's *The Artist and Her Mother* (Pl. XXVII). Male teachers have also been shown by female painters, as in Sofonisba Anguissola's *Bernardino Campi Painting the Portrait of Sophonisba* (Fig. IV.9), but to our knowledge there exist no male self-portraits with female preceptresses. The self-portrait of the female painter as a teacher also is self-evidently unique, in such representations as Adélaïde Labille-Guiard's *The Artist with Two Female Pupils* (Pl. XXII) or Berthe Morisot teaching her daughter.

Another category of female artists' painted self-portraits reflects uniquely a representation or identification of the painter as a female artist predecessor. This can be seen in Sharples's self-portrait with her mother (Pl. XXVII), who was also her teacher. Here, the artist depicts two generations of artists, the second continuing the profession of the first and emphasizing the spiritual obligation existing between mother and daughter. Likewise Marie-Victoire Lemoine's *Self-Portrait in the Studio of Vigée-Lebrun* (Fig. VI.13) and Miriam Schapiro's *Collaboration Series* with female artists of the past (for example, Pl. XLVII) portrays the bond between artist and teacher. An obvious reason for women artists to represent themselves with female predecessors is the valorization of the feminine, a self-aggrandizement of the female.

A traditional pattern of power relationships is reversed in the type of self-portrait that shows a female artist painting a male model. This can be seen in Judith Leyster's *Self-Portrait*, which shows her painting a male fiddler (Pl. XVII), as well as Elizabeth Butler's *Self-Portrait* of 1866 (collection of Mrs Marie Kingscote Scott), in which she is painting soldiers on a canvas.[2] A contemporary example is found in Paula Rego's *Joseph's Dream* of 1990 (Pl. XLIX), in which the artist shows herself painting a sleeping male model. A self-portrait of a female artist painting a male nude can be found in Sylvia Sleigh's *Philip Golub Reclining* (1971; private collection, New York). Sleigh also offers a new type of self-portrait – a group of female painters – in her *Artists of the SoHo 20 Gallery* (Pl. XLVI).

As a genre, the female nude as self-portrait includes Suzanne Valadon's *Adam and Eve* (Pl. XXXII), where she herself emerges or impersonates the mother of humankind, Paula Modersohn-Becker's and Alice Neel's works illustrated in this book (Pls XXXIV and LII), and Frida Kahlo, Florine Stettheimer, Joan Semmel, Heather Dorrough and Cynthia Mailman. A variant of this type is the pregnant nude self-portrait, as seen in paintings by Katy Schneider (Pepper Gallery, Boston) and Gilian Melling (Nicholas Treadwell Gallery, London). These contemporary self-portraits may have grown from the tradition of pregnant nude portraits established by Paula Modersohn-Becker and Alice Neel and from the art-historical convention of portraying the woman as nurturer.[3]

One creative depiction, by definition unique to female self-portraits, can be seen in the representation of mother and child images, such as those painted by Mary Beale with her two sons (Fig. V.12), Elisabeth Vigée-Lebrun in *Self-Portrait with Her Daughter* (Pl. XX) and self-portraits by Lily Martin Spencer, Suzanne Valadon, Berthe Morisot, Charlie Toorop and Käthe Kollwitz with their children. Evident in these self-portraits is a close identification with the offspring, a female bonding with the child as well as a demonstration of another form of creativity beside art. The theme of motherhood in a self-portrait has also had propaganda value in revealing the painter's double creativity and her identification with 'a woman's proper sphere'.

In the twentieth century, a number of female painters have executed self-portraits identifying themselves with archetypal figures, particularly those of a deity. Examples include Yolanda Lopez's *Self-portrait as the Virgin of Guadalupe* (Pl. XL), in Ana Mendieta's numerous self-portraits as the Great Goddess, and works by Maria Brito, Mary Beth Edelson, Janet Ellen Gilmore and Cynthia Mailman. These associational self-portraits and those including women artists of the past attempt to claim worship as a means of empowering contemporary female painters.

A claim to recognition and respect is the prevailing theme of many female painters' self-portraits. Those representations of self which appear unique to women painters frequently reverse the typical power structure of male dominance by showing women in positions of prestige, privilege and power. Understandably, until the later nineteenth century these self-portraits reflected a milieu of privilege and leisure. Sophonisba Anguissola, for example, presents an image of the painter as a *nobil donna*, surrounded by the paraphernalia of her class. Lavinia Fontana paints herself as a woman of culture and a collector, ensconced among books and art objects. In Adélaïde Labille-Guiard's *The Artist with Two Female Pupils*, the artist is represented in her triple status as painter, teacher and woman of fashion.

This history of female self-portraiture demonstrates how variously numerous painters have treated the genre through the ages: obviously, there have been significant differences in style and technique among the female painters of the past, reflections of each individual artist's time and place as well as of her social and political status. Nevertheless, a female concern with self-portraiture has been constant, from the earliest recorded instances. To the viewing public, it is the self-portraitist who seeks the closest connection between art, medium and artist. Most dramatically, the evolution of the female self-portraitist can be summed up by demonstrating that, in the beginning, the mirror in which the artist reflected herself included primarily the attributes through which she established herself in society. By the end of the twentieth century, her work has come to reflect the realities of her society at large, as she perceives it.

From the beginning of the female artist's expression of her quintessential self, she has concerned herself with physical beauty as well as the beauty of her soul. In earlier eras, this meant representations of grace, beauty, nobility, patronage and social skills, set in an iconography of accomplishment, qualities derived from established conventional and aesthetic values. By the end of the twentieth century, the painter has liberated herself from such constructs and constraints imposed by society. Instead, she now comments on her society from a more gender-aware, psychological plane. If, in the past, her search for artistic truth derived from visual truth, recognition and cultivation, her quest today is for inner truth, irrespective of how honest or painful. Now, female self-portraits express, through manipulation and even mutilation of the body, the transformation brought by a long voyage of recognition into a new world of forthrightness.

In more recent works, particularly those of the twentieth century, in sharing and continuing the quest for self-imaging, female painters have taken images from many sources. The unconscious, dreams, memory, personal history and archetypal figures have all been used to produce new configurations, based less on mirror images of themselves and more on projections of the artist's inner self, as a psychological and spiritual journey on which she creates icons of enablement. Ultimately, however, it is not true to say that female self-portraiture is intrinsically restricted by gender-related dictates. Above and beyond such recently developed perceptions stands the common desire of artists to bond with their art so that they can leave an understandable legacy for posterity. Female painters' self-portraiture creates a new and vital iconography as part of this legacy.

Notes

Introduction

1. Ernest Kris and Otto Kurz, *Legend, Myth, and Magic in the Image of the Artist* (London: Yale University Press, 1979), p. 2, n. 1, a fundamental book on the links between the legend of the artist in all cultures and the human psyche. See also Richard Brilliant, 'On Portraits', *Zeitschrift für Äesthetic und Allgemeine Kunstwissenschaft*, 16 (1971), pp. 11–26.

2. Leon Battista Alberti, *On Painting and On Sculpture: The Latin Texts of 'De Pictura', and 'De Statua'*, ed. and trans. Cecil Grayson (London: Phaidon, 1972), p. 61.

3. W. Shakespeare, *Hamlet*, III, ii, 19–20.

4. It is interesting to note that in ancient China the idea of the mirror was registered on oracle bones and bronzes in the eleventh century BC. See Eugene Yuejin Wang, 'Mirrors, Death, and Rhetoric: Reading Later Han Chinese Bronze Artifacts', *Art Bulletin*, LXXVI (September 1994), pp. 511–34.

5. See Paul Williamson, *et al., Images in Ivory: Precious Objects of the Gothic Age* (Detroit, Mi: Detroit Institute of the Arts, 1997), for ivory mirror illustrations, and Brigitte Buettner, 'Circular Arguments', a paper presented at the International Congress on Medieval Studies, 8 May 1997, where she discusses the splendors of ivory mirrors in the thirteenth century in France.

6. After 1839, with the assistance of photographs of many, the identification is sometimes readily available, but in many cases this source does not exist.

7. Shari L. Thurer, *The Myths of Motherhood: How Culture Prevents the Good Mother* (Boston: Houghton Mifflin, 1994), for a discussion of motherhood from the ancient concept of goddess to the Holy Virgin to the present activist mother. Bonnie S. Anderson and Judith P. Zinsser, *A History of Their Own: Women in Europe from Prehistoric to the Present*, Vol. II (New York: Harper and Row, 1988), for a historical approach on the study of the female in relation to the male. Marina Warner, *Monuments and Maidens: The Allegory of the Female Form* (London: Pan Books, 1987), for a discussion on why the female has been considered appropriate since the earliest days of Western civilization to personify a wide range of ideal concepts in the history of art and culture. Rosemary Agonito, *History of Ideas on Woman* (New York: Putnam's, 1977), for a selection of primary sources of Eastern culture on attitudes toward women. Renate Bridenthal, Claudia Koonz, and Susan Stuard, eds, *Becoming Visible: Women in European History* (Boston: Houghton Mifflin, 1987), an anthology of major writings on the history of women through an analysis of the social construction of gender over time and across cultures. Whitney Chadwick, *Women, Art and Society* (London: Thames and Hudson, 1990), for a general introduction to the history of women's involvement in the visual arts. Georges Duby and Michelle Perrot, eds, *A History of Women: From Ancient Goddesses to Christian Saints* (Cambridge: Harvard University Press, 1992), Clarisse Nicoïdski, *Une Histoire des femmes peintres* (Mesnil-sul-Estrée: J. C. Lattès, 1994), for an excellent global bibliography on women painters; and Fredrika H. Jacobs, *Defining the Renaissance Virtuosa: Women Artists and the Language of Art History and Criticism* (Cambridge: Cambridge University Press, 1997).

8. Kris and Kurz, *Legend, Myth, and Magic in the Image of the Artist*, p. 5.

9. Ibid., p. 39.

10. Ibid., p. 90.

11. Irving Sandler, *Art of the Postmodern Era* (New York: Icon Editions, 1996), p. xxi. See also Linda Nochlin's seminal article, 'Why Have There Been No Great Women Artists?', *Artnews*, LXIX, Jan. 1971, pp. 23–39, 67–9, where she discusses the many barriers put in the way of women trying to be professional artists.

12.. H. W. Janson, *History of Art* (New York: Abrams, 1995).

13. *Horace on the Art of Poetry*, ed. and trans. Edward Henry Blakeney (New York: Freeport, 1970).

14. Norman E. Land, *The Viewer as Poet: The Renaissance Response to Art* (University Park, Pa: Pennsylvania State University Press, 1994), and Leatrice Mendelsohn, *Paragoni: Benedetto Varchi's 'Due Lezzioni' and Cinquecento Art Theory* (Ann Arbor, Mi: UMI Research Press, 1982).

15. Rensselaer W. Lee, *Ut Pictura Poesis: The Humanistic Theory of Painting* (New York: Norton, 1967).

16. Elaine Hedges and Ingrid Wendt, *In Her Own Image* (Westbury, NY: The Feminist Press, 1980), plate 33.

17. Norma Broude and Mary D. Garrard, eds, *The Power of Feminist Art* (New York: Abrams, 1994), p. 175.

18. Sue Graze and Kathy Halbreich, *Elizabeth Murray: Paintings and Drawings* (New York: Abrams, 1987), p. 68.

Chapter I

1. E. F. Ellet, *Women Artists in All Ages and Countries* (London: Richard Bentley, 1859), pp. 1–4; Wendy Slatkin, *Women Artists in History: From Antiquity to the Present* (Upper Saddle River, NJ: Prentice-Hall, 1997), pp. 6–24; Pascal Bonafoux, *Portraits of the Artist: The Self-Portrait in Painting* (New York: Rizzoli, 1985), pp. 7–8; Norbert Schneider, *The Art of the Portrait* (Cologne: Benedikt Taschen, 1994), pp. 6–30; and Joan Kinneir, *The Artist by Himself: Self-Portrait Drawings from Youth to Old Age* (New York: Granada Publishing, 1980), pp. 12–20. For general bibliography on women artists, see Donna G. Bachmann and Sherry Piland, *Women Artists: An Historical, Contemporary and Feminist Bibliography* (London: The Scarecrow Press, 1978); Chris Petteys, *Dictionary of Women Artists: An International Dictionary of Women Artists Born before 1900* (Boston, Ma: G. K. Hall, 1985); and Delia Gaze, ed., *Dictionary of Women Artists*, 2 vols. (London: Fitzroy Dearborn, 1997). For an historical survey on ancient women, see Georges Duby and Michelle Perrot, eds, *A History of Women: From Ancient Goddesses to Christian Saints* (Cambridge, Ma: Harvard University Press, 1992).

2. Julia O'Faolain and Lauro Martines, eds, *Not in God's Image: Women in History from the Greeks to the Victorians* (New York: Harper and Row, 1973), for a historical overview on the documentation on women in Western societies, discussing women's status, social roles, degrees of freedom, and tutelage in writings by or about women of the respective periods. See Mary Kinnear, *Daughters of Time: Women in the Western Tradition* (Ann Arbor, Mi: University of Michigan Press, 1982), pp. 1–7, for an overall social-history view of the roles of women in Western society, such as rulers, reformers, models, artisans, entertainers, writers, teachers, intellectuals, wives, and mothers. See also Sarah B. Pomeroy, *Goddesses, Whores, Wives, and Slaves: Women in Classical Antiquity* (New York: Schocken Books, 1975), for a sociological perspective on the history of women recounted in Greek and Roman literary and biographical texts and the oral tradition.

3. Antiquity refers to the historical period from 3000 BC to AD 400, including ancient Near East, Egyptian, Greek, Etruscan and Roman art.

4. Ludwig Goldscheider, *Fünfhundert Selbstporträts: von der Antike bis zur Gegenwart* (Vienna: Phaidon, 1836), pp. 8–10, illustration on p. 9. For a discussion on the early self-portraits in Egyptian art, a noted painter was Ni-ankh-Ptah, whose *Self-Portrait* of 2650 BC, Third Dynasty, appears in a grave relief of Mereruke's tomb in Saqqara. The painter standing with hand raised points to her painted relief. A more explicit painter's *Self-Portrait* of 1300 BC, from a painted relief now in the Cairo Museum of Art, shows a painter kneeling with his hands raised pointing to his painted hieroglyphs. See also Barbara S. Lesko, 'Women of Egypt and the Ancient Near East', in Renate Bridenthal, Claudia Koonz and Susan Stuard, *Becoming Visible: Women in European History* (Boston: Houghton Mifflin, 1987), pp. 41–77, and further suggested readings on this topic.

5. Lesko, 'Women of Egypt and the Ancient Near East', p. 9, figs. 1 and 2. According to Plutarch, the sculptor Phidias portrayed himself in the marble shield of his statue of Athena in 438 BC for the Acropolis (now in the British Museum in London). See also Marylin Arthur, 'From Medusa to Cleopatra: Women in the Ancient World', in Bridenthal, Koonz and Stuard, *Becoming Visible*, pp. 79–106.

6. Richard Brilliant, *Portraiture* (Cambridge, Ma: Harvard University Press, 1991), G.M.A. Richter, *The Portraits of the Greeks*, abridged and revised edition by R. R. R. Smith (New York: Cornell University Press, 1984); and Jo Ann McNamara, 'Matres Patriae/Matres Ecclesiae: Women of the Roman Empire' in *Becoming Visible*, pp. 107–30.

7. Pliny the Elder, *Natural History*, eds. Antonio Corso, Rossana Mugellesi, and Gianpiero Rosati, translations and commentaries (Turin: Giulio Einaudi, 1988), Book 33, section 52, at present the most erudite translation and study of Pliny's discussion of the visual arts. See also K. Jex-Black and E. Sellers, *The Elder Pliny's Chapters on the History of Art* (Chicago: Argonaut, 1976), pp. 171–3, and Jacob Isager, *Pliny on Art and Society: The Elder Pliny's Chapters on the History of Art* (London: Routledge, 1991), p. 135, for English translations and commentaries.

8. Pliny, eds Corso *et al.*

9. Imhotep, architect and high priest in the court of Zozer, Third Dynasty, Old Kingdom, designed the palace, courts and step-pyramid for his pharaoh. In Book 34, section 12 of his *Natural History*, Pliny the Elder discusses the history of portraiture represented on shields, wax masks, and portrait busts; however, he deplores the Romans for the decline in the art of painting (*ars moriens*) and claims the quality of resemblance (*similitudo*) in portrait paintings to be lost. In Book 35, Pliny cites the vanished painted self-portraits of Apelles, Parrhasius, Hermes, and Phidias. See Jex-Black and Sellers, *The Elder Pliny's Chapters on the History of Art*, Book 35, section 118, Book 35, section 6–7 on Asinius Pollio's library of famous bust portraits; and Isager, *Pliny on Art and Society*, Book 34, pp. 114–17, for a discussion on Pliny's recording of Cicero's friend Atticus, who published a book on portraits, and Marcus Varro, who included 700 portraits of famous men in his book, *Imagines*. See also Richter, *The Portraits of the Greeks*, passim.

10. Elaine Fantham, Helene Peet Foley, Natalie Boyme Kampen, Sarah B. Pomeroy, and H.A. Shapiro, *Women in the Classical World* (Oxford: Oxford University Press, 1994), pp. 36–8, figs. 1.11 and 3.24, and for a complete study of written texts and visual representations of the women of ancient Greece and Rome, from slaves to prostitutes to Athenian housewives and the Roman imperial family. See also Ugo Enrico Paoli, *La donna greca nell'antichità* (Florence: Felice Le Monnier, 1955).

11. Fantham, Peet Foley, Boyme Kampen, Pomeroy, and Shapiro, *Women in the Classical World*, pp. 82–3, fig. 3.2.

12. Nancy Thomson de Grummond, 'The bronze mirrors by the Etruscans: Thy name is woman', *FMR* (October 1985), pp. 101–16, for an illuminating article on the subject.

13. Ibid., figs. 1 and 2 both at the Museo Nazionale of Villa Giulia, Rome.

14. Montserrat Saba Gody, *Los Cinco Sentidos y el Arte* (Madrid: Museo del Prado, 1997), for a significant study on the five senses, discussing the development of this concept from the time of antiquity, with the writings of Aristotle, to the nineteenth century. The traditional iconographical attributes for the sense of sight are the cat, the sun, the eagle and the mirror. See Hendrick Goltzius's engraving *Allegory of Sight and the Art of Painting* of 1617 (Graphische Sammlung Albertina, Vienna).

15. Anne Baring and Jules Cashford, *The Myth of the Goddess: Evolution of an Image* (Baltimore, Md: Arkana, Penguin Books, 1993), pp. 3–46. This study is significant for the mythological perspective on goddess myths or the regeneration principles of nature or women.

16. Gay Robins, *Women in Ancient Egypt* (Cambridge, Ma: Harvard University Press, 1993), pp. 11–20, fig. 28, for a significant study on women in ancient Egypt.

17. Abby Remer, *Pioneering Spirits: The Life and Times of Remarkable Women Artists in Western History* (Worcester, Ma: Davis Publications, 1997), p. 6.

18. Hugo Munsterberg, *A History of Women Artists* (New York: Clarkson N. Potter, 1975), pp. 1–9, and Joelynn Snyder-Ott, *Women and Creativity* (Milbrae, Ca: Les Femmes Publishing, 1978), pp.1–41; also Mirra Bank, *Anonymous Was a Woman* (New York: St Martin's Press, 1979), pp. 9–11.

19. Remer, *Pioneering Spirits: The Life and Times of Remarkable Women Artists in Western History*, pp. 2–3, and Mary R. Lefkowitz and Maureen B. Fant, *Women's Life in Greece and Rome* (Baltimore, Md: Johns Hopkins University Press, 1992, second edition), pp. 208–24, discuss the funerary inscriptions, legal texts, and fragments where women are associated with various occupations, as weavers, farmers, prostitutes, dancers, singers, musicians, actresses, servants, and sellers in markets.

20. Robert E. Bell, *Women in Classical Mythology* (Oxford: Oxford University Press, 1991) and Baring and Cashford, *The Myth of the Goddess: Evolution of an Image*, pp. 299–390, for references on their myths according to Hesiod, *Theogeny*, Homer, *Odyssey*, *Iliad*, and *Homeric Hymn to Aphrodite*, Callimachus, *Hymn to Delos* and *Hymn to Demeter*, and Pindar, *Olympian Odes*. See also Sue Blundell, *Women in Ancient Greece* (Cambridge, MA: Harvard University Press, 1995), pp. 25–46, and Jean Shinoda Bolen, *Goddesses in Every Woman* (New York: Harper and Row, 1971), a psychoanalytical study on the application of these mythical images of women in our present society.

21. Lefkowitz and Fant, *Women's Life in Greece and Rome*, pp. 16–54, on men's opinions about women.

22. Blundell, *Women in Ancient Greece*, pp. 47–57, 74–7 and 113–29.

23. Lefkowitz and Fant, *Women's Life in Greece and Rome*, pp. 55–93, on the legal status of women in Greece.

24. Pomeroy, *Goddesses, Whores, Wives, and Slaves: Women in Classical Antiquity*, pp. 42–56; Blundell, *Women in Ancient Greece*, pp. 82–91; and Lefkowitz and Fant, *Women's Life in Greece and Rome*, pp. 2–15, on women's voices.

25. Lefkowitz and Fant, *Women's Life in Greece and Rome*, pp. 166–7 and 215–26, on recorded fragments concerning the education of women, learning how to read and play an instrument, as well as noting their occupation, playing a cithara, trumpet or harp, acting in plays, and painting.

26. O'Faolain and Martines, eds, *Not in God's Image: Women in History from the Greeks to the Victorians*, pp. 34–71, and J.P.V.D. Balsdon, *Roman Women: Their History and Habits* (New York: Harper and Row, 1983), pp. 13–18.

27. Pomeroy, *Goddesses, Whores, Wives, and Slaves: Women in Classical Antiquity*, pp. 149–89, on women of the upper class, the matron role, and pp. 190–204, on women of the lower class.

28. Lefkowitz and Fant, *Women's Life in Greece and Rome*, pp. 94–128, 156 and 161.

29. Richard Brilliant, *Roman Art: From the Republic to Constantine* (London: Phaidon, 1974), pp. 166–87.

30. J.P.V.D. Balsdon, *Roman Women: Their History and Habits*, pp. 252–76, for a discussion of a Roman woman's daily life. Plautus' *Epidicus*, written in early second century BC, gives a poetic account of the variety of women's fashion. Also Anne Hollander, *Seeing Through Clothes* (Berkeley, Ca: University of California Press, 1993), pp. xi–xvi. For this writer, clothes reveal aspects of culture and personality as well as creative links between a tradition and image making.

31. Plato, *Republic*, Book 5, 542, and Aristotle's *Generation of Animals*, trans. by A.L. Peck (Cambridge, Ma: Harvard University Press, Loeb Classics, 1943), Book I, pp. 101, 103, 109, 113. Aristotle based his incorrect observations on a biological interpretation that the female contribution to fertilization was in the body's *menses* while the male provided the form (life or soul), the generative principle. By contrast, Plato's assumption of woman's inferiority is related to her being an object of desire; as a functional object she is not a perfect form.

32. Galen, *De Uteri Dissectione* (Basel, 1536), Book 1, p. 110.

33. P. R. Ackroyd, ed., *The Cambridge History of the Bible* (Cambridge: Cambridge University Press, 1063–70), Vol. III, pp. 79–93, 213–17, and Ian MacLean, *The Renaissance Notion of Woman: A Study in the Fortunes of Scholasticism and Medical Science in European Intellectual Life* (Cambridge: Cambridge University Press, 1980), pp. 6–8, for an excellent discussion on the ancient position on the inferiority of the woman, starting from biblical times and continuing with Aristotle viewing the female as an incomplete version of the male. See also Rozsika Parker and Griselda Pollock, 'Critical Stereotypes: The Essential Feminine or How Essential is Femininity?', in *Old Mistresses: Women, Art and Ideology* (New York: Pantheon Books, 1981), pp. 1–50, for a discussion on the concept of femininity. See also the copious editing and writings on this aspect by Norma Broude and Mary D. Garrard, eds, *Feminism and Art History: Questioning the Litany* (New York: Harper and Row, 1982) and *The Expanding Discourse: Feminism and Art History* (New York: Harper Icons, 1992).

34. Pliny, *Natural History*, Book 33, section 52.

35. See also Isager, *Pliny on Art and Society: The Elder Pliny's Chapters on the History of Art*, p. 135, and Jex-Black and Sellers, *The Elder Pliny's Chapters on the History of Art*, pp. 171–3.

36. Pliny, *Natural History*, Book 33, section 115, Book 35, section 149, and see Homer's *Iliad*, II, 144, 637. See Silvia Bordini, *Materia e imagine: Fonti sulle tecniche della pittura* (Rome: Leonardo-De Luca, 1991), fig. 4.5, for an illustration of the ancient instruments of painting found in the excavation of Saint Médard-des-Prés recorded by Cross-Henry in 1884 and for a history of painting techniques from ancient times to the present.

37. Pliny, *Natural History*, Book 35, section 122.

38. Ibid., section 147.

39. G. Gualandi 'Aristarete di Calypso' in *Annuario della Scuola Archeologica italiana di Atene*, LIV, 1976, pp. 88–96.

40. Ellet, *Women Artists*, p. 6.

41. Pliny, *Natural History*, Book 35, sections 104, 142 and 145.

42. Ellet, *Women Artists*, p. 6.

43. Pliny, *Natural History*, Book 35, section 147, and A. Pickard-Cambridge, *The Dramatic Festivals* (Oxford: Oxford University Press, 1968), pp. 286–319.

44. Pliny, *Natural History*, Book 35, section 147, and Ellet, *Women Artists*, p. 6.

45. Pliny, *Natural History*, Book 35, section 148.

46. Ellet, *Women Artists*, p. 6, and Anton Hirsch, *Die Frau in der bildenden Kunst* (Stuttgart: Verlag von Ferdinand Enke, 1905), p. 25.

47. Pliny, *Natural History*, Book 35, sections 59 and 147.

48. Mary T. Boatwright, 'The City Gate of Plancia Magna in Perge', in *Roman Art in Context*, p. 200. Plancia Magna, an upper-class woman, was highly respected and received high honors in society for her accomplishment as a patron of the arts.

49. Ellet, *Women Artists*, p. 7, and Hirsch, *Die Frau in der bildenden Kunst*, p. 25. In her book, Ellet mentions that an important sculptress was Lala (Laya or Lerla) (80 BC) of Greek origin and education, who resided in Rome and was celebrated for her busts in ivory. The Romans erected a statue in her honor.

50. Pliny, *Natural History*, Book 35, sections 147–8, and Franciscus Junius, *De Pictura Veterum*, trans. in 1638 as *The Painting of the Ancients*, edited by Keith Aldrich, Philipp Fehl and Raina Fehl, 2 vols. (Berkeley: University of California Press, 1991), Vol. I, entry 688, p. 219.

51. G. Becatti, *Arte e gusto negli scrittori latini* (Florence, 1951), p. 69, discusses at length the works of Iaia.

52. Pliny, *Natural History*, Book 35, sections 147–8, p. 171. See also sections 109, 110 and 121.

53. Pliny, *Natural History*, Book 35, sections 141–53 on Butade or Dibutade. A variation of this story was narrated by Athenagoras, a Christian Athenian of the second century AD, in *Legatio pro christianis*, XVII, 1st edn, pp. 65–7, referring to Kora as the Corinthian maiden, 'from the Corinthian maiden, came the art of modeling small figures'. See also Junius, *The Painting of the Ancients*, Vol. I, entry 457, p. 148.

54. For an eighteenth-century representation of this story, see Joseph Wright of Derby, *The Corinthian Maid*, 1783–4 (National Gallery of Art, Washington, DC), which shows a Corinthian maiden tracing the shadow of her lover's profile on a wall.

55. Pliny, *Natural History*, Book 35, section 151.

56. For further discussion on theory of art in antiquity, see the extensive bibliography in and comments of Isager, *Pliny on Art and Society*, and Pliny, *Natural History*, Book 35.

57. Gunter Schweikhart, 'Boccaccio's *De Claris Mulieribus* und die Selbstdarstellungen von Malerinnen im 16. Jahrhundert,' in *Der Künstler über sich in seinem Werk*, edited by Matthias Winner (Rome: Acta Humaniora, 1992), pp. 113–36. Jex-Blake and Sellers, *The Elder Pliny's Chapters on the History of Art*, pp. 170–71. Pliny the Elder comments on ancient women painters such as Timarete, Eirene, Kalypso, Aristarete, Olympias and Iaia (whom Boccaccio called Marcia). See *Noble and Famous Women*, 1401–2 (MS. Fr. 12420, Bibliothèque Nationale, Paris, and also MS Fr. 598, folio 86 recto, Bibliothèque Nationale, Paris).

58. Pascal Bonafoux, *Portraits of the Artist: The Self-Portrait in Painting* (New York: Rizzoli, 1985), p. 8. See also Lilian Armstrong, 'The Illustrations of Pliny's *Historia Naturalis* in Venetian Manuscripts and Early Printed Books', in *Manuscripts in the Fifty Years after the Invention of Printing*, ed. J. B. Trapp (London: Thames and Hudson, 1983), pp. 97–106.

59. Jex-Black and Sellers, *The Elder Pliny's Chapters on the History of Art*, pp. 170–71. Catherina King in her article 'Looking a Sight: Sixteenth-Century Portraits of Woman Artists', *Zeitschrift für Kunstgeschichte*, 59, 3 (1995), p. 383, erroneously states that 'Vasari reversed the story of Pliny [sic] and had the first modeler as a male lover.' Giorgio Vasari, trained in the classics, correctly interpreted Pliny's comment; see Pliny, 'Painting', in *The History of Art*, ed. Jex-Black and Sellers, p. 85: '*omnes umbra hominis lineis circumducta, itaque primam talem* (painting began with the outlining of a man's shadow).' See also Liana De Girolami Cheney, 'Vasari's Depiction of Pliny's Histories', in *Explorations in Renaissance Culture*, 1989, pp. 23–33.

60. Boccaccio's manuscript of 1401–2 also illustrates Marcia painting the Virgin and Child, a popular theme in Italian art during the fourteenth century. An early Christian legend has it that the Virgin, wanting to have herself portrayed, appeared in the studio of the painter St Luke, where she instructed and assisted him in the portraiture of herself. According to Michael Levey, although there was no muse of painting in the early Renaissance, the prominence of St Luke established the association of a founder figure with a patron saint of painters. Cennini calls St Luke *primo dipintore cristiano* (first Christian painter). See Cennino Cennini, *Il libro dell'arte*, ed. L. Magagnato, 1971, p. 5. Depictions of St Luke at this time show him seated and painting at an easel. The image portrayed in the painting is a *Madonna and Child*, the interior setting is surrounded with painter's paraphernalia – thus the environment alludes to a painter's studio. In *St Luke Painting the Virgin* by an anonymous Italian painter of the fourteenth century, the artist is not as aware or interested in the perspectival quests as Marcia. Even if we consider the fact that the Italian painter has presented the painted image – a *Madonna and Child* – to confront the viewer, still his overall

composition is tilted as in Marcia's design. See Michael Levey, *The Painter Depicted* (London: Thames and Hudson, 1981), pp. 14–16, and Dorothee Klein, *St Lukas als Maler der Maria* (Berlin, 1933).

Chapter II

1. Georges Duby and Michelle Perrot, eds, *A History of Women: From Ancient Goddesses to Christian Saints* (Cambridge, Ma: Harvard University Press, 1992), pp. 337–44, for a historical discussion on the woman's role in Early Christian society.

2. Anne Baring and Jules Cashford, *The Myth of the Goddess: Evolution of an Image*, pp. 447–546, for a discussion on the Old Testament and women, emphasizing the role of Eve as mother of all living things.

3. Tikva Frymer-Kensky, *In the Wave of the Goddesses: Women, Culture and the Biblical Transformation of Pagan Myth* (New York: Fawcett Columbine, 1992), pp. 1–6, for a discussion on the impact of the Judeo-Christian religion on the role of women.

4. A. Freidberg, ed. *Corpus Iuris Canonici*, 2 vols. (Leipzig, 1879–81), Vol. 1, Part II, Chapter 33, q. 12, 13, 17, and 18.

5. See the pioneer study on women's patronage by June Hall McCash, ed., *The Cultural Patronage of Medieval Women* (Athens, Ga: University of Georgia Press, 1996), pp. 1–49, for an excellent overview of the cultural patronage of medieval women.

6. McCash, ed., *The Cultural Patronage of Medieval Women*, pp. 1–50, and Madeline H. Caviness, 'Anchoress, Abbess, and Queen: Donors and Patrons or Intercessors and Matrons', in McCash, ed., *The Cultural Patronage of Medieval Women*, pp. 105–54, for a study on women and patronage in the visual arts; Angela M. Lucas, *Women in the Middle Ages: Religion, Marriage, and Letters* (New York: St. Martin's Press, 1983), for a study on the medieval woman, through wills, medical, theological and philosophical treatises as well as sermons and homilies; and Susan Mosher Stuard, ed., *Women in Medieval Society* (Philadelphia: University of Pennsylvania Press, 1976), for a study of the public roles, rights and responsibilities of women in the Middle Ages in Europe. See also Derek Baker, ed., *Medieval Women* (Oxford: Basil Blackwell, 1978), for a historical and literary study on Merovingian to Early medieval women in France, with the development of allegorical representations of women in the *artes liberales*.

7. Eileen Power, *Medieval Woman*, ed. M. M. Postan (Cambridge: Cambridge University Press, 1975), pp. 9–34, for a discussion on the medieval idea of woman: lady versus slave. See also Stuard, 'The Dominion of Gender: Women's Fortunes in the High Middle Ages', pp. 153–74.

8. Christine de Pizan, *The Book of the City of Ladies*, trans. Earl Jeffrey Richards with a foreword by Marina Warner (New York: Persea Books, 1982).

9. Power, *Medieval Woman*, ed. Postan, pp. 89–99, for a discussion on the functions of nunneries, and Tibbetts Schulenburg, 'The Heroics of Virginity: Brides of Christ and Sacrificial Mutilation', in *Women in the Middle Ages and the Renaissance: Literary and Historical Perspectives*, ed. Mary Beth Rose (Syracuse, NY: Syracuse University Press, 1986), pp. 29–72.

10. Quoted from Christine de Pizan, *Cité des Dames*, in Henry Martin, *Les Miniatures Françaises* (Paris: Fayard, 1906), p. 164; published lecture by Dorothy Miner on *Anastaise and Her Sisters: Women Artists of the Middle Ages* (Baltimore, Md: Walters Art Gallery, 1974), no pagination; and Annemarie Weyl Carr, 'Women as Artists in the Middle Ages,' *Feminist Art Journal*, I (Spring 1976), pp. 5–9 and 26.

11. *Apocalypse of Gerona*, facsimile edition with commentary by J. M. Casanovas, Cesar Dubles and Wilhelm Neuss (Olten-Lausanne-Freiburg: Urs Graf, n.d.); Max Hirmer and Pedro de Palol, *Early Medieval Art in Spain* (New York: Abrams, n.d.); and see Ann Sutherland Harris and Linda Nochlin, *Women Artists, 1550–1950* (New York: Knopf, 1976), p. 17, for support that the illuminations were painted by Ende.

12. Harris and Nochlin, *Women Artists, 1550–1950*, p. 17.

13. Karen Petersen and J. J. Wilson, *Women Artists: Recognition and Reappraisal from the Early Middle Ages to the Twentieth Century* (New York: Harper and Row, 1976), pp. 11–21, a pioneering study of this subject.

14. Thérèse B. McGuire, S.S.J., 'Monastic Artists and Educators of the Middle Ages', *Woman's Art Journal*, 9 (Fall 1988/Winter 1989), pp. 3–9, for an account of monastic culture as well for an excellent bibliography on the subject. See also Jean Leclerc, O.S.B., '*Otium Monasticum* as a Context for Artistic Creativity', in *Monasticism and the Arts*, ed. Timothy Gregory Verdon (Syracuse, NY: Syracuse University Press, 1984), pp. 63–80.

15. Pamela Berger, *The Goddess Obscured: Transformation of the Grain Protectress from Goddess to Saint* (Boston: Beacon Press, 1985), pp. 61–4, explains how a tradition of the miraculous grain legend was linked to the oral history about the life of the eighth-century nun Saint Walpurga, who traveled with her brothers, Willibald and Wynnevbald, from England to convert the Germans.

16. Thérèse B. McGuire, S.S.J., 'Monastic Artists and Educators of the Middle Ages', *Woman's Art Journal*, Vol. 9 (Fall 1988/Winter 1989), p. 4.

17. Ibid., p. 7.

18. Black and white photographs are preserved in the Rheinische Bildarchiv in Cologne and had been published in 'Les miniatures du "Scivias" de Sainte Hildegarde, conservées à la Bibliothèque de Wiesbaden', *Académie des Inscriptions et Belles Lettres: Monuments et mémoires*, vol. 18 (Paris: Leroux, 1911), pp. 49–119, and in Maura Böckler, *Hildegard of Bingen, Wisse die Wege, Scivias* (Berlin: Sankt Augustinus, 1928).

19. Clemencia H. Kessler, 'A Problematic Illumination of the Heidelberg *Lieber Scivias*', *Marsyas*, Vol. 8 (1957–9), pp. 7–21, for a discussion on the attribution of the illumination. Comparing two manuscripts of the *Scivias* suggests that Hildegard supervised the illustrations without painting them.

20. Madeline H. Caviness, 'Anchoress, Abbess, and Queen: Donors and Patrons or Intercessors and Matrons', in McCash, ed., *The Cultural Patronage of Medieval Women*, pp. 105–54, for a study on women in patronage in the visual arts, and p. 115, for a clear discussion on this issue, and Barbara Newman, *Sister of Wisdom: St Hildegard's Theology of the Feminine* (Berkeley, Ca: University of California Press, 1987), pp. 17–18. See also Matthew Fox, *Illuminations of Hildegard of Bingen* (Santa Fe: Bear, 1985), for good color reproduction of a facsimile manuscript in Lucca, Biblioteca Governativa, MS 1942.

21. Petersen and Wilson, *Women Artists: Recognition and Reappraisal from the Early Middle Ages to the Twentieth Century*, p. 15, and Lina Eckenstein, *Woman under Monasticism* (Cambridge, Ma: Harvard University Press, 1896), p. 264 for the quotation. See Adelgundis Fuhrkotter, *The Miniatures from the Book Scivias – Know the Ways – of St Hildegard of Bingen from the Illuminated Rupertsberg Codex*, trans. Father Hockey, O.S.B. (Belgium: Brepol-Turnhout, 1977), for a discussion on the imagery of the illumination, and Fiona Bowie and Oliver Davies, *Hildegard of Bingen, Her Life and Her Work* (Stockholm: Cordia, 1997), for a social and historical study of this Benedictine mystic.

22. McGuire, 'Monastic Artists and Educators of the Middle Ages,' p. 7; G. Cames, *Allégories et symboles dans l'Hortus Deliciarum* (Leyden, 1971); A. Straub and G. Keller, *Herrade de Landsberg, Hortus Deliciarum* (Strasbourg, 1879–99), reprinted, ed. and trans. Aristade D. Caratzas (New Rochelle, NY: Caratzas Brothers, 1977); for an excellent study with complete illustrations see Rosalie Green, Michael Evans, C. Bischoff and M. Curschmann, eds, *Herrad of Landesberg's Hortus Deliciarum* (London: Warburg Institute, 1979).

23. Charles Gérard, *Les Artistes de l'Alsace pendant le Moyen Age* (Nancy: Librairie des Arts et Métiers-Editions, 1977), p. 42.

24. Franz Saxl, 'Illustrated Medieval Encyclopedias II: The Christian Transformation,' in *Lectures* (London: Warburg Institute, 1957), p. 245.

25. McGuire, 'Monastic Artists and Educators of the Middle Ages', p. 8.

26. Eckenstein, *Woman under Monasticism*, pp. 254–5, for the quotation.

27. Hans Biedermann, *Dictionary of Symbolism: Cultural Icons and the Meanings behind Them*, trans. James Hulbert (Baltimore: Penguin Books, 1995), pp. 4–35.

28. Annemarie Weyl Carr, 'Women Artists in the Middle Ages', *The Feminist Art Journal*, Vol. V (1976), pp. 5–9. For an extensive bibliography on Guda, see Pietro d'Ancona and Erardo Aeschlimann, *Dictionnaire des miniaturistes* (Milan: Electa, 1940), p. 101 and pl. LI.

29. Power, *Medieval Woman*, ed. Postan, pp. 75–88, for a discussion of the cultivation of women and the treatises on comportment in the Middle Ages.

30. Millard Meiss, *French Painting in the Time of Jean de Berry: The Late 14th Century and the Patronage of the Duke* (New York: Abrams, 1976), p. 168. Regarding her writing, see Gland K. McLeod, ed., *The Redemption of Christine de Pizan from the Fifteenth through the Nineteenth Centuries* (London: Edwin Mellen Press, 1991).

31. Charity Cannon Willard, *Christine de Pizan: Her Life and Works* (New York: Persea Books, 1984), for a biography and her literary works.

32. Christine de Pizan, *The Book of the City of Ladies*, trans. Earl Jeffrey Richards with a foreword by Marina Warner (New York: Persea Books, 1982), pp. 83–4.

33. Christine de Pizan, *The Treasure of the City of Ladies or The Book of the Three Virtues*, trans. Sarah

Lawson (Baltimore: Penguin Books, 1985, first English translation) and Christine de Pizan, *A Medieval Woman's Mirror of Honor: The Treasury of the City of Ladies*, trans. Charity Cannon Willard, ed. Madeleine Pelner Cosman (New York: Persea Books, 1989, with illustrations).

34. Meiss, *French Painting in the Time of Jean de Berry: The Limbourgs and their Contemporaries*, Vol. I, pp. 3, 13–14 (New York edition). See also Miner on *Anastaise and Her Sisters: Women Artists of the Middle Ages*, no pagination.

35. Meiss, *French Painting in the Time of Jean de Berry*, Vol. I, p. 3, and Miner on *Anastaise and Her Sisters*.

Chapter III

1. Bruce Cole, *The Renaissance Artist at Work* (New York: Harper and Row, 1983), pp. 57–136, for a thorough discussion of the materials used by Renaissance painters.

2. Ian MacLean, *The Renaissance Notion of Woman: A Study in the Fortunes of Scholasticism and Medical Science in European Intellectual Life* (Cambridge: Cambridge University Press, 1980), pp. 92–6; P. R. Ackroyd, ed., *The Cambridge History of the Bible* (Cambridge: Cambridge University Press, 1963–70), Vol. III, pp. 79–93, 213–17.

3. For a discussion of this style and period see Frederick Hartt, *The History of the Italian Renaissance* (Englewood Cliffs, NJ: Prentice-Hall, 1995), and Sydney Freedberg, *High Renaissance in Italy* (New York: Harper Icons, 1985).

4. For a discussion of this style and period, see Sydney Freedberg, *Paintings in Italy: 1500–1600* (Baltimore: Penguin Books, 1994).

5. Eugenio Garin, ed., *Renaissance Characters*, trans. Lydia G. Cochrane (Chicago: University Press of Chicago, 1991), passim.

6. John Pope-Hennessy, *The Portrait in the Renaissance* (New York: Pantheon Books, 1966), p. 4; Stephen K. Scher, ed., *The Currency of Fame: Portrait Medals of the Renaissance* (New York: Abrams, 1994), pp. 15–21, and André Chastel, 'The Artist,' in Eugenio Garin, ed., *Renaissance Characters*, pp. 180–207.

7. Jean Alazard, *Le Portrait florentin de Botticelli à Bronzino* (Paris, 1951), p. 262, and Alistair Smith, *Renaissance Portraits* (London: Phaidon, 1973), p. 31, for discussions of the concept of visual realism not symbolism in High Renaissance portraits.

8. Richard Brilliant, 'Portraits', *Zeitschrift für Äesthetik und Allgemeine Kunstwissenschaft*, 16 (1971), pp. 11–26, and Richard Brilliant, *Portraiture* (London, 1991).

9. Chastel, 'The Artist', pp. 180–92, for a discussion on the term 'artist' in the Renaissance.

10. Andrew Martindale, *The Rise of the Artist in the Middle Ages and Early Renaissance* (New York: McGraw-Hill, 1972), pp. 97–116.

11. Judith Brown, 'Woman's Place Was in the Home: Women's Work in Renaissance Tuscany', in Margaret W. Ferguson et al., eds., *Rewriting the Renaissance: The Discourses of Sexual Difference in Early Modern Europe* (Chicago: University of Chicago Press, 1986), p. 209.

12. Joan Kelly-Gadol, 'Did Women Have a Renaissance?', in Renate Bridenthal and Claudia Koonz, eds., *Becoming Visible: Women in European History* (Boston: Houghton Mifflin, 1972), pp. 160–61.

13. Leon Battista Alberti, *The Family in Renaissance Florence*, trans. and introd by Renée N. Waltkins (Columbus, SC: University of South Carolina Press, 1969), pp. 208–13, and Leon Battista Alberti, *On Painting and On Sculpture: The Latin Texts of 'De Pictura' and 'De Statua'*, ed. and trans. Cecil Grayson (London: Phaidon, 1972), p. 61.

14. Margaret L. King, 'Book-Lined Cells: Women and Humanism in the Early Italian Renaissance', in Patricia Labalme, ed., *Beyond Their Sex: Learned Women of the European Past* (New York: New York University Press, 1984), no pagination, and Margaret L. King and Albert Rabil, Jr, eds, *Her Immaculate Hand: Selected Works by and about the Women Humanists of Quattrocento Italy* (Binghamton, NY: Medieval and Renaissance Texts & Studies, 1992). See also Rose, ed., *Women in the Middle Ages and the Renaissance: Literary and Historical Perspectives*, passim.

15. Ruth Kelso, *Doctrine for the Lady of the Renaissance* (Urbana, IL: University of Illinois Press, 1956), p. 77; see also p. 59.

16. Patricia Simons, 'Women in Frames: The Gaze, the Eye, the Profile in Renaissance Portraiture', in Norma Broude and Mary D. Garrard, eds, *The Expanding Discourse: Feminism and Art History* (New York: Harper and Row, 1992), pp. 39–45.

17. Boccaccio, *Noble and Famous Women*, 1401–2. See Chapter I, 'Self-portraits in antiquity', in the

present text.

18. Irene Graziani, 'La leggenda dell'artista donna', in Vera Fortunati, *La pittura in Emilia e in Romagna: Il Cinquecento* (Milan: Nuova Alfa Editoriale, 1994), p. 129, and her citations of F. Zanasi, 'Donne alla richerca della fama', in G. Roversi, *Donne celebri nell'Emilia Romagna e del Montefeltro* (Bologna: Alfa Editoriale, 1993), pp. 45–106.

19. Graziani, 'La leggenda dell'artista donna', p. 129–35, for a clear and well-documented study of the cultural milieu of Bologna and the importance of Saint Cecilia, the patron saint of musicians, as a source of inspiration for women painters depicting themselves as musicians.

20. Harris A.S., and Nochlin, L., *Women Artists: 1550–1950* (New York: Knopf, 1976), p. 20, n. 38.

21. Ellet, *Women Artists in All Ages and Countries* (London: Richard Bentley, 1859), p. 13.

22. Petteys, *Dictionary of Women Artists*, passim, for entries and bibliography of each of these painters, and Germaine Greer, *The Obstacle Race: The Fortunes of Women Painters and Their Work* (New York: Farrar Straus Giroux, 1979), chapter on cloisters, pp. 151–68, and its bibliography, pp. 345–6.

23. Karen Petersen and J. J. Wilson, *Women Artists: Recognition and Reappraisal From the Early Middle Ages to the Twentieth Century* (New York: Harper and Row, 1976), pp. 11–12.

24. Graziani, 'La leggenda dell'artista donna', p. 129, for a study on this artist and bibliography. See Walter Shaw Sparrow, ed., *Women Painters of the World: From the Time of Caterina Vigri 1413–1463 to Rosa Bonheur and the Present Day* (New York: Hacker Art Books, 1976, reprinted from 1st edition, London, 1905).

25. Clara Erskine Clement, *Women in the Fine Arts* (Boston: Houghton Mifflin, 1904), p. 351 (repr. New York: Hacker Art Books, 1974).

26. Laura M. Raggs, *The Women Artists of Bologna* (London: Methuen, 1907), p. 137; Ellet, *Women Artists in All Ages and Countries*, p. 16.

27. C. Foletti, 'Catharina Bononienis, S. "Le sette armi spirituali"', *Medievo e Umanismo*, 56, p. 1985; C. Leonardi, 'Caterina Vigri e l'obedienza del diavolo', *Medievo e Umanismo*, 72, p. 1988, and G. Pozzi and C. Leonardi, eds, *Scrittrice mistiche italiane* (Genoa: Grafis, 1988), pp. 261–86.

28. Jerildene Wood, 'Breaking the Silence: The Poor Clares and the Visual Arts in Fifteenth-Century Italy', pp. 262–86, in particular pp. 272–6.

29. Serena Martinelli Spanò, 'Per uno studio su Caterina di Bologna', *Studi Medievali*, 2 (1971), pp. 713–59, and 'La Biblioteca del "Corpus Domini" bolognese: l'inconsueto spaccato di una cultura monastica femminile', *La Bibliofilia*, 88 (1986), pp. 1–23.

30. Elsa Fine, *Women and Art* (London: Allanheld & Schram, 1978), pp. 6–9, and Wood, 'Breaking the Silence', pp. 262–86, in particular pp. 272–7.

31. Wood, ibid.

32. Her musical instrument (similar to a viola) is conserved in the convent of Corpus Domini, Bologna.

33. P. Lucius M. Nuñez, O. F. M., 'Descriptio Breviarii Manuscripti: S. Catharinae Bononiensis O. S. CL.', *Codiographia*, pp. 732–47, fig. 2, *Eiusdem Breviarii* MS. fol. 465 recto in the convent of Corpus Domini of Bologna.

34. Ellet, *Women Artists in All Ages and Countries*, p. 15. For a different point of view see Harris's evaluation of her style as 'naive, provincial and archaic', Harris and Nochlin, *Women Artists*, p. 20.

35. Clement, *Women in the Fine Arts*, p. 350.

36. Nuñez, 'Descriptio Breviarii Manuscripti S. Catharinae Bononiensis O.S. CL.,' pp. 732–47.

37. Raggs, *The Women Artists of Bologna*, pp. 137–51.

38. Ellet, *Women Artists in All Ages and Countries*, pp. 12–15; Greer, *Obstacle Race*, pp. 162–7; and Chris Petteys, *Dictionary of Women Artists: An International Dictionary of Women Artists Born before 1900*, and Gaze, ed., *Dictionary of Women Artists*, for respective entries for each name.

39. Tufts, *Our Hidden Heritage* (New York: Paddington Press, 1974), p.43. See Harris and Nochlin, *Women Artists*, pp. 102–4, for an evaluation of the art of this artist, a bibliography and understanding of English miniaturists; Roy Strong, *Artists of the Tudor Court: The Portrait Miniature Rediscovered 1520–1620* (London: Victoria and Albert Museum Publications, 1983), pp. 52–7, for a series of portrait miniatures attributed to her, including portraits of Elizabeth I and Mary I.

40. Clement, *Women in the Fine Arts*, p. 172; Petersen and Wilson, *Women Artists*, p. 34; and Petteys, *Dictionary of Women Artists*, p. 389.

41. Strong, *Artists of the Tudor Court*, p. 9 and pp. 10–27, for a clear analysis of limning art.

42. Simone Bergmans, 'The Miniatures of Levina Teerlinc', *Burlington Magazine*, XIV (1934), pp. 232–6. Harris and Nochlin, *Women Artists*, p. 102 and n. 5.

43. Bergmans, 'The Miniatures of Levina Teerlinc', pp. 232–6; for a study of her painted miniatures, Tufts, *Our Hidden Heritage*, pp. 43–9; and Harris and Nochlin, *Women Artists*, pp. 102–4.

44. Bergmans, 'The Miniatures of Levina Teerlinc', pp. 232–6.

45. E. Sambo, 'Giulio Clovio', in Giulio Bora, *I Campi* (Milan: Electa, 1985), p. 175.

46. Harris and Nochlin, *Women Artists*, p. 102, n. 10.

47. Joanna Wood-Marsden, 'Ritratto al Naturale: Questions of Realism and Idealism in Early Renaissance Portraits', *Art Journal* (Fall 1987), pp. 209–16.

48. Norbert Schneider, *The Art of the Portrait* (Cologne: Benedikt Taschen, 1994), pp. 42–3; and Günther Heinz and Karl Schutz, *Porträtgalerie zur Geschichte Österreichs von 1400 bis 1800* (Vienna: Kunsthistorisches Museum, 1982), passim.

49. Irving Lavin, 'On the Sources and Meaning of the Renaissance Portrait Bust', *Art Quarterly*, 33 (1970), pp. 207–26.

50. Petteys, *Dictionary of Women Artists*, p. 389.

51. Clements, *Women in the Fine Arts*, p. 172, and Petersen and Wilson, *Women Artists*, p. 34.

Chapter IV

1. E. F. Ellet, *Women Artists in All Ages and Countries* (London: Richard Bentley, 1859), p. 19, referring to Guhl's comment on the sixteenth century.

2. Mary Hollingsworth, *Patronage in Sixteenth-Century Italy* (London: John Murray, 1996), pp. 1-4; Paola Tinagli, *Women in Italian Renaissance Art: Gender Representation and Identity* (Manchester: Manchester University Press, 1997), pp. 112–14.

3. Liana De Girolami Cheney, ed., *Readings in Italian Mannerism* (London: Peter Lang Press, 1997), for a discussion on Italian art theory, patronage and artistic endeavors in the sixteenth century.

4. André Chastel, 'The Artist', in Eugenio Garin, ed., *Renaissance Characters*, trans. Lydia G. Cochrane (Chicago: University Press of Chicago, 1991), pp. 180–207, for a discussion on the meaning of 'artifex' and artist.

5. Baldassare Castiglione, *The Book of the Courtier*, trans. Charles S. Singleton (New York: Anchor Books, 1959), pp. 206–9, 211, and 214–15; and Pamela Joseph Benson, 'Il Libro del Cortegiano', in *The Invention of the Renaissance Woman: The Challenge of Female Independence in the Literature and Thought of Italy and England* (University Park, Pa: Pennsylvania State University Press, 1992), p. 90.

6. Christopher Hare, *The Most Illustrious Ladies of the Italian Renaissance* (Williamstown, Ma: Corner House Publishers, 1972).

7. Blamires, Pratt and Marx, eds, *Woman Defamed and Woman Defended: An Anthology of Medieval Texts*, for history on this topic, and Pamela Joseph Benson, 'From Paradise to Paradox: The First Italian Defense of Women', in *The Invention of the Renaissance Woman: The Challenge of Female Independence in the Literature and Thought of Italy and England* (University Park, Pa: Pennsylvania State University Press, 1992), pp. 33–64.

8. Boccaccio, *Concerning Famous Women*, trans. G. A. Guarino (London: Allen & Unwin, 1964); Brigitte Buettner, *Boccaccio, 'Des cleres et nobles femmes': System of Signification in an Illuminated Manuscript* (Seattle: University of Washington Press, 1996), pp. 4–7; Benson, 'Boccaccio's *De Mulieribus Claris*: An Ambiguous Beginning', in *The Invention of the Renaissance Woman: The Challenge of Female Independence in the Literature and Thought of Italy and England*, pp. 9–33; and Blamires, Pratt and Marx, eds, *Woman Defamed and Woman Defended: An Anthology of Medieval Texts*, pp. 166–77.

9. Liana De Girolami Cheney, 'Vasari's Interpretation of Female Beauty', in *Renaissance Concepts of Beauty*, ed. Francis Ames-Lewis and Mary Rogers (London: Scolar Press, 1997), pp. 180–90.

10. Lorenzetti, *La bellezza e l'amore nei trattari del cinquecento*, passim, and Nelson (Florence: Sansoni), *The Renaissance Theory of Love*, passim.

11. Rocchi, 'Per una nuova cronologia evaluazione del *Libro di natura de amore* di Mario Equicola', pp. 566–85, and Barocchi, 'Bellezza e grazia', pp. 1613–27.

12. Ebreo, *Dialoghi d'amore* (Rome, 1535), pp. 226–8, and Ebreo, *The Philosophy of Love (Dialoghi d'amore)*,

trans. F. Friedberg-Seely (London: J. H. Barnes, 1937), pp. 298–300 and 327–30.

13. Cited in Barocchi, 'Bellezza e grazia', p. 1672.

14. Agostino Nifo in *Del bello: il bello è nella natura* (Lugduni, 1549), XV–XX, pp. 15–20.

15. Castiglione, *Il Cortegiano*, Chapters XXVI and XXVIII of Book I in Barocchi, 'Bellezza e grazia',
     pp. 1609–1708; Luigi Baldacci, '*Gli Asolani* del Bembo e Venere celeste', *Il petrarchismo italiano nel
     '500* (Milan-Naples: Riccardi, 1957), pp. 107–10; Zorzi Pugliese, 'Variation on Ficino's *De Amore*:
     The Hymns to Love by Benivieni and Castiglione', pp. 113–21; and Rogers, 'The Decorum of
     Women's Beauty', pp. 47–87.

16. Wiener, *Dictionary of the History of Ideas*, Vol. III (New York: Charles Scribner's, 1968–73), p. 508.

17. For the theory of female beauty in Italian Renaissance art, see Cropper, 'On Beautiful Women:
     Parmigianino, Petrarchismo, and the Vernacular Style', pp. 374–94; Cropper, 'The Beauty of
     Woman: Problems in the Rhetoric of Renaissance Portraiture', *Art Bulletin* 58 (1976), pp. 175–90;
     Rogers, 'The Decorum of Women's Beauty: Trissino, Firenzuola, Luigini and the Representation of
     Women in Sixteenth-Century Painting', *Renaissance Studies* 2 (1988), pp. 47–87; and Firenzuola, *On
     the Beauty of Women*, 1548, passim.

18. Patricia Simons, 'Portaiture, Portrayal, and Idealization: Ambiguous Individualism in
     Representations of Renaissance Women', in *Language and Images of Renaissance Italy*, ed. Alison
     Brown (Oxford: Clarendon Press, 1995), pp. 263–313, for a provocative discussion on the
     visualization of female imagery.

19. Quoted in Jean Alazard, *Le Portrait florentin de Botticelli à Bronzino* (Paris, 1951), p. 262.

20. Craig H. Smyth, 'The Earliest Works of Bronzino', *Art Bulletin*, 31 (1949), pp. 184–210. Another
     commentator on Mannerist portraiture, Henri de Montherlant, states in his *Notebooks*: 'I love those
     Renaissance portraits in which the principal person points with one hand to his breast as if to
     indicate that he and none other, is important.' A quotation from Rémy G. Saisselin, *Style, Truth and
     the Portrait* (Cleveland, Oh: Cleveland Museum of Art, 1963), p. 24.

21. He was hired by Queen Isabella of Spain to teach her four daughters.

22. Corrado Gizzi, *Vittoria Colonna* (Turin: Electa, 1997), passim; Margaret F. Rosenthal, *The Honest
     Courtesan: Veronica Franco, Citizen and Writer in Sixteenth-Century Venice* (Chicago, Il: Chicago
     University Press, 1992).

23. Recently several books have appeared on sixteenth-century female painters: Vera Fortunati, *Lavinia
     Fontana, 1552–1614* (Milan: Electa, 1994 and 1998); Mina Gregori, ed., *Sofonisba Anguissola e le sue
     sorelle* (Milan: Leonardo Arte, 1994); Valeria Moretti, *Le più belle del reale: Pittrici in Autoritratto del
     Cinquecento all Ottocento* (Rome: Nuova Editrice Spada, 1993); Ilya Sandra Perlingieri, *Sofonisba
     Anguissola* (New York: Rizzoli, 1992); M. T. Cantaro, *Lavinia Fontana bolognese* (Milan: J. Sapi, 1989);
     Flavio Caroli, *Sofonisba Anguissola e le sue sorelle* (Milan: Arnoldo Mondadori, 1987); Nancy G.
     Heller, *Women Artists: An Illustrated History* (New York: Abbeville Press, 1987); Charity C. Willard,
     Christine de Pizan: Her Life and Works (New York: Persea Books, 1984); Anna Banti, *Quando anche le
     donne si misero a dipingere* (Milan: La Tartaruga Edizioni, 1982); and the pioneer work of M.
     Masciotta, *Autoritratti* (Milan: Electa, 1955).

24. John Pope-Hennessy, 'Humanism and the Portrait', in *The Portrait in the Renaissance* (New York:
     Pantheon Books, 1966), pp. 64–100; Jean Alazard, *The Florentine Portrait* (New York: Schocken
     Books, 1968), pp. 221–7; and Rab Hatfield, 'Five Early Renaissance Portraits', *Art Bulletin*
     (September 1965), pp. 316–33.

25. L. M. Sleptzoff, 'Men or Supermen', in *The Italian Portrait in the Fifteenth Century* (Jerusalem:
     Hebrew University, 1978), pp. 126–39; Patricia Simons, 'Women in Frames: The Gaze, the Eye, the
     Profile in Renaissance Portraiture,' *History Workshop Journal* (1988), pp. 4–29, with an excellent
     bibliography; and Ferguson, Quilligan, and Vickers, eds, *Rewriting the Renaissance, The Discourses of
     Sexual Difference in Early Modern Europe*, passim, and Catherina King, 'Looking a Sight: Sixteenth-
     Century Portraits of Woman Artists', *Zeitschrift für Kunstgeschichte*, 59, 3 (1995), pp. 381–407.

26. Pope-Hennessy, 'The Cult of Personality,' in *The Portrait in the Renaissance*, pp. 3–63, and Gottfried
     Boehm, *Bildnis und Individuum (Über den Ursprung der Porträtmalerei in der italienischen Renaissance*
     (Munich: Prestel-Verlag, 1985).

27. See n. 17, above.

28. Ellet, *Women Artists*, p. 7, and Katlijne van der Stighhelen, '"Een vrow en haar spiegel: van
     zelportret naar zelfbeeld"', in *Dietsche Warande & Bellfort* (Leuven: Luc Verlag, 1995), pp. 10–24.

29. Donna G. Bachmann and Sherry Piland, *Women Artists: An Historical, Contemporary and Feminist
     Bibliography* (London: The Scarecrow Press, 1978), pp. 61–2. See Simone Bergmans, 'Le problème
     Jan van Hemessen monogrammiste de Brunswich', *Revue Belge d'Archéologie et d'Histoire de l'Art*, 23
     (1955), pp. 133–57, for a discussion on the collaboration of father and daughter.

30. Harris and Nochlin, *Women Artists*, p. 105.

31. Carel van Mander, *Schilderboeck (1604): Dutch and Flemish Painters*, trans. Constant van de Wall (New York: Arno Press, 1969), pp. xxxi–xxxii; Anthony Blunt, *Artistic Theory in Italy 1450–1600* (Oxford: Oxford University Press, 1940), passim; Robert Klein and Henri Zerner, *Italian Art 1500–1600* (Englewood Cliffs, NJ: Prentice-Hall, 1969), pp. 4–35; Leatrice Mendelsohn, *Paragoni: Benedetto Varchi's Due Lezzioni and Cinquecento Art Theory* (Ann Arbor, Mi: UMI Research Press, 1982), passim, an excellent bibliography on this topic.

32. Susan Sturrock, ed., *Musical Instruments of the World* (New York: Unicef Fund, 1976), pp. 164–5 and 228–9, for a discussion on the history of chordophones.

33. Some art historians think that this painting is a portrait of her sister and a pendant to the painting of 1546. However, it is difficult to understand why the attire is the same in both portraits as well as the physiognomy. See Eleanor Tufts, *Our Hidden Heritage* (New York: Paddington Press, 1974), p. 51, and Harris and Nochlin, *Women Artists*, p. 105, and Valerio Gauzzoni, 'Entry 66', in Gregori, ed., *Sofonisba Anguissola e le sue sorelle*, p. 330.

34. See David R. Smith, *Mask of Wedlock: Seventeenth-Century Dutch Marriage Portraiture* (Ann Arbor, Mi: UMI Research Press, 1978), and Mario Praz, *Conversation Pieces* (London: Methuen, 1960), passim.

35. Pascal Bonafoux, *Portraits of the Artist: The Self-Portrait in Painting* (New York: Rizzoli, 1985), pp. 34–5; Norbert Schneider, *The Art of The Portrait* (Cologne: Benedikt Taschen, 1994), pp. 104–7; Joan Kinneir and David Piper, eds, *The Artist by Himself: Self-Portraits and Drawings from Youth to Old Age* (London: Granada Publishing, 1980), p. 23; and Ludwig Goldscheider, *Fünfhundert Selbsporträts* (Vienna: Phaidon, 1936), figs. 72 and 73, for Lucas Cranach's paintings.

36. Baldassare Castiglione, *The Book of the Courtier*, trans. C. S. Singleton. New York: Anchor Books, 1959.

37. Giulio Bora, *I Campi* (Milan: Electa, 1985).

38. Numerous articles by Maria Kusche have assisted in the understanding of Sofonisba Anguissola's sojourn in Spain in the court of King Philip II, culminating in the essay 'Sofonisba Anguissola al servizio dei re di Spagna', in Mina Gregori, ed., *Sofonisba Anguissola e le sue sorelle* (Milan: Leonardo Arte, 1994), pp. 117–85.

39. Perlingieri, *Sofonisba Anguissola*, pp. 151–2, for a discussion on the documentation of her dowry and the published document of 8 May 1572 in Camara de Castilla, Lib. 252, fol. 107, in the Archivo Historico Nacional of Madrid.

40. See Smith, *Mask of Wedlock*, passim, and Rose Wishneusky, 'Studien zum "Portrait historié" in den Niederlanden' (doctoral dissertation, University of Munich, 1967).

41. Bora, *I Campi*, pp. 53–8.

42. Only selected self-portraits by Sofonisba Anguissola will be discussed at this time. The *Self-Portrait* at the Poldi Pezzoli Museum in Milan, also in an oval frame, can be dated shortly after another self-portrait, in the Museum of Fine Arts, Boston, between 1552 and 1554. Stylistic and compositional elements support this dating. The other *Self-Portrait*, signed and inscribed 1554 (Brera Pinacoteca, Milan), shows a frontal view portrait of the artist as a genteel *donna*.

43. *Self-Portrait* of 1552 (Uffizi, Florence) and *Self-Portrait at the Easel* of 1552–4, W. Stirling Collection in Keir, UK.

44. Liana De Girolami Cheney, 'Self-Portraits of Renaissance Painters', lecture presented at the Renaissance Society of America conference in Tempe, Arizona, 1987, where I decipher the symbolism of the inscription.

45. An earlier date should be considered for the Boston portrait since it is stylistically similar to the Uffizi *Self-Portrait* (Pl. VIII). The other Uffizi *Self-Portrait* (Inv. 1246) in a tondo frame is attributed to her, but looks more like one of her sisters, perhaps Minerva, because of her spirited expression and elaborate attire, unlike the usually melancholic and somber dressing of Sofonisba. Compare this painting with Sofonisba's *Portrait of Minerva* (Milwaukee Art Museum, Mi).

46. Lasinio the Younger engraved the artist's self-portraits in the Uffizi collection. See *Reale Galleri di Firenze Illustrata* (Florence: Giuseppe Molini, 1817), Vol. III, pp. 197-200, fig. 43.

47. A similar drawing at Windsor Castle attributed to her by A. E. Popham and J. Wilde has been rejected by recent scholarship. See Bora, 'Disegni', *I Campi*, p. 303, and Ilya Sandra Perlingieri, 'Sofonisba Anguissola's Early Sketches', *Woman's Art Journal* (Fall 1988), pp. 10–14.

48. Sacchi, 'Entry 2', in Gregori, ed., *Sofonisba Anguissola e le sue sorelle*, p. 188, for archival documentation

49. Peter Burke, 'Artists and Writers', in *The Italian Renaissance: Culture and Society in Italy* (New York: Scribner, 1972), pp. 50–70.

50. In the Federico Zeri Collection (Mentana, Rome), Anguissola's *Self-Portrait* contains an inscription above the head of the artist: 'Musa Appellem A Suavi Sophonisba Puelle/ Coloribus Fungens/ Carminibusque Meis'. The other version at the William Stirling Collection, dated 1554–5, contains a signature on the easel: '*Sofonisfa Angusciola virgo cremonensi se ipsam pinxit.*' See Caroli, pp. 106–7, and subsequent commentaries, Sacchi, Entries 7 and 8 in Gregori, ed., *Sofonisba Anguissola e le sue sorelle*, pp. 198–201, for a discussion on the differences in representation in these versions.

51. See Ann Sutherland Harris and Linda Nochlin, *Women Artists: 1550–1950* (New York: Alfred A. Knopf, 1976), p. 105, and Varelio Gauzzoni, entry 66, in Gregori, ed., *Sofonisba Anguissola e le sue sorelle* (Milan: Electa, 1994), p. 330.

52. Michael Levey, *The Painter Depicted* (London: Thames and Hudson, 1981), pp. 14–16, fig. 7; Dorothee Klein, *St Lukas als Maler der Maria* (Berlin, 1933), for a thorough study on the iconography of this theme; Paul Binsky, *Painters* (London: British Museum Press, 1991), fig. 7, for Marcia; and Sally Fox, ed., *The Medieval Woman* (Boston: Little, Brown, 1985), for Timarete, calendar page, November.

53. Gregori, ed., *Sofonisba Anguissola e le sue sorelle*, pp. 27, 202, and 212; Caroli, *Sofonisba Anguissola e le sue sorelle*, pp. 100–101, 130 and 132; and Sylvia Feino-Pagden, *Sofonisba Anguissola, a Renaissance Woman* (Washington, DC: National Museum of Women in the Arts, 1995), plate 5.

54. Varelio Gauzzoni, 'Entry 66', in Gregori, ed., *Sofonisba Anguissola e le sue sorelle*, p. 330, for a questionable argument on the influence of Catherina van Hemessen's painting on Sofonisba Anguissola.

55. Sacchi, 'Entry 16', in Gregori, ed., *Sofonisba Anguissola e le sue sorelle*, p. 216, for the documentation.

56. For example, Adélaïde Labille-Guiard's *Self-Portrait with Two Pupils: Mlle Marie Gabrielle Capet and Mlle de Rosemond* of 1785 (Metropolitan Museum of Art, New York).

57. Giorgio Vasari, *Le vite dei più eccellenti pittori, scultori ed architetti*, ed. Gaetano Milanesi (Florence: G. C. Sansoni, 1906), referred to in this text as Vasari-Milanesi, Vol. IV, pp. 335–9; Graziani, Irene 'La leggenda dell'artista donna' in Vera Fortunata, *La pittura in Emilio e in Romagna: Il Cinquecento* (Milan: Nuova Alfa Editoriale, 1994), pp. 131–3; and Fredricka Jacobs, 'The Construction of a Life: Madonna Properzia de' Rossi "Scultrice" Bolognese', *Word & Image*, 9 (1993), pp. 122–32.

58. Vasari-Milanesi, Vol. V, p. 81. See Carlo Ridolfi, *Delle Meraviglie dell'Arte* (Venice, 1548), Vol. II, p. 11, praising women such as Lavinia Fontana, Chiara Varotari, and Giovanna Garzoni.

59. Vasari-Milanesi, Vol. VI, pp. 501, and 500, 502.

60. Ibid., p. 501.

61. Vasari is alluding to Alberti's concept of nature. See Leon Battista Alberti, *On Painting*, trans. John Spencer (New Haven, Ct: Yale University Press, 1966), p. 67.

62. Vasari-Milanesi, Vol. II, pp. 95–6, and Liana De Girolami Cheney, *The Paintings of the Casa Vasari* (New York: Garland Publishing, 1985), pp. 121–2.

63. Ibid.

64. Vasari-Milanesi, Vol. V, p. 81, and Vol. VI, p. 501, Licia Ragghianti Collobi, *Libro dei Disegni del Vasari* (Milan: Vallecchi, 1974), pp. 116 and 196; Perlinguieri, 'Sofonisba Anguissola's Early Sketches', pp. 10–14; and Giulio Bora, 'Entry 39', in Gregori, ed., *Sofonisba Anguissola e le sue sorelle*, pp. 274–7, for an emblematic connection.

65. Vasari-Milanesi, Vol. VI, p. 502: '*Le donne sì bene sanno fare gli uomini vivi, che maraviglia che quelle che viogliono sappiano anco fargli sì bene dipinti.*'

66. Gregori, ed., *Sofonisba Anguissola e le sue sorelle*, p. 32, plate 8, for a reproduction of Anthony van Dyck's drawing at the British Museum in London.

67. Pope Julius III, Farnese, also praised and thanked her after receiving her self-portrait in homage by writing in a letter on 15 October 1561: '*Comendando questa vostra virtù, la quale, ancora che sia maravigliosa*' ('I commend your artistic ability or creativity, that is, indeed, a wonderment'). See Vasari-Milanesi, Vol. VI, pp. 499–500, and Vol. VII, p. 133.

68. Vasari-Milanesi, Vol. VI, p. 501.

69. Ibid., '*Elena dopo essersi molto avanzata negli studi del disegno e del colorito, si volle far monaca*' ('Elena, having reached a high level of competency in drawing and painting, wished to become a nun').

70. Ibid. Some of her works were collected by Count Giuseppe Schinchinelli.

71. Ibid., p. 282.

72. Gregori, ed., *Sofonisba Anguissola e le sue sorelle*, p. 218, and Anastasia Gilardi, 'Entry 42', in Gregori, ed., *Sofonisba Anguissola e le sue sorelle*, p. 282.

73. Guazzoni, 'Entry 20', in Gregori, ed., *Sofonisba Anguissola e le sue sorelle*, p. 224.

74. Vasari-Milanesi, Vol. VI, p. 498, '*Minerva, che in pitture e in lettere fu rara.*'

75. Bachmann and Piland, *Women Artists*, pp. 58–61, quoting Vasari.

76. Carlo Pietrangeli, ed., *L'Accademia Nazionale di San Luca* (Rome: De Luca Editore, 1974), pp. 204 and 206. This study is fundamental on the academy's foundation, theory of art, teaching training, and collection of artists' works.

77. Carlo Galli, *Lavinia Fontana* (Rome, 1940), n. 1.

78. It is interesting to note that Lavinia signed all her paintings as 'unmarried or single' and with her family name, Lavinia Fontana Virgo, before her marriage, and after added her husband's last name de Zappi to hers: Lavinia Fontana de Zappi or Lavinia Fontana Zappi.

79. Cantaro, *Lavinia Fontana*, pp. 236–9, and Fortunati, *Lavinia Fontana*, pp. 208–9, for a discussion on the drawings of Lavinia and bibliographical data on them.

80. I am using Leon Battista Alberti's concept. See *On Painting*, trans. Spencer, p. 67.

81. This portrait was severely damaged and its restoration poorly executed: Liana De Girolami Cheney.

82. Gozzini-Lasinio's engraving representing Lavinia Fontana's self-portraits at the Raccolta Seletti at Castel Sforzesco in Milan. See also, Lasinio the Younger's engravings of two of Lavinia Fontana's *Self-Portraits* at the Uffizi in the *Reale Galleria di Firenze Illustrata*, Vol. II, pp. 19–22, fig. 64, for a painted copy and other reproductions. See Cantaro, *Lavinia Fontana*, pp. 274–5.

83. Cantaro, *Lavinia Fontana*, pp. 72–4, figs. 4 and 12, for illustrations of both portraits.

84. Hans Biedermann, *Dictionary of Symbols* (New York: Penguin Books, 1994), pp. 197–9.

85. Bonafoux, *Portraits of the Artist: The Self-Portrait in Painting*, p. 8.

86. Fortunati, *Lavinia Fontana*, p. 181. The marriage was arranged between her father, Prospero, and Severo Zappi, father of her future spouse.

87. Anne Hollander, *Seeing Through Clothes* (Berkeley, Ca: University of California Press, 1993), pp. 391–6, for a discussion on the use of mirrors in the sixteenth century.

88. This is the second Lasinio the Younger's engraving of Lavinia Fontana's *Self-Portrait* at the Uffizi in the *Reale Galleria di Firenze Illustrata*, Vol. II, pp. 19–22, fig. 65.

89. Tufts, *Our Hidden Heritage*, p. 31.

90. See n. 82, above, and Cantaro, *Lavinia Fontana*, 'Entry 4a.18', p. 87, and Fortunati, *Lavinia Fontana*, pp. 181–2.

91. Hollander, *Seeing Through Clothes*, pp. 237–311, for a discussion on costumes and clothing.

92. It has been suggested that the palette and brushes were added at a later time, in order to transform the painting into a self-portrait. See Cantaro, *Lavinia Fontana*, p. 88.

93. Elizabeth Vigée-Lebrun's *Self-Portrait with Straw Hat and Palette* of 1782 (private collection), and Adélaïde Labille-Guiard's *Self-Portrait with Two Pupils: Mlle Marie Gabrielle Capet and Mlle de Rosemond* of 1785 (Metropolitan Museum of Art, New York).

94. Veronese's drawing of a *Portrait of a Woman*, 1595, in the Biblioteca Reale, Turin, (Inv. n. 15681) has been identified by Cantaro, and with good reason, as a portrait of Lavinia Fontana. See Cantaro, *Lavinia Fontana*, p. 243.

95. Fortunati, *Lavinia Fontana*, pp. 49–50, for cartouche-portraits and effigies in C.C. Malvasia, *Felisina Pittrice* (1678) and in the Roman Accademia di San Luca's portrait series.

96. Liana De Girolami Cheney, 'Barbara Longhi', *Woman's Art Journal*, Fall 1987, pp. 10–14; Bachmann and Piland, *Women Artists*, pp. 53–8; and Graziani, 'La leggenda dell'artista donna', p. 144.

97. Vasari-Milanesi, Vol. VII, 1970, p. 421: '*Nè tacerò che e una sua figliuola ancor piccola fanciulletta, chiamata Barbara, disegna molto bene, ed a ha cominciato a colorire ancluna cosa con assai buona grazia e maniera.*'

98. J. Bentini, *Luca Longhi* (Bologna: Alfa Edition, 1982), p. 5; Nadia Ceroni, *La Donazione Levi* (Ravenna: Pinacoteca Comunale, 1995); and M. Manfredi, *Lettione ai colleghi Accademici Confusi* (Bologna, 1575), pp. 22–3.

99. Paola Barocchi, ed., *Scritti d'arte del Cinquecento* (Milan: Einaudi, 1977), Vol. III, pp. 1715–36, and Graziani, 'La leggenda dell'artista donna', p. 144.

100. Cantaro, *Lavinia Fontana*, p. 8, for Gozzini-Lasinio's engraving representing the portraits of women painters such as Maria Robusti, Lavinia Fontana, and Sofonisba Anguissola from the *Raccolta Seletti*, at the Castel Sforzesco in Milan, as well as Lasinio the Younger's engraving of Marietta Robusti's *Self-Portrait* at the Uffizi in the *Reale Galleri di Firenze Illustrata*, Vol. II, pp. 93–4, fig. 89.

101. Venezia, Archivio di Stato, Scuola Grande di San Rocco II, Consegna, Ba. 413, states that she married on 2 December 1583.

102. Ridolfo Borghini, *Il riposo* (Florence, 1584), note 1, pp. 558–9. '*Ha il Tintoretto una figliuola, chiamata Marietta, e detta da tutti Tintoretta, la quale oltre alla belleza, et alla gratia, et al saper sonare di gravicembalo, di liuto, e d'atri strumenti, dipinge benissimo.*'

103. Caterina Caneva, ed., *Autoritratti dagli Uffizi da Andrea del Sarto a Chagall* (Florence: Uffizi, 1990), catalogue note 37 and pp. 70–73, for discussion on the attribution of this *Self-Portrait*.

104. Trans. and intro. Catherine Enggass and Robert Enggass (London, 1984), Carlo Ridolfi, *Le meraviglie dell'arte*, ed. Detler Freiherrn von Hadelm (Berlin: G. Grotesche, 1924), Vol. II, pp. 78–80; and Fabio Maniago, *Storia delle belle arti friulane* (Undine, 1823); Franceso Sansovino, *Venetia città nobilissima et singolare descritta in Venetia 1581*, ed. D. Giustiniano Martinioni (Venice, 1663). See also the exhibition catalogue by Caterina Caneva, *Painters by Painters* (New York: National Academy of Design, 1988), 'Entry 6', and Caneva, *Autoritratti*, pp. 70–73.

105. Graziani, 'La leggenda dell'artista donna', p. 129, first made this connection; see also Mary D. Garrard, 'Here's Looking at Me: Sofonisba Anguissola and the Problem of the Woman Artist', *Renaissance Quarterly*, 47 (1994), pp. 556–622, pp. 591–7, and recent bibliography on this topic.

106. Although records show the existence of these latter two portraits in these locations, at present they have been misplaced. See Germaine Greer, *The Obstacle Race* (New York: Farrar Straus Giroux, 1979), p. 337, n. 4.

107. Ellet, *Women Artists*, pp. 25–6; Harris and Nochlin, *Women Artists*, p. 28; and Piland, *Women Artists*, pp. 65–6; E. Tietze-Conrat, 'Marietta, fille du Tintoret: peintre de portraits', *Gazette des Beaux-Arts*, 12 (December 1934), pp. 258–62.

108. Joachim von Sandrart, *Teutsch Academie de edlen Bau-Bild-un Mahlerey-Künstle* (Nuremberg, 1675).

109. For a list of other sixteenth-century Italian women artists with their respective bibliographical references from the sixteenth and seventeenth centuries, see Fredrika H. Jacobs, *Defining the Renaissance Virtuosa* (Cambridge: Cambridge University Press, 1997), pp. 165–8.

Chapter V

1. Helga Möbius, *Women of the Baroque Age* (Montclair, NJ: Abner Schram, 1982), for a general view on women's life in the seventeenth and (mostly) eighteenth centuries.

2. Ann Sutherland Harris, 'Women's Models', presentation at the College Art Association, New York, 1997.

3. William Monter, 'Protestant Wives, Catholic Saints, and the Devil's Handmaid: Women in the Age of Reformations', in Renate Bridenthal, Claudia Koonz and Susan Stuard, eds, *Becoming Visible: Women in European History* (Boston: Houghton Mifflin, 1987), pp. 203–19.

4. Pascal Bonafoux, *Portaits of the Artist* (Geneva: Skira, 1985), pp. 22–3.

5. In Italy, the Accademia di San Luca in Rome, Accademia del Disegno in Florence, and the Accademia of Bologna were leading institutions for artists.

6. Rensselaer W. Lee, *Ut Pictura Poesis: The Humanistic Theory of Painting* (New York: W. W. Norton, 1941), pp. 16–44.

7. Chris Petteys, *Dictionary of Women Artists: An International Dictionary of Women Artists Born before 1900* (Boston, Ma: G. K. Hall, 1985), p. 64, for bibliographical information.

8. Germaine Greer, *The Obstacle Race: The Fortunes of Women Painters and Their Work* (New York: Farrar Straus Giroux, 1979), pp. 219–22.

9. Mary D. Garrard, *Artemisia Gentileschi* (Princeton, NJ: Princeton University Press, 1989).

10. Gentileschi's *Judith and Holofernes* (1610, from the Lemme Collection in Rome), was auctioned at Sotheby's of London on April 6, 1977. The painting was included in *Artemesia*, an exhibition held at the Casa Buonarotti in Florence (18 June–4 November 1991). Gianni Papi's entry for the

catalogue clearly documents and discusses convincingly the provenance of the painting, its attribution and its stylistic merits and placement in Gentileschi's career. See Roberto Contini and Gianni Papi, *Artemisia* (pp. 106–9).

11. See Mary Garrard, *Artemisia Gentileschi: The Image of the Female Hero in Italian Baroque Art* (Princeton: Princeton University Press, 1989), p. 137, for the transalation of '*Ne l'intagliar le corna a mio marito/lasciai il pennello, e preso lo scapello,*' in *Cimiterio, epitafi giocosi di Giovan Francesco Loredano e Pietro Michele* (Venice, 1653).

12. Garrard, *Artemisia Gentileschi*, pp. 383–4.

13. Liana De Girolami Cheney, *The Paintings of the Casa Vasari* (New York: Garland Publications, 1985), pp. 121–2.

14. Cesare Ripa, *Iconologia* (Padua, 1625), 'Painting'. See Garrard, *Artemisia Gentileschi*, pp. 356–7, fig. 316.

15. Elizabeth Cropper, 'Artemisia Gentileschi', in Delia Gaze, ed., *Dictionary of Women Artists* (London: Fitzroy Dearborn, 1997), p. 579.

16. Ripa, *Iconologia*, 'Imitation'.

17. See Contini and Papi, *Artemisia*, pp. 172–5, and Garrard, *Artemisia Gentileschi*, pp. 87–8, for a discussion of the attribution of this painting.

18. For a documented portrait of Orazio Gentileschi, see Lucas Vosterman's engraving, after Anthony van Dyck's *Portrait of Orazio Gentileschi*, in Contini and Papi, *Artemisia*, p. 21, fig. 6.

19. D. Denise Minault, *Woman as Heroine* (Worcester, Ma: Worcester Art Museum, 1972), the pioneer exhibition on this subject.

20. Domenico Vaccolini, *Biography di Elis. Sirani* (Rome, 1844), and Adelina Modesti, 'Elisabetta Sirani "pittrice eronina": A Portrait of the Artist as a Young Woman', in *Identità ed appartenza*, Acts of the First International Congress of the Italian Society of Women Historians (Rimini: Tipografia Rimini, 1995), n.p.

21. Andrea Bianchini, *Il processo di avvelenamento fatto 1655–66 in Bologna contro Lucia Tolomelli per la morte di Elisabetta Sirani* (Bologna, 1854, reprinted 1904), and G. Baldi, *La farmacia nella breve mortale malattia della pittrice bolognese Elisabetta Sirani* (Pisa, 1958).

22. For example, Archangela Paladini, who painted *Self-Portrait* (Galleria degli Uffizi, Florence), was born in Pisa in 1599 and died in 1662 in Florence. She painted numerous portraits, training with her father, Filippo Paladini, who was also a musician. She married Jan Broomans. See Greer, *Obstacle Race*, pp. 71–2.

23. Originally attributed to Elisabetta Sirani as a portrait of Ginevra Cantofoli. See Greer, *Obstacle Race*, pp. 219–22.

24. Carlo Ridolfi, *Delle meraviglie dell'arte* (Venice, 1648), Vol. II, p. 83, and Greer, *Obstacle Race*, pp. 218–19.

25. Robert Enggass and Jonathan Brown, *Italy and Spain: 1600–1750*, Sources and Documents in the History of Art Series (Englewood Cliffs, NJ: Prentice-Hall, 1970), pp. 5–68.

26. Giovan Paolo Lomazzo, *L'Idea del tempio della pittura* (Milan, 1590), p. 163, and Giovan Paolo Lomazzo, *Rime* (Milan, 1587).

27. Paolo Morigia, *La Nobiltà di Milano* (Milan, 1595).

28. Flavio Caroli, *Fede Galizia* (Turin: Umberto Allemandi, 1989), p. 81; Ann Sutherland Harris and Linda Nochlin, *Women Artists: 1550–1950* (New York: Alfred A. Knopf, 1976), pp. 28, 31–3; for a discussion on the attribution of this painting, Liana De Girolami Cheney, 'Review of Caroli's Fede Galizia', in *Sixteenth Century Journal* (Fall 1998), pp. 257–8.

29. Archivio di Stato di Milano, fondo Religione, cart. 972, 1010–11; for a total quotation of the testament, see Caroli, *Fede Galizia*, pp. 20–21.

30. Harris and Nochlin, *Women Artists*, pp. 31–3, and Caroli, *Fede Galizia*, pp. 9–17.

31. Gerard Casale, *Giovanna Garzoni, 'Insigne miniatrice' 1600–1700* (Milan: Jandi Sapi, 1991), and Gerard Casale, ed., *Gli incanti dell'iride: Giovanna Garzoni pittrice nel Seicento* (Milan: Silvana Editoriale, 1966), pp. 32–100 and bibliography on this painter.

32. Casale, ed., *Gli incanti dell'iride*, p. 33, for an illustration of this painting, and see Sancro Scoccianti's commentary on the date, p. 32. See Liana De Girolami Cheney, 'Review of Casale's *Gli incanti dell'iride*', in *Sixteenth Century Journal* (Spring 1998), pp. 257–8.

33. Carlo Pietrangeli, ed., *L'Accademia Nazionale di San Luca* (Rome: De Luca Editore, 1974), p. 255, document ASSL Vol. 69, fasc. 303, letter 3 April 1633, for a list of the new members where she is included.

34. Casale, *Giovanna Garzoni*, for a copy of the full testament, made on 3 June 1666, but not disclosed until after her death on 15 February 1670; Pietrangeli, ed., *L'Accademia Nazionale di San Luca*, p. 227, K. Noehles, *La Chiesa di SS Luca e Martina* (Rome, 1970), pp. 116 and 369, and Harris and Nochlin, *Women Artists*, p. 135, n. 7, for a discussion on the arrangements and difficulties of the delayed erection of this monument, finally designed by Mattia de' Rossi, Bernini's favorite assistant, in 1698.

35. Mina Gregori, 'Giovanna Garzoni e l'arte del suo tempo', in Casale, ed., *Gli incanti dell'iride*, p. 13, concerning the influence of Jacopo Ligozzi's natural studies (1623–6) on her work.

36. Casali, *Gionnna Garzoni*, pp. 16 and 120, Casali, ed., *Gli incanti dell'iride*, pp. 36–7.

37. Pietrangeli, ed., *L'Accademia Nazionale di San Luca*, pp. 227 and 212, for an illustration of her portrait by Giuseppe Ghezzi, and Casali, ed., *Gli incanti dell'iride*, p. 28.

38. Casali, ed., *Gli incanti dell'iride*, pp. 29 and 31, for illustrations of these portraits.

39. Another Italian still-life painter was Margherita Caffi (1662–1700), see Harris and Nochlin, *Women Artists*, pp. 151–2. In the eighteenth century, Teresa Berenice Vitelli was active from 1706–29 in Florence.

40. Luís Filipe Marques de Gama, *O Testamento Inédito da Pintora Josefa D'Óbidos* (Óbidos: Câmara Municipal de Óbidos, 1986), pp. 1–20; *Arquitectura e Urbanismo, Sec. XVI e XVII* (Óbidos: Câmara Municipal de Óbidos, 1986), pp. 99–101; Barbara von Barghahn, Victor Serrão and Luis de Moura Sobral, *The Sacred and the Profane: Josefa de Óbidos of Portugal* (Lisbon: Gabinete de Relações Internacionais, 1997). This exhibition catalogue represents the first comprehensive study in English on Josefa de Ayala D'Óbidos.

41. Barbara von Barghahn, Vitor Serrão, and Luís de Moura Sobra, *The Sacred and the Profane: Josefa de Óbidos of Portugal* (Lisbon: Gabinete de Relaçōnes Internacionales, 1997), for an excellent study and bibliography on this painter; Jordana Pomeroy, 'Josefa de Óbidos of Portugal', *Women in the Arts* (Summer 1997), pp. 6–9; Luís Reis-Santos, *Josefa d'Óbidos* (Lisbon, 1956), the first comprehensive study, with a list of signed and dated works; Edward J. Sullivan, 'Josefa de Ayala: A Woman Painter of the Portuguese Baroque', *Journal of the Walters Art Gallery* (1978), pp. 22–35; and Liana De Girolami Cheney, 'The Self-Portraits of Josefa de Ayala D'Óbidos', presented at the International Mediterranean Congress in Lisbon, Portugal, 26–8 May 1998.

42. Cesare Ripa, *Iconologia* (Padua, 1618), trans. and ed. by Jan Barja and Yago Barja (Madrid: Ediciones Akal, 1987), pp. 279–92.

43. Barghahn, Serrão, and Sobra, *The Sacred and the Profane: Josefa de Óbidos of Portugal*, p.102.

44. Donna G. Bachmann and Sherry Piland, *Women Artists* (London: The Scarecrow Press, 1978), pp. 89–91, for an excellent bibliography of this French painter.

45. Montserrat Sabán Godoy, ed., *Los Cinco Sentidos y el Arte* (Madrid: Museo del Prado, 1997), pp. 29–58, and Sylvia Ferino-Pagden, *I cinque sensi nell'arte: Immagini del sentire* (Cremona: Leonardo Arte, 1996), pp. 122–9.

46. Pamela Hibbs Decoteau, *Clara Peeters, 1594 – ca. 1640, and the Development of Still-Life Painting in Northern Europe* (Lingen: Luca Verlag, 1992), pp. 51 and 183, for a questionable attribution.

47. Wayne E. Franits, *Paragons of Virtue: Women and Domesticity in Seventeenth-Century Dutch Art* (Cambridge: Cambridge University Press, 1995), passim. Although this scholar focuses on Dutch society, similar ideas on woman's role in marriage are applicable to Flemish culture.

48. Ibid., pp. 104–8.

49. Harris and Nochlin, *Women Artists*, fig. 1, from the collection of the Comte de Normand, Nice, France, to the Galerie J. Charpentier, Paris, and as of 1 June 1951 in a private collection in Belgium, then Newhouse Galleries in New York

50. Elis Kloek, 'Women Painters in Seventeenth Century Holland', in James A. Welu, ed., *Judith Leyster: A Dutch Master and Her World* (Worcester, Ma: Worcester Art Museum, 1993), pp. 62–3, nn. 35 and 42. Women whose works have been unfortunately forgotten but whose names are recorded in the painters' Haarlem Guild of Saint Luke include Sara van Baalbergen, Gerritje Jans, Geertruit van Veen, Anna Snellings and Sara Vrooms. Other painters among the 6,000 recorded are listed by Kloek.

51. Ibid.

52. Judith Leyster was also an accomplished painter of botanical subjects. However, her historical contribution to art history is in the genre paintings. See Welu, ed., *Judith Leyster*, pp. 214–16; and

Kloek, 'Women Painters in Seventeenth Century Holland,' in Welu, ed., *Judith Leyster*, pp. 62–5, nn. 34 and 35, for additional bibliography on Dutch women painters.

53. Harris and Nochlin, *Women Artists*, p. 137, nn. 1 and 2, for cited documents on Judith's life and career.

54. Welu, ed., *Judith Leyster*, p. 11.

55. Franits, *Paragons of Virtue*, passim.

56. Liana De Girolami Cheney, ed., *The Symbolism of Vanitas in the Arts, Literature, and Music* (New York: Edwin Mellen Press, 1993), pp. 113–76.

57. Welu, ed., *Judith Leyster*, pp. 162–7, for information regarding the physical treatment of this painting and its provenance.

58. Welu, ed., *Judith Leyster*, pp. 190–92, for an excellent discussion on the polarity of musical instruments in Dutch paintings.

59. Norman E. Land, *The Viewer as Poet* (University Park, Pa: Pennsylvania State University Press, 1994), pp. 3–24, for a historical discussion on this topic, and pp. 81–97, for a discussion of the poems on portraits, such as Dante on artists, Petrarch, Bembo, and Aretino.

60. Raupp, *Untersuchungen zu Künsterbildinis und Künstlerdarstellung in dem Niederlanden im 17. Jahrhundert*, pp. 133–7, explains how the painted fiddler suggests joy in performing and in relation to Judith, the painter, the joy of creativity.

61. Welu's position is that this painting was referred to in the Haarlem inventories as 'modern figures (*moderne beelden*)'. See Welu, ed., *Judith Leyster*, p. 166.

62. Wheelock, quoted in Welu, ed., *Judith Leyster*, p. 166.

63. Welu, ed., *Judith Leyster*, p. 166, nn. 22 and 23, for his comments on van Mander's *Het Schilder-Boeck* of 1604, chapter 1:23, citing the total passage and reiterating the popular Dutch proverb. I question whether a woman painter at this time, such as Leyster, would have viewed or thought of herself in this manner.

64. Franits, *Paragons of Virtue*, p. 140.

65. Jeffery Daniels, 'The Excellent Ms Mary Beale', *Art News*, 74 (October 1975), pp. 100–101, for a summary of her life's work; Henry S. Reitlinger, 'The Beale Drawings in the British Museum', *Burlington Magazine*, 41 (September 1922), pp. 143–7; and Elizabeth Walsh, 'Mrs Mary Beale, Paintress', *Connoisseur*, 131 (April 1953), pp. 3–8; Sibylla J. Flower, 'The Excellent Ms Mary Beale', *Connoisseur*, 190 (December 1975), p. 302; and *The Excellent Ms Mary Beale* (London: Geffrye Museum, 1975), p. 22, exhibition catalogue.

66. Greer, *The Obstacle Race*, pp. 256–7.

67. Charles Beale's notebook for 1677 is in the Bodleian Library, Oxford (Ms Rawl 8° 572); his notebook for 1681 and Richard Jeffree's *Mary Beale* with miscellaneous documentary and letters are in the National Portrait Gallery Archives, London.

68. Flower, *The Excellent Ms Mary Beale*, p. 45.

Chapter VI

1. Germaine Greer, *The Obstacle Race: The Fortunes of Women Painters and Their Work* (New York: Farrar Straus Giroux, 1979), p. 73.

2. Ibid., p. 74.

3. Quoted in Clara Erskine Clement, *Women in the Fine Arts* (Boston: Houghton, Mifflin, 1904; repr. Hacker Art Books, New York, 1974).

4. 'Chéron, Elizabeth Sophie' in *Dossier de L'Art*, April 1997, p. 61.

5. Bernardina Sani, *Rosalba Carriera* (Turin: Umberto Allemande, 1987), p. 276.

6. Wendy Slatkin, *Voices of Women Artists*, The National Museum of Women in the Arts (New York: Abbeville Press, 1995), p. 19.

7. Bice Viallet, *Gli Autoritratti Femminili R.R. Gallerie degli Uffizi in Firenze* (Rome: Luigi Alfieri, n.d.), p. 53.

8. For a further discussion of this work see Viallet, *Autoritratti*, p. 60, and Sani, *Rosalba Carriera*, p. 312.

9. Slatkin, *Voices of Women Artists*, p. 19.

10. Michael Levey, *Painting in XVIIIth Century Venice* (London: Phaidon, 1959), p. 140.

11. Other self-portraits by Carriera are located in the Ospedale Civico, Castel Delpino and the Ca Rezzonico, Venice, and in a private collection, which has a pencil and brown ink drawing which is reproduced by Russell in 'Drawings by Rosalba', *Burlington Magazine*, March 1997, p. 196.

12. *Gli Uffizi: Catalogo generale* (Florence: Centro Di, 1979), entry A366.

13. For a discussion of these works see Viallet, *Autoritratti* and Uffizi, *Catalogo generale*.

14. Greer, *Obstacle Race*, p. 89.

15. Valeria Moretti, *Le più belle del reale: Pittrici in Autoritratto dal Cinquecento all Ottocento* (Rome: Nuova Editrice Spada, 1983), p. 85.

16. For further information on Lama see Rodolfo Pallucchini, 'Di una pittrice veneziana del settecento: Giulia Lama', *Rivista d'arte*, July 1933, pp. 399–413.

17. *Uffizi: Painters by Painters* (New York: National Academy of Design, 1988), pl. 24.

18. *Diderot et l'art de Boucher à David* (Paris: Editions de la Réunion des Musées Nationaux, 1984), p. 359.

19. Ibid., p. 360.

20. Horace Walpole, *Anecdotes of Painting in England* (New Haven, Ct: Yale University Press, 1937), p. 4 and pp. 136–7.

21. Greer, *Obstacle Race*, p. 278.

22. Ibid.

23. Walpole, *Anecdotes*, p. 137.

24. Nancy G. Heller, *Women Artists: An Illustrated History* (New York: Abbeville Press, 1987), p. 82.

25. Pierre Rosenberg, *Fragonard* (New York: Metropolitan Museum, 1988), p. 593.

26. Linda Nochlin and Ann Sutherland Harris, *Women Artists: 1550–1950* (New York: Knopf, 1984), p. 197.

27. Jeanne Doin, 'Marguerite Gérard', *Gazette des Beaux Arts* (1912), p. 431.

28. Rosenberg, *Fragonard*, p. 565.

29. Rosenberg (*Fragonard*, p. 564) discusses attributions by both Wells-Robertson and Williams of the painting as a self-portrait by Gérard.

30. Ibid., p. 563.

31. George Levitine, 'Marguerite Gérard and her Stylistic Significance', *Studies in Honor Of Gertrude Rosenthal. The Baltimore Museum of Art Annual III* (Baltimore, 1968), pp. 21–31.

32. Doin, 'Marguerite Gérard', p. 452.

33. Greer, *Obstacle Race*, p. 103.

34. See Marianne Roland Michel, *Anne Vallayer-Coster 1744–1818* (Paris: C.I.L., 1979), p. 42 for a discussion of self-portraits by Vallayer-Coster.

35. The following discussion of Vigée-Lebrun was originally presented by Kathleen Russo as a paper in Amsterdam in 1996 and published in the *VRA Bulletin*, Vol. 23, New York, Winter, 1996. Additional information on Vigée-Lebrun and images of her work may be found on Kevin Kelly's website www.az.starnet.com/%7Ekjkelly/vigeepaints.html. Thanks to Kevin Kelly and Charles Stein for bibliographical material.

36. Elisabeth Vigée-Lebrun, *Memoirs*, translated by Lional Strachey (New York: George Braziller, 1989), p. 22.

37. Joseph Baillio, *Elisabeth Louise Vigée-LeBrun* (Fort Worth: Kimbell Art Museum, 1982), p. 44.

38. Vigée-Lebrun, *Memoirs*, p. 34. The original of this self-portrait is in a private collection; the National Gallery painting is an autograph copy.

39. W.H. Helm, *Vigée-Lebrun 1755–1842: Her Life, Works and Friendships* (Boston: Small, Maynard, 1915), p. 38.

40. Mary Sheriff, *The Exceptional Woman: Elisabeth Vigée-Lebrun and the Cultural Politics of Art* (Chicago: University of Chicago Press, 1996), p. 215.

41. Michael Levey, *Painting and Sculpture in France, 1700–1789* (New Haven, Ct: Yale University Press, 1993), p. 282.

42. Helm, *Vigée-Lebrun*, p. 110.

43. Anne Marie Passez, *Adélaïde Labille-Guiard 1749–1803* (Paris: Arts et Métiers Graphiques, 1973), p. 90.

44. Passez, *Labille-Guiard*, p. 21.

45. Slatkin, *Voices of Women Artists*, p. 104.

46. Passez, *Labille-Guiard*, p. 158.

47. These lodgings included a house on the rue de Richelieu, lodgings in the Louvre and a country house in Pontault-en-Brie.

48. For a photograph and discussion of all of these works see Comte Arnauld Doria, *Une Émule d'Adélaïde Labille-Guiard, Gabrielle Capet portraitiste* (Paris, 1934).

49. Joseph Baillio, 'Vie et oeuvre de Marie Victoire Lemoine', *Gazette des Beaux-Arts*, ser. 6, vol. 127, (April 1996), p. 135.

50. Greer, *Obstacle Race*, p. 135.

51. Margaret Oppenheimer, 'Nisa Villers, neé Lemoine, 1774–1821', *Gazette des Beaux-Arts*, ser. 6, vol. 127 (April 1996), p. 167.

52. Oppenheimer, 'Villers', p. 173.

53. Nochlin and Harris, *Women Artists*, p. 217.

54. Charles Sterling, 'A Fine "David" Reattributed', *Metropolitan Museum of Art Bulletin*, Vol. 9, no. 5 (1951), p. 124.

55. Sterling, '"David" Reattributed', p. 132.

56. Oppenheimer, 'Villers', p. 170.

57. Sterling, '"David" Reattributed', p. 125.

58. Marie Juliette Ballot, *La Comtesse Benoist, l'Emilie de Demoustier 1768–1826* (Paris: Librarie Plon, 1914).

59. Nochlin and Harris, *Women Artists*, p. 210.

60. Bouliar is often erroneously spelled 'Bouliard' due to Jouin's use of this spelling in *Mlle Marie-Geneviève Bouliard* (Paris, 1891). She herself spelled it 'Bouliar'.

61. Wendy Wassyng Roworth, 'Biography, Criticism, Art History: Angelica Kauffmann in Context', in *Eighteenth-Century Women and the Arts*, ed. Frederick Keener (London: Greenwood Press, 1988), p. 210.

62. See Stefano Susinno, *I Ritratti degli Accademia Nazionale di San Luca* (Rome: de Luca, 1974), p. 269.

63. Eleanor Tufts, *Our Hidden Heritage* (New York: Paddington Press, 1974), p. 118.

64. Ibid., p. 120.

65. Louise Rice and Ruth Eisenberg, 'Angelica Kauffmann's Uffizi Self-Portrait', *Gazette des Beaux-Arts*, ser. 6, vol. 117 (March 1991), pp. 123–6.

66. Roworth, *Eighteenth-Century Women and the Arts*, p. 217.

67. Ibid., p. 213.

68. Gill Perry, 'The British Sappho: Borrowed Identities and the Representation of Women Artists in Late Eighteenth-Century British Art', *Oxford Art Journal*, vol. 18, no. 1 (1995), pp. 44–57.

69. Ibid., p. 50.

70. Albert Boime, *Art in an Age of Revolution 1750–1800* (Chicago: University of Chicago Press, 1987), p. 114.

71. Ibid., p. 114.

72. Karen Petersen and J. J. Wilson, *Women Artists: Recognition and Reappraisal from the Early Middle*

Ages to the Twentieth Century (New York: New York University Press, 1976), p. 44.

73. Peter Tomory, *The Life and Art of Henry Fuseli* (New York: Praeger, 1972), p. 41.

74. In Perry, 'The British Sappho', p. 53.

75. Clement, *Women in the Fine Arts*, pp. 89–90.

76. Constance Scheerer, 'Maria Cosway: Larger Than Life Miniaturists', *Feminist Art Journal* (April 1997), pp. 10–13. The 'Macaroni' works are pictured here.

77. Nochlin and Harris, *Women Artists*, p. 214.

78. Greer, *Obstacle Race*, p. 37.

Chapter VII

1. Abby Remer, *Pioneering Spirits: The Lives and Times of Remarkable Women Artists in Western History* (Worcester, Ma: Davis Publications, 1997), p. 80.

2. Jan Marsh, 'Art, Ambition and Sisterhood in the 1850s', in Clarissa Campbell Orr, ed., *Women in the Victorian Art World* (Manchester: Manchester University Press, 1995), p. 35.

3. *The Artist* (May 1880), p. 154.

4. *La Gazette des Femmes*, Vol. 10, 3 (10 February 1883).

5. William M. Rossetti, *Dante Gabriel Rossetti: His Family Letters and A Memoir*, Vol. 1 (London: Ellis and Levee, 1895), p. 175.

6. W. Rossetti, *Family Letters*, Vol. 1, pp. 171 and 174.

7. Oswald Doughty and John Robert Wahl, eds., *Letters of Dante Gabriel Rossetti*, Vol. 1 (Oxford: Clarendon Press, 1965), p. 244.

8. Henry James, *The Painter's Eye: Notes and Essays on the Pictorial Arts* (Cambridge, Ma: Harvard University Press, 1956), p. 92.

9. Henrietta Ward, *Memories of Ninety Years* (London: Hutchinson, 1922), p. 124.

10. Doughty and Wahl, eds, *Letters*, Vol. 1, p. 384.

11. Ibid., p. 383.

12. Susan Fisher Sterling, *Women Artists, The National Museum of Women in the Arts* (New York: Abbeville Press, 1995), p. 84.

13. Josephine Withers, 'Artistic Women and Women Artists', *Art Journal*, Vol. 35, 4 (Summer 1976), p. 333. All the letters quoted in this article are taken from the Spencer papers, Archives of American Art, Washington, DC.

14. Robert Bolton-Smith and William H. Truettner, *Lilly Martin Spencer 1822–1902, The Joys of Sentiment* (Washington, DC: Smithsonian Institution, 1973), p. 196.

15. May Alcott Nieriker, *Studying Abroad and How to Do It Cheaply* (Boston, 1879), p. 48.

16. Germaine Greer, 'A tout prix, devenir quelqu'un: The Women at the Académie Julien', in *Artistic Relations*, Peter Collier and Robert Lethbridge, eds. (New Haven, Ct: Yale University Press, 1994), p. 53.

17. Tamar Garb, *Sisters of the Brush* (New Haven, Ct: Yale University Press, 1994), p. 103.

18. Garb, *Sisters*, p. 92.

19. Charlotte Yeldham, *Women Artists in Nineteenth Century France and England*, Vol. 1 (New York: Garland, 1984), p. 45.

20. J. Diane Radycki, 'The Life of Lady Art Students: Changing Art Education at the Turn of the Century', *Art Journal*, Vol. 42 , 1 (Spring 1982), p. 13.

21. Yeldham, *Women Artists*, p. 31.

22. Lynda Nead, *The Female Nude* (London: Routledge, 1992), p. 50.

23. Susan Waller, *Women Artists in the Modern Era: A Documentary History* (Metuchen, NJ and London: The Scarecrow Press, 1991), p. 238.

24. Elizabeth Butler, *An Autobiography* (London: Constable, 1923), p. 5.

25. Ibid., p. 3.

26. Paul Usherwood and Jenny Spencer-Smith, *Lady Butler, Battle Artist 1846–1933* (London: National Army Museum, 1987), p. 57.

27. Butler, *Autobiography*, p. 112.

28. E. T. Cook and Alexander Wedderburn, *The Works of John Ruskin*, Vol. 14 (London, 1904), pp. 308, 309.

29. W. Meynell, 'The Life and Work of Lady Butler', *The Art Annual* (1898), p. 31.

30. Alain Clairet, Delphine Montalent and Yves Rouart, *Berthe Morisot 1841–1895: Catalogue raisonné de l'oeuvre peint* (CERA – nrs éditions, France, 1997).

31. Ibid., p. 16.

32. Carnet of notes by Berthe Morisot, Mézy, 1890, p. 34, at the Musée Marmottan, noted in Marianne Delaford and Caroline Genet-Bandeville, *Berthe Morisot ou L'Audace raisonné* (Paris: Musée Marmottan Claude Mont, 1997), p. 50.

33. Barbara Ehrlich White, *Impressionists Side by Side* (New York: Alfred A. Knopf, 1996), p. 260.

34. Ibid., p. 260.

35. Louisine Havemeyer, 'The Cassatt Exhibition', *Pennsylvania Museum Bulletin* (May 1927), p. 378.

36. Achille Segard, *Mary Cassatt, un peintre des enfants et des mères* (Paris: Ollendorf, 1913), pp. 184, 185.

37. Denise Bauer, 'Suzanne Valadon by Thérèse Rosinsky', *Women's Art Journal*, Vol. 17, 1 (Spring/Summer 1996), p. 56.

38. Thérèse Diamond Rosinsky, *Suzanne Valadon* (New York: Universe Publishing, 1994), p. 13.

Chapter VIII

1. Quoted in Whitney Chadwick, *Women, Art and Society* (London: Thames and Hudson, 1990), p. 279.

2. *Gwen John* (Arts Council of Great Britain, London, 1968), p. 8.

3. John Rothenstein, *Modern English Painters: Sickert to Smith* (London: Eyre & Spottiswoode, 1952), pp. 166–7.

4. Susan Chitty, *Gwen John 1876–1939* (London: Hodder and Stoughton, 1981), pp. 62, 77.

5. Augustus John, *Chiaroscuro* (London: Cape, 1952), pp. 254–5.

6. Olga S. Opfell, *Special Visions* (Jefferson, NC, and London: McFarland, 1991), p. 160.

7. Regina Marler, ed., *Selected Letters of Vanessa Bell* (New York: Pantheon Books, 1993), p. 235.

8. Gillian Parry, *Paula Modersohn-Becker* (New York: Harper and Row, 1979), p. 26.

9. Paula Modersohn, *Letters and Journals*, trans. and annotated by J. Diane Radycki (Metuchen, NJ, and London: The Scarecrow Press, 1980), p. 279.

10. Gabrielle Buffet, 'Marie Laurencin', *Arts* (June 1923), p. 96.

11. Patrick Waldberg, *Surrealism* (New York: Oxford University Press, 1978), p. 11.

12. André Breton, *Manifestos of Surrealism*, trans. Richard Seaver and Helen R. Lane (Ann Arbor: University of Michigan Press, 1972), p. 26.

13. Quoted in William Rubin, *Dada, Surrealism and their Heritage* (New York: Museum of Modern Art, 1968), p. 19.

14. Quoted in Waldberg, *Surrealism*, p. 27.

15. *Gil Blas*, 14 May 1910.

16. *L'Intransigeant*, 15 May 1910.

17. André Breton, 'Frida Kahlo', brochure for the Frida Kahlo exhibition at the Johan Levy Gallery, New York, in 1938.

18. Sarah M. Lowe, ed. *The Diary of Frida Kahlo* (New York: Abrams, 1995), p. 215.

19. Janet A. Kaplan, *Unexpected Journeys: The Art and Life of Remedios Varo* (New York: Abbeville, 1988), p. 169.

20. Bice Curriger, *Meret Oppenheim* (Zurich: Plackett, 1989), p. 43.

21. Ibid., p. 8.

22. Ibid., pp. 130–31.

23. Laura Knight, *The Magic of a Line* (London: William Kimber, 1965), p. 307.

24. Caroline Fox, *Dame Laura Knight* (Oxford: Phaidon, 1988), p. 31.

25. Sacha Craddock, 'No clear dividing line', *The Times* (London), 7 March 1995.

Chapter IX

1. Charles Jencks, *What is Post-Modernism?* (London: Academy Editions, 2nd revised edn, 1987), p. 8.

2. Michelle Wallace, 'Daring to Be Unpopular', *Ms*, Vol. 11, 3 (September 1973), p. 24.

3. Calvin Tompkins, 'Righting the Balance', in Randy Rosen and Catherine Brauer, eds, *Making Their Mark: Women Artists Move into the Mainstream* (New York: Abbeville, 1988), p. 45.

4. Maya Ying Lin, 'An Interview with Maya Lin', *Art in America* (April 1983), p. 108.

5. Heather Dorrough, 'Self-Portraits: Recent Work by Heather Dorrough', *Craft Australia*, pt 4 (1982), p. 36. The article contains illustrations of the work mentioned in the text.

6. For reproductions of these works, see Mary Jane Jacob, *Ana Mendieta: The 'Silueta' Series 1973–1980* (New York: Galerie Lelong, n.d.).

7. Joy Harjo, 'Creation Story: The Jaune Quick-To-See Smith Survey', in *Jaune Quick-To-See Smith Subversions/Affirmations* (Jersey City: Jersey City Museum, 1996), p 67.

8. Harmony Hammond and Jaune Quick-To-See Smith, *Women of Sweetgrass, Cedar and Sage* (New York: Gallery of the American Indian Community House, 1985).

9. Derrickson Moore, 'Quick-To-See Smith Offers Art with a Conscience and a Message', *Sun-News*, 25 January 1997, B7.

10. Audrey Flack, *Audrey Flack on Painting* (New York: Abrams, 1981), p. 54.

11. Sue Graze and Kathy Halbreich, *Elizabeth Murray: Paintings and Drawings* (New York: Abrams, 1987), p. 64.

12. Ibid., p. 8.

13. *Watchful Eyes: Native American Women Artists* (Phoenix, Az: Heard Museum, 1994), p. 34.

14. Therese Harlan, 'To Watch, to Remember and to Survive', in ibid., p. 12.

15. Allison Arieff, 'Cultural Collisions: Identity and History in the Work of Hung Liu', *Woman's Art Journal*, Vol. 17, 1 (Spring/Summer 1996), p. 39.

16. John McEwen, *Paula Rego* (London: Phaidon, 1993), p. 195.

17. *Howardena Pindell: Paintings and Drawings. A Retrospective Exhibition 1972–1992* (Potsdam, New York: Roland Gibson Gallery, Potsdam College, 1992), p. 85.

18. *The Heart of the Question: The Writings and Paintings of Howardena Pindell* (New York: Midmarch Arts Press, 1997), p. 76.

19. *Emma Amos Paintings and Prints 1982–1992* (Wooster, Oh: College of Wooster Art Museum, 1993), p. 28.

20. Conversation with the artist, summer 1997.

21. Joan Arbeiter and Sally Swenson Shearer, *Lives and Works: Talks with Women Artists*, Vol. 2. (Metuchen, NJ, and London: The Scarecrow Press, 1995), p. 209.

22. Erin Valentino, 'Mistaken Identity: Between Death and Pleasure in the Art of Kay WalkingStick', *Third Text* (Spring 1994), p. 64.

23. Cindy Nemser, *Art Talks* (New York: Scribner's, 1975), p. ii.

24. 'Annette Messager', *Art News* (May 1997), p. 142.

25. Ruth Iskin, 'Anita Steckel's Feminist Fantasy: The Making of a New Ideology', *Chrysalis*, 3 (1977), p. 91.

26. Arlene Raven, 'The Archaic Smile', *New Feminist Criticism*, Joanna Frueh, Cassandra Langer and Arlene Raven, eds (New York: HarperCollins, 1994), p. 5.

27. Joan Semmel and April Kingsley, 'Sexual Imagery in Women's Art', *Woman's Art Journal* Vol. 1, 1 (Spring/Summer 1980), p. 3.

Chapter X

1. Mary D. Garrard, 'Artemisia Gentileschi's Self-Portrait as the Allegory of Painting', *Art Bulletin*, 62 (March 1980), pp. 97–112.

2. Reproduced in Charlotte Yeldham, *Women Artists in Nineteenth-Century France and England*, Vol. 2 (New York: Garland, 1984), illus. 137. In 1873 Butler did preliminary sketches for *The Roll Call* using a number of male models posed in pink 'shell jackets' so she could draw the figures before putting them in uniform. See Paula Gillett, *The Victorian Painter's World* (Gloucester: Alan Sutton, 1990), p. 187.

3. Patricia Hills, *Alice Neel* (New York: Harry N. Abrams, 1983), pp. 120, 126, 133, 162 and 163, and Pamela E. Allara, 'Matter of Fact: Alice Neel's Pregnant Nudes', *American Art*, Vol. 8, No. 2 (Spring 1994), pp. 6–31.

Select bibliography

General works: books and articles

Anderson, Janet A. *Women in the Fine Arts: A Bibliography and Illustration Guide*. London: McFarland, 1991

Bachmann, Donna G. and Piland, Sherry. *Women Artists: An Historical, Contemporary and Feminist Bibliography*. London: The Scarecrow Press, 1978

Bonafoux, Pascal. *Portraits of the Artist: The Self-Portrait in Painting*. New York: Rizzoli, 1985

Broude, Norma and Garrard, Mary O. D., eds. *Feminism and Art History: Questioning the Litany*. New York: Harper and Row, 1982
    The Expanding Discourse: Feminism and Art History. New York: Harper Icons, 1992
    The Power of Feminist Art. New York: Harry N. Abrams, 1994

Cedarholm, Theresa Dickason. *Afro-American Artists, A Bio-bibliographical Directory*. Boston Public Library, 1973

Chadwick, Whitney. *Women, Art and Society*. London: Thames and Hudson, 1990

de Piles, Roger. *Abrégé de la vie des peintres*. 2nd edition, Paris, 1715

Dunford, Penny. *A Biographical Dictionary of Women Artists in Europe and America since 1850*. Philadelphia: University of Pennsylvania Press, 1989

Elliot, Bridget and Wallace, Jo-Ann. *Women Artists and Writers*. London and New York: Routledge, 1994

Fine, Elsa. *Women and Art*. London: Allanheld & Schram, 1978
    The Afro-American Artist. New York: Holt, Rinehart and Winston, 1973
    American Women Artists: The 20th Century. Knoxville: Knoxville Museum of Art, 1989

Goldman, Shifra and Ybarran-Frausto, Tomas. *A Comprehensive Annotated Bibliography of Chicano Art, 1965–1981*. Berkeley, Ca: Chicano Studies Library Publications, University of California, 1985

Gouma-Peterson, Thalia and Mathews, Patricia. 'The Feminist Critique of Art History', *Art Bulletin* LXIX (1987), pp. 326–57

Greer, Germaine. *The Obstacle Race: The Fortunes of Women Painters and Their Work*. London: Secker and Warburg, and New York: Farrar Straus Giroux, 1979

Harris, Ann Sutherland and Nochlin, Linda. *Women Artists: 1550–1950*. New York: Alfred A. Knopf, 1976

Hedges, Elaine and Wendt, Ingrid. *In Her Own Image*. Westbury, NY: The Feminist Press, 1980

Heller, Jules and Heller, Nancy G., eds. *North American Women Artists of the Twentieth Century; A Biographical Dictionary.* New York and London: Garland Publishing, 1995

Heller, Nancy G. *Women Artists: An Illustrated History.* New York: Abbeville Press, 1987

Hollander, Anne. *Seeing Through Clothes.* Berkeley, Ca: University of California Press, 1993

Ireland, Norma Olin. *Index to Women of the World from Ancient to Modern Times: Bibliographies and Portraits.* Westwood, Ma: F. W. Faxon, 1970

Jacobs, Fredrika H. *Defining the Renaissance Virtuosa.* Cambridge: Cambridge University Press, 1997

Kelly, Joan. *Women, History, and Theory.* Chicago: University of Chicago Press, 1984

Kinnear, Mary. *Daughters of Time: Women in the Western Tradition.* Ann Arbor, Mi: The University of Michigan Press, 1982

Kinneir, Joan and David Piper, eds. *The Artist by Himself: Self-Portraits and Drawings from Youth to Old Age.* New York: Granada Publishing, 1980

Laduke, Betty. *Africa Through the Eyes of Women Artists.* Trenton, NJ: Africa World Press, 1991

MacLean, Ian. *The Renaissance Notion of Woman: A Study in the Fortunes of Scholasticism and Medical Science in European Intellectual Life.* Cambridge: Cambridge University Press, 1980

Mitchell, Sally. *Victorian Britain: An Encyclopedia.* New York and London: Garland Publishing, 1988

Munro, Eleanor. *Originals: American Women Artists.* New York: Simon and Schuster, 1980

Nochlin, Linda. *Women, Art and Power.* New York: Harper and Row, 1988
    The Politics of Vision. New York: Harper and Row, 1989

Parker, Rozsika and Pollock, Griselda. 'Critical Stereotypes: The Essential Feminine or How Essential is Femininity?', in *Old Mistresses: Women, Art and Ideology.* New York: Pantheon Books, 1981, pp. 1–50

Partner, Nancy F. *Studying Medieval Women: Sex, Gender, Feminism.* Cambridge: Cambridge University Press, 1993

Petteys, Chris. *Dictionary of Women Artists: An International Dictionary of Women Artists Born before 1900.* Boston, Ma: G.K. Hall, 1985

Piland, Sherry. *Women Artists: An Historical, Contemporary and Feminist Bibliography.* London: The Scarecrow Press, 1994

Pollock, Griselda. *Vision and Difference.* London: Routledge, 1988

Pope-Hennessy, John. *The Portrait in the Renaissance.* New York: Pantheon Books, 1966

Remer, Abby. *Pioneering Spirits: The Life and Times of Remarkable Women Artists in Western History.* Worcester, Ma: Davis Publications, 1997

Rubenstein, Charlotte S. *American Women Artists.* Boston, Ma: G.K. Hall, 1982

Russo, Alexander. *Profiles of Women Artists.* Frederick, Md: University Publications of America, 1985

Schneider, Norbert. *The Art of the Portrait.* Cologne: Benedikt Taschen, 1994

Slatkin, Wendy. *Women Artists in History: From Antiquity to the Present.* Upper Saddle River, NJ: Prentice-Hall, 1997

Sterling, Susan Fisher. *Women Artists. The National Museum of Women in the Arts.* New York: Abbeville Press, 1995

Tickner, Lisa. 'Feminism, Art History and Sexual Difference', *Genders* 3 (1988), pp. 92–128

Tufts, Eleanor. *Our Hidden Heritage.* New York: Paddington Press, 1974
    American Women Artists, Past and Present: A Bibliography. 2 vols. New York: Garland, 1984–9

Turner, James Grantham. *Sexuality and Gender in Early Modern Europe.* Cambridge: Cambridge University Press, 1993

Waller, Susan. *Women Artists in the Modern Era*. Metuchen, NJ: The Scarecrow Press, 1991

Witzling, Mara R., ed. *Voicing Our Visions: Writings by Women Artists*. New York: Universe, 1991

Woodhall, Joanna, ed., *Portraiture: Facing the Subject*. Manchester: Manchester University Press, 1997

Antiquity

Bell, Robert E. *Women in Classical Mythology*. Oxford: Oxford University Press, 1991

Blundell, Sue. *Women in Ancient Greece*. Cambridge, Ma: Harvard University Press, 1995

    On Portraiture. London: Phaidon, 1992

Cheney, Liana De Girolami. 'Vasari's Depiction of Pliny's Histories', *Explorations in Renaissance Culture* (1989), pp. 23–33

Duby, Georges and Perrot, Michelle, eds. *A History of Women: From Ancient Goddesses to Christian Saints*. Cambridge, Ma: Harvard University Press, 1992

Fantham, Elaine; Foley, Helene Peet; Kampen, Natalie Boyme; Pomeroy, Sarah B.; and Shapiro, H.A. *Women in the Classical World*. Oxford: Oxford University Press, 1994

Lesko, Barbara S. 'Women of Egypt and the Ancient Near East', in Renate Bridenthal, Claudia Koonz and Susan Stuard, *Becoming Visible: Women in European History*. Boston: Houghton Mifflin Company, 1987

Robins, Gay. *Women in Ancient Egypt*. Cambridge, Ma: Harvard University Press, 1993

The Middle Ages

General works, books and articles

Baker, Derek, ed. *Medieval Women*. Oxford: Basil Blackwell, 1978

Caviness, Madeline H. 'Anchoress, Abbess, and Queen: Donors and Patrons or Intercessors and Matrons', in June Hall McCash, ed. *The Cultural Patronage of Medieval Women*. Athens, Ga: The University of Georgia Press, 1996, pp. 105–54

Eckenstein, Lina. *Woman under Monasticism*. Cambridge, Ma: Harvard University Press, 1896

Erickson, Carolly and Casey, Kathleen. 'Women in the Middle Ages: A Working Bibliography', *Medieval Studies* (Toronto: Pontifical Institute of Medieval Studies), V (1975), pp. 340–59

Hamburger, Jeffrey F. *Nuns as Artists*. Berkeley, Ca: University of California Press, 1997

Lucas, Angela M. *Women in the Middle Ages: Religion, Marriage, and Letters*. New York: St Martin's Press, 1983

McCash, June Hall, ed. *The Cultural Patronage of Medieval Women*. Athens, Ga: University of Georgia Press, 1996

Phillips, John A. *Eve: The History of an Idea*. New York: Harper and Row, 1984

Stuard, Susan Mosher ed. *Women in Medieval Society*. Philadelphia: University of Pennsylvania Press, 1976

Monographs and articles on individual painters

Ende

Aznar, José Camón. 'Art in the Beatos and the Codex of Gerona', *Beati in Apocalipsin: Codex Gerundensis* (facsimile with commentaries). Madrid, 1975, pp. 17–178

Carr, Annemarie Weyl. 'Women Artists in the Middle Ages', *Feminist Art Journal*, I (Spring 1976), pp. 5–10

Williams, John W. *The Illustrated Beatus: A Corpus of the Illustrations of the Commentary on the Apocalypse, II: The Ninth and Tenth Centuries*, London: Harvey Miller, 1994 (contains comprehensive bibliography on the Girona *Beatus*)

Hildegard of Bingen

Bowie, Fiona and Davies, Oliver. *Hildegard of Bingen, Her Life and Her Work*. Stockholm: Cordia, 1997

Davidson, Audrey Ekdahl. *The Ordo Virtutum of Hildegard of Bingen: Critical Studies in Early Drama, Art and Music*. Kalamazoo, Mich.: Medieval Institute, 1992

Fox, Matthew. *Illuminations of Hildegard of Bingen*. Santa Fe, N. Mex: Bear, 1985

Klaes, Monika, ed. *Vita Hildegardis*, Corpus Christianorum Continuatio Medievalis, 126, Turnhout: Brepols, 1993

Mumford, Marilyn R. 'A Feminist Prolegomenon for the Study of Hildegard of Bingen', in Ronald Dotterer and Susan Bowers, eds, *Gender, Culture and the Arts*. Selinsgrove, Pa: Susquehanna University Press, 1993, pp. 44–53

Newman, Barbara. *Sister of Wisdom: St. Hildegard's Theology of the Feminine*. Berkeley, Ca: University of California Press, 1987

Sur, Carolyn Wöman. *The Feminine Images of God in the Visions of Saint Hildegard of Bingen's Scivias*. Lewiston, NY: Mellen Press, 1993

Christine de Pizan

Christine de Pizan, *The Treasury of the City of Ladies or The Book of the Three Virtues*, trans. Sarah Lawson. Baltimore, Md: Penguin Books, 1985

    A Medieval Woman's Mirror of Honor: The Treasury of the City of Ladies, trans. Charity Cannon Willard, ed. Madeleine Pelner Cosman. New York: Persea Books, 1989

    The Book of the City of Ladies, trans. Earl Jeffrey Richards with a foreword by Marina Warner. New York: Persea Books, 1982

McLeod, Gland K., ed. *The Redemption of Christine de Pizan from the Fifteenth through the Nineteenth Centuries*. London: Edwin Mellen Press, 1991

Miner, Dorothy. *Anastaise and Her Sisters: Women Artists of the Middle Ages*. Baltimore, Md: Walters Art Gallery, 1974

Quilligan, Maureen. *The Allegory of Female Authority: Christine de Pizans's Cité des Dames*. Ithaca, NY: Cornell University Press, 1991

Willard, Charity Cannon. *Christine de Pizan: Her Life and Works*. New York: Persea Books, 1984

The Renaissance

General works, books and articles

Ackroyd, P. R., ed. *The Cambridge History of the Bible*. Cambridge: Cambridge University Press, 1963–70

Alazard, Jean. *Le Portrait Florentin de Botticelli à Bronzino*. Paris, 1951

    The Florentine Portrait. New York: Schocken Books, 1968

Alberti, Leon Battista. *The Family in Renaissance Florence*, trans. and introd. Rénée N. Waltkins. Columbus, SC: University of South Carolina Press, 1969

    On Painting and On Sculpture: The Latin Texts of 'De Pictura' and 'De Statua', ed. and trans. Cecil Grayson. London: Phaidon Press, 1972

Alcoff, Linda. 'Cultural Feminism versus Post-Structuralism: The Identity Crisis in Feminist Theory'. *Signs* 13 (1988), pp. 405–36

Bergmans, Simone. 'The Miniatures of Levina Teerling'. *Burlington Magazine*, 64 (1934), pp. 232–6

Berrigan, Joseph R. 'Saint Catherine of Bologna: Franciscan Mystic', in Katharina M. Wilson, ed., *Women Writers of the Renaissance and Reformation*. Athens, Ga: University of Georgia Press, 1987

Boehm, Gottfried. *Bildnis und Individuum über den Ursprung der Porträtmalerei in der italienischen Renaissance*. Munich: Prestel-Verlag, 1985

Brown, Judith. 'Woman's Place Was in the Home: Women's Work in Renaissance Tuscany', in Margaret W. Ferguson et al., eds, *Rewriting the Renaissance: The Discourse of Differences in Early Modern Europe*. Chicago: University of Chicago Press, 1986, p. 209

Chastel, André. 'The Artist', in Eugenio Garin, ed., *Renaissance Characters*, trans. Lydia G. Cochrane. Chicago: University Press of Chicago, 1991, pp. 180–92

Cole, Bruce. *The Renaissance Artist at Work*. New York: Harper and Row, 1983

de Voragine, Jacobus. 'The Eleven Thousand Virgins', *The Golden Legend*, trans. Granger Ryan and Helmut Ripperger. New York: Arno Press, 1969

Freedberg, Sydney. *High Renaissance in Italy*. New York: Harper Icons, 1985
        Paintings in Italy: 1500–1600. Baltimore, Md: Penguin Books, 1994

Garin, Eugenio, ed., *Renaissance Characters*, trans. Lydia G. Cochrane. Chicago: University Press of Chicago, 1991

Graziani, Irene. 'La leggenda dell'artista donna', in Vera Fortunati, *La pittura in Emilia e in Romagna: Il Cinquecento*. Milan: Nuova Alfa Editoriale, 1994

Guhl, Ernest. 'Die Frauen in der Kunstgeschichte', *Westminster Review* (July 1858), p. 96

Hartt, Frederick. *The History of the Italian Renaissance*. Englewood Cliffs, NJ: Prentice-Hall, 1995

Heinz, Gunther and Schutz, Karl. *Porträtgalerie zur Geschichte Österreichs von 1400 bis 1800*. Vienna: Kunsthistorisches Museum, 1982

Jordan, Constance. *Renaissance Feminism: Literary Texts and Political Models*. Ithaca, NY: Cornell University Press, 1990

MacLean, Ian. *The Renaissance Notion of Woman: A Study in the Fortunes of Scholasticism and Medical Science in European Intellectual Life*. Cambridge: Cambridge University Press, 1980

Raggs, Laura M. *The Women Artists of Bologna*. London: Methuen, 1907

Rose, Mary Beth, ed. *Women in the Middle Ages and the Renaissance: Literary and Historical Perspectives*. Syracuse, NY: Syracuse University Press, 1986

Wiesner, Merry E. 'Women's Defense of their Public Role', in Mary Beth Rose, ed., *Women in the Middle Ages and the Renaissance: Literary and Historical Perspectives*. Syracuse, NY: Syracuse University Press, 1986, pp. 1–27

Wood-Marsden, Joanna. 'Ritratto al Naturale: Questions of Realism and Idealism in Early Renaissance Portraits', *Art Journal* (Fall 1987), pp. 209–16

Monographs and articles on individual painters

Caterina de Vigri

Berrigan, J. 'Catherine of Bologna: Franciscan Mystic', *Women Writers of the Renaissance and Reformation*, ed. Katharina M. Wilson, Athens: University of Georgia Press, 1987, pp. 81–95

Wood, Jeryldene M. 'Breaking the Silence: The Poor Clares and the Visual Arts in Fifteenth-Century Italy', *Renaissance Quarterly* 47 (Summer 1995), pp. 262–86
        Women, Art and Spirituality: The Poor Clares of Early Modern Italy, Cambridge: Cambridge University Press, 1996

Levina Teerlinc or Teerling

Bergmans, Simone. 'The Miniatures of Levina Teerlinc', *Burlington Magazine*, lxiv (1934), pp. 232–6

King, Catherine. 'Looking a Sight: Sixteenth-Century Portraits of Women Artists', *Zeitschrift für Kunstgeschichte*, LVIII (1995), pp. 381–406

Weale, W.H.J. 'Simon Bennink, Miniaturist', *Burlington Magazine*, VII (1906), pp. 355–6

Mannerism

General works, books and articles

Benson, Pamela Joseph. 'From Paradise to Paradox: The First Italian Defense of Women', in *The Invention of the Renaissance Woman: The Challenge of Female Independence in the Literature and Thought of Italy and England*. University Park, Pa: Pennsylvania State University Press, 1992, pp. 33–64

Boccaccio. *Concerning Famous Women*, trans. GA. Guarino. London: Allen & Unwin, 1964

Campbell, Lorne. *Renaissance Portraits: European Portrait-Painting in the 14th, 15th, and 16th Centuries*. New Haven, Ct: Yale University Press, 1990

Caneva, Caterina. *Autoritratti degli Uffizi da Andrea del Sarto a Chagall*. Florence: Uffizi, 1990

Castiglione, Baldassare. *Il Cortegiano* (1528): *The Book of the Courtier*, trans. Charles S. Singleton. New York: Anchor Books, 1959

Cheney, Liana De Girolami. 'Self-Portraits of Renaissance Painters', lecture presented at the Renaissance Society of America Conference in Tempe, Arizona, 1987
    'Vasari's Interpretation of Female Beauty', in *Renaissance Concepts of Beauty*, ed. Francis Ames-Lewis and Mary Rogers. London: Scolar Press, 1997

Cropper, Elizabeth. 'On Beautiful Woman: Parmigianino, Petrarchismo, and the Vernacular Style', *Art Bulletin* 58 (1976), pp. 374–94
    'The Beauty of Woman: Problems in the Rhetoric of Renaissance Portraiture', in *Rewriting the Renaissance: The Discourses of Sexual Differences in Early Modern Europe*, eds. Margaret Ferguson, Maureen Quilligan and Nancy Vickers. Chicago: University of Chicago Press, 1986, pp. 175–90
    'The Place of Beauty in the High Renaissance and its Displacement in the History of Art', in *Place and Displacement in the Renaissance*, ed. Albin Vos. Binghmaton, NY: CEMERS, 1994, pp. 159–205

King, Catherine. 'Looking a Sight: Sixteenth-Century Portraits of Woman Artists', *Zeitschrift für Kunstgeschichte*, 58, 3 (1998), pp. 381–407

King, Margaret L. and Rabil, Albert Jr., eds. *Her Immaculate Hand: Selected Works by and about the Women Humanists of Quattrocento Italy*. Binghamton, NY: Medieval and Renaissance Texts and Studies, 1992

Rogers, Mary. 'The Decorum of Women's Beauty: Trissino, Firenzuola, Luigini and the Representation of Women in Sixteenth-Century Painting', *Renaissance Studies* 2 (1988), pp. 47–87

Schutte, Anne Jacobson. 'Irene di Spilimbergo: The Image of a Creative Woman in Late Renaissance Italy', *Renaissance Quarterly* 44 (1991), pp. 42–61

Simons, Patricia. 'Portaiture, Portrayal, and Idealization: Ambiguous Individualism in Representations of Renaissance Women', in *Language and Images of Renaissance Italy*, ed. Alison Brown. Oxford: Clarendon Press, 1995, pp. 263–313

Tinagli, Paola. *Women in Italian Renaissance Art: Gender, Representation, Identity*. Manchester: Manchester University Press, 1997

Monographs and articles on individual painters

Sofonisba Anguissola

Caroli, Flavio. *Sofonisba Anguissola e le sue sorelle*. Milan: Arnoldo Mondadori, 1987
    'Aggiunte a Sofonisba Anguissola e Fede Galizia', *Notizie da Palazzo Albani*, XX (1991), pp. 143–8
Feino-Pagden, Sylvia. *Sofonisba Anguissola, a Renaissance Woman*. Washington, DC: National Museum of Women in the Arts, 1995
Garrard, Mary D. 'Here's Looking at Me: Sofonisba Anguissola and the Problem of the Woman Artist', *Renaissance Quarterly*, 47 (1994), pp. 556–622
Gregori, Mina, ed. *Sofonisba Anguissola e le sue sorelle*. Milan: Leonardo Arte, 1994
Jacobs, Fredrika H. 'Woman's Capacity to Create: The Unusual Case of Sofonisba Anguissola', *Renaissance Quarterly* 47 (1994), pp. 74–101
Kusche, Maria. 'Sofonisba Anguissola al servizio dei re di Spagna,' in Mina Gregori, ed., *Sofonisba Anguissola e le sue sorelle*. Milan: Leonardo Arte, 1994, pp. 117–85
Perlingieri, Ilya Sandra. *Sofonisba Anguissola: The First Great Woman Artist of the Renaissance*. New York: Rizzoli, 1992

Lavinia Fontana

Cantaro, Maria Teresa. *Lavinia Fontana bolognese, pittore singolare, 1552–1614*, Milan: J. Sapi, 1989
Cheney, Liana De Girolami. 'Lavinia Fontana's Boston *Holy Family*', *Woman's Art Journal*, Spring 1984, pp. 12-16
Fortunati, Vera. *Lavinia Fontana, 1552–1614*. Milan: Electa, 1994 and 1998
    Pittura bolognese del '500, 2 vols, Bologna: Grafis, 1986
Murphy, Caroline P. 'Lavinia Fontana: The Making of a Woman Artist', in *Women of the Golden Age*, ed. Els Kloek and others. Hilversum: Verloren, 1994, pp. 171–81.

Barbara Longhi

Cheney, Liana De Girolami. 'Barbara Longhi', *Woman's Art Journal*, Fall 1987, pp. 10–14
    'Self-Portraits of Renaissance Women', *Visual Resources Association Journal* December (1996), pp. 67–74

Marietta Robusti, La Tintoretta

Cheney, Liana De Girolami. 'Self-Portraits of Renaissance Women Painters', *Discovery*, Fall 1997, pp. 2–5

Catherina van Hemessen

Bergmans, Simone. 'Le problème Jan van Hemessen monogrammiste de Brunswick, Le Collaborateur de Jan van Hemessen: L'Identité du monogrammiste', *Revue Belge d'Archéologie et d'Histoire de l'Art*, xxiv (1955), pp. 133–57
    'Le problème du Monogrammiste de Brunswich', *Bulletin, Musées Royaux des Beaux-Arts de Belgique*, XI (1965), pp. 143–62
De Clippel, Karolein. 'Catharina van Hemessen', PhD dissertation, University of Leuven (in preparation)
Wallen, Burr. *Jan van Hemessen: An Antwerp Painter Between Reform and Counter-Reform*. Ann Arbor, Mi: UMI Research Press, 1983

The Baroque

General works, books and articles

Chambers, D. S. and Quiviger, F. *Italian Academies of the Sixteenth Century*. London: Warburg Institute, University of London, 1995

Cheney, Liana De Girolami, ed. *The Symbolism of Vanitas in the Arts, Literature, and Music*. New York: Edwin Mellen Press, 1993

Félibien, André. *Entretiens sur les vies et sur les ouvrages des plus excellens peintres anciens et modernes*. 5 vols, Paris, 1666–88

Franits, Wayne E. *Paragons of Virtue: Women and Domesticity in Seventeenth-Century Dutch Art*. Cambridge, Ma: Cambridge University Press, 1995

Land, Norman E. *The Viewer as Poet*. University Park, Pa: Pennsylvania State University Press, 1994

Möbius, Helga. *Woman of the Baroque Age*. Montclair, NJ: Abner Schram, 1982

Monographs and articles on individual painters

Josefa d'Ayala d'Óbidos

Cheney, Liana De Girolami. 'The Self-Portraits of Josefa de Ayala d'Óbidos, *Mediterranean Studies Journal* (1999)

Días, José Hernández. *Josefa de Ayala: Pintora ibérica del siglo XVII*, Lisbon: Editorial Estampas, 1967

Reis-Santos, Luis. *Josefa d'Óbidos (Ayala)*, Lisbon: Artes Graficas [1956] (first comprehensive study, with list of signed and dated works)
    Josefa de Óbidos e o Tempo Barroco, exh. cat., Galeria de Pintura, Lisbon, 1991

Serrão, Vitor. 'Josefa d'Ayala e a pintura portuguesa do século XVII', *Estudos de Pintura Manierista e Barroca*, Lisbon: Caminho, 1986, pp. 181–203

Sobral, Luis de Moura. 'Três *bodegones* do Museu de Evora: Algumas considerações', *Colóquio: Artes*, 55 (1982), pp. 5–13
    'Un nuevo cuadro de Josefa de Ayala', *Archivo Español de Arte*, LVII (1984), pp. 386–7

Sullivan, Edward J. 'Josefa de Ayala: A Woman Painter of the Portuguese Baroque', *Journal of the Walters Art Gallery*, XXVII (1978), pp. 22–35
    'Obras de Josefa de Ayala', *Archivo Español de Arte*, LIV (1981), pp. 87–93
    '*Herod and Salome with the Head of John the Baptist* by Josefa de Ayala', *Source*, II/I (1982), pp. 26–9

Mary Beale

Flower, Sibylla J. *The Excellent Ms. Mary Beale*. London: Geffrye Museum, 1975
    'The Excellent Ms. Mary Beale', *Connoisseur*, 190 (December 1975), p. 302

Mrs. Mary Beale, Paintress, 1633–1699, exh. cat., Manor House Museum, Bury St. Edmunds, 1994

Fede Galizia

Caroli, Flavio. *Fede Galizia*. Turin: Umberto Allemandi, 1989
    Fede Galizia, 2nd edition, Turin: Allemandi, 1991

Giovanna Garzoni

Casale, Gerard, *Giovanna Garzoni, 'Insigne miniatrice' 1600–1700*. Milan: Jandi Sapi, 1991

Pascoli, Lione. *Vite de' pittori, scultori et architetti moderni*, 2 vols, Rome: Antonio de' Rossi, 1730–6; ed. Alessandro Marabottini, Perugia: Electa Umbri, 1992

Artemisia Gentileschi

Banti, Anna. *Artemisia*. Shirley D'Ardia Caracciolo, trans. Lincoln: University of Nebraska Press, 1988

Garrard, Mary D. *Artemisia Gentileschi: The Image of the Female Hero in Italian Baroque Art*, Princeton: Princeton University Press, 1989

   'Artemisia Gentileschi's "Corsica and the Satyr"', *Burlington Magazine*, cxxxv (1993), pp. 34–8

Judith Leyster

Hofrichter, Frima Fox. 'Judith Leyster's *Self-Portrait*: Ut Pictura Poesis', in *Essays in Northern European Art, Presented to Egbert Havercamp Begemann On His Sixtieth Birthday*. Doornspijk, 1983

   Judith Leyster: A Woman Painter in Holland's Golden Age, Doornspijk: Davaco, 1989

Welu, James A., ed. *Judith Leyster: A Dutch Master and Her World*. Worcester, Ma: Worcester Art Museum, 1993

Clara Peeters

Docoteau, Pamela Hibbs. *Clara Peeters, 1594–ca.1640, and the Development of Still-Life Painting in Northern Europe*. Lingen: Luca, 1992

Elisabetta Sirani

Bellini, P. 'Elisabetta Sirani: Catalogue des gravures', *Nouvelles de L'Estampe*, November–December 1976, pp. 7–12

Modesti, Adelina. 'Elisabetta Sirani "Pittrice eroina": A Portrait of the Artist as a Young Woman', *Identità ed appartenza: Donne e relazioni di genere dal mondo classico all'età contemporanea*. Acts of the First International Congress of the Italian Society of Women Historians, Rimini: Tipographia Rimini, 1995

The eighteenth century

General works, books and articles

Dayot, Armand. *La peinture française au XVIII siècle*. 3 vols., Paris, 1909
   Les femmes peintres au XVIII siècle. Castes: Musée Goya, 1973

Mariette, P. J. *Abécédario de P. J. Mariette et autres notes inédites de cet amateur sur les arts et les artistes*, edited by Ph. de Chennevière and A. de Montanglon. 8 vols., Paris, 1851–60

Oulmont, C. *Les femmes peintres au dix-huitième siècle*. Paris, 1908

Runte, R. *French Women and the Age of Enlightenment*. Bloomington, In: Indiana University Press, 1984

Monographs and articles on individual painters

Lady Diana Beauclerk

Erskine, Beatrice Caroline (Mrs. Steuart). *Lady Diana Beauclerk: Her Life and Work*, London: Fisher Unwin, 1903

Hardie, Martin. *Water-Colour Painting in Britain*, ed. Dudley Snelgrove, I, London: Batsford, 1966

Comtesse Benoist

Ballot, Marie Juliette. *La Comtesse Benoist, l'Emilie de Demoustier 1768–1826*. Paris: Librarie Plon, 1914

Cameron, Vivian. 'Woman as Image and Image-Maker in Paris during the French
    Revolution'. PhD dissertation, Yale University, 1983

Marie-Geneviève Bouliar
Cameron, Vivian. 'Woman as Image and Image-Maker in Paris during the French
    Revolution'. PhD dissertation, Yale University, 1983
Jouin, Henry. *Mademoiselle Marie-Geneviève Bouliard*, Paris, 1891

Gabrielle Capet
Passez, Anne-Marie. *Adélaïde Labille-Guiard (1749–1803): Biographie et catalogue raisonné
    de son oeuvre*, Paris: Arts et Métiers Graphiques, 1973

Rosalba Carriera
Bionda-Schwok, Claire-Lise. 'Rosalba Carriera: pastelliste et portraitiste', *L'Œil*,
    March 1993, pp. 32–9
Cessi, Francesco. *Rosalba Carriera*. Milan: Fabbri, 1965
Sani, Bernardina. *Rosalba Carriera: Lettere, diari, frammenti*. Florence, 1985
    *Alcune precisazioni sugli autoritratti di Rosalba Carriera, 'per Maria Cionini Visani-
        Scritti di Amici'*. Turin: Allemandi, 1977
    Rosalba Carriera. Turin: Allemandi, 1987
    Rosalba Carriera, Turin: Allemandi, 1988

Elizabeth Sophie Chéron
Brodsky, Judith. 'Rediscovering Women Printmakers, 1550–1850', *Counterproof*, I
    (Summer 1979), p. 7
'Chéron, Elizabeth Sophie,' *Dossier de L'Art*, April 1997, p. 61
Hilgar, Marie-France. 'The Val-de-Grâce Cupola in Painters' and Writers' Quarrels',
    Laurels, LII (Fall 1981), pp. 171–80
    'Les multiples talents d'Elisabeth Sophie Chéron', *Cahiers du Dix-Septième*, II
        (Spring 1988), pp. 91–8

Maria Cosway
Lloyd, Stephen. 'The Accomplished Maria Cosway: Anglo-Italian Artist, Musician,
    Salon Hostess and Educationalist (1759–1838)', *Journal of Anglo-Italian Studies*, II
    (1992), pp. 108–39
Richard and Maria Cosway: Regency Artists of Taste and Fashion, exh. cat., Scottish
    National Portrait Gallery, Edinburgh, and National Portrait Gallery. London, 1995
    (contains extensive bibliography)
Scheerer, Constance, 'Maria Cosway: Larger Than Life Miniaturists', *Feminist Art
    Journal*, April 1997, pp. 10–13

Marguerite Gérard
Ananof, Alexandre, 'Propos sur les peintures de Marguerite Gérard', *Gazette des
    Beaux-Arts*, Dec. 1979, pp. 211–18
Levitine, George, 'Marguerite Gérard and her Stylistic Significance', *Studies in Honor
    of Gertrude Rosenthal. The Baltimore Museum of Art Annual*, III (1968), pp. 21–31
Wells-Robertson, Sally. 'Marguerite Gérard'. PhD dissertation, New York University,
    1978

Angelica Kauffmann
Bionda-Schwok, Claire-Lise. 'Angelika Kauffmann', *L'Oeil*, Dec. 1992, pp. 22–9
Baumgärtel, Bettina. 'Freiheit-Gleichheit-Schwesterkeit: Der Freundschaftskult der
    Malerin Angelika Kauffman', *Sklavin oder Bürgerin Französische Revolution und*

Neue Weiblichkeit, 1760–1838, exh. cat., Historisches Museum. Frankfurt am Main,
1989, pp. 325–39
  *Angelika Kauffmann (1741–1807): Bedingungen weiblicher Kreativität in der Malerei
    des 18 Jahrhunderts*. Weinheim and Basel, 1990
Clark, Anthony. 'Roma mi è sempre in pensiero', *Studies in Roman Eighteenth-Century
  Painting*, ed. E.P. Bowron. Washington, DC: Decatur House Press, 1981, pp. 125–38
De Rossi, Giovanni Gherardo. *Vita di Angelica Kauffmann, pittrice 1754–1827*. Florence:
  A. Spese di Molini, 1810; reprinted London: Cornmarket, 1970
Hammer, Sabine. *Angelica Kauffman*. Vaduz: Haas, 1987
Mayer, Dorothy Moulton. *Angelica Kauffmann, R.A. 1741–1807*. Gerrards Cross,
  England, 1972
Rice, Louise and Eisenberg, Ruth. 'Angelica Kauffmann's Uffizi Self-Portrait', *Gazette
  des Beaux-Arts*, March 1991, pp. 123–6
Rosenthal, A. *Angelika Kauffmann: Bildnismalerei im 18. Jahrhundert*. Berlin: Reimer,
  1996
  'Anatomy is Destiny: Regarding the Body in the Art of Angelica Kauffmann',
    Femininity and Masculinity in Eighteenth-Century Art and Culture, ed. Gill
    Perry and Michael Rossington. Manchester: Manchester University Press,
    1994, pp. 41–62
Roworth, Wendy Wassyng, ed. *Angelica Kauffmann: A Continental Artist in Georgian
  England*. London: Reaktion Books, 1992

Adélaïde Labille-Guiard
Bonnet, Marie-Jo. 'La révolution d'Adélaïde Labille-Guiard et Elisabeth Vigée-Lebrun
  ou deux femmes en quête d'un espace dans la société', *Les Femmes et la Révolution
  française*, ed. Marie-France Brive. Toulouse: Presses Universitaires du Mirail, 1991,
  pp. 337–44
Rice, Danielle. 'Vigée-Lebrun vs Labille-Guiard: A Rivalry in Context', *Proceedings of
  the XIth Annual Meeting of the Western Society for French History*. Riverside, Ca 1983,
  pp. 130–38
Suellen, Diaconoff. 'Ambition, Politics and Professionalism: Two Women Painters',
  Eighteenth-Century Women and the Arts, ed. Frederick M. Keener and Susan E.
  Lorsch. New York: Greenwood, 1988, p. 208

Giulia Lama
Fiocco, Giuseppe. 'Il ritratto di Giulia Lama agli Uffizi', *Rivista d'arte*, XI (1929),
  pp. 113–17
Pallucchini, Rodolfo. 'Per la conoscenza di Giulia Lama', *Arte Veneta*, XXIV (1970),
  pp.161–72

Marie-Victoire Lemoine
Baillio, Joseph, 'Vie et oeuvre de Marie Victoire Lemoine', *Gazette des Beaux-Arts*,
  April 1996, pp. 125–64

Constance Mayer
Pilon, Edmond. *Constance Mayer (1775–1821)*. Paris: Delpleuch, 1927
Weston, Helen. 'The Case for Constance Mayer', *Oxford Art Journal*, III/I (1980),
  pp. 14–19

Mary Moser
Mitchell, Peter. *Great Flower Painters: Four Centuries of Floral Art*. Woodstock, NY:
  Overlook Press, 1973

Catharine Read

Archer, Mildred. *India and British Portraiture, 1770–1825*. London and New York: Sotheby Parke Bernet, 1979

Manners, Lady Victoria. 'Catherine [sic] Read: The "English Rosalba"', *Connoisseur*, LXXXVIII (1931), pp. 376–86; LXXXIX (1932), pp. 35–40, 171–8

Sophie Rude

Geiger, Monique. 'Sophie Rude (1797–1867): Une élève de David et son évolution artistique (avec essai de catalogue de son oeuvre)', *Bulletin de la Société de l'Histoire de l'Art Français*, 1987, pp. 167–90

Vautier, Dominique. 'Sophie Rude', *Autour de Neo-classisme en Belgique*, exh. cat., Musée d'Ixelles, Brussels, 1985, pp. 252–4

Anna Dorothea Therbusch-Lisiewska

Berckenhagen, Ekhart. 'Anna Dorothea Therbusch', *Zeitschrift des Deutschen Vereins für Kunstwissenschaft*, XLI (1987), pp. 118–60

Reidemeister, Leopold. 'Anna Dorothea Therbusch: Ihr Leben und ihr Werk', PhD dissertation, Berlin, 1924

Elisabeth Vigée-Lebrun

Sheriff, Mary. *The Exceptional Woman: Elisabeth Vigée-Lebrun and the Cultural Politics of Art*, Chicago: Chicago University Press, 1996.

Sontag, Susan. *The Volcano Lover: A Romance*. New York: Farrar Straus Giroux, and London: Cape, 1992

Anne Vallayer-Coster

Michel, Marianne Roland. *Anne Vallayer-Coster 1744–1818*. Paris: C.I.L., 1970

Marie Denise Villers

Oppenheimer, Margaret, 'Nisa Villers, née Lemoine, 1774–1821', *Gazette des Beaux-Arts*, April 1996, pp. 165–80

The nineteenth century

General works, books and articles

Aureli, Annamaria. *The Portrait in Impressionism*. London: Park Lane, 1993

Casteras, Susan P., and Peterson, Linda H. *A Struggle for Fame: Victorian Women Artists and Authors*. New Haven: Yale Center for British Art, 1994

    Images of Victorian Womanhood in English Art. London and Toronto: Associated University Presses, 1987

Cherry, Deborah. *Painting Women: Victorian Women Artists*. London and New York: Routledge, 1993

Dunford, Penny. *A Biographical Dictionary of Women Artists in Europe and America since 1850*. Philadelphia: University of Pennsylvania Press, 1989

Faxon, Alicia Craig. *Dante Gabriel Rossetti*. New York: Abbeville Press, 1989; Oxford: Phaidon Press, 1989

    and Moore, Sylvia, eds. *Pilgrims and Pioneers: New England Women in the Arts*. New York: Midmarch Arts Press, 1987

Herold, Martine. *L'Académie Julian à cent ans*. Paris: Académie Julian, 1968

Marsh, Jan. *Pre-Raphaelite Sisterhood*. London, Melbourne, New York: Quartet Books, 1985

    The Legend of Elizabeth Siddal. London, New York: Quartet Books, 1989

Pre-Raphaelite Women. New York: Harmony Books, 1987
and Nunn, Pamela Gerrish. *Women Artists and the Pre-Raphaelite Movement*.
  London: Virago Press, 1989
Mitchell, Sally. *Victorian Britain: An Encyclopedia*. New York and London: Garland,
  1988
Nunn, Pamela Gerrish. *Problem Pictures: Women and Men in Victorian Painting*.
  Aldershot, Hants: Scolar Press, 1995
Orr, Clarissa Campbell, ed. *Women in the Victorian Art World*. Manchester and New
  York: Manchester University Press, 1995
Tappert, Tara Leigh. *Cecilia Beaux and the Art of Portraiture*. Washington and London:
  National Portrait Gallery, 1995
Yeldham, Charlotte. *Women Artists in Nineteenth-Century France and England*. 2 vols.
  New York and London: Garland, 1984

Monographs and articles on individual painters

Lady Elizabeth Butler
Usherwood, Paul. 'Elizabeth Thompson Butler: A Case of Tokenism.' *Woman's Art
  Journal*, Fall 1990, pp. 14–18
    'Elizabeth Thompson Butler: The Consequences of Marriage,' *Woman's Art
      Journal*, Spring/Summer 1988, pp. 30–34
    and Jenny Spencer-Smith. *Lady Butler, Battle Artist, 1846–1933*. London: Alan
      Sutton, 1987

Mary Cassatt
Art Institute of Chicago. *Mary Cassatt: Modern Woman*. New York: Harry N. Abrams,
  1998
Mathews, Nancy Mowll. *Mary Cassatt: A Life*. New York, Villard, 1994
Pollock, Griselda. *Mary Cassatt*. London: Thames and Hudson, 1998
Sweet, Frederick A. *Miss Mary Cassatt: Impressionist from Philadelphia*. Norman:
  University of Oklahoma Press, 1966

Berthe Morisot
Adler, Kathleen and Garb, Tamar. *Berthe Morisot*. Oxford: Phaidon, and Ithaca, NY:
  Cornell University Press, 1987
Edelstein, T. J. *Perspectives on Morisot*. New York: Hudson Hills, 1990
Higonnet, Anne. *Berthe Morisot: A Biography*. New York: Harper and Row and
  London: Collins, 1990
    Berthe Morisot's Images of Women. Cambridge, Ma: Harvard University Press, 1992

Emily Mary Osborn
Casteras, Susan P. *Images of Victorian Womanhood in British Art*. London and Toronto:
  Associated University Presses, 1987
Nunn, Pamela Gerrish. *Victorian Women Artists*, London: Women's Press, 1987

Rolinda Sharples
Metz, Kathryn. 'Ellen and Rolinda Sharples, Mother and Daughter Painters', *Woman's
  Art Journal*, 16, no. 1 (Spring/Summer 1995), pp. 3–11

Elizabeth Siddal
Ashmolean Museum. *Rossetti's Portraits of Elizabeth Siddal*. ed. Virginia Surtees.
  Oxford: Ashmolean Museum/Scolar Press, 1991
Marsh, Jan. *Elizabeth Siddal 1829–1862*. Sheffield: Ruskin Gallery, 1991

Williams, Isabel. 'Elizabeth Siddal: The Health Issue', *The Journal of Pre-Raphaelite Studies*, New Series, 5 (Spring 1996), pp. 53–70

Lilly Martin Spencer
Johns, Elizabeth. *American Genre Painting: The Politics of Everyday Life*. New Haven and London: Yale University Press, 1991
Langa, Helen S. 'Lilly Martin Spencer: Genre, Aesthetics and Gender in the Work of a Mid-nineteenth century American Woman Artist', *Athanor*, IX (1990), pp. 37–45

Marie Spartali Stillman
Christian, John. 'Marie Stillman', in *The Last Romantics*. London: Lund Humphries and Barbican Art Gallery, 1989, pp. 86–7
Elzea, Rowland. 'Marie Stillman in the United States: Two Exhibitions: 1908 and 1982'. *Journal of Pre-Raphaelite and Aesthetic Studies*, 2, no. 1 (Spring 1989), pp. 56–72

Suzanne Valadon
Bayliss, Sarah. *Utrillo's Mother*. London: Pandora, 1987, and New Brunswick, NJ: Rutgers University Press, 1989
Betterton, Rosemary. 'How Do Women Look? The Female Nude in the Work of Suzanne Valadon', in *Looking On: Images of Femininity in the Visual Arts and Media*, ed. Rosemary Betterton. London and New York: Pandora, 1987, pp. 217–34
Mathews, Patricia. 'Returning the Gaze: Diverse Representaions of the Nude in the Art of Suzanne Valadon', *Art Bulletin*, 73, no. 3 (Sept. 1991), pp. 415–30
Rose, June. *Mistress of Montmartre: A Life of Suzanne Valadon*. London: Cohen, 1997
Rosinsky, Thérèse Diamond. *Suzanne Valadon*. New York: Universe Publishing, 1994

The twentieth century

General works, books and articles

Allen, Paula Gunn. *The Sacred Hoop: Recovering the Feminine in American Indian Traditions*. Boston: Beacon Press, 1992
Atkinson, J. Edward, ed. *Black Dimensions in Contemporary American Art*. New York: New American Library, 1971
Bataille, Gretchen M. and Kathleen Mullen Sands. *American Indian Women: A Guide to Research*. New York: Garland, 1991
Beardon, Romare and Harry Henderson. *A History of African-American Artists from 1792 to the Present*. New York: Pantheon Books, 1994, pp. 382–8
Bearing Witness: Contemporary Works by African-American Women Artists. New York: Spellman College and Rizzoli International Publications, 1996
Bontemps, Anna Alexander, ed. *Forever Free: Art by African-American Women, 1862–1980*. Alexandria, Va: Stephenson, 1980
Brown, Betty Ann and Raven, Arlene. *Exposures: Women and Their Art*, Pasadena, Ca: New Sage Press, 1989
Caws, Mary Ann. 'Ladies Shot and Painted: Female Embodiment in Surrealist Art', in *The Female Body in Western Culture: Contemporary Perspectives*. ed. Susan Suleiman. Cambridge, Ma: Harvard University Press, 1986, pp. 262–87
and Kuenzli, Rudolf E. and Raaberg, Gwen., eds. *Surrealism and Women*. Cambridge, Ma: M.I.T. Press, 1991
Chadwick, Whitney. *Mirror Image: Women, Surrealism and Self-Representation*. Cambridge, Ma: M.I.T. Press, 1998
Women Art and Society. London and New York: Thames and Hudson, 1990

Cooey, Paula M. *Religious Imagination and the Body: A Feminist Analysis*. New York: Oxford University Press, 1994

Donnell, Radka. *Quilts as Women's Art*. North Vancouver, BC: Gallerie Publications, 1990

Elliott, Bridget, and Wallace, Jo-Ann. *Women Artists and Writers; Modernist (Im)positionings*. London and New York: Routledge, 1994

Gasser, Maurice. *Self-Portraits*. New York: Appleton Century, 1961

Hartman, Diane. A. *The Soaring Spirit: Contemporary Native American Art*. Morristown, NJ: Morris Museum, 1987

Highwater, Jamake. *The Sweet Grass Lives On: Fifty Contemporary North American Indian Artists*. New York: Crowell, 1980

hooks, bell. *Yearning: Race, Gender and Cultural Politics*. Boston: South End Press, 1990

Hubert, Renée Riese. *Magnifying Mirrors: Women, Surrealism and Partnership*, Lincoln: University of Nebraska Press, 1994

Hunt, Lynn, ed. *Eroticism and the Body Politic*. Baltimore: Johns Hopkins University Press, 1991

King, Leslie, ed., *Gumbo YaYa: An Anthology of African-American Women Artists*. New York: Midmarch Arts Press, 1995

LaDuke, Betty. *Women Artists: Multicultural Visions*. Trenton, NJ: Red Sea Press, 1992

Lippard, Lucy, *Mixed Blessings: New Art in a Multicultural America*. New York: Pantheon Books, 1990
    Overlay: Contemporary Art and the Art of Prehistory. New York: Pantheon Books, 1983

Marsh, Jan. *Bloomsbury Women*. London: Pavilion, 1995, New York: Henry Holt, 1996

Meisel, Louis K. *Photorealism since 1980*. New York: Abrams, 1993

Miller, Lynn F. and Sally S. Swenson. *Lives and Works: Talks with Women Artists*. Metuchen, NJ, and London: The Scarecrow Press, 1981

Minh-ha, Trinh T. *Women, Native, Other: Writing Post Coloniality and Feminism*. Bloomington: Indiana University Press, 1989

Morrison, Keith. *Art in Washington and its Afro-American Presence, 1940–1970*. Washington, DC: Washington Project for the Arts, 1985

Murray, Elizabeth. *Artist's Choice: Modern Women*. New York: Museum of Modern Art, 1995

Naylor, Gillian, ed. *Bloomsbury: Its Artists, Authors and Designers by Themselves*, London: Pyramid, and Boston: Little Brown, 1990

Neilson, Winthrop and Frances Neilson. *Seven Women: Great Painters*. Philadelphia: Chilton Book Company, 1969

O'Neill, Eileen. '(Re)presentations of Eros', in *Gender/Body/Knowledge*, ed. Alison M. Jagger and Susan P. Bordo. New Brunswick, NJ: Rutgers University Press, 1986

Opfell, Olga S. *Special Visions*. Jefferson, NC, and London: McFarland, 1991, pp. 148–64

Penney, David. *Native American Art Masterpieces*. Southport, Cn: Hugh Lauter Leun Associates, 1994

Perry, Gill. *Women Artists and the Parisian Avant-Garde*, Manchester: Manchester University Press, and New York: St Martin's Press, 1995

Pollock, Griselda, 'What is Wrong with "Images of Women"'?, *Framing Feminism*, ed. Roziska Parker and Griselda Pollock. London and New York: Pandora, 1987

Powell, Richard. *Black Art and Culture in the 20th Century*. London: Thames and Hudson, 1997

Raven, Arlene, Cassandra Langer and Joanna Frueh. *Feminist Art Criticism: An Anthology*. Ann Arbor: U.M.I. Press, 1989
    'The Archaic Smile', in *New Feminist Art Criticism*, ed. Joanna Frueh, Cassandra Langer and Arlene Raven. New York: HarperCollins, 1994

Robins, Corinne. *The Pluralist Era: American Art, 1968–1981*. New York: Harper and Row, 1984

'Elizabeth Murray: Deconstructing our Interiors', *Art Journal*, 1 (1991), pp. 57–9

Rubinstein, Charlotte Streifer. *American Women Artists*. New York: Avon, 1982

Russo, Alexander. *Profile on Women Artists*. Frederick, Md: University Publications of America, 1985

Sandler, Irving. *Art of the Postmodern Era*. New York: Icon Editions, 1996, pp. 247–9, 279

Smith, Beryl, Arbeiter, Joan and Swenson, Sally Shearer. *Lives and Works: Talks with Women Artists*, Vol. II. Metuchen, NJ, and London: The Scarecrow Press, 1995

van Wagner, Judy Kay Collischan. *Lines of Vision: Drawings by Contemporary Women*. New York: Hudson Hills Press, 1989

Walters, Margaret. *The Nude Male: A New Perspective*. New York and London: Paddington Press, 1978

Witzling, Mara R., ed. *Voicing Our Visions: Writings by Women Artists*. New York: Universe, 1991, and London: Women's Press, 1992

Voicing Today's Visions: Writings by Contemporary Women Artists, New York: Universe, 1994

Monographs and articles on individual painters

Alice Bailly

Butler, Judith. 'Alice Bailly: Cubo-Futurist Poineer (1872–1938)', *Oxford Art Journal*, 3 (April 1980), pp. 52–5

Jaccard, Paul André. 'Alice Bailly et l'introduction du Cubisme en Suisse', *Etudes des Lettres*. Lausanne, 1975

Peillex, Georges, *Alice Bailly*. Geneva: Editions Pierre Cailles, 1968

Vanessa Bell

Ball, Colin Franck. *Vanessa Bell: A Bibliography*. Canterbury: Canterbury College of Art, 1983

Casteras, Susan P. *Vanessa Bell*. Poughkeepsie, NY: Vassar College Art Gallery, 1984

Caws, Mary Ann. *Women of Bloomsbury: Virginia, Vanessa and Carrington*. New York and London: Routledge, 1990

Dunn, Jane. *A Very Close Conspiracy: Vanessa Bell and Virginia Woolf*. London: Cape, and Boston: Little Brown, 1990

Gillespie, Diane F. *The Sister Arts: The Writing and Painting of Virginia Woolf and Vanessa Bell*. Syracuse, NY: Syracuse University Press, 1988

Marler, Regina, ed. *Selected Letters of Vanessa Bell*. New York: Pantheon Books, 1993

Spalding, Frances. *Vanessa Bell*. London: Weidenfeld and Nicolson, and New Haven, Ct: Ticknor and Fields, 1983

Romaine Brooks

Barney, Natalie. *Adventures of the Mind*. New York: New York University Press, 1992 (French original, 1929)

Chastain, Catherine McNickle. 'Romaine Brooks: A New Look at the Drawings', *Woman's Art Journal*, 17, no. 2 (Fall 1996/Winter 1997), pp. 9–14

de Montera, Pierre. 'Gabriele D'Annunzio, Romaine Brooks et Natalie Barney', *D'Annunzio e il simbolismo europeo*. Milan: Il Saggiatore, 1976

Wernet, Françoise. *Romaine Brooks*. Paris: Plon, 1990

Gwen John

Foster, Alicia. 'She Shopped at the Bon Marché', *Women's Art Magazine*, 65 (July–August 1995), pp. 10–14

Langdale, Cecily. *Gwen John: With a Catalogue Raisonné of the Paintings and a Selection of the Drawings*. New Haven and London: Yale University Press, 1987

and Fraser Jenkins, David. *Gwen John: An Interior Life*. London: Barbican Art
 Gallery, and New York: Rizzoli, 1986
Lloyd-Morgan, Ceridwen. *Gwen John Papers at the National Library of Wales*.
 Aberystwyth: National Library of Wales, 1988
Taubman, Mary. *Gwen John: The Artist and Her Work*, London: Scolar Press, and Ithaca,
 NY: Cornell University Press, 1985

Frida Kahlo
Baddeley, Oriana. '"Her Dress Hangs Her": De-frocking the Kahlo Cult', *Oxford Art
 Journal*, XIV (1991), pp. 10–17
Comisarenco, Dina. 'Frida Kahlo, Diego Rivera, and Tlazolteotl', *Woman's Art Journal*,
 17, no. 17 (Spring/Summer 1996), pp. 14–21
Drucker, Malka. *Frida Kahlo: Torment and Triumph in Her Life and Art*. New York:
 Bantam, 1991
Herrera, Hayden. *Frida Kahlo*. New York: Rizzoli, 1992
 Frida Kahlo: The Paintings. New York: HarperCollins, and London: Bloomsbury,
 1991
Lowe, Sarah M., ed. *The Diary of Frida Kahlo*. New York: HarperCollins, and London:
 Bloomsbury, 1995
Ketterman, Andrea. *Frida Kahlo, 1907–1954: Pain and Passion*. Cologne: Benedikt
 Taschen, 1993
Zamora, Martha. *Frida Kahlo: The Brush of Anguish*. New York and San Francisco:
 Chronicle, 1990 (Spanish original, 1987)

Laura Knight
Bolling, G. Frederick and Valerie A. Withington. *The Graphic Work of Laura Knight*.
 London: Ashgate/Scolar Press, 1993
Fox, Caroline. *Dame Laura Knight*. Oxford: Phaidon, 1988
Grimes, Teresa, Collins, Judith and Baddeley, Oriana. *Five Women Painters*. London:
 Lennard, 1989

Käthe Kollwitz
Hinz, Renate, ed. *Käthe Kollwitz: Graphics, Posters, Drawings*. London: Writers and
 Readers, and New York: Pantheon, 1981 (German original, 1980)
Jansen, Elmar. *Ernst Barlach – Käthe Kollwitz: Die Geschichte einer verborgenen Nähe*.
 Berlin, 1988
Kearns, Martha Mary. *Käthe Kollwitz: Woman and Artist*. Old Westbury, NY: Feminist
 Press, 1976
Klein, Mina C. and Klein, H. Arthur. *Käthe Kollwitz: Life in Art*. New York: Holt,
 Rinehart and Winston, 1976

Marie Laurencin
Fagan-King, Julia. 'United on the Threshold of the Twentieth-Century Mystical
 Ideal: Marie Laurencin's Integral Involvement with Guillaume Apollinaire
 and the Inmates of the Bateau Lavoir', *Art History*, 11 (March 1988), pp.
 88–114
Marchesseau, Daniel. *Catalogue raisonné of the Paintings of Marie Laurencin*. San
 Francisco: Alan Wofsy Fine Arts, 1986 (French original, 1980)
McPherson, Heather, ed., *Marie Laurencin: Artist and Muse*. Exh. cat., March 18–April
 30, 1989 Birmingham, Al: Birmingham Museum of Art, 1989
Radycki, Diane. 'Pretty/Ugly: Morphing Paula Modersohn-Becker and Marie
 Laurencin', *Make: The Magazine of Women's Art*, 72 (1996), pp. 19–21

Paula Modersohn-Becker

Busch, Günter, *Paula Modersohn-Becker: Malerin, Zeichnerin*. Frankfurt am Main:
Fischer, 1981
  and von Reinken, Liselotte, *Paula Modersohn-Becker: The Letters and Journals*, ed.
  and trans. Arthur S. Wesinger and Carole Clew Hoey. Evanston, Il:
  Northwestern University Press, 1990
Davidson, Martha. 'Paula Modersohn-Becker: Struggle between Life and Art', *The
Feminist Art Journal*, Winter 1973–4, pp. 1, 3–5
Modersohn-Becker, Paula. *Letters and Journals*, trans. and annotated by J. Diane
Radycki. Metuchen, NJ, and London: The Scarecrow Press, 1980
Murken-Altrogge, Christa. *Paula Modersohn-Becker: Leben und Werk*. Cologne:
DuMont, 1980

Meret Oppenheim

Belton, Robert J. 'Androgyny: Interview with Meret Oppenheim', *Surrealism and
Women*, ed. Mary Ann Caws, Rudolf E. Kuenzli and Gwen Raaberg. Cambridge,
Ma, and London: M.I.T. Press, 1991, pp. 63–75
Brandt, Bettina. '*Meret Oppenheims Inkognito: (De)maskierung und Reflexion in Meret
Oppenheims Filmskript* Kaspar Hauser oder die Goldene Freiheit', *Der Imaginierte
Findling Studien zur Kaspar-Hauser Rezeption*, ed. Ulrich Struve. Heidelberg:
Universitätsverlag C. Winter, 1995, pp. 144–62
Burkhardt, Jacqueline and Curriger, Bice. *Meret Oppenheim: Beyond the Teacup*. New
York: Independent Curators Incorporated, 1996
Curriger, Bice. *Meret Oppenheim*. Zurich: Plackett, and Cambridge, Ma: M.I.T. Press,
1989. With catalogue raisonné by Meret Oppenheim and Dominique Bürgi, trans.
Catherine Schelbert
  et al. *Meret Oppenheim: Defiance in the Face of Freedom*. Cambridge, Ma: M.I.T.
  Press, 1989 (German original, 1982)
Helfenstein, Josef. *Meret Oppenheim und der Surrealismus*. Stuttgart: Hatje, 1993
Hubert, Renée Riese. 'From "Déjeuner en Fourrure" to "Caroline": Meret
Oppenheim's Chronicle of Surrealism', in *Surrealism and Women*, ed. Mary Ann
Caws et al. Cambridge, Ma: M.I.T. Press, 1991, pp. 37–49
Schulz, Isabel. *Edelfuchs und Morgenrot: Studien zum Werk von Meret Oppenheim*.
Munich: Silke Schreiber, 1993

Kay Sage

Krieger, Regine. *Kay Sage (1898–1963)*. Ithaca, NY: Cornell University Press, 1977
Miller, Stephen Roberson. 'The Surrealist Imagery of Kay Sage', *Art International*, 26
(Sept.–Oct. 1983), pp. 32–47, 54–6
Suther, Judith D. 'Separate Studios: Kay Sage and Yves Tanguy', in *Significant Others:
Creativity and Intimate Partnership*, ed. Whitney Chadwick and Isabelle de
Courtivron. New York and London: Thames and Hudson, 1993, pp. 136–53
  A House of Her Own: Kay Sage, Solitary Surrealist. Lincoln: Nebraska University
  Press, 1997

Remedios Varo

Haynes, Deborah J. 'The Art of Remedios Varo: Issues of Gender, Ambiguity and
Religious Meaning', *Woman's Art Journal*, 16, no. 1 (Spring/Summer 1995), pp.
26–37
Kaplan, Janet. *Unexpected Journeys: The Art and Life of Remedios Varo*, 2nd edition. New
York: Abbeville, 1994 (contains extensive bibliography and illustrations)
Ovalle, Ricardo, et al. *Remedios Varo: Catálogo Razonado*. Mexico City: ERA, 1994

Contemporary art

Monographs and articles on individual painters

Emma Amos

Faxon, Alicia Craig. 'Emma Amos: Paintings and Prints 1982–1992', *Woman's Art Journal*, Spring/Summer 1996, pp. 43–5

Fox, Catherine. 'Sculptor Will Evoke Abernathy, But Not Re-create Him', *The Atlanta Journal, The Atlanta Constitution*, 24, September 1995, p. L6

Lippard, Lucy R. 'Floating Falling Landing: An Interview with Emma Amos', *Art Papers*, Nov./Dec. 1991, pp. 13–16

Audrey Flack

Brigham, David R. 'The New Civic Art: An Interview with Audrey Flack', *American Art*, IX (Winter 1994), pp. 2–21

Casteras, Susan P. *Audrey Flack: A Pantheon of Female Deities*. New York: Louis K. Meisel Gallery, 1991

Flack, Audrey. *Art and Soul: Notes on Creating*. New York: Harry N. Abrams, 1981
    Audrey Flack on Painting. New York: E.P. Dutton, 1986
    Audrey Flack: The Daily Muse. New York: Harry N. Abrams, 1989

Gouma-Peterson, Thalia. *Breaking The Rules: Audrey Flack, A Retrospective 1950–1990*. New York: Harry N. Abrams, 1992

Lois Mailou Jones

Benjamin, Tritobia Hayes. 'Lois Mailou Jones', in *Gumbo YaYa: Anthology of Contemporary African-American Women Artists*. New York: Midmarch Arts Press, 1995, pp. 126–9
    The Life and Art of Lois Mailou Jones. San Francisco: Pomegranate, 1994

Bontemps, Anna Alexander, ed. *Forever Free: Art by African-American Women 1862–1980*. Alexandria, Va: Stephenson, 1980

Clark, Marjorie. 'Lois Jones Pierre-Noel', *Women Artists in Washington Collections*. ed. Josephine Withers. College Park, Md: University of Maryland Art Gallery, 1979

Faxon, Alicia Craig. 'Lois Mailou Jones', *Dictionary of Women Artists*. London: Fitzroy Dearborn, 1997, Vol. 2, pp. 750–2

Fine, Elsa Honig. *The Afro-American Artist*. New York: Holt, Rinehart and Winston, 1973
    American Women Artists: The 20th Century. Knoxville, Tenn: Knoxville Museum of Art, 1989

Forever Free: Art by African-American Women, 1862–1980, exh. cat. Alexandria, Va: Stephenson, 1980

Gaither, Edmund Barry. *Reflective Moments: Lois Mailou Jones Retrospective 1930–1972*. Boston: Museum of Fine Arts, 1973

Laduke, Betty. 'Lois Mailou Jones: The Grande Dame of African-American Art', *Woman's Art Journal*, 8, no. 2 (1987–8), pp. 28–32

Strickland, Edward. 'Director's Notes', in *Lois and Pierre: Two Master Artists*. Boston: Museum of the National Center of Afro-American Artists, 1983

Hung Liu

Arieff, Allison. 'Cultural Collisions: Identity and History in the Work of Hung Liu', *Woman's Art Journal*, 17, no. 1 (Spring/Summer 1996), pp. 35–40

Atkins, Robert. 'Hung-Liu: Sensing the Self', in *The Year of the Dog: Hung Liu*. New York: Steinbaum Krauss Gallery, 1994

Clark, Trinkett. *Parameters*. Norfolk, Va: Chrysler Museum of Art, 1995

Yolanda Lopez
Blanc, Julio V. 'When You Think of Mexico: Latin American Women in the Decade
    Show', *Arts Magazine*, April 1990, p. 17
Goldman, Shifra. '"Portraying Ourselves": Contemporary Chicana Artists', in
    Feminist Art Criticism. ed. Arlene Raven, Cassandra Langer and Jeanna Frueh. Ann
    Arbor: U.M.I. Press, 1988, pp. 187–205
Mesa-Bains, Amalia. 'El Mundo Femenino: Chicana Artists of the Movement', in *Cara
    Chicano Art: Resistance and Affirmation*. Los Angeles: University of California,
    Wight Art Gallery, 1991, pp. 137–8
Peterson, Jeanette Faust. 'The Virgin of Guadalupe: Symbol of Conquest or
    Liberation?' *Art Journal*, 51, no. 4 (Winter 1992), pp. 39–56
Yolanda Lopez. *Works: 1975–1978*. La Jolla, Ca: Mandeville Center for the Arts, 1978

Juanita McNeeley
Alloway, Lawrence. 'Women Artists in the 70's,' *Art in America*, May 1976
Azara, Nancy. 'Women Artists Found', *Ms. Magazine*, January 1973
Semmel, Joan and Kingsley, April. 'Sexual Imagery in Women's Art', *Woman's Art
    Journal*, Spring/Summer 1980, pp. 1–6
Siblering, Dorothy. 'The Female View of Erotica', *New York Magazine*, 11, Feb. 1974
Steckel, Anita. 'McNeely Paints the Dark Side of Life', *New Directions for Women*, 1990

Ana Mendieta
Clearwater, Bonnie, ed. *Ana Mendieta: A Book of Works*. Miami Beach: Grassfield Press,
    1993
Faxon, Alicia. 'Ana Mendieta: Sacrifice and Transcendence', *Art New England*,
    Oct./Nov. 1992, pp. 18–19
Helsinki City Art Museum. *Ana Mendieta, 1948–1985*. Finland, 1996
Katz, Robert. *Naked by the Window: The Fatal Marriage of Carl Andre and Ana Mendieta*.
    New York: Atlantic Monthly Press, 1990
Perrault, John and Barreras, Petra del Rio. *Ana Mendieta: A Retrospective*. New York:
    New Museum of Contemporary Art, 1987–8
Spero, Nancy. 'Tracing Ana Mendieta', *Artforum*, April 1992, pp. 75–7

Annette Messager
Conkelton, Sheryl and Eliel, Carol S. *Annette Messager*. Los Angeles: County Museum
    of Art, and New York: Museum of Modern Art, 1995
Foray, Jean-Michel. 'Annette Messager: Collectionneuse d'histoires', *Art Press*, May
    1990, pp. 14–19
Gourmelon, Mo. 'Arbitrated Dissections: The Art of Annette Messager', *Arts
    Magazine* (November 1990), pp. 66–71
Gumpert, Lynn. 'Annette Messager: Comédie, tragédie', *Galeries Magazine*, 35 (1990),
    pp. 86–9
Pohlen, Annelie. 'The Utopian Adventures of Annette Messager', *Artforum*, Sept.
    1990, pp. 111–16
Rochelle, Anne and Saunders, Wade. 'Savage Mercies', *Art in America*, March 1994,
    pp. 78–83
Rowlands, Penelope. 'Art That Annoys', *Artnews*, Oct. 1995, pp. 132–5
Troncy, Eric. 'Annette Messager', *Flash Art*, 159 (1991), pp. 103–5

Elizabeth Murray
Adams, Brooks. 'Elizabeth Murray at Paula Cooper', *Art in America*, LXXX (Dec.
    1992), pp. 100–111
Simon, Roberta, ed. *Elizabeth Murray: Paintings and Drawings*. Dallas: Dallas Museum
    of Art, 1987

Theresa Musoke
Court, Elizabeth. 'Margaret Trowell and the Development of Art Education in East
    Africa', *Art Education*, November 1985, pp. 36, 37
Kingdom, Jonathan. *Theresa Musoke*, exh. cat. Uganda Museum of Art, 1965
Tesfagiouris, Freida High. 'In Search of a Discourse and Critiques that Center the Art
    of Black Women Artists', in *Theorizing Black Feminism*, ed. Stanlie M. Jones and
    Abena Busia. New York: Routledge, 1993
Wangbojie, Solomon Irein. 'Cultural Identity and Realisation Through the Arts',
    Journal of Art and Design Education, 5, nos. 1 and 2 (1986)

Alice Neel
Alice Neel: Paintings since 1970. Philadelphia: Pennsylvania Academy of Fine Arts,
    1985
Allara, Pamela. *Pictures of People: Alice Neel's American Portrait Gallery*. Hanover and
    London: University Press of New England, 1998
Board, Marilyn Lincoln. 'The Legend of Alice Neel: Re-envisioning the Cinderella
    Story', in *Images of the Self as Female: The Achievement of Women Artists in Re-
    envisioning Feminine Identity*, ed. Kathryn N. Benzel and Lauren Pringle de la Vars.
    Lewiston, NY: Edwin Mellen Press, 1992
Hills, Patricia. *Alice Neel*. New York: Harry N. Abrams, 1983

Howardena Pindell
Barnwell, Andrea D. 'Been to Africa and Back: Contextualizing Howardena Pindell's
    Abstract Art'. *The International Review of African American Art*, 13, no. 3, pp. 43–9
Kozloff, Joyce, ed. *Interview with Women in the Arts, Part 2*. New York: Tower Press,
    1976
Pindell, Howardena, *Autobiography*, exh. cat., New York: Cyrus Gallery, 1989
    'Breaking the Silence: Art World Racism – the Glaring Omission', *New Art
        Examiner*, Oct./Nov. 1990, pp. 18–27, 50–51

Paula Rego
Almeida-Matos, Lucia. *Review of Paula Rego* by John McEwen, *Woman's Art Journal*,
    Spring/Summer 1996, pp. 47–8
McEwen, John. *Paula Rego*. New York: Rizzoli, 1992; London: Phaidon, 1993 (contains
    bibliography)
Obalk, Hector. *Paula Rego*. Kyoto: Art Random, 1991
Bradley, Fiona, Victor Willing, Ruth Rosengarten, Judith Collins. *Paula Rego*. London:
    Thames and Hudson, 1997
Pointon, Marcia. *Paula Rego: New Work*. New York: Marlborough Gallery, 1997

Miriam Schapiro
Broude, Norma. 'Miriam Schapiro and "Femmage"', *Arts Magazine*, Feb. 1980,
    pp. 83–7
Frank, Elizabeth. 'Miriam Schapiro: Formal Sentiments', *Art in America*, May 1982,
    pp. 106–11
Gouma-Peterson, Thalia. 'Miriam Schapiro: An Art of Becoming', *American Art*, 11
    no. 1 (Spring 1997), pp. 11–45
Haynes, Deborah J. 'Miriam Schapiro's Collaboration Series: "Mother Russia"'.
    Woman's Art Journal, 17, no. 1 (Spring/Summer 1996), pp. 57–8

Sylvia Sleigh
Bowman, Russell and Adrian, Dennis. *Sylvia Sleigh: Invitation to a Voyage and Other
    Works*. Milwaukee, Wis: Milwaukee Art Museum, 1990
Johnson, Ken. 'Sylvia Sleigh at Stiebel Modern', *Art in America*, XII (Dec. 1994), p. 98

Loughery, John. 'Sylvia Sleigh: Invitation to a Voyage and Other Works', *Woman's Art Journal*, XII, no. I (1991), pp. 69–71

Jaune Quick-To-See Smith

Abbott, Lawrence, ed. *I Stand in the Center of the Good: Interviews with Contemporary Native American Artists*. Lincoln: University of Nebraska Press, 1994

Anreus, Alejandro. 'A Conversation with Jaune Quick-To-See Smith', in *Jaune Quick-To-See Smith Subversions/Affirmations*. Jersey City: Jersey City Museum, 1996, pp. 108–13

Hammond, Harmony, and Smith, Jaune Quick-To-See. *Women of Sweetgrass, Cedar and Sage*. New York: Gallery of the American Indian Community House, 1985

Harjo, Joy. 'Creation Story: The Jaune Quick-To-See Smith Survey', in *Jaune Quick-To-See Smith Subversions/Affirmations*. Jersey City: Jersey City Museum, 1996, pp. 63–9

Lippard, Lucy. 'Jaune Quick-To-See Smith's Public Art', in *Jaune Quick-To-See Smith, Subversions/Affirmations*. Jersey City: Jersey City Museum, 1996, pp. 79–92

Nash, Ann. 'Native American Women Artists: Claiming Identity', *Proteus: A Journal of Ideas*, 10, no. 2 (Fall 1993), pp. 33–7

Smith, Jaune Quick-To-See. *Our Land/Ourselves*. Albany, NY: University Art Gallery, State University of New York, 1990

Tremblay, Gail. 'When Word and Image Dance Together: The Work of Jaune Quick-To-See Smith', in *Jaune Quick-To-See Smith Subversions/Affirmations*. Jersey City: Jersey City Museum, 1996

Anita Steckel

Basker, J. Taylor. *Anita Steckel's 'The Tribe'*. New York: Kenkelaba Gallery, 1986

Nead, Lynda. *The Female Nude: Art, Obscenity and Sexuality*. London and New York: Routledge, 1992

Rosser, Phyllis. 'Anita Steckel: Pioneer', *New Directions for Women*, 17 (Nov./Dec. 1988)

Semmel, Joan, and Kingsley, April. 'Sexual Imagery in Women's Art', *Woman's Art Journal* (Spring/Summer 1980), pp. 1–6

Kay WalkingStick

Abbott, Lawrence. *I Stand in the Center of the Good: Interviews with Contemporary Native American Artists*. Lincoln: University of Nebraska Press, 1994

Kay WalkingStick: Paintings, 1974–1990, exh. cat. Brookville, NY: Hillwood Art Museum of Long Island University, 1991

Land, Spirit, Power: First Nations at the National Gallery of Canada, exh. cat. Ottawa: National Gallery of Canada, 1992

Morgan, Anne Barclay. 'Kay Walkingstick', *Art Papers*, Nov. Dec. 1996, pp. 12–15

Traugott, Joseph. 'Native American Artists and the Postmodern Cultural Divide', *Art Journal*, 51, no. 3 (Fall 1992), pp. 36–43

Valentino, Erin. 'Mistaken Identity: Between Death and Pleasure in the Art of Kay Walkingstick', *Third Text* (Spring 1994), pp. 61–73

WalkingStick, Kay. *Autobiography: In Her Own Image*, New York: INTAR, Latin American Gallery, 1988

'Native American Art in the Postmodern Era', *Art Journal*, 51, no.3 (Fall 1992), pp.15–17

Melanie Yazzie

Harlan, Theresa. 'To Watch, to Remember and to Survive', *Watchful Eyes: Native American Women Artists*. Phoenix, Az: Heard Museum, 1994, pp. 7–14

Rickard, Jolene. 'Frozen in the White Light', *Watchful Eyes: Native American Women Artists*. Phoenix, Az: Heard Museum, 1994, pp. 15–19

Roessel, Ruth. *Women in Navajo Society*. Rough Rock, Navajo Nation: Navaho Resource Center, Rough Rock Demonstration School, 1981

Index

References in **bold** type indicate illustrations